RAF Bomber Command Squadron Profiles

101 Squadron

Other Bomber Command books from Mention the War

Striking Through Clouds – The War Diary of 514 Squadron RAF
(Simon Hepworth and Andrew Porrelli)
Nothing Can Stop Us – The Definitive History of 514 Squadron RAF
(Simon Hepworth, Andrew Porrelli and Harry Dison)
Lancasters at Waterbeach – Some of the Story of 514 Squadron
(Harry Dison)

A Short War – The History of 623 Squadron RAF
(Steve Smith)
A Stirling Effort – Short Stirling Operations at RAF Downham Market 1942-1944
(Steve Smith)

RAF Bomber Command Profiles by Chris Ward:
83 Squadron
103 Squadron (with David Fell)
106 Squadron (with Herman Bijlard)
138 Squadron (with Piotr Hordyra)
300 (Masovian) Squadron (with Grzegorz Korcz)
617 Squadron

'…and in the morning…' Bomber Command Casualty Records compiled by Barry Hope:
57 Squadron RAF
514 Squadron RAF
617 Squadron RAF
630 Squadron RAF

Trusty to the End: The History of 148 (Special Duties) Squadron, 1918 – 1945
(Oliver Clutton-Brock)
A Special Duty – A Crew's Secret War with 148 (SD) Squadron
(Jennifer Elkin)
Wig's Secret War – The Biography of an SOE Air Operations Expert
(Gavin Wigginton)
Skid Row to Buckingham Palace
(Ed Greenburgh)
The Boy and the Bomber
(Francois Ydier)
The Pendulum and the Scythe
(Ken Marshall)

War Stories

The Dark Part of the Sky – A Collection of Bomber Command Ghost Stories (Simon Hepworth)
Late Shift (Simon Hepworth)

The above books are available through Amazon worldwide, as well as from the publisher. For further details or if you would like to purchase a signed and dedicated copy, please contact *bombercommandbooks@gmail.com* or visit www.bombercommandbooks.com

RAF Bomber Command Squadron Profiles

101 Squadron

by Chris Ward

Bomber Command Books

From

MENTION
THE WAR
PUBLICATIONS

This edition first published 2017 by Mention the War Ltd., 32 Croft Street, Farsley, Leeds, LS28 5HA. Copyright 2017 © Chris Ward.

Cover design: Topics - The Creative Partnership www.topicsdesign.co.uk

A CIP catalogue reference for this book is available from the British Library.

ISBN 978-1-911255-21-5

Contents

Introduction

RAF Bomber Command Squadron Profiles first appeared in the late nineties, and proved to be very popular with enthusiasts of RAF Bomber Command during the Second World War. They became a useful research tool, particularly for those whose family members had served and were no longer around. The original purpose was to provide a point of reference for all of the gallant men and women who had fought the war, either in the air, or on the ground in a support capacity, and for whom no written history of their unit or station existed. I wanted to provide them with something they could hold up, point to and say, "this was my unit, this is what I did in the war". Many veterans were reticent to talk about their time on bombers, partly because of modesty, but perhaps mostly because the majority of those with whom they came into contact had no notion of what it was to be a "Bomber Boy", to face the prospect of death every time they took to the air, whether during training or on operations. Only those who shared the experience really understood what it was to go to war in bombers, which is why reunions were so important. As they approached the end of their lives, many veterans began to speak openly for the first time about their life in wartime Bomber Command, and most were hurt by the callous treatment they received at the hands of successive governments with regard to the lack of recognition of their contribution to victory. It is sad that this recognition in the form of a national memorial and the granting of a campaign medal came too late for the majority. Now this inspirational, noble generation, the like of which will probably never grace this earth again, has all but departed from us, and the world will be a poorer place as a result.

RAF Bomber Command Squadron Profiles are back. The basic format remains, but, where needed, additional information has been provided. Squadron Profiles do not claim to be comprehensive histories, but rather detailed overviews of the activities of the squadron. There is insufficient space to mention as many names as one would like, but all aircraft losses are accompanied by the name of the pilot. Fundamentally, the narrative section is an account of Bomber Command's war from the perspective of the bomber group under which the individual squadron served, and the deeds of the squadron are interwoven into this story. Information has been drawn from official records, such as group, squadron and station ORBs, and from the many, like myself, amateur enthusiasts, who dedicate much of their time to researching individual units, and become unrivalled authorities on them. I am grateful for their generous contributions, and their names will appear in the appropriate Profiles. The statistics quoted in this series are taken from The Bomber Command War Diaries, that indispensable tome written by Martin Middlebrook and Chris Everitt, and I am indebted to Martin for his kind permission to use them.

Finally, let me apologise in advance for the inevitable errors, for no matter how hard I and other authors try to write "nothing but the truth", there is no such thing as a definitive account of history, and there will always be room for disagreement and debate. Official records are notoriously unreliable tools, and yet we have little choice but to put our faith in them. It is not my intention to misrepresent any person or RAF unit, and I ask my readers to understand the enormity of the task I have undertaken. It is relatively easy to become an authority on single units or even a bomber group, but I chose to write about them all, idiot that I am, which means 128 squadrons serving operationally in Bomber Command at some time between the 3rd of September 1939 and the 8th of May 1945. I am dealing with eight bomber groups, in which some 120,000 airmen served, and I am juggling around 28,000 aircraft serial numbers, code letters and details of provenance and fate. I ask not for your sympathy, it was, after all, my choice, but rather your understanding if you should find something with which you disagree. My thanks to you, my readers, for making the original series of RAF Bomber Command Squadron Profiles so popular, and I hope you receive this new incarnation equally enthusiastically.

My thanks also, as always, to my gang members, Andreas Wachtel, Steve Smith and Greg Korcz for their unstinting support, without which my Profiles would be the poorer. Finally, my appreciation to my publisher, Simon Hepworth of Mention the War Publications, for his belief in my work, untiring efforts to promote it, and for the stress I put him through to bring my books to publication. During the writing of this wartime squadron history, I was privileged to meet "Rusty" Waughman, whose tour of operations with 101 Squadron between December 1943 and June 1944 is detailed in the narrative. While talking about his time in Bomber Command, he mentioned a mid-air collision during an operation to Hasselt in Belgium in May 1944. He had no idea as to the identity and ultimate fate of the other Lancaster and crew, other than it did not survive the encounter. I was pleased to be able to provide Rusty with the details 73 years after the incident through my good friend Wim Govaerts. Rusty kindly gave me access to his photo collection, and permission to use it in this book. I am pleased to dedicate this book to him and his crew. I am also grateful to Gary Weightman, a serving officer at RAF Cranwell, who is the official historian of the 101 Squadron Association and provided photos from his extensive archives. My good friend David Fell also contributed photos of former 103/576 Squadron crews. I would also like to thank Pat Hickton's granddaughter, Jackie Ridgway and great-granddaughter, Hayley Wesche, for the photographs and information about the escapades of Pat's crew.

Chris Ward. Lutterworth. September 2017.

Vic Redfern was a member of the groundcrew at Ludford Magna and took many of the photographs now held in the 101 Squadron archives, and now reproduced in this book with the permission of the 101 Squadron Association.

This 101 Squadron Profile is dedicated to F/O Russell "Rusty" Waughman and his crew, who completed a tour of operations between December 1943 and June 1944.

Pilot;   F/O Russell Reay Waughman. "Rusty"
Flight Engineer;   Sgt John Ormerod. "Curly"
Navigator;   P/O Alec Cowan. "Jumbo"
Bomb-Aimer;   Sgt Norman Westby. "Babe"
Wireless Operator;   Sgt Idris Arndell. "Taffy"
Mid-upper Gunner;   Sgt Thomas Dewsbury. "Tommy"
Rear Gunner;   Sgt Harold Nunn (Canada). "Harry"
ABC Operator;   Sgt Edward Manners. "Ted"

Rusty

Curly

Jumbo

Babe

Taffy

Tommy

Harry

Ted

A Bristol Blenheim IV over France in 1939. The bravery of the aircrew could not make up for the vulnerability of the Blenheims when they encountered the ferocious flak and the Luftwaffe during the battles for the Low Countries and France (GW).

Pre-War History

Blenheim IVs line up in 1939. Until the outbreak of war in September that year, the squadron's designator was LU, which helps date this photo. It was SR from September 1939 onwards (GW).

The history of 101 Squadron dates back to the 12th of July 1917, when it was formed as a night bomber unit, carrying out operations from French bases. On the last day of 1919 it underwent disbandment, and remained on the shelf until March 1928, when it was reformed as a day bomber squadron. June 1938 saw the arrival of Mk I Blenheims, and replacement of these with the Mk IV began in April 1939, at the same time that W/C Hargroves was appointed as the commanding officer. He was an experienced officer, who had held a similar post with 37 Squadron during 1938.

This, then, was how 101 Squadron entered the Second World War on the 3rd of September 1939 as part of 81 Wing in 2 Group. It was stationed at West Raynham in Norfolk, to where it had moved from Bicester on the 9th of May. It had on charge a complement of twenty-one Blenheims in two flights of eight, commanded by S/Ls Hartwright and Morton, with five aircraft in reserve. As part of the general "scatter" arrangement for the whole Command in these very early days, when enemy air attacks were expected, eight aircraft were detached to Brize Norton. These returned on the 11th, by which time the squadron had not been called on to mount any operational sorties. It was placed on standby on the morning of the 12th, for possible attacks on elements of the enemy fleet, but was stood down again thirteen hours later. From the 17th, the Group assigned a designated unit as Duty Squadron on a rota basis, but 101 Squadron's turn never once resulted in operational activity. The squadron's chances of getting into the war had been further reduced by the decision on the 4th to install additional fuel tanks in the Blenheim's outer wing section, and modification of aircraft already in service had to be undertaken on station. While this was in progress, Group Pool Training squadrons were introduced, to handle the transition of new crews from training station to squadron. This meant that each Group was to take one of its squadrons out of the line, and designate it as a Reserve Squadron, and as 101 had not yet modified its Blenheims, it was selected to fulfil this role, and was stood down on the 25th.

In view of the fact that 101 Squadron had to support six frontline units, its complement of aircraft increased to twenty-seven, and inevitably, during the course of its work, some of these would be lost to accidents. The first occurred on the 2nd of November, when L4809 crashed on landing in the hands of P/O Keedwell, and was written off. L4900 lost the use of its port engine during a height test on the 14th, but P/O Goodbody ultimately landed safely at Mildenhall, after initially ordering his two crew members to bail out at 8,000 feet. One did so, before the order was rescinded, and landed in a field at Soham with a torn parachute, after it snagged on the aircraft. On the 20th of November, P/O Newman crash-landed L4887 in Staffordshire, but all on board emerged without injury. There were no other incidents during what remained of the year, and it would not be long before the harsh winter closed in, to freeze the aircraft to the ground. Elsewhere during this period, elements of 1, 3 and 5 Groups sustained bloody noses at the hands of enemy fighters during a number of daylight operations against warships off Germany's coast. Not only did this shocking outcome lead to restricted offensive flying, which gave the reserve squadrons time to prepare their charges for the battles ahead, it also forced a rethink in tactics. Before the war, it had always been assumed, that the Douhet theory would prevail, that self-defending bombers would always get through in sufficient numbers in daylight, to deal with the target, and training had reflected that viewpoint. The loss of five Hampdens on the 29th of September, five of twelve Wellingtons on the 14th of December, and twelve out of twenty-two Wellingtons four days later, shattered that notion. Only 4 Group had trained its crews to fly at night, but soon, the rest of the Command would have to become largely nocturnal, and even 2 Group would occasionally fly at night.

Top: Three Blenheims silhouetted against cumulus clouds in 1938 Above: Another pre-war photo of a Blenheim IV, this aircraft being LU-V. The serial number is indecipherable (GW).

January to July 1940

The winter seemed to deepen as the year progressed, and it would be towards the end of February before the freezing conditions began to loosen their grip. P/O Gilling wrote off N6178 in a landing accident on the 12th of January, and this was the last incident for two months. On the 16th of February, 2 Group was ordered to select volunteer crews to ferry twelve Mk I Blenheims to Finland, to help in its conflict with Soviet forces, and five such crews were to be found at 101 Squadron. All the necessary preparations were made, but the whole plan was suddenly scrubbed, and Finland capitulated a few days later. The first fatalities incurred by the squadron resulted from a training flight on the 7th of March. N6165 collided with high tension cables and crashed into the Norfolk countryside four miles south-west of Diss, killing F/O Mottram and one other, and injuring the survivor. The training role continued as before with bombing practice and formation flying, and the lack of offensive activity prompted the American press to dub this period as the "Phoney War". The first genuine bombing attack was delivered by Whitleys of 4 Group and Hampdens of 5 Group against the Seaplane base at Hörnum on the island of Sylt on the night of the 19/20th of March. The attack, which was spread over six hours, was in retaliation for the inadvertent slaying of a civilian on the island of Hoy, during a Luftwaffe assault on elements of the Royal Navy in Scapa Flow two nights earlier. The RAF effort made headline news, and was heralded as a major success, a claim not supported by photographic reconnaissance on the 6th of April.

The "Phoney War ended abruptly on the 9th of April, when German forces marched unopposed into Denmark, and began an air and sea invasion of Norway. British and French forces were ordered to slow Germany's advance, by carrying out air attacks on shipping and airfields in the south, while an expeditionary force was dispatched to land at Narvik in the north. Bomber Command set about its task with enthusiasm, but the long range and enemy fighters resulted in further heavy losses, and the whole affair was over by the time that other events captured the attention of the world. At first light on the 10th of May, enemy forces began their advance into the Low Countries, swallowing up Luxembourg, Belgium and the Netherlands, and, by the end of the month, the surviving British and French armies were trapped on the beaches of Dunkerque. The Advanced Air Striking Force had been committed to the fray from its bases in France, along with 2 Group Blenheims from home stations, but the obsolete Fairey Battles were no match for the BF109s and ME110s, and were hacked from the sky in frighteningly large numbers. Many others fell victim to the ground defences, which had been allowed to become established before any air attacks were carried out, and a number of squadrons were, literally, knocked out of the battle within days. During the course of May, the squadron carried out training sweeps over the sea, and also practiced high-level, low-level and dive bombing over the range at Wainfleet on the Lincolnshire coast.

On the 4th of June, a directive was issued by Bomber Command, which the 2 Group Air-Officer-Commanding (A-O-C) set out as 2 Group Operations Order 11, calling for sporadic daylight attacks on specific objectives, when conditions of sufficient cloud existed. June also brought two more accidents for 101 Squadron, both of which involved total loss of life. On the 6th, P4912 stalled over Oxfordshire during a height test, and span in to crash at Stanton St Johns with the crew of P/O Buller on board. On the 12th, L9258 dived into the ground near Hilborough in Norfolk, during a transit flight from Watton, where it had landed on the previous afternoon in bad weather following formation practice. Only two people were on board, the pilot, P/O Fletcher, and his observer, Sgt Matthews. S/L Singer became attached to the squadron from XV Squadron on the 15th, having recently completed a brief spell in command of 10 Squadron, and he would soon find himself in command.

The fall of France on the 22nd of June, and the introduction of Operational Training Units back in April, released 101 Squadron from its training role, and catapulted it into 2 Group's front line.

The squadron's first sorties in anger were launched in line with G.O.O.11 against oil targets in northern Germany on the 4th. Three crews from B Flight were involved, S/L Morton and crew taking off first, at 15.05, to head for Harburg, situated on the south bank of the Elbe, opposite Hamburg, but returned early through lack of cloud cover. F/L Little and F/O Messervey got away at 15.25 in L8870 and P6924 respectively, the former bound for the Oslebshauser district of Bremen, situated in the docks area on the northern bank of the Weser, while the latter set course for Ostermoor, an industrial region nestling on the northern bank of the Elbe Estuary. F/L Little also failed to find sufficient cloud and turned back, while F/O Messervey reached his target area, and made an attack, only to find that his four 250lb bombs had failed to release. Despite heavy defensive fire from the ground, he made a second run at 2,000 feet at 17.25, and observed bomb blasts among pipelines running between storage tanks and the Kiel Canal. On the following day, the 5th, the day on which the Air Ministry ordered the return of all reserve squadrons to operational status, three more Blenheims were dispatched individually to attack the same targets. F/L Monroe took off at 14.20 in P6924, and Sgt Brown thirty minutes later, leaving W/C Hargrove as the last to depart in N6140. The first two turned back because of a lack of cloud cover, and Sgt Brown attacked three small vessels off the Dutch coast on the way home, claiming to have hit one of them. W/C Hargrove's Blenheim crashed into the sea without survivors, and thus were registered the first three names in what, by the end of the war, would be the longest Roll of Honour of any squadron in Bomber Command.

The task for P/Os Miles and Ferguson and Sgt Balmer on the afternoon of the 6th was to reconnoitre parts of northern France and Belgium, for which they took off between 14.23 and 15.00. P/O Miles flew over the mouth of the Scheldt and took some photographs, but all three returned to base in the face of insufficient cloud cover. Four crews were briefed for similar operations to be carried out on the morning of the 8th, and Sgt Lorrimer was first away at 06.08. He returned after finding insufficient cloud cover, while F/O Ducker turned back at the Dutch coast when his rear gun jammed. P/O Bicknell dropped a dozen 40lb bomblets amongst ten Heinkel 111 on Ledeghem aerodrome, and F/O Messervey did likewise, and added two 250 pounders in a stick from 3,500 feet among around twenty enemy aircraft assembled on the airfield at Soissons. P/O Watson force-landed N6176 near Wyton at 16.00 on the 9th, writing off the airframe and slightly injuring himself, but the engines were repairable. West Raynham was bombed on the 10th in a cloud-cover attack, which resulted in the destruction of three Ansons and a Gladiator. The ORB speaks of six aircraft being prepared for operations over northern Germany that morning, but details only Sgt Brown and crew, who took off at 11.15 in N6238. They found no cloud on arrival at the Dutch coast, and decided to head for a search area north of Heligoland, where they attacked two small ships that fired upon them. No results were observed. Six Blenheims were made ready to attack shipping in harbours and canals on the Dutch and Belgian coasts on the 11th, but only two took off to carry out weather reconnaissance, P/O McLaren at 04.05 and S/L Morton at 14.08. They brought back reports of clear skies, and operations were cancelled.

W/C Singer's attachment to the squadron was made permanent on the 15th, and he was installed as the new commanding officer, at a time when the Battle of Britain was beginning to gather momentum overhead. As the spectre of invasion increased, twelve crews at each station were ordered to stand by at twenty minutes readiness each morning until sunrise, to attack invasion craft at their point of departure and at sea, and to repel any attempts to carry out landings. The 18th brought four sorties against enemy airfields in northern France, beginning with the departure of F/L Monroe and crew in N6141 at 10.30, bound for Le Crotoy. A lack of cloud cover, and the failure of the forward gun, persuaded them to abandon the attempt and return to base. It was a similar story for P/Os Miles and Ferguson, who took off at 12.25 and 12.45 to attack Douai and Arras aerodromes respectively. We do not know what time F/O Ducker and crew departed West Raynham in P6924, and headed for Cherbourg, where, although the ORB records the target as the aerodrome, it may, in fact, have been the invasion barges being assembled in the port. In the event, the Blenheim failed to return, and no trace of it or its crew was ever found.

Six aircraft were made ready for shipping sweeps off the Dutch coast on the 20th, 21st and 22nd, but weather conditions proved unsuitable, and they were cancelled. However, conditions over northern France on the afternoon of the 22nd were considered favourable, and six Blenheims were dispatched to attack the aerodromes at Inglevert, Boulogne and St Omer. F/L Little was the senior pilot on duty as they took off between 12.19 and 13.07, with two aircraft assigned to each target, but all turned back after failing to find sufficient cloud cover. Nine aircraft were prepared for operations on the 25th, their crews briefed to carry out photographic reconnaissance over north-western Germany and France, and attack selected targets. The weather intervened once more, and, in the event, only P/O Short and crew took off at 16.20 to carry out a weather recce over the Channel and Cherbourg, and, if conditions allowed, to attack oil installations at Cherbourg. N6174 failed to return, as the unequal contest continued between the Blenheims of 2 Group and the German defences, and its fate and that of its crew remains a mystery. A further nine crews were briefed in the early hours of the following day for similar operations over north-western Germany, Holland and France, but just three eventually took off. The uncoordinated manner of conducting operations in the early days of the war is demonstrated by the take-off times. F/O Palmer was the senior pilot on duty, and departed at 05.40 in P6955 to photograph Wilhelmshaven and bomb a specific objective, probably a major warship. He reached the target area, but was unable to carry out his brief because of poor visibility. Sgt Brown and crew took off at 07.00 in N6142, and headed for the coast, climbing to 9,000 feet over the North Sea and encountering icing conditions in the cloud layer, which persuaded them to turn back. It was 11.25 before P/O Hill and crew departed West Raynham in N6182 to attack Schiphol, upon which they dropped two 250 pounders and eighteen 40lb bomblets from 4,000 feet at 12.30, but failed to observe the results. Six Blenheims were prepared for operations against aerodromes in north-western France and Holland on the 29th, but, only N6141 actually took off, doing so at 11.55 with the crew of S/L Morton on board. They had been briefed to attack Leeuwarden in northern Holland, but returned a little over ninety minutes later after being denied cloud cover.

August 1940

The new month began with three sorties directed at aerodromes on the morning of the 1st. F/O Smythe was the senior pilot on duty, and took off at 04.56 for his primary target, which he failed to locate. He bombed Leeuwarden instead, and Sgt Lorrimer, who took off almost four hours later, also attacked Leeuwarden as an alternative. Sgt Riddick took to the air at the same time as Sgt Lorrimer, but failed to find sufficient cloud cover, and turned back. On the following morning, P/O Miles, P/O Ferguson and F/L Little took off at 08.47, 09.27 and 09.35 respectively, to attack aerodromes, two bombing Schiphol, one as an alternative, and both claiming damage, while P/O Ferguson dropped his bombs on Waalhaven airfield, also as an alternative, but did not observe the results. P/O Dunnicliffe undertook the only sortie on the 5th, taking off in P6955 at 05.25 to bomb Le Bourget aerodrome. He was back home within ninety minutes after failing to find the hoped-for cloud cover. F/O Messervey carried out his final sortie with the squadron on the 6th, when setting out in R3846 for Kamen, an oil town situated on the north-eastern edge of the Ruhr. He was also unable to find sufficient cloud cover, and was forced to turn back. He and his crew would be posted to 82 Squadron on the 14th.

A landing accident occurred at Wittering during training on the morning of the 8th, when P/O Miles crashed into a dispersal pan in L9250, and F/L Monroe ran into him in T1866, after failing to pull up in time. Happily, there were no human casualties. Five sorties were dispatched on the 11th, the crews having been briefed to attack targets in France, Belgium and Germany. W/C Singer at 05.35, but he returned ninety minutes later after failing to find cloud, and, perhaps, should have delayed his take-off, as three other crews enjoyed better luck. F/L Monroe took off at 09.25, and, although not reaching his primary target, attacked enemy destroyers making out to sea off Den Helder. P/O Bicknell and crew were airborne at 09.45, but returned early through lack of cloud. It was almost three hours later, when F/O Smythe and crew departed for Brest aerodrome, which was attacked with two 250lb bombs from 25,000 feet. S/L Hartwright was last away at 12.20 in T1825, and dropped his two 250 pounders onto Caen aerodrome from 20,000 feet.

From the 14th of August, the squadron was switched to night operations, and from now on, an increasing proportion of the Command's effort would be directed towards anti-invasion measures until the threat diminished. Airfields continued to be primary targets for both daylight and night operations, and 101 Squadron was also assigned to attack long-range guns in the Pas-de-Calais along with 18 Squadron, which had resumed operations at the same time as 101 Squadron, following its return from France. Alongside these requirements, the G.O.O. 11 was still in force, and this had been revised to include attacks on aluminium and aircraft

A formation of Blenheim IV aircraft of 101 Sqn, now recoded SR, which the squadron used for the rest of the war (GW).

16

assembly plants, oil, and shipping in German ports. P/O Hill and crew were one of two representing the squadron on the evening of the 14th, and departed West Raynham at 21.10. They could not locate the unspecified aerodrome primary target, and dropped a stick of bombs across an alternative one. Sgt Brown and crew took off in L9421 at 21.15 to attack Antwerp aerodrome, and dropped two 250 pounders and twelve 40lb bomblets on it from 8,000 feet. The gunner also managed to extinguish a searchlight with a burst of fire.

The 15th was the day on which the Luftwaffe began its campaign against RAF fighter airfields, an event which signalled the main phase of the Battle of Britain. That evening, 101 Squadron dispatched six Blenheims to a number of targets, with S/L Morton, P/O Miles and P/O Bicknell assigned to heavy gun emplacements at Cap Gris-Nez, a few miles along the coast south-west of Calais. They took off at roughly thirty-minute intervals from 20.55, and each delivered a stick of four delayed-action bombs, before returning safely home. Sgt Lorrimer took off at 22.15 to attack an aerodrome, and observed his stick of two 250 and twelve 40 pounders score a direct hit on hangars and a parked aircraft. P/O Wade could not identify his primary target in Holland because of haze and searchlight dazzle, and released his bombs on an alternative. P/O Ferguson and crew were last away, at 23.40, but were also thwarted by ground mist and searchlight dazzle, and jettisoned their bombs into the sea.

The 101 Squadron and 2 Group ORBs become somewhat confused concerning events on the nights of the 17/18th and 18/19th. The group record states that the squadron put up twelve Blenheims on the latter date, when the Bomber Command War Diaries shows no Blenheims in action. The squadron record cites the former date, but has two entries for W/C Singer and crew, both assigned to the same target, but in different aircraft with different take-off times. However, by counting the commanding officer twice, we arrive at the correct total of twelve sorties under the date of the 17th, and must assume that his second entry actually refers to a different crew, perhaps that of S/L Morton. W/C Singer was the first to take off, at 20.50, on a night when more than a hundred crews had been briefed for targets in Germany, and aerodromes in France, Holland and Belgium. The 101 Squadron targets were the aerodromes at Schiphol, De Kooy (two), Hingene, Flushing (two), St Inglevert (two), Lille (two), Waalhaven and Evere. The commanding officer's sortie was curtailed through the failure of the air supply while over the North Sea, and the bombs were jettisoned. S/L Hartwright was thwarted by haze and intense searchlight activity, while Sgt Sellars returned early with engine failure. The other nine participants, F/L Little, F/O Palmer, P/Os Bicknell, Hill, Miles and Wade and Sgts Balmer and Skipworth, and one other, possibly S/L Morton, delivered their two 250lb and dozen 40lb delayed-action bombs onto their targets, and a number were able to confirm hits, while others were blinded by searchlight dazzle.

Another large effort was mounted on the night of the 19/20th, when 120 aircraft were drawn from 2, 3, 4 and 5 Groups, and sent against multiple targets in Germany and the occupied countries. The objectives for the twelve 101 Squadron crews were once more aerodromes, and F/O Palmer led the way at 20.40, bound for Soesterberg. He was followed by F/L Little (Evere), P/O Hill (Leeuwarden), F/L Monroe (Flushing), Sgt Chelmick (Eindhoven), P/O Wade (Hingene), Sgt Balmer (Lille), Sgt Sellars (Waalhaven), P/O Miles (St Inglevert), P/O Ferguson (Leeuwarden), Sgt Skipworth (Soesterberg), and P/O Bicknell (Antwerp). All those who were coming home were back on the ground by 23.35, and this initially left two unaccounted for. Sgt Bicknell and his crew had set off for Antwerp in N3574 at 22.05, but having lost an engine while over the North Sea, they elected to bomb Haamstede airfield on the island of Schouwen in the Scheldt Estuary, and carried out an attack from 5,000 feet. Unable to maintain height on the way home, the Blenheim was ditched in rough seas off the Suffolk coast close to a trawler, and, although the pilot and observer made strenuous and heroic attempts to free the unconscious gunner, who was trapped in the cockpit, they were unsuccessful, and he went down with the aircraft. In recognition of their gallantry, the two survivors were awarded a DFC and a DFM respectively at the end of the month. Sgt Chelmick and his crew failed to return in L9419, and news eventually reached the squadron, that they were alive and in enemy hands.

Shortly after 21.00 on the 21st, F/O Palmer and P/O Hill took off to attack the aerodromes at Leeuwarden and Soesterberg, but both turned back before reaching the Dutch coast, after encountering severe electrical storms. Eleven crews were briefed on the 24th, for a late take-off that night to carry out attacks on coastal batteries at Cap Gris-Nez and aerodromes in Holland and Belgium. Those heading for airfields mostly took off first, between 22.45 and 00.53, but S/L Morton had a compressed air connection break, and jettisoned his bombs into the sea before returning safely home. P/O Miles failed to locate his primary target, and attacked what he believed to be a flare path near Brussels, while S/L Hartwright and Sgt Balmer also went for alternatives, in the form of searchlights. P/O Hill claimed hits on airfield buildings, and F/O Palmer's gunner saw two blinding flashes in response to his attack at Hingene. F/L Monroe, F/O Smyth, P/Os Brown and Wade and Sgt Skipworth all took off after midnight, making their way individually to the target area, and all dropped their bombs at Cap Gris-Nez without observing results. On the night of the 25/26th, the squadron dispatched six crews, again after midnight, to attack aerodromes in France at Fecamp, Le Touquet, St Inglevert, Boulogne, Berck-sur-Mer and St Malo. F/O Smyth was the senior pilot on duty, and he observed his bombs to fall onto his target at Fecamp. On the way home from St Malo, L8870 struck a balloon cable at 04.20, and crashed a mile south-east of Eastleigh in Hampshire, killing Sgt Balmer and his crew. Airfields were again the objectives on the night of the 29/30th, when the squadron sent out five Blenheims after midnight. Sgt Sellars and F/O Palmer failed to locate their targets, the latter at Morlaix, while P/O Brown started a huge and brilliant fire at Dinard, and F/L Little and Sgt Lorrimer were unable to observe the results of their efforts at St Malo and Fecamp respectively. W/C Singer was the senior pilot on duty on the 31st, when he, F/L Monroe and P/O Wade took off in mid-evening to attack the coastal batteries at Cap Gris-Nez, while P/Os Brown, Ferguson and Hill headed for Emden. All returned safely, and only P/O Ferguson was able to report observing the results of his bombs, which fell into a canal five hundred yards north-east of the target.

September 1940

The new month began for 101 Squadron with the promotion to acting flight lieutenant rank of F/Os Palmer and Monroe. The first operational activity took place on the night of the 4/5th, when four crews were briefed to attack the marshalling yards at Hamm, one of Germany's most important railway centres, situated just to the north-east of the Ruhr. Two others, P/Os Westcott and Cave, were assigned to the aerodrome at Berck-sur-Mer, and departed first, at 20.00 and 20.05, to be followed into the air by the Hamm-bound element between 20.20 and 20.35. The only crew to positively identify their target was that of P/O Cave, who delivered two 250lb delayed action bombs along with a load of incendiaries, but did not observe the results. P/O Westcott was unable to identify the target himself, but bombed on the burst of the incendiaries dropped by P/O Cave. F/L Smyth was the senior pilot on duty of the Hamm contingent, but not one located the target, despite its size. P/O Miles bombed on ETA, and might have been in the right place, while the others bombed an aerodrome, a searchlight and flak battery, and a ship in the North Sea off Alkmaar, before returning safely.

A further six Blenheims were made ready for operations on the night of the 6/7th, four to attack the coastal guns at Cap Gris-Nez, and two the aerodrome at Foret-de-Guines. S/Ls Hartwright and Morton were the senior pilots on duty, and the former was first away at 20.10 bound for Cap Gris-Nez. He reported starting eight fires in the target area, four of them visible from fifteen miles into the return journey. S/L Morton reported three fires, while P/O Brown's bombs straddled the target, and Sgt Skipworth was unable to observe the results of his efforts. F/L Palmer was unable to locate the aerodrome, but F/L Monroe reported starting two small fires. The campaign against invasion barges continued on the night of the 8/9th, when the squadron dispatched ten Blenheims to attack those assembled at Boulogne. The ORB page, that lists seven of those taking part, appears to be missing, but, according to the 2 Group ORB, three crews carried out an attack, four others returned early because of the weather conditions, which included icing, another turned back with engine problems, and two failed to return. P6955 and R2788 both crashed into the sea, and there were no survivors from the crews of F/L Palmer and Sgt Cooke respectively. Eleven Blenheims were made ready for operations on the 10th, and the crews were told at briefing, that their target was to be a concentration of barges at Flushing, on the southern coast of Walcheren. W/C Singer was the senior pilot on duty, and was the first to take off at 20.58, followed by the others at intervals until Sgt Skipworth and crew brought up the rear at 21.50. F/L Monroe and P/Os Brown, Ferguson and Westcott were the only ones to locate and attack the target on a night of unfavourable weather conditions, characterised by rain and heavy cloud, and S/L Hartwright was defeated by a troublesome starboard engine.

Five crews were briefed for a similar operation at Dunkerque on the night of the 14/15th, when S/Ls Hartwright and Morton were the senior pilots on duty, taking off first and last at 22.51 and 23.45 respectively. In the event, both senior officers abandoned their sorties in the face of adverse weather conditions, and it was left to P/Os Cave and Hill and Sgt Skipworth to carry out attacks, the results of which were not observed. All three were afflicted by severe electrical storms as they departed the target area, and came home with minor damage. Later on the 15th, the Battle of Britain reached its crescendo, and Fighter Command inflicted a heavy defeat on the Luftwaffe. W/C Singer and crew set out alone at 05.10 on the 17th, once more to attack barge concentrations at Dunkerque, this time under cover of cloud. They crossed the coast at Orford Ness, and encountered a 200-foot-thick band of three-tenths cloud at 3,000 feet, which had largely dispersed by the time they were thirty miles out over the Channel. They were left with four-tenths medium cloud at 9,000 feet, which was insufficient for the task in hand, and the sortie was abandoned. On the way home, three barrage balloons were seen to be drifting in the Orford Ness area, upon which, two Blenheims were dispatched at 06.40 to shoot them down, but failed to do so. Fourteen aircraft are listed as involved in two further operations against invasion barges at Dunkerque on the night of the 18/19th, the first section of four departing West Raynham between 19.50 and 20.40, with S/L Hartwright taking the lead. The second section of ten, among which, W/C Singer was the senior pilot on duty, took off between 23.54 and 01.17, and made its way to the enemy coast in bright moonlight and good visibility. The attacks were carried out from between 7,000 and 12,000 feet, most crews adopting a glide approach in the face of a very limited searchlight and flak response, and returning crews claimed good results. The ten aircraft involved in a return to Dunkerque harbour on the night of 20/21st, took off between 21.10 and 21.56, carrying four 250 pounders each, and were led away by S/L Hartwright. P/O Cave turned back with a faulty ASI, but the others pressed on to carry out glide attacks from 12,000 down to 7,000 feet in clear skies and under a full moon, and all returned safely home.

At 03.05 on the 23rd, the first of nine aircraft took off at five-minute intervals to attack the docks at either Zeebrugge or Calais. Six were assigned to the former, and were led by S/L Hartwright, while F/L Monroe headed the trio bound for Calais. All carried out attacks as briefed, in good visibility, delivering four 250 pounders each and a few incendiaries in a glide approach from between 14,000 and 7,000 feet, some observing bomb bursts in Nos 1, 2 and 4 basins at Zeebrugge, and fires visible from twenty miles into the return journey. There was another very early start on the 25th, for eight crews briefed to attack the docks at Ostend. F/Ls Smyth and Monroe were the senior pilots on duty as they took off between 03.12 and 03.59, and all but Sgt Tucker and crew were able to locate the target in fine weather conditions. Attacks were carried out mostly in a straight-and-level run from between 11,000 and 14,000 feet, although P/O Wade glided down from 10,000 to 6,000 feet to deliver his four 250 pounders. Sgt Lorrimer and his crew were killed, when P6905 crashed at Swaffham in Norfolk on the way home. The pattern of early take-offs continued on the 27th, when six Blenheims were dispatched to bomb the docks at Calais. S/L Hartwright was the senior pilot on duty as they departed West Raynham between 03.14 and 04.15, and all reached the target area to find fine weather conditions and good visibility. Attacks were delivered from between 6,000 and 14,000 feet, and a number of hits were observed.

The 101 Squadron ORB does not refer in detail to the operation on the evening of the 28th, when nine Blenheims were dispatched to attack the coastal batteries at Cap Gris-Nez. We do not know, therefore, which crews were involved, and we have little detail of their efforts. The 2 Group ORB states that aircraft began departing at 21.06 at five-minute intervals, and two failed to complete the operation, one as a result of low cloud, and the other through engine trouble. Five aircraft carried out an attack on the gun emplacements, and bomb bursts were observed at Floringzelle, Le Vivier and Haringzelles, while one aircraft attacked Wimereux and another Calais, without observing results. All returned safely to home airspace, and the last one landed at 23.55, but, it seems that Sgt Tucker crashed on landing, and damaged two other aircraft in the process. The final operation of the month took place on the evening of the 30th, when the squadron dispatched seven Blenheims at five-minute intervals from 18.52 to attack the docks at Boulogne. S/L Hartwright was the senior pilot on duty, and was one of five to bomb as briefed in good visibility, although he did not observe the fall of his 250 pounders. The attacks were carried out from between 9,000 and 11,000 feet, and some explosions were seen. F/L Smyth and P/O Wade attacked Calais as an alternative target, and the former's T2234 had a flak shell pass through the rear fuselage.

October 1940

A change of Commander-in-Chief on the 5th of October saw the departure of Sir Charles Portal to become Chief of the Air Staff, and he was replaced by ACM Sir Richard Peirse, who was to have an uncomfortable time at the helm. The new month was to require 101 Squadron to continue operations under G.O.O.11, while also attacking Channel ports, industrial and communications targets in Germany and heavy gun emplacements in the Pas-de-Calais. The weather proved to be a major problem, and heavy cloud obscured the ground in 2 Group's theatre of operations most of the time. P/O Miles took off for Calais at 19.00 on the 2nd to open the squadron's account for the new month, but found the target area to be obscured by ten-tenths cloud, and dropped his bombs on an unspecified alternative. Later, P/O Brown took off for the same target at 23.31, but also encountered ten-tenths cloud in a solid layer from 1,000 up to 15,000 feet, and he abandoned his sortie. F/L Smyth took off at 06.25 on the 5th, intending to attack a Ruhr oil target under cover of cloud, but, on reaching the English coast, it was clear that there was insufficient, and, on his return, the five other planned sorties were cancelled. On the 7th, F/O Cree and Sgt Sellars set out at 06.45 to attack targets in the Ruhr under cover of cloud, but, again, when they were fifty miles out from the coast the cloud was found to be dispersing, and the sorties were abandoned.

S/L Hartwright was the senior pilot on duty as eight 101 Squadron Blenheims began to depart West Raynham at 18.55 on the 8th, three to attack Flushing, and five Boulogne. S/L Hartwright began to experience problems with his port engine, and turned back, while the remainder continued on, two of them failing to locate their objectives. Two crews attacked Flushing, and observed bombs falling onto the Walcheren Canal, and, although two others bombed in the Boulogne area, they were unable to make a positive identification because of cloud and poor visibility, and did not see their bombs burst. One crew joined in the 82 Squadron attack on the docks at Calais, and watched their bombs find the mark. W/C Singer and crew started the ball rolling on the evening of the 10th, when taking off at 18.40 as one of two assigned to attack a target at Schwerte, situated just south of Dortmund in the Ruhr. The other crew was that of F/O Cree, who took off at 20.45, but neither located the primary target in cloudy and wet conditions. W/C Singer aimed his bombs from 9,000 feet at a blast furnace at nearby Oberhausen, while F/O Cree attacked the marshalling yards at Gelsenkirchen from 10,000 feet. P/Os Westcott and Hill and Sgt Skipworth were sent to southern Germany to attack a target in Mannheim, and only Sgt Skipworth got close in cloudy conditions, delivering his bombs on approach from 6,000 feet. P/O Westcott bombed a fire seen burning on the north bank of the Mosel River, while P/O Hill bombed a railway bridge five miles south of Liege on the way home. The remaining seven crews were briefed for Boulogne, but Sgt MacDonough became ill, and was forced to turn back. Three of the others carried out glide attacks, releasing their bombs from between 6,000 and 8,000 feet, while Sgt Tucker flew in straight-and-level at 10,000 feet. P/O Cave was thwarted by cloud on his first attempt, and returned thirty minutes later to drop his bombs onto the inner harbour from 10,000 feet. P/O McLaren was unable to locate the primary target, so made his way to Calais at 18,000 feet, before gliding down to 7,000 feet to bomb searchlights in the general area of the port.

Among the crews posted to the Middle East on the 12th, were those of F/L Smyth, and P/Os Ferguson, Miles and Wade. That night, three aircraft were sent to attack the marshalling yards at Cologne-Eifeltor, while nine others attended to the docks at Le Havre. W/C Singer took off at 18.24 at the head of the Le Havre-bound contingent of nine aircraft, and S/L Hartwright was the senior pilot on duty for Cologne, with P/O Brown and Sgt Skipworth following over the ensuing thirty minutes. P/O Brown and Sgt Skipworth identified the target from 11,000 and 14,000 feet respectively, and descended a few thousand feet each, before watching their bombs fall across the marshalling yards. S/L Hartgrove failed to locate either the primary or secondary targets, and, instead, bombed the airfield at Hangelar, ten miles to the south from 14,000 feet. Eight crews attacked Le Havre from between 4,000 and 12,000 feet, and explosions were observed in the docks area, along with many fires. The briefed targets for the evening of the 15th were at Le Havre, Krefeld and Soest, for which take-off began at 18.25, and continued for an hour. Six crews were assigned to Le Havre, where cloud hampered the efforts of some to locate the aiming-point, but four bombed it from between 2,000 and 9,000 feet, those from the lower levels adopting a glide approach, and some bomb bursts were observed. Sgt Tucker and P/O McLaren failed to identify the primary, and followed the coast to Cap Gris-Nez, where they bombed the coastal batteries without observing the results. Ground mist obscured much of the Ruhr region, and Soest proved difficult to locate, forcing the three assigned crews to find alternatives. F/O Cree bombed a railway in the general target area from 14,000 feet, Sgt Skipworth attacked the marshalling yards at Hamm from 10,000 feet, and P/O Hill dropped his load from 11,000 feet onto a railway junction at Münster. P/Os Brown and Cave managed to locate Krefeld, and delivered their bombs from 8,000 and 9,000 feet respectively after gliding down, while F/L Monroe found a target at Duisburg-Ruhrort, and delivered a stick of bombs from 6,000 feet, which fell within a hundred yards of a blast furnace.

On the 19th, the squadron bade farewell to S/L Morton, who was posted to 13 O.T.U. The evening of the 20th found nine 101 Squadron Blenheims taking off between 18.12 and 19.31 to attack the airfields at Flushing and St Omer. W/C Singer was the senior pilot on duty, and his was one of four crews bound for the latter, while F/L Monroe led those assigned to Flushing. In the event, F/L Monroe became indisposed and turned back, and P/O McLaren failed to find a suitable target for his bombs. The remainder attacked their briefed objectives, three at Flushing from between 7,000 and 11,000 feet, and two at St-Omer from 5,000 and 10,000 feet, or found alternatives at Mardyck and Dunkerque. Fog at home meant using every kind of flare device available, and all eventually landed safely, although the last two set pulses racing as they arrived at the airfield boundary almost simultaneously, and touched down with a mere fifty yards between them. Nine Blenheims were prepared on the 23rd, five for operations that night against a warehouse and munitions ship in the Hook of Holland docks, three, it is believed, for a target at Herringen, west of Hamm, and one for Mannheim. Take-offs began with that of S/L Hartwright at 01.12, bound for Herringen. He was unable to locate the target in the face of ten-tenths cloud, but, on his way home, came across the Hook of Holland, and joined in the attack there, as did F/L Monroe. All five assigned to this target managed to find it, and bombed the warehouse from 4,000 to 6,000 feet, but failed to hit the ship. F/O Graham found Mannheim obscured by cloud, and dropped his bombs on Coblenz from 8,000 feet on his way home.

Visibility was sufficiently good on the night of the 25/26th for three crews to locate the heavy guns at Cap Gris Nez. This was intended to be a nuisance raid, for which F/L Cree, P/O Hill and Sgt Skipworth took off in the early evening, with orders to remain over the target for thirty minutes, releasing bombs singly, while they awaited the arrival of elements from another squadron. Each made four runs across the target from between 4,000 and 14,000 feet, and a number of bursts were observed. The remaining crews took off between 01.40 and 02.46 to attack aerodromes at Schiphol and Antwerp-Deurne, and a railway target at Soest. The two crews heading for Belgium ran into conditions of severe icing, and turned back, while P/O McLaren bombed Schiphol airfield from 10,000 feet, two others attacked searchlights at Hamm and Krefeld, and another the docks at Medemblik on the eastern coast of the Den Helder peninsular. F/L Monroe was promoted to the acting rank of squadron leader on the 26th, and would assume the flight commander role vacated by S/L Morton. On the 27th, it was the turn of the Luftwaffe to retaliate to 101 Squadron's aggression, by bombing West Raynham airfield at 18.15, having bombed Great Massingham some fifteen minutes earlier. The airfield was put out of action by craters, and some aircraft were slightly damaged, but there were no human casualties. The Luftwaffe returned on the evening of the 29th, and again rendered the airfield temporarily unusable. Six Blenheims were made ready for operations on the evening of the 30th, four to attack Duisburg-Ruhrort, and two the new Ruhrort harbour. They took off between 17.11 and 17.55, but S/L Monroe became indisposed, and had to return. Apart from Sgt Sellars, who returned early with instrument failure, the other crews found the target area to be obscured by ten-tenths cloud at between 2,000 and 4,000 feet, which forced them to seek out alternatives in that part of the Ruhr. The return of P/O Cave and crew in T2246 was overdue, when news eventually came through, that the Blenheim had crashed at 23.00 into a wood at Coleby in north Lincolnshire, and all on board had lost their lives.

November 1940

The new month began for the squadron with attacks on six airfields, each assigned to a single crew carrying two instant-fused 250 pounders and two delayed-action. The target airfields in Holland were at De Kooy, Flushing, Schillingwoude and Waalhaven, and were handed to W/C Singer, F/L Graham and P/Os Brown and Hill, not necessarily in that order, while those in France were at St-Omer and Le Touquet, for which the crews of S/L Hartwright and F/L Cree had been briefed. The commanding officer was the first to take off, at 17.10, and he observed the flash from his exploding bombs. F/L Graham attacked Schillingwoude from 6,500 feet, and believed his bombs to have fallen into the harbour entrance. P/O Hill made five approaches before delivering his bombs from 7,500 feet, but was unable to assess the results. P/O Brown dropped his bombs from 8,000 feet, again without being able to plot their fall. Meanwhile, in France, S/L Hartwright made his attack at Le Touquet from 10,000 feet, and saw bomb bursts across the flare-path. F/L Cree released his four 250 pounders from 5,000 feet onto St-Omer airfield, and saw two explosions. All returned safely before 21.00, although S/L Hartwright landed by mistake on the dummy airfield at Bircham Newton, but got away with it. It seems that operations were being launched at the time from the satellite airfield at Great Massingham, which became waterlogged through persistent rain during the first week of the month, and was consequently declared unfit for operations.

The 8th brought fine weather, and, according to the 2 Group ORB, ten 101 Squadron Blenheims were made ready for operations that night, nine of the crews briefed to attack an oil plant at Gelsenkirchen, while a singleton was assigned to the docks at Le Havre. P/O Brown took off at 18.58 to head for the French coast, and bombed the docks from 10,000 feet, observing detonations in the Bassin Bellot. The Squadron ORB lists eight crews for the main target, with S/L Hartwright the senior pilot on duty. He took off at 19.37, but was forced to return early after his wireless operator became indisposed. P/O Hill had been the first to depart West Raynham, at 18.55, but he was unable to locate the target because of cloud over the Ruhr, and bombed the Rhine docks at Duisburg-Ruhrort as an alternative objective. Only three aircraft, those of F/L Cree and P/Os McLaren and Waugh attacked at Gelsenkirchen, from 12,000 to 13,000 feet, while Sgt Tucker, unable to locate the primary, bombed searchlights in the general target area. P/O Westcott was blinded by searchlight activity in the target area, and ultimately aimed his bombs at a railway bridge over the Rhine at an unspecified location from 8,000 feet. They failed to hit the bridge, and exploded on the eastern bank of the river. Sgt Sellars experienced problems with the fuel mixture control while outbound over the North Sea, and, in attempting to bomb the docks in the Hook of Holland as an alternative, hit the railway station adjacent to them.

The conditions at Great Massingham forced the squadron to fly its Blenheims back to West Raynham, and this took place over the 10th and 11th. Five sorties were dispatched between 19.50 and 21.17 on the 14th, each with a crew briefed to attack the airfields at Rennes and Evreau in France. S/L Hartwright saw no activity at Evreau, and bombed St Pierre from 16,000 feet as an alternative at 21.35. P/O Brown attacked Rennes from 4,500 feet at 23.40, observing three bomb bursts on the runway, and the fourth possibly hitting a hangar. F/L Graham ran out of time to reach Evreau, and dropped his hardware onto Etaples aerodrome from 10,000 feet at 22.05 instead, without observing any results. Sgt Skipworth was unable to locate his target, despite searching, and bombed Le Havre docks from 6,000 feet on the way home at 22.38, observing four bursts. P/O Westcott became indisposed while outbound, and failed to reach his primary target. On the way home at 22.45, he attacked the harbour at Dunkerque from 8,000 feet, and observed bursts among ships moored in the outer harbour. Three Blenheims took off between 17.38 and 17.50 on the 15th to bomb airfields in France. F/L Cree attacked an airfield north of Chartres from 700 feet, and strafed an aerial lighthouse and beacon with front and rear guns. Sgt Skipworth headed first for Etampes, before flying on to a second objective at St-Cyr, where the landing ground was identified as the only objective worthy of attention. The 2 Group ORB makes reference to an attack at Voves-Villars, which was south of Chartres, but who might have been responsible for this cannot be determined. S/L Monroe failed to find anything to bomb in his assigned target area, and dropped his 250 pounders on the airfield at Abbeville from 500 feet as an alternative on the way home, and also gave his gunners free rein. All arrived safely home, the last one landing at 22.17.

Eleven crews were briefed on the 16th, nine for an objective in Hamburg, and two freshmen for Schiphol airfield. W/C Singer was the first away of the main contingent at 17.15, followed closely by the others, with Sgt Sellars bringing up the rear at 17.49. S/L Hartwright returned early with engine trouble, P/O McLaren because of severe icing, and Sgt Sellars was also defeated by the weather conditions, he ultimately landing at Leuchars in Scotland after receiving incorrect W/T bearings from West Raynham. The remaining six aircraft, captained by W/C Singer, F/Ls Cree and Graham, P/Os Brown and Thompson and Sgt Skipworth reached Hamburg to bomb between 19.17 and 20.14 from 9,000 to 14,000 feet through almost complete cloud cover, which prevented any assessment of the outcome. Schiphol was bombed by Sgts Clarke and Palmer from between 4,500 and 5,000 feet in the face of a flak defence, which prevented them from observing the results. The target for the evening of the 20th was the docks at Duisburg-Ruhrort, for which five crews were briefed. Take-offs took place between 21.37 and 22.15, with F/Ls Cree and Graham the senior pilots on duty. F/L Graham's navigator became indisposed, and the sortie was abandoned. Sgt Sellars also felt unwell, and he, too, returned early. The three remaining aircraft reached the target to deliver their two 250 pounders and one container each of 40lb bomblets and incendiaries from 10,000 to 15,000 feet between 23.14 and 23.25. They arrived home optimistic about the results of their efforts, reporting bomb bursts and fires. Six Blenheims began taking off at 08.23 on the 22nd to carry out cloud-cover attacks on shipping at Antwerp and Rotterdam, but fifty miles out over the sea it became clear that the cloud was insufficient, and all returned to base. P/O Brown was awarded the DFC on the 23rd, and his two crew members a DFM each for their great skill and determination in locating their targets and pressing home their attacks, usually in the face of heavy anti-aircraft fire.

There is a little confusion concerning operations on the nights of the 23/24th and 24/25th. According to Bill Chorley in Bomber Command Losses Vol 1, Sgt Redmond and crew went to Wanne-Eickel on the 23rd, and crashed on return. The squadron and group ORBs make no reference concerning this event, or of 101 Squadron operating on this night. The 2 Group ORB refers to eight Blenheims being dispatched to Hamburg on the evening of the 24th, but makes no reference to the crash of the Redmond crew. The 101 Squadron ORB, however, records nine Blenheims departing for Hamburg, and details the events leading to the crash. They took off between 17.00 and 17.19, with F/L Graham the senior pilot on duty, but he turned back because of ice accretion, and P/O Thompson had his fixed aerial break away from the mast and become wrapped around the tail-plane, forcing him also to turn back. Five crews returned home to report attacking the target through eight to ten-tenths cloud from 12,000 to 14,000 feet, between 19.08 and 19.25, and some observed the reflections of exploding bombs. It is believed, that Sgt Redmond and crew carried out their attack, and it was during the return flight across the North Sea that the lock nut on the spider of the starboard engine reduction gear worked loose, causing the casing to be churned away. The propeller eventually sheared off, leaving N6236 to limp home on one engine, and it was in the West Raynham circuit when control was lost and it crashed. The pilot and gunner sustained minor head injuries, but the observer suffered a fractured skull, and lost his fight for life, according to the ORB, on the 26th, and according to Bill Chorley, on the 28th. N6238 failed to return after disappearing into the sea somewhere off the English coast. It had taken off at 17.03, and was last heard from on R/T at 19.05. Only the body of the pilot, F/O Waugh, was eventually washed ashore on the English coast some ten weeks later.

Eight Blenheims were made ready for operations on the 26th, three each to attack marshalling yards at Hamm and Schwerte, and two for a similar target at Soest. S/L Monroe took off first at 16.55 bound for Hamm, but R3803 developed a problem with his starboard engine, and it was decided to bomb Schiphol airfield as an alternative. This was carried out from 6,000 feet at 17.45, after which the Blenheim returned safely home to land at 19.00. F/L Cree and P/O McLaren were also assigned to Hamm, and took off at 18.25 and 20.11, carrying out their attacks from 14,000 and 15,000 feet at 20.13 and 21.46 respectively. Sgt Rickinson, F/L Graham and Sgt Palmer took off for Schwerte at 17.15, 18.40 and 20.19 respectively, but only the last-mentioned was able to identify the target in conditions of nine-tenths cloud. His success was probably the result of coming down to below the cloud base to deliver his attack from 2,000 feet, where searchlight dazzle and flak prevented an assessment of results. This aircraft eventually crashed on landing at Cottesmore after failing to locate West Raynham, but all on board emerged unscathed. The other two bombed in the general target area, and had no idea where their bombs fell. Sgt Clarke and crew attacked Soest from 12,000 feet at 22.20, after which, wireless problems resulted in them landing at Digby. The second crew assigned to this target is not mentioned in the Squadron ORB, but there is a report, that they bombed Emmerich from 10,000 feet at 19.01 as an alternative, after the wireless operator became ill.

Seven Blenheims were dispatched on the evening of the 29th, six to attack a target in Bremen, while the freshman crew of Sgt Caunt was sent to bomb the docks at Boulogne. The last-mentioned took off at 16.53, bombed the target from 14,000 feet at 18.17, and returned safely to report being unable to determine the results. The others took off between 16.45 and 17.20, with F/O McLaren the senior pilot on duty, accompanied by P/Os Brown and Hill and Sgts Clarke, Rickinson and Skipworth. All reached the target area in conditions of excellent visibility, which enable them to pick up land marks to assist navigation. They bombed from 8,500 to 14,500 feet between 19.04 and 20.15, and returned to report bursts in the vicinity of the aiming-point. This was the final activity of the month, during the course of which seventy sorties had been dispatched.

December 1940

Sgt Palmer and crew were detached to Thorney Island on the 1st, pending their posting to the Middle-East, and the ORB records them as missing on a flight from Thorney Island on the 2nd. Fog and then generally inclement weather conditions caused the cancellation of operations on the 2nd and 3rd, and it was between 03.25 and 03.50 on the 5th before the month's first six operational sorties were launched. S/Ls Hartwright and Monroe were the senior pilots on duty as they headed for Düsseldorf, but none located the target in the conditions of heavy cloud and icing. P/O Hill dropped his bombs from 15,500 feet at 04.31 onto a concentration of flak batteries in the Wesel area, and S/L Hartwright released his over Duisburg from 19,000 feet at 04.58. S/L Monroe dropped his bombs in the general target area from 18,000 feet at 05.03, Sgt Skipworth attacked two flare-paths at Vught in Holland, causing one to be switched off, and P/O Brown bombed a flare-path and beacon at Hasselt in Belgium from 2,000 feet at 06.22. F/O McLaren was unable to find a recipient for his bomb load, and brought it back. Eight aircraft were prepared for operations against a target in Düsseldorf on the night of the 7/8th, for which W/C Singer was to be the senior pilot on duty. They took off between 18.57 and 20.11, but the commanding officer and P/O McLaren were forced to bring their bombs home after the former's wireless operator/gunner became indisposed, and the latter's communications system failed. Of the others, Sgts Rickinson and Clarke attacked the primary target from 14,000 feet, and P/O Hill from 15,000 feet, between 20.58 and 21.10, and observed bomb bursts. F/L Cree was unable to find the target because of ten-tenths cloud, and bombed the docks at Boulogne from 10,000 feet as an alternative. P/O Brown admitted to becoming lost, and bombed a factory at Coblenz from 11,000 feet at 22.03, proving him to be well to the south of his intended target area. Sgt Caunt's sortie was compromised by icing conditions while outbound over Holland, and he dropped his bombs onto fifteen searchlights two miles south-west of Rotterdam.

Seven 101 Squadron Blenheims took off between 03.18 and 04.40 on the 11th, three of them assigned to a railway target in Soest, and four to an objective at Stockum-Lippe, some fifty miles south-east of Cologne. S/L Hartwright was the senior pilot on duty for the latter, and he returned early after his wireless operator/gunner became indisposed. None of the others located this target in the face of ten-tenths cloud, P/O Brown bombing a flare-path at Soesterberg in Holland, and Sgt Clarke releasing his load over the Bochum area, before running into a severe electrical storm on the way home near Amsterdam. This caused his starboard engine to fail, and he had to cross the North Sea on the other one, eventually landing safely at Langham. F/L Cree failed to locate Soest, and brought his bombs back, while Sgt Caunt and P/O Brown bombed on ETA, without observing results.

Blenheim IV N6142 survived her time with 101 Sqn., despite a wheels-up landing in December 1940. The aircraft was later transferred to No. 5 Bombing and Gunnery School, Jurby, Isle of Man (GW).

The night of the 16/17th was one of significance for Bomber Command for a number of reasons. Operation Abigail Rachel was an attack on the centre of the southern German city of Mannheim, and was, therefore, a blatant area raid, and was mounted in response to recent devastating Luftwaffe assaults on British cities, Coventry and Southampton in particular. It was also to be the largest attack yet on a single target, for which 134 aircraft were made ready. The figure would have been higher, had meteorologists not threatened deteriorating weather conditions over the bomber stations as the crews' return was due. A total of nine Blenheims represented 2 Group, seven from 101 Squadron and two from 114 Squadron, the former taking off between 20.45 and 21.25, led away by W/C Singer. It was not to be a successful night for the Command, or a happy one for 101 Squadron, which would register its final casualties of the year. The attack was opened by Wellingtons, which were supposed to drop incendiaries to set fire to the city centre as a beacon for those following behind, but, despite favourable conditions of clear skies and moonlight, they failed to achieve any concentration, and the bombing was scattered. 240 buildings were destroyed, mostly in residential districts, at a cost to the Command of just three aircraft, while four more crashed at home. W/C Singer was blown off course by a wrongly forecast wind, and bombed a small town with a railway instead. P/Os Brown and Hill and F/L Graham were the only ones from the squadron to reach the target area, and bombed from between 12,000 and 15,000 feet at around 23.10. Ten-tenths cloud caused major navigational problems on the way home, forcing P/O Hill and his crew to abandon their fuel starved Z5801 near Plymouth. They had sent an SOS, and received a response from Plympton with a course to steer, but ran out of fuel after eight hours and forty minutes aloft. They, at least, landed safely between Brixham and Plymouth, but their colleagues, Sgt Skipworth and his crew, were less fortunate, and all died when P6953 crashed near Hastings in Sussex, and was destroyed by fire. P/O Brown pulled off a wheels-up landing at Cornwood, near Plymouth, damaging N6142, but not its occupants. The return of T2039 was awaited in vain, after an SOS signal had provided a fix in the region of St Quentin in France. No trace of it or the crew of Sgt Clarke was ever found, suggesting that it had gone down over the sea.

The squadron had a few days to lick its wounds before the next operations, which were mounted on the night of the 20/21st, although it was well into the 21st before they actually got away from West Raynham. Four crews were assigned to an unspecified target at Gelsenkirchen, and two to the docks at Dunkerque, and the former, F/L Cree, F/Os Thompson and McLaren and Sgt Rickinson, took off first, between 04.02 and 04.17. They were followed into the air an hour later by P/O Westcott and Sgt Langrish. Three crews located and bombed the primary target from between 10,000 and 17,000 feet, and flashes were observed on the ground, but Sgt Rickinson failed to locate it, and dropped his bombs close to a railway line in Duisburg. Both of the Dunkerque-bound crews found their target, delivering their 250 pounders from 10,000 feet, and observing bomb bursts across Nos 4 and 5 Docks. On the 23rd, F/L Cree and F/O McLaren took off twenty minutes apart either side of 17.00 briefed to attack aerodromes in the Lille region of France. F/L Cree abandoned his sortie in the face of ten-tenths cloud and rain, and brought his bombs home. F/O McLaren found Lille-Nord airfield, and bombed the flare-path from 1,000 feet, although an incorrect bomb selection resulted in only four flares, six 40lb bomblets and a single delayed action 250 pounder falling away. On Christmas Day, the acting rank of flight lieutenant was bestowed upon him, while F/Ls Graham and Cree were elevated to acting squadron leaders to take over the roles of A and B Flight commanders respectively.

The final operation of the year was reserved for New Year's Eve, and involved four crews taking off between 12.45 and 13.32 to attack an unspecified target in Emmerich, situated on the German/Dutch border, under cover of cloud. F/L McLaren and Sgts Rickinson and Caunt turned back when thirty miles out over the sea because of insufficient cloud, but S/L Cree pressed on in the hope of reaching Flushing. On the way, he came across a one-thousand-ton patrol vessel in the western entrance to the port, and carried out a beam attack from 400 feet, scoring a direct hit amidships. As he left the scene, the ship was seen to be listing to port and sinking by the stern with steam escaping. It had been a backs-to-the-wall struggle for the Command since the fall of France, and, without the means to carry the offensive to the enemy, this was to continue for the foreseeable future. Prospects were bleak in the face of an, as yet, all-conquering Nazi war machine, but, at least, Britain had survived far longer than the three weeks offered by the prophets of doom. The crews of Bomber Command were the embodiment of the nation's defiant face and bold heart, nightly undergoing an ordeal of unbelievable discomfort for hours on end in their cramped, unheated aircraft, or flying by daylight into the teeth of ferocious flak and fighter defences. Ominously, the coming year could promise only more of the same.

January 1941

101 Squadron group photograph, taken at Weasingham on January 12th 1941. Back row, left to right: Sgts Rickinson, Kniveton, Wilde, Cainaerts, De Ath, Chesterman, Woodruff, Wakefield, Langnish, Rampley, Gray, Canant, Kidle, Loughlin, Chell. Middle row, left to right: P/O Annandale, Sgts Meadows, Redmond, Symondson, F/Sgts Screech, Croft, W/O Burke, F/Sgts Gosney, Hoyle, Sgts Jefferies, Martin, Archer-Crump, P/O Pearse. Seated, left to right: P/O's Brown, Westcott, Arthur, F/Lt. MacLaren, S/Ldr. Cree, W/Cdr. Singer, F/Lt. Blackmore (Adj.), S/Ldr. Graham, F/Lt. Hill, P/O Glover, F/O Baker, P/O Rogers (GW).

The year began with German ports as the main focus of attention, Bremen bearing the brunt during the first week, and Wilhelmshaven during the second, and later in January. The Blenheim squadrons were largely inactive throughout the month, and most of the sorties that did take place resulted in failure to bomb the assigned targets. 101 Squadron dispatched two Blenheims shortly after 08.30 on New Year's Day, P/O Westcott to attack Emmerich, and F/L McLaren an airfield near the French coast. The former returned early because of insufficient cloud, while the latter ran into a ME110 just inland, about six miles south-west of Cherbourg, and brought his bombs back after escaping into cloud. Promotions continued with the elevation of the long-serving P/O Hill to acting flight lieutenant rank. Unfavourable weather conditions prevented operations from taking place on the 2nd, 3rd and 4th, but P/O Brown managed to sneak in a cloud-cover attack on Flushing airfield on the 5th, taking off at 11.50 and bombing two hours later from 7,000 feet, without observing results. On the 7th, the newly promoted W/C Hartwright was posted to 13 Empire Flying Training School (EFTS).

There were no further operations until mid-month, as the weather continued to make flying conditions uncomfortable. Six Blenheims were made ready on the 16th for an attack on Wilhelmshaven, and took off between 17.34 and 17.50, with S/L Graham last away and the senior pilot on duty. He encountered a large bank of cloud a hundred miles off the English coast, and turned back, while Sgts Caunt and Rickinson each experienced engine problems, which caused them to abandon their sorties. Sgt Rickinson dropped his bombs on the docks at Den Helder from 11,000 feet, but Sgt Caunt brought his back, and overshot the flare path, ending up close to the airfield boundary fence with a collapsed undercarriage. While this operation was in progress, the freshman crews of Sgts Kiddle and Redmond were heading for Boulogne to bomb the docks. The former found the target to be obscured by ten-tenths cloud, and brought his bombs home, while the latter was able to deliver four 250 pounders and two 40 pounders from 10,000 feet, and watch them straddle docks 4 and 7. This proved to be the final operational activity of the month for the squadron.

Between the 22nd of January and the 10th of February, no night bombing operations were undertaken by Blenheims, and, anyway, their limited range and small bomb load precluded them from conducting effective attacks on targets in Germany. Never-the-less, under an Operations Instruction issued on the 25th of January, they were still to participate in night attacks against oil, industrial, railway and airfield targets during the moon period, if weather conditions were deemed to be suitable. This was in line with a new Air Ministry directive issued ten days earlier, which claimed that the next six months would bring a critical period for Germany's oil situation, and that a concerted effort against this industry could have an impact on the enemy's war effort. A list of seventeen oil related sites was drawn up accordingly, the top nine of which represented 80% of all synthetic oil production. It would be February before Peirse could implement this policy properly, although he had already despatched a record force of 135 aircraft to Gelsenkirchen on the 9/10th of January, barely a third of which had reached it to bomb.

February 1941

The squadron's first casualty of the year came not through operations, but via a training accident on the 2nd of February. It involved N3570, which crashed on the beach near Freiston, south of Boston, killing one of Sgt Langrish's crew outright, and fatally injuring another who succumbed on the following day. The body of F/O Waugh, who had been lost on the 24th of November, was washed ashore at this time at Eccles on the Norfolk coast. The first operational activity of the new month took place on the evening of the 5th, when six crews were sent to attack airfields in "beats" 1 and 2. The targets were at Lille-Rochin, Lille-Nord, Vitry-en-Artois in France, Willemstaad in Holland and Antwerp-Deurne in Belgium. They took off between 17.30 and 18.00, with S/Ls Cree and Graham the senior pilots on duty and last away from West Raynham. The former attacked an unidentified airfield south of Willemstaad from 2,000 feet, but it wasn't enough to extinguish the flare-path. The latter found a flare-path at Lille-Rochin, and bombed it from 900 feet, whereupon all of the lights went out. F/L McLaren bombed at Lille-Nord from 11,000 feet without observing any results, and P/O Brown descended to 400 feet to deposit his bombs on Vitry-en-Artois, and watched them straddle the runway and two aircraft about to take-off. Sgt Rickinson attended to Antwerp-Deurne from 800 feet, before dropping leaflets over Antwerp. Only P/O Westcott returned with nothing to report, having found no activity in his target area.

A new record force of 222 aircraft, including thirty-four Blenheims, set off for Hannover on the evening of the 10th, to attack industrial targets. 183 returning crews claimed to have attacked as briefed, and reported good results. 101 Squadron was not involved in this main event, but W/C Singer took off at 18.05 in the lead Blenheim of four, bound for oil storage tanks at Rotterdam. A fifth aircraft, captained by Sgt Kiddle, took off much later for the same target, but abandoned the sortie at Lowestoft because of communications problems. W/C Singer and Sgts Redmond, Caunt and Burrows carried out attacks from between 7,000 and 21,000 feet, and all reported bomb bursts in the target area. The night of the 14/15th was devoted to attacks on Germany's

29

The theoretical efectiveness of the standard camouflage scheme is demonstrated in this photograph of Blenheim IV SR-C (GW).

oil industry at two sites, both by forces of forty-four aircraft. Gelsenkirchen was an all-Wellington affair, while those heading for Homberg, a north-western district of Duisburg, were Wellingtons and Blenheims in equal numbers. Seven 101 Squadron crews were detailed, and departed West Raynham between 18.10 and 18.35, with F/L McLaren the senior pilot on duty. He was unable to locate the target because of cloud and ground haze, and bombed on ETA from 12,000 feet. P/O Brown and Sgts Rickinson and Kiddle also bombed on ETA, from 11,000 feet, and saw flashes on the ground. Sgt Redmond dropped his bombs on Duisburg docks from 10,000 feet, Sgt Burrows bombed a flare-path at A in Holland from 12,000 feet, while Sgt Caunt brought his bombs home after failing to identify a suitable target. The operation was not successful, and was scheduled again for the following night, when a force of seventy Hampdens and Blenheims was made ready, including seven representing 101 Squadron. They took off between 18.10 and 18.45, while the freshman crew of Sgt Cook departed at 18.10, bound for the docks at Boulogne. Sgt Rickinson returned early with engine trouble, and P/O Brown and Sgts Caunt and Kiddle failed to locate the primary target because of searchlight activity and ground haze. They dropped their bombs on alternative targets of opportunity in the Ruhr area, while F/L Hill and Sgts Burrows and Redmond did manage to locate the primary, and delivered their bombs from between 10,000 and 16,000 feet. Sgt Cook returned safely from Boulogne to report bombing from 6,000 feet and observing bursts in the target area. The final operation of the month involved 116 assorted aircraft on the evening of the 28th, whose task was to try to hit the battleship Tirpitz in the port of Wilhelmshaven. 101 Squadron's contribution was seven Blenheims, which took off between 21.35 and 22.00, by which time, P/O Jones had been to Boulogne to bomb the docks, and had returned safely. S/Ls Cree and Graham were the senior pilots on duty, and both reached the target, along with F/L McLaren and Sgts Kiddle, Redmond and Rickinson, to bomb from between 10,000 and 14,000 feet through nine-tenths cloud. Sgt Caunt was the only one not to reach the target following instrument failure, and he dropped his bombs on Papenburg instead. No one was able to assess the results, and the Tirpitz was not hit.

March 1941

There were no operations for the first two weeks of the new months, as persistent adverse weather conditions restricted flying to training and army co-operation exercises. West Raynham became unserviceable for a time, and arrangements were made to operate from Bodney. In response to the mounting losses of Allied shipping to U-Boots in the Atlantic, a new Air Ministry directive was issued on the 9th of March, which changed the priority from oil to maritime matters. From now on, the U-Boot, and its partner in crime, the Focke-Wulf Kondor long-range reconnaissance bomber, were to be hunted down where-ever they could be found, at sea, in their bases, at the point of their manufacture and in the component and engine factories, and a new list of targets was drawn up accordingly. This was headed by the German ports containing U-Boot construction yards, Kiel, Hamburg, Vegesack and Bremen, the last named also boasting a Focke-Wulf factory. The French ports of Lorient, St Nazaire and Bordeaux were also included, as homes to U-Boot bases.

The first operations of the month for 101 Squadron were mounted on the night of the 14/15th, when eight Blenheims took off to attack targets in Düsseldorf, while Sgts Hart and Deane went for the oil storage tanks at Rotterdam. The latter took off first, at 19.30 and 19.40, to be followed by the others between 19.50 and 20.20. S/L Graham was the senior pilot on duty, and he bombed the target from 12,000 feet at 21.45, and saw only his incendiaries burning on the ground. The others bombed from 11,000 to 13,000 feet between 21.45 and 22.40 in conditions of brilliant moonlight, before returning safely. The Rotterdam duo also attacked as briefed, and reported fires burning in the target area. W/C Addenbrooke was posted in from 18 Squadron on the 15th, as the new commanding officer, pending the posting of W/C Singer to 2 Group HQ at the end of the month. Thirteen Blenheims were made ready for operations on the 18th, nine to attack Wilhelmshaven, and three for the oil storage tanks at Rotterdam. S/L Cree was the senior pilot on duty as the main section took off between 19.30 and 20.01 and headed east. Sgt Burrows was forced to turn back with a failed port engine, but the others pressed on to reach and bomb the target from 10,000 to 15,000 feet between 20.50 and 21.26. All but one returned to report fires burning in the target area, one of which was visible seventy minutes into the homeward flight. The experienced P/O Brown and crew failed to return in R3846, which presumably disappeared into the sea on the way home, and was the only loss from among the forty-four Blenheims dispatched. The Rotterdam trio also reported bombing as briefed between 21.10 and 22.05, and fires were observed in the target area.

The night of the 23/24th was one of marginal weather conditions and no moon, and was considered suitable for what can best be described as nuisance raids against major urban areas. The destinations on this night were Berlin, Kiel and Hannover, and it was to the last-mentioned that ten 101 Squadron Blenheims took off between 19.50 and 20.25, led for the first time by W/C Addenbrooke. They were part of a force of twenty-six Blenheims, and only Sgt Cooke of the 101 Squadron participants failed to reach the target area, after engine problems persuaded him to turn back when already over Germany. He dropped his bombs on a concentration of searchlights at Diepholz, some fifty miles short of Hannover, before returning safely. The others attacked the target from between 10,000 and 15,000 feet, but were unable to plot the fall of their bombs, because of the fires already burning and searchlight dazzle. On the 25th, Operations Order 20 was issued to the 2 Group stations, signalling the start of the anti-shipping campaign, but it would be sometime yet before 101 Squadron became involved.

On the 29th of March, the German cruisers, Scharnhorst and Gneisenau were reported to be off Brest, and by the following day they had taken up residence. Their presence would be a constant thorn in the flesh of the Admiralty for a further twelve months, and Bomber Command would find itself tasked with the job of trying to incapacitate them, and prevent them from breaking out to attack convoys. Many gallant crews would lose their lives before the warships' daring escape in February 1942 resolved the matter once and for all. An attempt on the night of the 30/31st by over one hundred aircraft would fail in its purpose and set a frustrating trend. Fourteen 101 Squadron Blenheims were detailed, and flew down to St Eval in Cornwall, arriving at 17.45. The crews were briefed to attack the warships with two 250lb SAP bombs and two 40 pounders each, between 21.00 and 22.00, but three failed to take off after a Hurricane obstructed the flare-path. The remaining eleven, of which S/Ls Cree and Graham were the senior pilots, managed to carry out their orders, and ten returned safely to report fires in the target area. T2281 overshot its landing, and crashed into a field beyond the runway, killing Sgt Kiddle and one of his crew. Later that day, W/C Singer was officially posted from the squadron to take up his new appointment. Sadly, his successor's period of tenure would be brief in the extreme.

April 1941

Brest was once more the target for the squadron's first operation of the new month, for which the ORB records eleven aircraft as detailed to take part. W/C Addenbrooke was the senior pilot on duty, supported by S/L Cree, and they took off between 19.00 and 19.41 as part of a force of ninety aircraft, made up of Wellingtons, Whitleys, Blenheims and a single Stirling. Weather conditions outbound were poor, and some crews turned back early as a result. Only three 101 Squadron crews reached the target to bomb, those of F/L Hill and Sgts Redmond and Rickinson, and they returned safely to land at Boscombe Down. S/L Cree abandoned his sortie over Bath because of the weather, and he landed at South Cerney. Sgt Taylor put down at Shrewton, on Salisbury Plain, while F/O Craig and Sgts Cook and Deane landed at West Raynham, all after abandoning their sorties through the weather conditions. Sgt Caunt experienced instrument failure, forcing him to turn back early, and land also at West Raynham. Sgt Burrows was apparently heading for Boscombe Down, when T2439 crashed at Frampton in Dorset, and blew up, killing all on board. An unhappy night was completed by the failure to return of W/C Addenbrooke and crew, who disappeared without trace in N3552. Wellington R1161 of 75(NZ) Squadron force-landed at Boscombe Down on return, and F/O Prichard and crew reported colliding in the target area with a Blenheim. The only Blenheim failing to return from this operation was that of W/C Addenbrooke, the commanding officer of 101 Squadron, and it is possible, therefore, that it was the aircraft involved in the collision.

Ten crews were briefed for operations on the evening of the 6th, and the first five took off between 20.05 and 20.45 to patrol enemy airfields at Schiphol, Soesterberg, Gilze-Rijen and Deelen. S/L Cree was the senior pilot on duty as they headed out across the sea, but adverse weather conditions persuaded him to abandon the operation, and the five crews waiting to take off at West Raynham had their sorties cancelled. W/C McDougall was posted in from 13 O.T.U on the 7th as the new commanding officer, and he, too, would enjoy only a brief period with the squadron, although not as the result of an untimely end. S/L Cree was again the senior pilot on duty that night, as ten 101 Squadron Blenheims took off for Bremerhaven between 20.30 and 21.00. The operation was an all-Blenheim affair involving twenty-four aircraft, and all but one from the squadron reached and bombed in the target area from 9,000 to 15,000 feet between 22.30 and 23.00. Sgt Taylor and crew were intercepted by an enemy night fighter while outbound, and, after evading it, dropped their bombs onto a searchlight concentration at an unidentified location, before returning safely along with the others. Bremerhaven was the target again twenty-four hours later, for which seven crews were briefed, with S/L Graham the senior pilot among them. They took off between 20.25 and 20.45, and all reached the target to bomb from between 9,000 and 13,000 feet. A number of returning crews broke cloud close to a friendly convoy steaming twenty miles off Happisburgh, and were fired upon, but escaped without damage.

Since the 10th of January, 2 Group aircraft had been used in a new type of operation known as Circus. These required them to act as bait by attacking targets on the occupied coast or a few miles inland in daylight, with the intention of drawing up enemy fighters for a battle of attrition with the Spitfire escorts. The squadron was officially switched to these operations from the 10th, but it would be the 17th before the crews experienced their first taste of this kind of action. In the meantime, six crews were briefed to attack Brest at first light on the 11th, and took off between 01.20 and 01.45, with W/C McDougall taking the lead for the first time. S/L Cree turned back because of adverse weather conditions, but the others pressed on to bomb the target through ten-tenths cloud from 10,000 to 15,000 feet at around 04.00, before returning safely, ignorant of the results of their efforts. On the evening of the 13th, F/O Craig and Sgts Caunt and Cooke took off to carry out a sea search for a missing 18 Squadron crew, but failed to find any trace. F/L Hill was posted to 17 O.T.U on the 15th for a well-earned rest at the end of his tour, although, there were those who considered training establishments to be more dangerous than operations. Five crews were briefed later that day for a patrol operation in Beat 13, starting from Shoreham. S/L Graham took the lead as they departed West Raynham between 12.33 and 12.39, but F/L McLaren lost contact with the formation and returned early. The others observed no activity, and all were back on the ground by 15.40.

At 14.30 on the 17th, W/C McDougal led a dozen 101 Squadron Blenheims into the air to form into two boxes of six, together with a box of six from 18 Squadron. They were to rendezvous with six squadrons of Spitfires and head for Cherbourg to bomb the docks in a Circus operation. The enemy rarely reacted to such provocation, and again failed to do so on this occasion. All aircraft attacked the target from 13,000 feet between 16.33 and 16.35, and explosions were seen across docks 4 and 5. Sgt Allen's bombs failed to release, so he remained with the formation and brought them home. S/L Cree and F/O Jones went to 14 O.T.U at Benson on the 18th, to "gen up" on the Wellington, the type onto which the squadron would shortly be converting, and the first examples of the type, R1700 and R1701, arrived at West Raynham with the returning S/L Cree and F/O Jones on the 20th. As already mentioned, the Battle of the Atlantic had become the overriding priority as far as the government was concerned, and this included a tightening of the blockade around Germany. The Blenheims of 2 Group were now pitched headlong into a fierce and uncompromising head-to-head battle with well-armed enemy shipping along the occupied coast. "Channel Stop" was implemented to close the Straits of Dover to enemy shipping, and 101 Squadron flew its first ten sorties on the morning of the 19th, six assigned to Beat 10 and four to Beat 9. W/C McDougall led the Beat 10 contingent away at 08.49, and they were followed three minutes later by the second section, led by F/L McLaren. W/C McDougall, F/O Craig and Sgt Caunt found no activity, but a convoy of five ships was sighted in Beat 10, one of which, a 5000-tonner, was attacked by Sgts Deane and Redmond in N6141 and T2047 respectively at 10.00, and left on fire and down by the stern. Sgt Allen went wide on his run, and was unable to bomb, but attacked with his guns, and had his starboard wing damaged by flak. The other vessels were bombed and machine-gunned, and near-misses were reported. The Beat 9 section found two ships of around 2,500 tons and seven trawlers, which were attacked with bombs and guns, and near-misses were reported.

Twelve Blenheims took to the air at 06.30 on the 21st, and formed up into two boxes of six, led by W/C McDougall and S/L Cree. Their target was to be the power station at Le Havre, but, on arrival in the target area, excessive amounts of cloud prevented W/C McDougall from making a positive identification. A convoy of four ships of around 2,000 tons each was spotted close to the mouth of the River L'Orne, and was attacked by the leading section from 8,500 feet at 08.59. No hits were scored, but a number of near misses were reported. The second section found a number of small ships in Quettehou harbour on the eastern side of the Cherbourg peninsular, and attacked them at 08.55 from 7,000 feet. The bombs overshot the harbour, and burst along the railhead adjacent to the docks. S/L McDonald was posted in from 17 O.T.U on the 24th, the day on which S/L Graham led a flight of nine 101 Squadron aircraft on detachment to Manston, to put them closer to the action and a Spitfire escort. F/L McLaren had now completed his tour, and was posted to 13 O.T.U on the 25th. The newly promoted F/L Jones spent the day engaged in dual instruction in a Wellington, as A Flight began conversion. S/L Cree, another 101 Squadron Stalwart, was posted to 2 Group HQ on the 26th at the end of his highly successful tour.

A section of three 101 Squadron Blenheims departed Manston at 09.19 on the 28th, bound for Dunkerque to attack shipping, but failed to rendezvous with its fighter escort, and returned to land a little over thirty minutes later. It seems that the same three crews, captained by P/O Brown and Sgts Ridgman-Parsons and Redmond, took off again at 10.54 to attack a convoy of nine trawlers between Calais and Cap Gris-Nez. As they carried out their attacks at 13.00 from a mere 50 feet, they were met by a hail of anti-aircraft fire from shore batteries and the target ships. V5493 was hit, it is believed, after releasing its four 250lb eleven-second delay bombs, and crashed into the sea without survivors from the crew of Sgt Ridgman-Parson. The two surviving crews returned home to claim one vessel as sunk and one damaged by machine-gun fire. On the following morning, the crews of F/O Craig and Sgts Allen and Deane took off at 08.26, to attack one large and three small merchant vessels steaming between Gravelines and Dunkerque. The convoy was intercepted when three miles off Niewport at 09.08, upon which, Sgt Allen dropped one bomb onto a 2,000 tonner from 50 feet, causing smoke. There were also claims that a battery on one ship was silenced by fire from a Blenheim rear gun. A BF109 arrived on the scene, and was claimed as damaged, while Sgt Deane's L9421 sustained damage to both wings, the fuselage and the rudder, and the observer was shot in the arm.

May 1941

The Manston detachment stood by all day on the 1st, but was not called into action. S/L Graham took off at 19.00 to carry out a lone patrol of the Gravelines to Dunkerque stretch of coastal water, but found nothing to attack. There was no activity either on the 2nd, but six Blenheims were dispatched from Manston at 13.30 on the 3rd to attack a 2,000-ton steamer, being escorted off Ostend by four trawler-type vessels and five E-boats. They flew out in two sections of three under a close escort of a dozen Spitfires from 74 Squadron, but S/L McDonald was forced to turn back with an unserviceable rear gun. The others, P/O Brown and Sgts Caunt, Cooke, Deane and Hart, carried out attacks with bombs and guns, and P/O Brown, flying as the leader of the second section, claimed to have hit and sunk the large vessel with three 250 pounders. Two of the escort boats were also claimed as sunk. They were called into action again that evening, when a further two sections of three, led by S/L Graham and P/O Brown, took off at 19.29 to attack a convoy ten miles south-south-west of Boulogne. S/L Graham and Sgts Caunt and Hart targeted the largest ship, estimated at between five and six thousand tons, and the leader pressed home his attack from 50 feet, achieving direct hits with all four of his bombs. On his return, he claimed the ship as sunk, and this was confirmed later. P/O Brown and Sgts Deane and Hart attacked a 2,000 tonner in the same convoy, also from 50 feet, and near misses were claimed. T1825 was hit by flak and crashed into the sea, taking with it P/O Brown and his crew. T2234 was also damaged by flak, and had to be ditched nineteen miles off Dungeness on the Kent coast. Sgt Deane and his observer were seen to climb out of the Blenheim, and F/O Craig and Sgt Allen took off at dawn to carry out a sea search, which, sadly, failed to locate them, and they were lost.

W/C McDougall departed the squadron on the 5th, to take command of 2 Group's newly reforming 90 Squadron, which was to introduce the Boeing B17C to operations. The type, which was designated Fortress I by the RAF, had a pressurised crew compartment, and was intended as a high-level bomber, operating at altitudes of around 30,000 feet, beyond the reach of enemy fighters. In the event, it would prove to be a failure, and, following a number of losses, would be quickly phased out of Bomber Command. Back at Manston, S/L McDonald and Sgts Caunt and Hart took off at 13.52 on the 6th, intent on attacking a 4,000-ton merchant vessel and two trawler-type escort vessels reported to be off Gravelines. They were set upon by three BF109s, despite the presence of six Spitfires from 74 Squadron, and, having sustained damage to his port engine during the engagement, and with no enemy shipping in sight, S/L McDonald led the trio home, where they landed safely. What would prove to be the last offensive action carried out by the squadron in Blenheims took place on the night of the 8/9th, when five NCO crews took off in an eight-minute slot from 22.17 to attempt to block the Kiel Canal at Holtenau by sinking shipping. The operation descended into chaos, when they were engaged by a large friendly convoy off Cromer, despite carrying out the correct identification procedure. Four of the Blenheims abandoned their sorties and returned home, while Sgt Caunt continued on, until reaching the west coast of the Schleswig-Holstein peninsular in the area near Büsum, where intense searchlight activity forced him to seek alternative options. He turned his attention upon Beat 7, and came upon a 3,000-tonner accompanied by eight smaller vessels. He carried out an attack from 1,500 feet at 01.50, and claimed near misses on the large ship.

The Manston detachment returned to West Raynham on the 9th, where working up to operational status on Wellingtons had been under way for some time. On the 16th, W/C Biggs was posted in from 107 Squadron as the new commanding officer, and S/L McDonald was posted in the opposite direction. F/L Colenso was posted in from 13 O.T.U on the 19th, and would soon be given the acting rank of squadron leader to enable him to replace S/L McDonald as a flight commander. By the 22nd, the squadron had on charge a complement of eighteen Wellingtons, and would remain, for the time-being, in 2 Group, and, thus, would be the only Wellington unit to conduct operations with that Group.

101 Squadron photograph, taken in Summer 1941 (GW)

35

June 1941

The first eleven days of June were taken up at West Raynham with intensive training, and the induction of airmen posted in to fill the extra crew positions in the Wellington. French and German ports would feature prominently during the month, as would industrial towns and cities in the Ruhr, and most nights brought relatively small-scale attacks on multiple targets. This practice of spreading the available resources thinly, would not bring dividends, and the period, generally, would be one of poor returns. Cologne and Düsseldorf became a major focus during the second half of the month, and were attacked simultaneously on no fewer than nine nights, and not once effectively. What was not known by those planning and executing operations during June and July, was that the Command's performance was being scrutinised by a civil servant, who would compile a report to present to the highest authorities in August. The first 101 Squadron Wellington operation took place on the night of the 11/12th, when W5716 and R1780 took off at 23.20 and 23.30 in the hands of S/L Jones and Sgt Caunt respectively, their brief, to attack the docks at Rotterdam. They each carried six 500 pounders, which were delivered according to instructions, the former from 12,000 feet at 00.45, and the latter from 10,000 feet forty minutes later, and both returned safely. The briefing of seven crews for the same target took place on the 17th, when S/L Jones and F/L Colenso were selected to be the senior pilots on duty. Six took off either side of 23.30, and, for whatever reason, it was fifteen minutes after midnight before Sgt Hart and crew got away. S/L Jones turned back with intercom failure some fifty miles out from Southwold, but the others pressed on to deliver their twelve 250 pounders each from 8,000 to 14,000 feet between 00.50 and 01.24. Sgt Hart bombed from 10,000 feet at 01.42, and, like the others, was prevented by ground fog from assessing the outcome. Ten Wellingtons were dispatched by the squadron on the night of the 21/22nd, six to join an all-Wellington force of sixty-eight aircraft to attack Cologne, while four freshmen crews cut their teeth on the docks at Dunkerque. Take-off of both contingents took place between 23.19 and 00.03, but Sgt Kethro-Schonbach turned back with a wandering compass, and, although he set off again, he became ill, and abandoned the sortie. The others all reached their respective targets, the Cologne crews bombing from 10,000 to 16,000 feet between 01.16 and 01.58, before returning safely to report observing flashes on the ground. Dunkerque was located by the three remaining crews, and two bombed from 13,000 to 14,000 feet, while the observer in the third one pressed the wrong button, and the bombs were brought home. Of five hundred high-explosive bombs and five thousand incendiaries supposedly dropped on Cologne, not one fell within the city boundaries.

Bremen was the target for a force of fifty-six Wellingtons and eight Whitleys on the night of the 25/26th, for which the squadron contributed five aircraft. They took off between 23.20 and 23.52, with F/L Colenso the senior pilot on duty, supported by P/Os Rickinson, Redmond and Todd and Sgt Fooks. They encountered severe electrical storms on the way out, which persuaded most of the force to abandon their attempt to reach the intended target. F/L Colenso and P/O Rickinson each dropped their ten 250lb bombs from 17,000 and 6,000 feet respectively onto a flashing beacon at Den Helder shortly after 01.00, while P/O Todd joined in a raid on Rotterdam, to which the three freshman crews of Sgt Fisher, P/O Bundey and F/O Robertson had been sent. Low cloud there prevented any sight of the ground, and the bombs were aimed at searchlights. Later on the 26th, F/L Colenso was granted the acting rank of squadron leader. Bremen was the target once more on the night of the 27/28th, for which the squadron put up eight Wellingtons as part of a Wellington/Whitley force of 108 aircraft. It was another night of adverse weather conditions, with electrical storms and icing, and many of the crews battling their way to northern Germany found themselves in the Hamburg area by mistake. S/Ls Colenso and Jones were the senior 101 Squadron pilots on duty, as they departed West Raynham between 23.21 and 00.16. Taking off among them at 23.33 were P/O Hardie and crew, who were bound for the docks at Dunkerque, until their electrical system failed and forced them to return. Once on the ground, they changed aircraft, and set off again at 01.49, but were recalled by group. Sgts Caunt, Redmond and Rickinson, P/O Todd and S/L Jones all located the primary target area, and the first four-mentioned carried out an attack from 11,000 to 15,000 feet between 01.26 and 01.45. S/L Jones' bombs failed to release, but he managed to dislodge them over Den Helder on the way home. Of the others, S/L Colenso and Sgt Taylor bombed Den Helder also, while Sgt Fooks delivered his load onto Oldenburg. Returning crews reported fierce night fighter activity for the first time, which coincided with the loss of fourteen aircraft, eleven of them Whitleys, and this represented the heaviest night loss of the war to date.

On return from the above operation, commissions were announced for Sgts Allen, Caunt, Cook, Hart and Taylor. The focus on Bremen was maintained on the night of the 29/30th, when nine 101 Squadron Wellingtons took off between 23.20 and 23.42, but a navigational error led to P/O Rickinson attacking Den Helder, while P/O Hart experienced trim problems, and abandoned his sortie at Happisburgh. The senior pilots on duty were S/Ls Colenso and Jones, and they were among the seven who reached the target area, to deliver their two 500 pounders and six SBCs of incendiaries from 11,000 to 16,000 feet between 01.30 and 02.45. Conditions over the target were good, and fires were already burning as they arrived.

July 1941

The squadron was immediately into action on the first night of the new month, when Brest was the target for a force of fifty-two Wellingtons, of which, nine took off from West Raynham between 23.11 and 23.26, led by S/Ls Colenso and Jones. Each aircraft was carrying ten 250 pounders, which were delivered from 11,000 to 16,000 feet between 01.50 and 02.47. All crews returned safely, mostly to report being unable to assess the results because of ground haze and searchlight glare. A bomb found its way into the Prinz Eugen, causing extensive damage and killing the executive officer and sixty sailors. Twelve crews were briefed on the 5th, six each for operations that night against Bielefeld and Rotterdam, which would prove to be the last under the banner of 2 Group. Details for this night's activities are scant, but, we are told that S/L Colenso and P/Os Todd, Redmond, Rickinson and Hart all successfully attacked Bielefeld, while P/Os Hardie, Bundey, Cook and Taylor and F/O Robertson did likewise at Rotterdam. In all, the squadron carried out twelve operations on eight nights as 2 Group's only Wellington unit, and these involved sixty-six sorties without loss.

On the 6th, S/L Jones flew the advanced party over to Oakington to begin the move to the squadron's new home, which it would share with 7 Squadron, the first Stirling unit, and the squadron officially joined 3 Group on the following day. A new Air Ministry directive was issued on the 9th, which referred to the morale of the enemy civilian population and Germany's transportation system as its weakest points, and, until further notice, the emphasis of operations was to fall upon these. During the moon period, this would require attacks to be carried out against the major railway centres ringing the Ruhr, in an attempt to isolate the region from the rest of Germany, and prevent the movement in of raw materials, and the export of finished goods. On moonless nights, the Rhine cities of Cologne, Düsseldorf and Duisburg would be easier to locate, and on dark nights with less favourable weather conditions, Peirse was to send his forces further afield, to urban centres in northern, eastern and southern Germany. That night, operations began for the squadron under the banner of 3 Group, and seven crews took off between 23.16 and 23.33 bound for the marshalling yards at Osnabrück. The senior pilots on duty were S/Ls Colenso and Jones, supported by P/Os Allen, Caunt, Cook, Redmond and Rickinson, and all but one arrived over what they believed to be the target to bomb from 10,000 to 14,000 feet at around 01.45. Bomb bursts were observed by some crews across the yards, but local reports would suggest that no bombs fell in Osnabrück. P/O Caunt admitted to bombing Münster railway station in error from 12,500 feet, but was prevented by ground haze from assessing the results.

The main operation for 3 Group on the night of the 14/15th was at Bremen, for which it contributed the bulk of the Wellingtons involved. 101 Squadron did not take part, but sent three aircraft to Rotterdam to attack the docks. F/O Craig, P/O Hardie and Sgt Fisher took off between 23.19 and 23.47, the last-mentioned with S/L Colenso on board as second pilot. F/L Craig abandoned his sortie three miles out from Aldeburgh on the Suffolk coast because of instrument failure, and Sgt Fisher turned back when thirty miles short of the Dutch coast citing the weather conditions as the reason. P/O Hardie made it to the target, but was held in searchlights for a considerable time, and opted to dump rather than aim his six 500 pounders, which, he claimed, started fires visible for twenty minutes into the return journey. Five crews were briefed on the 16th for an attack that night on Hamburg, while two others learned they would be going to Boulogne. S/Ls Colenso and Jones were the senior pilots on duty, and they would be accompanied to northern Germany by F/L Todd, F/O Robertson and P/O Cook, while Sgts Davey and Fisher headed for the French coast. The first element took off between 23.07 and 23.30, and joined up with the rest of the one-hundred-strong force, most of which failed to find the target in the face of nine to ten-tenths cloud. S/L Colenso and P/O Todd returned to claim bombing the target from 17,000 and 14,000 feet at 02.20 and 02.14 respectively, through gaps in the cloud, and observed two large explosions. S/L Jones was unable to locate the primary target, and bombed the docks at Ijmuiden from 10,000 feet as an alternative. F/O Robertson dropped his 500 pounders from 17,000 feet over the Bremen area, while P/O Cook delivered his over Wilhelmshaven from 14,000 feet. Local reports from Hamburg speak of four small fires and no major damage. The ORB reported that Sgt Davey successfully attacked Boulogne docks, but provided no details, while Sgt Fisher was unable to identify the French coast, and brought his bombs home.

Cologne provided the target for a force of more than a hundred aircraft on the night of the 20/21st. 3 Group's contribution amounted to twenty-nine Wellingtons and three Stirlings, eight of the former provided by 101 Squadron. S/L Colenso was the senior pilot on duty as he took off in R1801 at 23.12, with F/L Craig acting as second pilot. They bombed the target from 15,000 feet, but failed to observe any bursts. On the way out of the target area, two large explosions were noted at the confluence of two rivers in the Vogelsang district, west of the city centre. There are no details of the remaining sorties, other than that F/L Todd, F/O Robertson and P/Os Allen, Cook, Hardie, Redmond and Rickinson attacked the target successfully. Taking off ahead of the main element, between 22.46 and 22.53, were P/O Millson and Sgts Davey and Fisher, who were bound for the docks at Boulogne. They all reported reaching the target and bombing from between 9,000 and 15,000 feet, before returning safely. The main target on the night of the 22/23rd was Mannheim in southern Germany, a 3 Group show, for which seven 101 Squadron crews were briefed as part of an overall force of twenty-nine Wellingtons. Details in the squadron ORB for this operation are incomplete, but we know that F/L Todd failed to take off, and that S/L Jones, F/O Robertson, and P/Os Allen, Hardie, Redmand and Rickinson all claimed to have attacked the target in conditions of cloud and thunderstorms, and some fires were reported. While this operation was in progress, F/L Craig and Sgt Davey attacked the docks at Dunkerque.

A major attempt to solve the problem of the German Cruisers at Brest was mounted by daylight on the 24th of July. The original plan for Operation Sunrise was based almost on a "Circus" concept, and involved Fortresses of 90 Squadron opening proceedings at 30,000 feet to draw up the enemy fighters. Meanwhile, 5 Group Hampdens would act as further bait at a less rarefied altitude under the umbrella of a fighter escort, which, it was hoped, would clear a path for seventy-nine Wellingtons of 1 and 3 Groups to run in on the ships. In the event, it was discovered that the Scharnhorst had moved to La Pallice a day or so earlier, and a 3 Group contingent had been sent to attack her there on the evening of the 23rd, one claiming a direct hit on the stern with a 2,000lb bomb. A new plan was devised for the 24th, which incorporated all of the original elements for Brest, while a contingent of Halifaxes was sent to deal with Scharnhorst at La Pallice. Just three 101 Squadron crews were briefed, and S/L Colenso, F/L Craig and P/O Rickinson took off between 11.28 and 11.36 to join up with the main formation. For an unspecified reason, F/L Craig fell behind the others, who waited for him to catch up south of Pointe-St-Mathieu, at the western-most point of the ten-mile run-in to Brest, and, in so doing, lost contact with the main formation. R1702 was seen to be attacked twice by a BF109, and the Wellington crashed into the sea, killing F/L Craig MiD, and three of his crew, while two others survived to be taken prisoner. Despite the diversions, there was a stronger-than-expected presence of enemy fighters, and the Wellingtons were forced to fly through a fierce barrage of flak. S/L Colenso wisely decided not to take his section into the attack alone, and they returned home with their bombs. This was the squadron's first loss of a Wellington, and whilst claims were made for hits on the Gneisenau, these remained unconfirmed, and the operation was yet another failure in this long-running saga.

Operations were not yet over for the 24/25th, and six Wellingtons lined up for take-off either side of 23.00, five bound for Kiel and a freshman for Rotterdam. P/O Bundey and Sgt Gilbert, the fresher, turned back early on with technical difficulties, and P/O Allen lost his bearings while evading searchlights near Kiel, and dropped his bombs on Wilhelmshaven from 14,000 feet at 02.10. Sgt Fisher, Sgt Fooks and P/O Millsom all located Kiel, and delivered their bombs in good visibility from 13,000 to 15,600 feet between 01.44 and 01.51, before returning home safely to report explosions and fires. Ten aircraft were made ready for operations on the night of the 27/28th, but all other than a freshman trip to Dunkerque were cancelled because of adverse weather conditions. Sgt Gilbert and crew took off at 22.57 and attacked the docks through nine-tenths cloud from 14,500 feet at 00.36, observing two large, red flashes. The final operation of the month for 101 Squadron came on the night of the 30/31st, when nine crews took off between 23.59 and 00.27, as part of an overall force of 116 aircraft, bound for Cologne. P/O Allen was the first to drop out, turning back when ten miles south-east of Clacton with engine problems. F/O Robertson also experienced a problem, in his case with his port engine supercharger, and abandoned his sortie when six miles out from the Kent coast. P/O Bundey had travelled further before the icing conditions persuaded him to turn back. The others pressed on in difficult weather conditions, which included electrical storms, and Sgt Fooks bombed at Aachen from 8,000 feet at 02.30, after being unable to identify Cologne. P/Os Hardie, Millson, Redmond and Rickinson and Sgt Fisher attacked the primary target with seven 500 pounders each from 11,500 to 16,000 feet between 02.08 and 02.52, and returned safely. P/O Hardie's rear gunner was temporarily blinded, presumably by lightning, but made a full recovery in hospital at West Malling.

August 1941

Throughout the year, there had been a general policy of splitting the available forces, to enable multiple targets to be attacked simultaneously. The result was, in many cases, to dilute the effectiveness of the raids, and the damage was frequently not commensurate with the effort and cost. On the night of the 2/3rd of August, Hamburg, Berlin, Kiel and Cherbourg all received attention, but none suffered a telling blow. Seven 101 Squadron crews were briefed for Hamburg, as part of an overall force of eighty aircraft, and they departed Oakington between 22.34 and 22.46, with F/L Todd the senior pilot on duty. P/O Bundey was unable to locate the primary target, and bombed at Bremen from 14,000 feet at 02.15, before returning home to crash-land near Ashford in Kent at 05.23. R1088 was written off, but crew members were able to walk away from the burning wreckage without injury. Less fortunate were their colleagues, Sgt Davey and his crew in R1800, which was shot down by a night fighter flown by Feldwebel Siegfried Ney of 4./NJG1. The Wellington crashed into the Ijsselmeer, killing all on board, and just two bodies were eventually recovered for burial. The remaining crews all attacked the primary target from 13,000 to 16,400 feet between 01.33 and 02.10, and returned safely to report bomb bursts and fires. While this operation was in progress, Sgt Gilbert attacked Cherbourg docks from 13,500 feet with six 500 pounders, one 250 pounder and two SBCs of incendiaries, and observed one large fire.

August would be a month devoted almost entirely to the industrial centres of Germany, but rarely with forces large enough to make an impact. The night of the 5/6th was devoted to cities in southern Germany, at Mannheim, Karlsruhe and Frankfurt, and it was for the first-mentioned that seven 101 Squadron Wellingtons took off between 22.29 and 23.09, with F/L Todd the senior pilot on duty. All reached and identified the primary target on the eastern bank of the Rhine, but F/L Todd's R1781 began to ice-up, and he ultimately bombed at Schifferstadt, about six miles to the south-west at 01.10. The others carried out their attacks from 11,000 to 18,300 feet between 00.45 and 01.39, before returning to report large explosions and many fires. Local reports suggest that this was an effective attack, which caused damage in both Mannheim and Ludwigshafen on the other side of the Rhine. F/L Todd was again the senior 101 Squadron pilot on duty for a 3 Group operation against the important marshalling yards at Hamm on the night of the 7/8th. The squadron's eight Wellingtons took off between 00.31 and 00.47, but F/O Robertson returned immediately, after W5716 sustained damage to its undercarriage. P/O Rickinson had just crossed the Suffolk coast, when X9601 was attacked by night fighters at 01.20 at 9,500 feet. The second pilot was hit in the right hand, while the rear gunner, Sgt Thompson, bailed out over the sea, and was lost. The bombs were jettisoned into the sea, and a safe return carried out. The remainder pressed on towards the Dutch coast, where Sgt Fooks and P/O Cook were intercepted and engaged by BF109s. The assailants were eventually evaded, and Sgt Fooks bombed the docks at Rotterdam from 12,000 feet as an alternative. It is believed that P/O Cook did likewise, and both made it safely home, the latter with a wounded rear gunner. This left P/Os Allen, Millson and Redmond, and F/L Todd to continue on to the primary target, which they attacked with a 1,000 pounder and five 500 pounders each from 10,000 to 16,000 feet between 02.12 and 03.04, and returned to report large fires and smoke rising to 11,000 feet.

P/O Rickinson departed the squadron on the 11th, on posting to 11 O.T.U. Unfavourable weather conditions restricted operations until the night of the 12/13th, when Hannover, Berlin, Magdeburg and Essen provided the main targets, the last-mentioned for six 101 Squadron crews as part of an overall force of thirty-five mostly 3 Group aircraft. The senior pilots on duty were S/Ls Colenso and Jones, and take-off took place between 21.27 and 21.41. S/L Jones dropped his seven 500 pounders on Duisburg from 13,000 feet at 23.28, and P/Os Allen and Bundey were unsure of their precise position, and reported attacking the Ruhr area generally from 12,500 and 17,000 feet at 23.26 and 00.05 respectively. S/L Colenso and P/Os Millson and Redmond pushed on the extra miles to the primary target to bomb from 13,000 to 17,500 feet between 23.16 and 00.10, before returning home to report bomb bursts and fires. S/L Jones was the senior pilot on duty on the night of the 14/15th, when six Wellingtons prepared to take off for Hannover between 21.25 and 21.55. They were to join up with 146 other aircraft for the night's largest operation, but matters began to go awry for P/O Millson early on, when his front gunner attempted to gain access to his turret once airborne, and found the bulkhead door jammed. They were forced to turn back, as were P/O Bundey and crew on reaching Enschede in Holland, after the oxygen supply and intercom failed. The others all reached the target area to find fairly good conditions, although cloud drifted across to obscure the ground on occasions. S/L Jones, P/Os Allen and Hardie and Sgt Fisher delivered their mixed loads of HE from 13,500 to 15,000 feet between midnight and 00.39, and returned safely to English air space. P/O Hardie carried out a wheels-up landing in R1701, and both aircraft and crew would be available for the next operation. F/L Todd had set out at 21.30 to bomb the docks at Dunkerque, but failed to locate it in the face of ten-tenths cloud, and was attacked inconclusively by an enemy fighter on the way home.

Railway installations at Cologne and Duisburg were the principal targets on the night of the 16/17th, and it was for the latter that eight 101 Squadron Wellingtons took off between 23.55 and 00.30, with S/L Colenso the senior pilot on duty. P/O Redmond abandoned his sortie when just south of Eindhoven because of engine trouble, and jettisoned his bombs from 11,000 feet at 01.21. The remaining seven Wellingtons reached the target to attack it from 13,000 to 17,000 feet between 01.54 and 02.48, and returned safely to report difficult bombing conditions, and uncertainty as to the outcome. While this operation was in progress, P/O Ashton went to Dunkerque to bomb the docks, but dropped his load from 13,500 feet onto a flare-path near the port at 01.55.

It was on the 18th, that civil servant, Mr D M Butt, delivered his analysis of recent Bomber Command operations to those who had commissioned it, and its disclosures would send shock waves resounding around the Cabinet Room and the Air Ministry. Having studied around four thousand photographs taken during a hundred-night operations in June and July, he concluded, that only a small fraction of bombs was falling within miles of their intended targets. These revelations swept away at a stroke the belief that the Command was striking at the heart of the Nazi war machine, and showed the claims of crews to be wildly optimistic. The report would also forever unjustly blight the period of tenure as C-in-C of Sir Richard Peirse, and provide ammunition for the critics, who were calling for the dissolution of an independent bomber force, and the employment of its aircraft against the U-Boot menace, and to redress reversals in the Middle East.

A force of 108 aircraft set off for Kiel on the night of the 19/20th, among them a contingent of six Wellingtons provided by 101 Squadron, led by S/L Jones. They departed Oakington between 20.46 and 21.04, and reached the target area to encounter foul weather conditions and ten-tenths cloud, which prevented any from positively identifying their position. Five 101 Squadron crews bombed on estimated positions, from 13,000 to 19,000 feet, between 23.30 and 23.47, before returning safely. Sgt Fisher and crew failed to arrive back in W5715, and were lost without trace. According to local reports, had a number of incendiaries not fallen onto a swimming baths, the raid would probably have gone unnoticed. While this operation was in progress, P/Os Ashton and Pelmore carried out a freshman operation against the docks at Le Havre, and delivered their loads from 9,000 to 12,000 feet either side of 23.00. Eight Wellingtons were made ready for operations on the 22nd, six to participate in a raid by more than a hundred Wellingtons and Hampdens on Mannheim, and two for Le Havre. The main contingent departed first, between 22.45 and 23.49, and it is not clear why Sgt Fooks and S/L Colenso took off almost half an hour and an hour respectively after the first four. As a result, S/L Colenso abandoned his attempt to reach the primary target, and bombed a road or railway near Trier from 17,000 feet at 02.05 instead. The others attacked the primary target between 00.54 and 01.45 from 13,000 to 18,000 feet, and returned safely to report fires burning, although local authorities recorded just six high explosive bombs falling. P/O Ashton and F/O Robertson left Oakington at 01.50 and 02.30 respectively, and bombed the docks at Le Havre from around 12,000 feet, before returning to claim successful sorties.

P/O Redmond was posted to 21 O.T.U at Moreton-in-Marsh on the 25th, at the end of what had been a successful tour. S/L Colenso was the senior pilot on duty again that night, when leading a contingent of eight 101 Squadron Wellingtons to Karlsruhe in southern Germany, as part of an overall force of thirty-seven Wellingtons and a dozen Stirlings. They took off between 20.27 and 21.10, and set course for the Belgian coast, where S/L Colenso's aircraft developed engine problems while taking evasive action. Forced to abandon his sortie, he dropped his bombs onto a flare-path near Ostend, before returning home. The others encountered electrical storms, which contributed to the decision by Sgt Fooks to turn back, when fifteen miles south-west of Charlerois. R1778 demonstrated a reticence to climb, and it was decided to bomb the docks at Dunkerque on the way home. The others reached the target area in weather conditions that continued to challenge them, and delivered their bombs through cloud from 12,000 to 15,000 feet between 23.11 and 00.15. Eight crews attended briefings on the 28th, six to learn, that they would be attacking railway targets in Duisburg that night, while the freshman crews of P/O Imeson and Sgt Luin were to use the docks at Ostend to gain operational experience. The latter took off first, shortly after 21.00, and dropped their six 500 pounders each, along with 4lb incendiaries, according to instructions from 14,000 to 15,000 feet either side of 22.30. It was shortly before 00.30, when the participants in the main action began to take off, led by F/L Todd, as part of an overall force of 118 aircraft. All of the 101 Squadron crews reached the target area, and carried out their part in the plan from 13,000 to 16,000 feet between 02.05 and 02.25. P/O Ashton's bombs failed to release, and he eventually dropped them onto an aerodrome some eight miles east of The Hague.

The gentle introduction to operations continued for P/O Imeson and Sgt Luin on the night of the 30/31st, when they took off along with P/O Reynolds between 21.08 and 21.20, to bomb the docks at Cherbourg. P/O Reynolds and crew got as far as Rampton, two miles north-east of Oakington, before Z8860 crashed and burned out, killing one of the crew. P/O Reynolds and two others were admitted to Addenbrookes hospital, where second pilot, P/O Crichton RAAF, succumbed to his injuries on the 1st of September. On the following night, the squadron dispatched seven Wellingtons to Cologne, as part of a force of almost one hundred aircraft. They took off between 20.07 and 20.18, with F/L Todd the senior pilot on duty. P/O Pelmore abandoned his sortie because of technical issues, and tried to locate Rotterdam as an alternative target. He was thwarted in that regard by ten-tenths cloud, and jettisoned his bombs into the sea. R1703 came down in Belgium, it is believed, while outbound, killing P/O Ashton and two of his crew, while the Canadian second pilot was captured, and the two gunners evaded a similar fate. The remainder reached the target area to bomb through cloud on estimated position from 14,000 to 16,000 feet between 22.13 and 22.17.

September 1941

The squadron remained on the ground on the first night of the new month, and then called six crews to briefing on the 2nd, to learn that Frankfurt would be their target that night, while a second force went to Berlin. F/L Todd was the senior pilot on duty as they took off between 20.07 and 20.30 as part of an overall force of 126 aircraft. The weather conditions in the target area were described as fair, as the 101 Squadron contingent bombed from 14,000 to 17,000 feet between 23.05 and 23.30, and observed explosions on the ground. P/O Bundey attacked Mainz from 16,000 feet at 23.10, believing it to be the primary target, and he reported a large red explosion occurring fifteen minutes after leaving the area. The squadron's first trip to Berlin was scheduled for the night of the 7/8th, and seven crews were briefed to join an overall force of 188 aircraft, while two others from the squadron took part in a smaller raid against Kiel, where the U-Boot yards were the principal objective. Sgt Luin and P/O Imeson took off shortly before 19.30 for the latter, and bombed the target from 16,500 and 19,500 at 23.20 and 23.23 respectively, the former observing his bombs to fall across the shipyards. It was always a momentous moment when writing Berlin in a log book for the first time, having returned safely, and the aircraft and crew captains preparing for take-off between 19.34 and 20.04 were; R1781 F/L Todd, Z8842 F/O Robertson, T2846 P/O Pelmore, R1699 P/O Allen, R1780 P/O Hillson, X9828 P/O Hardie, and R1778 Sgt Fooks. All seven reached the target area to find clear skies, and they carried out their attacks from 15,000 to 18,000 feet between 22.55 and 23.38. Frustratingly for P/O Allen and crew, their bombs failed to release, and had to be brought back. On the way home, Sgt Fooks and crew were intercepted by a JU88, which rear gunner, Sgt Balshaw, shot down, a fact corroborated by two other crews, and, for which, he would soon be awarded a coveted DFM. Some useful damage was inflicted upon housing and a number of war-industry factories in the Lichtenberg and Pankow districts, in what could be described as a reasonably effective raid for the period, but it cost fifteen aircraft, eight of them Wellingtons.

Italian targets were generally considered to be a soft option, unless, of course, one happened to be in an aircraft that failed to return. Five 101 Squadron crews were briefed on the 10th, for an operation that night by a force of more than seventy aircraft on Turin, where the Fiat steelworks were the main attraction. F/L Todd was the senior pilot on duty as they took off from Oakington between 19.24 and 19.40. It is believed that all from the squadron reached the target, where ground haze and smoke from developing fires created some difficulties, and bombed from 17,000 feet between 22.55 and 23.23. A message was received at 01.14 from P/O Allen and crew, to the effect that, the starboard engine on R1699 had failed, and that the propeller had fallen away. A final message was picked up at 01.45, which stated "cannot make it", and it would be learned later, that a crash-landing had been carried out at Les Riceys, between Paris and Dijon. On the credit side, the crew managed to evade capture by the Germans and all eventually returned to the squadron by a variety of routes.

Sergeant H. T. Hickton, of Palmerston North, missing on operations.

Sgt Pat Hickton and his crewmates survived their crash-landing and eventually made it back to England (Jackie Ridgway and Hayley Wesche).

Sgt Pat Hickton, the rear gunner in the Allen crew, had suffered a cut to his head on landing, as he was still in his turret rather than at his crash position. After a brief period he and Christensen were captured, possibly by the Vichy French authorities and interned. After nearly a year's incarceration, on 25th August 1942, Hickton and a number of other internees escaped through the vents in the roof. They were followed on 5th September by 58 other internees in a mass breakout, 25 of whom, along with Hickton's group, were evacuated to Gibraltar on a Polish freighter and made it back to England.

The night of the 12/13th brought operations to Cherbourg and Frankfurt for four and seven crews respectively. 130 aircraft were made ready for the latter, the 101 Squadron element taking off between 19.34 and 19.53, with F/O Robertson the most senior pilot on duty. Three of the four Cherbourg-bound Wellingtons had taken off a few minutes earlier, leaving Sgt Parker to find a slot among the Frankfurt brigade, but Sgt Williams was forced to turn back, when X9806 proved incapable of maintaining height. The others pressed on to bomb the target from 10,000 to 13,200 feet between 21.50 and 22.20, and returned to report observing some explosions. Those bound for southern Germany all reached the target area, but F/O Robertson was unable to positively identify the aiming-point because of cloud, and he released his bombs over Mainz instead, from 16,500 feet at 22.54. The others attacked the primary target from 15,200 to 18,000 feet between 22.10 and 22.40, and contributed to a modestly effective raid, which caused thirty-eight fires in Frankfurt and nearby Offenbach, and damaged mostly housing.

Above left: Interned servicemen exercising in the yard of Fort de la Rivere, from where Sgt Pat Hickton and fifteen others made their escape on 23rd August, 1942. Right: A group of escapees from Fort de la Rivere. Back row, l to r: Sgt RD Porteous, Sgt Harold Burrell, Sgt Leslie Pearman, Sgt Robert Saxton, Sgt Doug Walsh. Front row, l to r: (two unidentified), Sgt Melville Dalphond, Sgt Pat Hickton. Sgts Porteous and Burrell were interned after force-landing on 5/6th August 1941 at Antwerp airport in their Wellington W5421 of 12 Sqn. Sgt Saxton was navigator in Sgt Hickton's crew. Below left: Sgt Ross Christensen RAAF meets King George VI following his return to England. At this time he was with No. 1456 Flight. Right: Sgt Hickton's forged identity document (Jackie Ridgway and Hayley Wesche).

Wellington R1781, here bearing squadron code SR-C, was another aircraft to survive her time with 101 Sqn., despite sustaining flak damage over the Ruhr on 20/21ˢᵗ September 1941. She later went on to 12 OTU to train new crews (GW).

Ten crews were called to briefing on the 15th, seven to learn the details of that night's main operation to Hamburg, and three freshmen for a raid by forty-five aircraft on the docks at Le Havre. Sgts House, Parker and Williams took off between 19.01 and 19.11, before heading for the French coast, and locating the target in favourable weather conditions. They each delivered six 500lb bombs and two SBCs of 4lb incendiaries from 11,000 to 15,500 feet between 20.35 and 21.20, and returned safely to report fires in the town as well as the docks. S/L Colenso was the senior pilot on duty as the participants in the main operation departed Oakington between 19.26 and 19.49. All reached the target to find clear skies, but intense searchlight glare, which prevented them from identifying ground detail. They bombed from 14,500 to 18,000 feet between 22.45 and 23.32, and returned safely to report many fires and bomb bursts, some of which were thought to be in the area of the shipyards. Local reports confirmed this to be an effective raid at a cost of eight aircraft, including the 75 (NZ) Squadron Wellington of Sgt James Ward VC RNZAF. The freshman crews of Sgts Dil and Betts undertook their maiden operations on the night of the 18/19th, when participating in a small-scale raid on the docks at Le Havre, the only representatives of the squadron in action that night. They took off shortly before 19.00, and returned either side of 23.00 to report bombing as briefed from around 13,000 feet.

The night of the 20/21ˢᵗ descended into chaos, after the threat of worsening weather conditions over the stations at landing times, caused a recall order to be issued shortly after take-off to the forces heading for Berlin and Frankfurt. 101 Squadron dispatched five crews to Berlin, one to Frankfurt and four freshmen to Ostend, taking off between 19.03 and 20.08, none of which heard the recall signal. Sgt Fooks got only as far as Eye in Suffolk, before turning back with an ailing rear gunner. P/O Millson's communications system broke down, and he bombed an aerodrome seventeen miles east of Katwijk in Holland from 13,000 feet at 20.55. F/L Todd was the senior pilot on duty, and he had reached the northern rim of the Ruhr, when he stumbled into the searchlight belt, and was forced down to 200 feet in the endeavour to evade attention. R1781 sustained flak damage, and the sortie was abandoned, the bombs ultimately being jettisoned over Germany from 9,000 feet at 21.45. F/O Robertson was caught in searchlights twenty miles south of Berlin, and jettisoned his bombs from 14,000 feet at 23.15. Only P/O Bundey reached Berlin, where he dropped his two 500 pounders and six SBCs of 4lb incendiaries on the south side from 16,500 feet at 23.30, starting fires which were visible sixty miles into the return trip. Sgt Parker made his way to Frankfurt, where he delivered his load at 22.50 from 13,000 feet, and he, too, observed bomb bursts. Sgts Betts, Callender, Dil and Wilson all reached Ostend to carry out their attacks from 12,500 to 16,000 feet between 20.30 and 21.40, before returning safely to English airspace. X9922 had lost the means to communicate, and Sgt Dil RNZAF had descended in an attempt to establish his position. The Wellington hit trees at Preston Deanery, some five miles south of Northampton, and crashed, killing four of the crew outright, and fatally injuring the pilot. This was not an isolated example of a crew being lost before it had time to gain the necessary experience that might see it through.

A few days of rest preceded the next operation, which, for 101 Squadron, was to the port of Emden, one of four targets scheduled for the night of the 26/27th. It was a freshman "do", for which Sgts Callender, Raybould, Williams and Wilson took off between 19.08 and 19.15. Doubts about the weather for returning crews brought another recall signal, which was picked up by Sgts Callender and Wilson, and complied with. Sgts Raybould and Williams, however, continued blissfully on, the latter reaching the target to bomb from 16,700 feet at 21.55, setting off fires that were still visible fifteen minutes into the return journey. The former arrived a little later, at 22.23, and delivered his bombs across the town in three sticks from 15,000 feet. The ports of Stettin and Hamburg were the principal targets for the night of the 29/30th, and seven 101 Squadron crews were briefed for the former, while three freshmen prepared for a much later departure for Le Havre. S/Ls Colenso and Jones were the senior pilots on duty for the long slog to Germany's north-eastern coast, the take-off for which was completed by five crews between 18.30 and 18.50. Sgt Fooks reached the Norfolk coast before turning back with wireless failure, and it was a similar problem that forced the early return of F/L Todd, whose take-off had been delayed until 19.25. He had reached the mid-point of the North Sea between the Norfolk coast and the Dutch Frisians, when wireless failure ended his sortie. The others all reached the target, and delivered their bombs and incendiaries from 14,000 to 16,500 feet between 22.56 and 23.25, before returning safely to report observing a number of bomb bursts and fires. It was 01.30 before Sgts Betts, Callender and Raybould took off for Le Havre, and they all reached the target to bomb from 12,000 to 15,000 feet between 03.23 and 03.43, observing some explosions across the docks.

October 1941

There was little activity at the start of October, and it was left to the freshmen to start the ball rolling for the new month on the night of the 3/4th. Eight crews were briefed for Antwerp and a singleton, Sgt Watts, for Dunkerque, and they all got away safely between 18.46 and 19.01. P/O Imeson turned back with aileron trouble, but the others all arrived in the target area to find good bombing conditions, and attacks were carried out from 12,500 to 17,500 feet between 20.30 and 20.57. All returned to report observing bomb bursts across the docks, and it was a similar story for Sgt Watts, who had delivered his load from 10,000 feet at 20.20. The first major night of operations came on the 10/11th, when the strength was divided between Cologne and the Krupp works at Essen. Nine 101 Squadron crews were briefed for the former, most of them having now emerged from their freshman status. P/O Hardie was the senior pilot on duty, and he, and the recently commissioned P/O Imeson, were the only officer captains involved. They took off either side of midnight to join up with sixty other aircraft, and arrived in the target area to encounter cloud and the usual blanket of

Three Wellingtons bore the squadron code SR-K and it is not known which of these is shown in this photograph. Sgt Bundey and X9828 failed to return from Frankfurt on 24/25.10.41, whilst R1701 (P/O Hardie) was lost attacking Berlin on 7/8.11.41 and X3654 (Sgt EH Brown) similarly came to grief against Osnabrück on 17/18.8.42 (GW).

industrial haze. It was impossible to pick out ground detail, and the conditions were sufficient to persuade P/O Hardie and Sgt Callender to give up and bring their bombs home. The remainder carried out their attacks on estimated positions from 11,000 to 18,000 feet between 02.02 and 02.42, observing the odd bomb burst, but nothing more. Only Sgt Parker had more to offer on his return with a wounded rear gunner in a flak-damaged X9818. He believed that his bombs had fallen in the Wesseling area, south of the city, where the oil refinery would become a major target in 1944. The return of R1219 was awaited in vain, the last contact with it placing it over Belgium on its way home. News eventually came through, that P/O Imeson and four of his crew were in enemy hands, and that one crew member had lost his life.

The 12/13th was a big night, and, in fact, involved 373 sorties, the largest number in a single night to date. The main objective was Nuremberg, for which 152 aircraft took off, while other forces of moderate size were sent to Bremen and Hüls, while a number of minor operations were also mounted. 101 Squadron had detailed seven Wellingtons for Nuremberg and one for Boulogne, but visibility at Oakington fell to six hundred yards, and the participation of the squadron, and that of 7 Squadron, was scrubbed. As if to lend weight to the Butt Report, some of the bombs intended for Nuremberg fell over sixty miles away, and the other raids were conducted in conditions of thick cloud and could not be assessed. It was a frustrating period for the under-pressure Peirse, who was constantly being thwarted by a protracted spell of bad weather both at home and in the target areas, and, as has already been recorded, it was not uncommon for recall signals to be transmitted, while the crews were outbound over the North Sea.

Fifty-three Wellingtons and seven Stirlings were made ready for an operation to Düsseldorf on the 13th, the majority provided by 3 Group. 101 Squadron contributed seven aircraft, six with NCO captains, and P/O Hardie the senior pilot on duty. They took off between 18.30 and 18.45, but not all would reach the Ruhr. Sgt Raybould turned back when twenty miles from the Belgian coast, after his starboard engine overheated, and Sgt Williams was north of Louvain when he ran into searchlights, and jettisoned his bombs to aid evasion. Sgts Parker, Callender and House and P/O Hardie attacked the primary target from 14,000 to 17,500 feet, between 20.45 and 21.09, and they observed a number of bomb bursts and fires. It is not known whether or not Sgt Betts reached the target, but he and his crew failed to return in T2846, and it was learned later, that five were in enemy hands, and a gunner had managed to evade a similar fate. A return to Nuremberg by eighty aircraft on the night of the 14/15th fared no better in the absence of a 101 Squadron presence, and in the prevailing very poor conditions of thick cloud and icing. The squadron was back in action on the night of the

15/16th, when sending five Wellingtons on a small-scale operation to Cologne, and two freshmen to Boulogne. The Germany-bound aircraft took off between 18.15 and 18.28, with P/Os Millson and Pelmore the senior pilots on duty. Sgts Watts and MacKenzie followed close behind on their way to the French coast, and all seven crews reached their respective targets. Sgt MacKenzie was the only one not to carry out an attack, and reported ten-tenths cloud as the reason for bringing his bombs home. Bombing took place at Cologne from 15,000 to 18,300 feet, between 20.27 and 21.00, and all returned safely, not all to Oakington, to report bomb bursts and fires in various districts of the city. Sgt Watts stirred up some flak activity after bombing at Boulogne from 16,000 feet at 20.34, and Sgt Callender's R1801 sustained damage when flying over the port on his way home to land at Manston.

101 Squadron remained on the ground when Duisburg was targeted again on the night of the 16/17th. Eighty-seven aircraft failed to positively locate the target lying beneath ten-tenths cloud, and the city's charmed life continued. Another large force, this one of 153 aircraft, was despatched to Bremen on the night of the 20/21st, but the effort was again wasted as most of the bombs missed the mark. 101 Squadron launched just two sorties on this night, both by freshman crew against the docks at Antwerp. Sgt Page was approaching the Dutch coast, when engine problems forced him to turn back, and Sgt Willison reached the target area, only to be thwarted by ten-tenths cloud. The Bremen operation was repeated on the following night, with scarcely any improvement, and then Mannheim was selected to host a raid by 123 aircraft on the night of the 22/23rd. Seven 101 Squadron crews attended briefing for this operation, with none of the pilots above the rank of pilot officer. They took off between 18.24 and 18.39, and headed towards the French coast. It was shortly after crossing it, that P/O Pelmore noticed an engine overheating, and decided to turn back when near Lille in north-eastern France. The others pressed on into southern Germany, despite thick cloud and icing conditions that persuaded many crews to seek alternative objectives. They delivered their attacks from 15,000 to 19,000 feet between 20.36 and 20.55, before returning home with little to report, other than bomb bursts and a few fires. While this operation was in progress, Sgt Willison and crew bombed Le Havre from 14,500 feet, and reported large, red fires and heavy explosions.

Difficult weather conditions persisted over Germany on the night of the 24/25th, when seventy aircraft set out for Frankfurt. Five 101 Squadron crews took off between 18.09 and 18.29, and two of them were among only eight who claimed to have reached and bombed the primary target. Sgt House and P/O Millson attacked from 18,000 and 19,200 feet at 21.53 and 21.40 respectively, and both described vivid flashes beneath the cloud, and a succession of large explosions. Sgts Fooks and Raybould also made it as far as the target area, but could not identify their precise location, and the former dropped his bombs on Mainz from 16,500 feet. Sgt Raybould lost power in one engine while approaching to land at Manston, and undershot the runway. X9818 was damaged, but would be returned to service, and the crew emerged unscathed. Sgt Bundey and his crew, who had survived a crash at the start of August, failed to arrive home in X9828, after sending a message stating that they had lost their starboard propeller during the return flight. The Wellington went down in the North Sea, and despite a search by two 101 Squadron crews and Spitfires from 11 Group, no sign of the aircraft and crew was sighted. One body would eventually wash ashore near Ostend, and be buried there.

There was no further operational activity for the squadron until the night of the 28/29th, when P/O McCrorie and crew carried out a freshman sortie to Cherbourg, which they attacked with 500 pounders and incendiaries from 13,700 feet, causing explosions and fires. Two nights earlier, over a hundred aircraft had attacked Hamburg in bright moonlight, and achieved a modicum of success, and the month ended with a further raid on Hamburg, by an initial 123 aircraft, on the night of the 31st, while a smaller scale operation was directed at Bremen. 101 Squadron supported the latter with four crews, led by F/L Todd, and they departed Oakington between 17.38 and 18.00. P/O Hardie turned back from a position east of Amsterdam, after encountering icing conditions, and suffering the failure of the heating system. F/L Todd, Sgt Callender and P/O Pelmore reached the target, but were defeated by ten-tenths cloud, and the first two-mentioned dropped their bombs on Emden, while the last-mentions released his over a flak concentration at Vechta. While this operation was in progress, P/O McCrorie and Sgts Diemer and Dowling raided Boulogne from 15,500 to 18,000 feet between 22.20 and 22.33, and returned to report bomb bursts, fires and an explosion. This was the final activity of a fairly low-key month, which had seen fifty-five sorties dispatched.

November 1941

November began inauspiciously for the Command, when a raid on Kiel by an intended 134 aircraft on the night of the 1/2nd, missed the town entirely. 101 Squadron sat this one out, and rewarded P/O Millson for his good work with promotion to the acting rank of flight lieutenant. The remainder of the first week of the month was devoted to minor operations, and the squadron launched its first three sorties on the night of the 4/5th, when Ostend was the destination for the freshman crews of P/O McCrorie and Sgts Dowling and Willison. They took off either side of 17.45, and the first two-mentioned delivered their 500 pounders and incendiaries onto the primary target from around 17,000 feet, while Sgt Willison bombed Nieuwpoort to the south-west, setting off explosions that lasted for around five minutes. Later on the 5th, the officers were moved from Oakington to take up accommodation at Bourn, some eight miles to the south-west.

There is no question that Peirse needed some good results after the recent frustrations, and he planned a major night of operations for the 7/8th. Berlin was to provide the main course, for which over two hundred aircraft were initially detailed, but doubts about the weather brought an objection from the 5 Group A-O-C, as the result of which, he was allowed to withdraw his contribution, and send it instead to Cologne. A third force of fifty-three Wellingtons and two Stirlings from 1 and 3 Groups was assigned to Mannheim, while minor operations involved more than ninety other aircraft. The total number of sorties, at 392, was a new record, but sadly, this massive effort was not to be rewarded with success. Despite the ominous weather warnings, the operations were allowed to go ahead, only now, the Berlin force had been reduced to 169 aircraft. 101 Squadron detailed five crews, those of P/O Hardie in R1701, P/O Pelmore in R3295, Sgt Callender in R1801, Sgt Luin in X9920 and Sgt Raybould in X9601, and they set off between 17.32 and 17.41. Sgt Luin was soon back in the circuit after his heating system failed, before even reaching the English coast. The others pressed on in the difficult conditions, Sgt Raybould and crew, to their eternal credit, doing so despite also losing their heating system early on. So cold was it, that the pump on the overload oil tank froze, and was thawed by having hot coffee poured onto it. They and the crews of Sgt Callender and P/O Pelmore reached and bombed the estimated position of the Capital through ten-tenths cloud, from a height of 15,000 to 19,500 feet between 20.40 and 20.55, and returned home safely. The ORB surmises that P/O Hardie and crew reached Berlin, but the timing of the receipt of an SOS message at 19.55 suggests otherwise. A second message, "Landing in sea", was received at 20.15, and a fix based on that transmission placed the Wellington some forty-two miles due west of the Hook of Holland. Despite a search by S/L Colenso and Sgt Fooks, and three motor torpedo boats, no trace of R1701 or the crew of P/O Hardie was found. While this operation was in progress, the freshman crews of P/O Laing and Sgts Denning and Winfield were engaged in an operation to Ostend. Sgt Denning brought his bombs back, after failing to identify the target in the cloudy conditions, but the other two crews carried out their attacks from 13,000 and 15,000 feet, and observed explosions across the docks.

The night's main operation was not successful, and certainly not worth the cost of twenty-one aircraft. The seventy-five strong 5 Group contingent landed only eight high-explosive bombs and sixty incendiaries on Cologne, but, at least, lost no aircraft. The Mannheim force failed to land any bombs within the city, and suffered the loss of seven Wellingtons for its pains, which, together with those missing from the minor operations, produced a record casualty figure for a single night of thirty-seven, more than twice the previous highest. This was the final straw for the War Cabinet, and Peirse was summoned to a meeting with Churchill to make his explanations. On the 13th, he was ordered to restrict further operations, while the future of Bomber Command was considered at the highest level, amid calls for its aircraft to be assigned to other theatres.

The remainder of the month was devoted largely to minor operations, the exception being an attack on Hamburg on the night of the 9/10, for which 103 aircraft were made ready. 101 Squadron was not invited to take part, but briefed and dispatched five freshman crews between 17.34 and 17.54 to bomb the docks at Dunkerque. Sgts Denning, Diemer, Dowling and McKenzie and P/O Laing all reached the target area, where Sgt McKenzie decided to carry out a glide attack, which he misjudged, and lost too much altitude before reaching the aiming-point. He abandoned the attempt, while the others bombed from 14,000 to 16,000 feet between 19.00 and 19.20, and returned safely to report bomb bursts and fires. Sgt Fooks was commissioned on the 10th, and from that day until the evening of the 15th, there were no operations involving the squadron. Only the freshman crew of Sgt Winfield was committed to action on that night, to raid the port of Emden. In the event, ten-tenths cloud prevented the target from being identified, and the bombs were dropped from 17,000 feet onto a flak concentration. Sgt Hunt and crew took off from Bourn on the 18th, to carry out a training sortie in X9601, but instrument failure caused the Wellington to crash almost immediately and burn out, fortunately, without injury to the occupants. The ports of Lorient, Brest and Dunkerque hosted small-scale raids on the night of the 23/24th, providing 101 Squadron with the opportunity to blood a few more freshman crews, and ease other recent arrivals further into their tours on less demanding targets. Six crews were briefed for Dunkerque, and they took off between 17.18 and 17.28 to head south. Sgt Willison returned early after making a navigational error, and the others returned later, all to report abandoning their sorties in the face of ten-tenths cloud over the target.

Eighty Wellingtons and twenty Hampdens were made ready for an operation to Emden on the night of 26/27th, five of the former provided by 101 Squadron. They took off between 17.06 and 17.32, with P/O Pelmore the senior pilot on duty, and they were followed away by a trio of freshmen bound for Ostend. Cloudy conditions over the German coast made life difficult for the crews, and only fifty-five reported bombing in the target area. Among these were all five 101 Squadron participants, two of which were carrying a single 1,000 pounder, along with five 500 pounders and one 250 pounder, while two others were loaded with three 500 pounders, one 250 pounder and six SBCs of 4lb incendiaries. P/O Pelmore's bomb bay held eight 500 pounders, and these loads were delivered through ten-tenths cloud from 11,500 to 17,000 feet between 19.15 and 19.39. P/O Clough and Sgts Chapman and Moran all encountered complete cloud-cover over the Belgian coast, and abandoned their sorties. Düsseldorf provided the target for a mixed force of eighty-six aircraft on the following night, when conditions again proved to be unhelpful. Over fifty crews claimed to have bombed in the target area, but the local authorities reported only very minor damage and no casualties. 101 Squadron sat this one out, and the entire Command remained on the ground for the next two nights.

Thus far, since joining the night-bombing brigade, 101 Squadron's losses had been relatively light, while all around them, other units had become accustomed to frequent and often multiple losses. The squadron's turn came on the last night of the month, when a force of 181 aircraft was made ready for an assault on Hamburg. Ten Wellingtons lined up for an early take-off, all with NCO captains, and got away safely between 16.30 and 16.55. Once they were airborne, P/O Clough and Sgts Chapman and Moran departed for an attack by fifty aircraft on Emden. Sadly, the effort expended by the squadron would not be rewarded with success, and the first to turn back was Sgt Wickens with a failed rev-counter. Sgt Dowling's cabin heating failed, and he was the next to abandon his sortie and bring his bombs home. Sgt Callender and crew dropped their bombs on Cuxhaven after a navigational error threw them off course, while Sgt Williams attacked Emden in the belief that he would be late arriving at the primary target. Sgt House failed to locate Hamburg, and delivered his load onto the Frisian island of Nordstrand on the way home. Sgt Diemer was attacked by three night fighters, from which he escaped, before making a run for home, and, in the event, only two 101 Squadron aircraft reached and bombed the primary target. Sgts Luin and Raybould carried out their attacks from 16,500 and 17,000 feet at 20.03 and 20.45 respectively, and returned home to report that searchlight glare had prevented an assessment of results. Two crews failed to return home, those of Sgt Willison in R1778, and Sgt Winfield in R3295. An SOS signal was received from the former, along with the message that they were landing in the sea, a fix providing an approximate location of 150 miles north-east of Cromer. It was learned later, that they had ditched in the North Sea at 20.00, some forty-five miles west-north-west of Esbjerg in Denmark, killing the pilot and three others. Two members of the crew survived, and drifted in their dinghy, until being rescued on the 2nd of December by a Danish fishing boat. They were suffering from exposure, and were taken to hospital, where they were handed over to the enemy. Sgts Moran and Chapman, meanwhile, had bombed Emden from 13,500 and 18,300 feet respectively, either side of 20.00, while P/O Clough had experienced temporary engine failure, and had jettisoned his bombs.

The following account of the fate of R3295 is taken from the book Gevleugeld Verleden (Winged History), written by leading Dutch historian, Ab Jansen, and published in 1975. It is based on an interview with rear gunner, Sgt Adrian Heath, and is an abridged version translated by Andreas Wachtel from Dutch into German, with the kind permission of Ab Jansen, and by this author from German into English. The original text appears on pages 157 to 163 in the chapter entitled Twee Wellingtons (Two Wellingtons).

Sgt Winfield, a Londoner, and his crew were on their third operation together, and outbound for Hamburg, when R3295 lost an engine about half an hour before reaching the German coast. The crew decided to press on, and reached the Hamburg area at around 20.00, having, by this time, lost a considerable amount of altitude. Shortly before running in on the target, they were ensnared by a searchlight, which Sgt Winfield managed to shake off through evasive action. He pulled out of the dive at 3,000 feet, and, realising that they were right over the aiming point, ordered the bombs to be dropped. At that moment, the dead engine suddenly sprang back into life, enabling them to quickly recover the lost height and reach 18,000 feet as they turned for home, still over the centre of the city, with the Binnen-Alster Lake beneath them. At that point, the engine failed again, this time for good, and they set course for home, sending out an SOS message at 21.36. The issue was decided when the second engine failed over the sea, and the Wellington became a rapidly-sinking glider. To parachute into the freezing North Sea meant certain death, so the crew searched frantically for somewhere to carry out an emergency landing. At 22.55, wireless operator Sgt Cook sent out his final message, "Landing in the sea close to the shore". As they glided down, they were fired upon by flak, but not hit. The sea was coming with undue haste towards them, when, at the last moment, second pilot, Sgt Johnson RCAF, a native of New York, spotted a flat, wet sandbank, and, without further thought, turned the Wellington to port and performed a perfect belly-landing. The rear gunner, Sgt Heath, was trapped in his turret by jammed doors, and had to be freed by use of the emergency axe. All crew members survived uninjured, and were taken into captivity in the morning. They were informed then, that they had come down at Het Balg (The Bellows), on the most easterly point of the Frisian island of Schiermonnikoog. Before the war, Burma-born Sgt Heath had studied art, and would become celebrated post-war as, perhaps, the finest abstract artist to work in the UK. (Bomber Command Losses 1941, Bill Chorley.)

It had been a relatively quiet month for the squadron, during the course of which, just forty-four sorties were dispatched.

Wellington R3295 was captured, along with her crew, by the Germans after a forced landing on the Frisian island of Schiermonnikoog (GW).

December 1941

An unidentified Wellington and crew (GW)

The Wellington squadrons were kept relatively active during December on small scale operations, and no less than thirteen such raids were directed at Brest and its lodgers, although not always in the presence of a Wellington contingent. It would be a quiet month for 101 Squadron, however, with no operations until the evening of the 7th, when six Wellingtons were dispatched to bomb the docks at Boulogne. They took off between 17.00 and 17.10, with P/Os Clough and Laing the senior pilots on duty. P/O Clough failed to identify the primary target, and bombed a nearby flare-path instead. The others delivered their five 500 and six 250 pounders each, as briefed, from 15,000 to 18,300 feet, between 18.27 and 19.02. There were no further operations for the squadron until the evening of the 17th, when a force of 121 aircraft was assembled for the latest attempt to damage the warships at Brest. 101 Squadron's contribution was six Wellingtons, while two others joined in a small effort at Le Havre. The two elements took off either side of 17.00, with P/Os Laing and Pelmore the senior pilots on duty for Brest, and P/O Clough and St Attwood bound for Le Havre. Sgt Williams failed to carry out an attack at the primary target because of ten-tenths cloud, but the others bombed on estimated positions from 16,000 feet either side of 19.00. It was a similar story at Le Havre, where just one among fourteen participants bombed in the face of complete cloud cover

After a few more days of operational inactivity, eight 101 Squadron crews were briefed for Brest on the 23rd. They were to make up a force of thirty-eight Wellingtons and nine Stirlings, and, after some time on the side-

53

lines, the senior officers, S/Ls Colenso and Jones and F/L Todd, were back on the Order of Battle. They took off between 16.00 and 16.30, but Sgt Chapman returned almost immediately with oil pressure failure. The others pressed on to the target, where they encountered the usual fierce opposition from flak and searchlights. They carried out their attacks from 13,000 to 17,500 feet between 18.35 and 19.50, and most were too busy taking evasive action to assess the results. The Command's largest effort of the month was reserved for Düsseldorf on the night of the 27/28th, for which 132 aircraft were despatched, among them eleven Wellingtons representing 101 Squadron. They took off either side of 17.00, with F/L Todd the senior pilot on duty, but P/O Fooks had W/C Biggs alongside him on a rare venture into the operational arena. Technical issues soon forced a spate of early returns, and it was engine trouble that caused Sgt Moran to turn back at the English coast at Orford Ness, before a similar problem afflicted Sgt Attwood's aircraft fifteen miles out from the same location. Sgt Diemer was twenty miles short of the Dutch coast at Haamstede, when the cabin heating failed, and Sgt Chapman turned back with oxygen and intercom failure, when mid-way between the Kent and Belgian coasts. P/O Laing had the target in sight, when temporary engine failure persuaded him to drop his bombs on the neighbouring town of Neuss. This left F/L Todd, P/O Fooks and Sgts Callender, Luin and Raybould to fly the squadron flag over Düsseldorf, which they attacked from 14,500 to 19,500 feet between 19.12 and 19.30, before returning safely to report bomb bursts and fires. Sadly, the effort was not rewarded with success, and damage within the city was light, at a cost to the Command of five Whitleys and two Wellingtons. The squadron posted missing the experienced P/O Pelmore and his crew in Z1115, which came down in or close to the Ruhr, killing all on board, and this was the squadron's final loss of the year. The final sortie of the year was carried out by P/O Clough and crew on the evening of the 28th, when Dunkerque was the target. They turned back when about two miles short of the Belgian coast, citing temporary engine failure as the cause, and, had, thereby, failed to complete a single sortie thus far.

1941 had brought change to the squadron, and 1942 would do likewise, but generally, it had been a bad year for the Command, with few advances made on the previous year. The new types introduced to operations early in the year had all failed to meet expectations, and each had spent lengthy periods of grounding to enable essential modifications to be carried out. A dark cloud hung over the Command and its commander-in chief, who had striven to fulfil the often-unrealistic demands placed upon him by his superiors. Undoubtedly, the greatest change in the year ahead would be occasioned by the arrival at the helm of Bomber Command of a new commander-in-chief, a man who was not only able to provide direction, purpose and firm leadership, but also possessed the self-belief and obstinacy to fight his corner against all-comers. He would be assisted in his efforts by the advent of the "shining sword" in the form of the Lancaster, which was currently undergoing operational trials in the hands of 5 Group's 44 Squadron.

January 1942

The year began with a continuation of the obsession with the German cruisers at Brest, and no less than eight raids would be carried out against the port during the first eleven days of the new year, with a further three right at the end. 101 Squadron would expend energy on this fruitless task, beginning on the evening of the 2nd, when five of its Wellingtons took off between 16.05 and 16.15 as part of a small effort. P/O Clough was the only officer captain, and he finally completed a sortie by delivering six 500 pounders and two SBCs of incendiaries over the target onto flares dropped by the early arrivals. The others were also successful, and, thus, five of the seven returning crews who claimed to have bombed as briefed, belonged to 101 Squadron. Sadly, it seems that a new scribe was responsible for maintaining the squadron record, and details of times on target and bombing heights have been omitted. Four NCO crews took off for Brest either side of 03.30 on the 6th, some carrying recently posted-in pilots as "second dickies" to gain experience, before being let loose with their own crews. The target area was largely hidden by cloud, but a number of flashes were observed, and fires were beginning to take hold as they retreated homeward. Sgt House took off almost two hours after the others, and headed for Cherbourg, where he dropped a dozen 250 pounders and two SBCs of 4lb incendiaries.

There was a very early start for eleven 101 Squadron crews on the morning of the 9th, as the enemy warships at Brest beckoned once more, although the port's Arsenal Power Station was the objective for the 3 Group element of twenty-seven aircraft. S/L Colenso was the senior pilot on duty as they took off between 04.25 and 04.45, and headed for the south coast. Sgt Attwood turned back at Reading because of severe icing, which caused his engines to falter, but the remainder pressed on to reach the target and deliver their ordnance. Six were carrying seven 500 pounders, while four had three 500 pounders in their bomb bay, along with one 250 pounder and six SBCs of 4lb incendiaries. The target lay beneath eight to nine-tenths cloud, but many crews saw bomb bursts, and the consensus was of a successful operation. There was a change at the top of Bomber Command on the 10th, AM Sir Richard Peirse having vacated his post as commander-in-chief a few days earlier. His future lay in commands in India and south-east Asia, and it would fall to the 3 Group A-O-C, AVM Baldwin, to stand in as C-in-C Bomber Command, until a permanent successor to Peirse was appointed. An early evening take-off on the 10th involved eight crews bound for Wilhelmshaven as part of a force of 124 aircraft, while a single freshman, Sgt Hunt, set off to bomb the docks at Boulogne. The main element was airborne between 16.30 and 16.40, with F/L Millson the senior pilot on duty, and the Boulogne-bound singleton followed on an hour later. All reached their respective targets to encounter good bombing conditions, and returned safely to report bomb bursts and fires.

A force of ninety-five aircraft was made ready on the 14th, for an attack that night on shipyards and an airframe factory in Hamburg. There were no commissioned captains on duty, but a number of officer pilots were flying as "second dickies" to gain experience. Sgt Attwood was approaching the mid-point of the outward flight, and was about fifty miles north of the Frisians, when he started jettisoning incendiaries to maintain height. Soon afterwards, he abandoned the sortie, and brought part of his bomb load home. The remainder found the target area to be free of cloud, and were among forty-eight crews to report delivering their bomb loads as briefed, and observing explosions and fires. Local reports confirmed that Altona railway station had been hit in the west of the city, and that seven large fires had broken out. Acting W/C Biggs departed the squadron on posting to 26 O.T.U on this day, and W/C Nicholls became his successor on the 15th. S/L Jones was posted to 99 Squadron on the 20th, and S/L Eaton, a future commander of the squadron, came in the opposite direction.

The focus remained on northern Germany on the evening of the 20th, when the squadron dispatched six Wellingtons to the port of Emden, as part of an overall force of twenty-five aircraft. They took off either side of 18.00, with P/O Clough the senior pilot on duty. Sgt Dowling was about sixty miles out from the Norfolk coast, when his heating system failed, and his starboard engine began to show signs of a problem. Sgt Callender was a little further into the outward flight, some forty miles short of the Frisians, when rising oil temperature in the starboard engine combined with an intermittently-functioning port engine to persuade him also to turn back. Sgt Hunt's efforts to reach Emden were hampered by a navigational error, which put him in the Wilhelmshaven area. He headed south from there, and found himself over a town, which he identified by a river, railway lines and an aerodrome, as Oldenburg. He dropped his six 500 pounders and two SBCs of 40lb incendiaries, and saw them all burst. Sgt Denning was the first to arrive over the intended target, before any searchlight and flak activity began, and he saw his bombs burst close to the aiming-point, just north of the docks. P/O Clough claimed to be the second to arrive, by which time Sgt Denning's bombs had stirred up some defensive response from the ground. As he was making his bombing run, he saw other bombs and incendiaries burst near the aiming-point, and he added his own a little to the east. Sgt Chapman and crew failed to arrive back in Z1110, and no trace of the Wellington and crew was ever found. On board was P/O Curtis, who was flying his third sortie as second pilot.

The single sortie on the evening of the 21st involved the freshman crew of Sgt Cowley, with P/O Lewis on board as second pilot. They took off at 18.10 for Boulogne, but abandoned the attempt to locate it because of ten-tenths cloud, and bombed a flare-path about eight miles south-west of Calais instead. Eight crews were briefed on the 22nd, seven to join forty others to attack Münster, and the freshman crew of Sgt Ward to cut their teeth at Dunkerque. The main element, of which F/L Millson was the senior pilot on duty, took off between 17.35 and 18.00, to be followed by the freshman twenty minutes later. P/O Laing suffered engine failure immediately after take-off, and jettisoned his bombs on Berner's Heath, south of Mildenhall. X9819 had a gun turret become unserviceable, and Sgt House bombed Dunkerque as an alternative. Sgt Hunt lost his port engine while over enemy territory outbound, and jettisoned his bombs onto open country. The others reached the target, and watched their bombs fall into the town and around the railway station. Returning crews claimed good results, for which there is no confirmation in local reports, which recorded five fatalities. This proved to be the final operation of a relatively quiet month, during the course of which fifty-three sorties had been dispatched.

February 1942

February was a time of limited activity, broken by the hectic, after-the-horse-had-bolted-attempt to compromise the breakout of the Scharnhorst, Gneisenau and Prinz Eugen from Brest on the 12th. The month began slowly for 101 Squadron, which would undertake no operations until the end of the second week as crews were familiarized with the new Mk III Wellingtons that were arriving on station. 419 Squadron RCAF had been formed in 3 Group in mid-December, and a number of aircrew postings took place between it and 101 Squadron, beginning with the departure of P/O Clough on the 1st, the day on which F/L Todd was posted to the Central Flying School at Uphaven. Brest was visited inconclusively on the night of the 6/7th, and P/O Laing was posted to 419 Squadron on the 8th. Crews were sent to Blackpool and Dumfries by air on the 9th to collect the new aircraft, and they would arrive back over the next three days. The change of address to Bourn, a satellite of Oakington, was completed on the 11th, and the air and ground staff set about the task of turning it into home.

A small-scale raid on Brest on the evening of the 11th, proved to be the final one, as Vice Admiral Otto Cilliax, the Brest Group commander, whose flag was on Scharnhorst, put Operation Cerberus into action shortly afterwards. The Scharnhorst, Gneisenau and Prinz Eugen slipped anchor at 21.14, and headed into the English

Channel under an escort of destroyers and E-Boats. It was an audacious bid for freedom, covered by widespread jamming and meticulously planned support by the Kriegsmarine and the Luftwaffe, all of which had been practiced extensively during January. The planning, and a little good fortune, allowed the fleet to make undetected progress until spotted off Le Touquet by two Spitfires piloted by G/C Victor Beamish, the commanding officer of Kenley, and W/C Finlay Boyd, both of whom maintained radio silence, and did not report their find until landing at 10.42 on the morning of the 12th. 5 Group was standing by at four hours readiness when Operation Fuller, which had been planned well in advance for precisely this eventuality, ground slowly into action. The problem seemed to be, that few people in the areas that mattered had been fully briefed on the operation's requirements, and some, it seems, were totally ignorant of it. The first of a record number of 242 daylight sorties were despatched at 13.30, and were followed by others throughout the day, but the squally conditions and low cloud prevented all but a few crews from catching sight of their quarry, and those attacks that did take place failed to find the mark. 101 Squadron dispatched four Wellingtons at 15.00, with F/L Millson the senior pilot on duty, and he and Sgts Callender and Williams reached the Dutch coast to receive a welcome from waving civilians on bicycles and on foot. Sgt Diemer stopped some twenty-five miles short of the Scheldt Estuary before turning back, but none of the 101 Squadron contingent sighted the enemy vessels, which passed unscathed through the Straits of Dover, to make good their escape into open sea. Both Scharnhorst and Gneisenau struck mines recently laid by 5 Group aircraft, and this slowed their progress to an extent, but all had arrived safely in home ports by the following day. The "Channel Dash" caught the British off guard, and despite the heroic efforts of Bomber and Coastal Commands, the episode was a huge embarrassment to the government and the nation. It had cost the Command a further fifteen crews, on top of all those lost over the past eleven months in the long running saga, but at least, this annoying itch had been scratched for the last time, and the Command could now concentrate its efforts against targets to which it was better suited.

Sgt Cowley and crew were sent off shortly after 18.00 on the 13th, with the intention of bombing the docks at Le Havre, but had got as far only as Halton in Buckinghamshire when the IFF system failed. They turned towards the east coast, and jettisoned the bombs safe some ten miles east of Southwold at 20.08. On the 14th, a new Air Ministry directive reaffirmed the assault on the morale of the enemy's civilian population, particularly its workers, by authorizing the blatant area bombing of Germany's urban areas, without the pretence of aiming for industrial and military objectives. Waiting in the wings, in fact, already steaming away from America's eastern seaboard in the armed merchantman, SS Alcantara, was the man who would pursue this policy with a will. Meanwhile, back at Bourn, 101 Squadron launched its final sortie of the month on the evening of the 16th. It was a nickelling (leaflet) trip undertaken to Lille in north-eastern France by the freshman crew of Sgt Cowley, and was probably to compensate them for the failure of their previous effort to gain experience. This time they made it all the way to the target area, where they delivered eight packages of leaflets on ETA through ten-tenths cloud.

ACM Sir Arthur T Harris took up his appointment as Commander-in-Chief on the 22nd, and arrived at the helm with firm ideas already in place, about how to win the war by bombing alone. He recognized the need to overwhelm the enemy defences by pushing the maximum number of aircraft across an aiming-point in the shortest possible time. This would signal the birth of the bomber stream, and bring to an end the former practice, whereby squadrons and crews largely determined for themselves the details of their sorties. He also knew that urban areas are most efficiently destroyed by fire rather than blast, and it would not be long before the bomb loads carried by his aircraft reflected this thinking. For the remainder of the month, Harris continued with small-scale raids on German ports, and it was during one of these operations, that the war threw up one of its ironies. On the night of the 26/27th, an attack was launched against the Gneisenau, now moored at the floating dock at Kiel, where she was now supposedly in safe haven, after enduring eleven months of constant bombardment at Brest. One of the participating Wellingtons, Hampdens and Halifaxes landed a high explosive bomb on her bows, ending her sea-going career for good, after which, her main armament was removed for use as a coastal battery.

March 1942

Harris made his first impression early in March, when sending a new record force for a single target, to attack the Renault lorry factory at Billancourt in Paris on the evening of the 3rd. 235 aircraft took off for this carefully planned raid, which was to be conducted in three waves, led by experienced crews, and with extensive use of flares to provide illumination. In the face of what was expected to be scant defence, bombing was to be carried out from low level to ensure accuracy, and to avoid unnecessary casualties among French civilians in adjacent residential districts. 101 Squadron despatched three crews at 19.00, those of W/C Nicholls, F/S Raybould and Sgt Attwood, who each carried eight 500 pounders. They were among the 223 crews who deposited their bomb loads into the target area, destroying 40% of the factory's buildings, and halting production of lorries for four weeks. It was estimated that the loss of production amounted to almost 2,300 vehicles. The operation was concluded for the loss of just one Wellington, and the satisfaction at this outstanding success was marred only by the heavy casualties inflicted upon nearby civilians, of which 367 were killed. It was somewhat paradoxical, that Harris, as a champion of area bombing, should gain his first major victory by way of a precision target.

Essen, as a major centre of war production, and the home of the giant Krupp armaments complex, was to feature prominently in Harris's future plans, and he intended to attack it frequently. The first of an initial five raids during the month took place on the night of the 8/9th, and was the first operation in which the leading aircraft were equipped with the Gee navigation device. It was also another ideal opportunity to employ flares to provide illumination and perhaps negate the ever-present industrial haze. Eight 101 Squadron Wellingtons began taking off at midnight as part of an overall force of 211 aircraft, with F/Ls Millson and Watts the senior pilots on duty, although, for an undisclosed reason, F/L Millson did not depart until 01.20. Sgts Attwood, Diemer and House each carried twelve bundles of flares, and the others, nine SBCs each, containing ninety 4lb incendiaries, and all seven of the returning crews claimed to have released their loads, as briefed, over the target. X3656 went missing without trace, and took with it to their deaths P/O Luin and his crew. The Essen authorities described this as a light raid, which destroyed a few houses and a church, and it would be the start of a frustrating period for Harris. He had to come to terms with the fact, that Essen, and, indeed, the entire Ruhr Valley, was effectively untouchable under its blanket of industrial haze, and until the means was developed to "see" through it, attacks on this region were a lottery.

Harris was a stubborn man, however, and would persist with his campaign against Essen, launching the second raid within twenty-four hours of the first. A force of 187 aircraft was made ready, which included six 101 Squadron Wellingtons, led by S/L Colenso. They began taking off at 19.30, but S/L Colenso and Sgt Llewelyn turned back at the Dutch coast, the former with Gee-equipment (TR1335) failure, and the latter for an undisclosed reason. Sgts Cowley and Early were carrying twelve bundles of flares each, while Sgts Hunt and Ward had incendiaries on board, and all carried out their briefs before returning home safely. Sgt Ward crash-landed a flak-riddled X3642 at Oakington, but all of the occupants scrambled clear before the Wellington was consumed by fire, and just one crew member was admitted to hospital. For his dedication to duty, Sgt Ward received an immediate award of the DFM. The operation was another failure, in which only two houses were classed as destroyed. For the third consecutive night, Essen was the target on the 10/11th, for a force, this time,

The wreckage of Wellington X3651, SR-Z, at Bourne after she crashed short of the runway during a training flight. Sgt Hunt and his crew were fortunate to survive the escapade, (GW).

of 126 aircraft, and it again escaped all but the most superficial damage, demonstrating that Gee was useful as a navigation device, but was too imprecise to use as a blind bombing aid. 101 Squadron sat this one out, and remained on the ground also on the night of the 12/13th, when the town area and the shipyards of Kiel were attacked to good effect.

Cologne was the target for the next attempt to employ Gee as a blind-bombing device, which took place on the night of the 13/14th. 101 Squadron briefed nine crews, who took off between 19.25 and 19.45 led by S/L Colenso. All were part of the flare-force, and each delivered their twelve bundles over the target, mostly on the basis of a Gee-fix (TR-fix), although some were able to make a visual identification of ground detail. F/Sgt Callender crash-landed X3648 at Newmarket, but the crew walked away, and the Wellington was soon back in harness. The raid caused damage to fifteen hundred houses and a number of important war-industry factories, where vital production was lost, and thus made it many times more effective than any other attack on this target, and the first one successfully led by Gee. Sgt Hunt walked away from the wreckage of X3651, after undershooting while trying to land during training on the 15th, but the rest of his crew needed attention for their injuries. The idiotic practice of sending individual crews out on daylight sorties under the cover of cloud, would cost the lives of many crews, until someone in High Command recognised the folly of "moling" operations, and ended them. S/L Colenso undertook one such sortie on the 19th, departing Bourn at 12.45 to "test the water" for five other crews waiting to hear of cloud conditions. He turned back some fifty miles out from Overflakee, after assessing the cloud to be insufficient for a flight over the Ruhr, and the other sorties were cancelled. This proved to be S/L Colenso's swansong with the squadron, his tour having come to an end. He was posted out on the following day, and replaced as A Flight commander by F/L Watts.

59

F/L Millson carried out a weather sortie on the afternoon of the 22nd, to assess the conditions for operations over Germany that night, but his report of fog led to them being cancelled. On the following day, F/Sgt Raybould was attempting a one-engine landing, but could not maintain height, and came down south of the airfield, apparently without damage to the aircraft or occupants. Nine crews were called to briefing on the 25th, to learn that Essen was to be their target that night. They were to be part of the largest force yet sent to a single target, consisting of 254 aircraft, and they took off between 19.45 and 20.40, led by F/L Millson, with B Flight commander, S/L Eaton, the senior pilot on duty. Six flew with the flare force, and the remainder carried nine SBCs, each containing ninety 4lb incendiaries. Sgts Attwood and Early turned back at the Dutch coast with overheating engines, but the others pressed on to reach the target area, and play their part in the proceedings. Weather conditions over the target were favourable, and many returning crews claimed to have found the mark. Unfortunately, many had been deceived by a decoy fire site at Rheinberg, eighteen miles away, and relatively little damage was inflicted upon Essen. F/L Millson was the senior pilot on duty on the following night, when six 101 Squadron Wellingtons joined ninety-eight others and eleven Stirlings for another crack at Essen. They departed Bourn between 20.00 and 20.35 as part of the flare force, but Sgts Attwood and Llewelyn turned back at the Dutch coast with TR and communications failures. The others carried out their assigned tasks and returned safely from midnight onwards, while eleven aircraft from other units failed to make it home, after encountering a fierce flak defence and many night fighters.

Harris understood the problems facing his crews with regard to target location over a blacked-out country that was invariable cloud-covered. He had confidence in their ability to hit a target effectively, if they could see it, and a coastal location would provide the best pinpoints. 234 aircraft set off on the night of the 28/29th, to attack the Baltic port city and Hansastadt (free-trade city) of Lübeck, in an operation that would be a signpost for things to come for the Reich's urban areas in the years ahead. It was selected for its close proximity to an easily identifiable coastline, the paucity of its defences, for its access, without the need to traverse large tracts of enemy territory, and for the fact that it was an old city, with narrow streets and half-timbered buildings, which would aid the spread of fire. The attack was to be conducted along similar lines to those employed against the Renault factory early in the month, and the high proportion of incendiaries carried in the bomb bays, reflected Harris's fire-raising intent. 101 Squadron contributed eight Wellingtons to the operation, led by F/L Watts and taking off either side of 20.00. F/L Millson and F/Sgt Callender flew with the flare force, while Sgts Attwood, Cowley, Early and Llewelyn carried incendiaries, and F/L Watts and F/Sgt Raybould a 1,000 pounder each and six 500 pounders. It was, for the period, an outstandingly successful operation, which destroyed over fourteen hundred buildings, and devastated an estimated 30% of the city's built-up area. It represented the first major success for the area bombing policy, and was concluded for the modest loss of twelve aircraft, none of which was from 101 Squadron. This was the final operation of the month, during the course of which fifty-one sorties had been dispatched. S/L Eaton was promoted to the temporary rank of wing commander on the 31st.

April 1942

The squadron was in action on the first night of the new month, sending four freshman crews to bomb the docks at Le Havre. They took off in a five-minute slot from 20.10, but F/Sgt Machin returned early with engine trouble, and landed at Feltwell. P/O Gardner and Sgts Weaver and Chaundy continued on to find clear skies and good visibility, and the first two-mentioned delivered their seventeen 250 pounders each in two sticks from 17,500 feet and 13,500 feet between 21.35 and 21.55 respectively, while Sgt Chaundy let his go in a salvo from 14,000 feet at 21.37, and all claimed to have hit the target. Hampdens and Wellingtons went mining in the Quiberon Bay region off St Nazaire on the night of the 2/3rd, and this would be a first "gardening" operation for 101 Squadron. The appropriately named P/O Gardner, and Sgt Weaver were again called into action, and they were joined by Sgt Machin. They took off at 19.40, carrying two 1,500lb parachute mines each, which P/O Gardner and Sgt Machin reported dropping into the briefed location from under 1,000 feet, the latter claiming to have shot at three searchlights also. X3709 failed to return with the crew of Sgt Weaver, having crashed into the sea, killing all on board. Three bodies eventually came ashore near Lorient, and they were interred there.

A new record force of 263 aircraft was made ready for an operation to Cologne on the night of the 5/6th, 101 Squadron providing nine Wellingtons. F/S Machin and Sgt Chaundy became bogged down while taxying, and failed to take off, but the others got away safely, six of them between 23.45 and 00.05, while P/O Gardner, the senior pilot on duty, departed an hour later. F/Sgt Raybould and Sgts Diemer, Early and Llewelyn were part of the flare force, while F/Sgt Callender and Sgt Attwood each carried nine SBCs of incendiaries, and P/O Gardner a 1,000 pounder and six 500 pounders. They arrived at the target to find five to eight-tenths cloud with tops ranging from 2,000 to 10,000 feet, and delivered their loads from between 17,400 and 19,000 feet. All returned safely to report observing some fires and bomb bursts, but it was not possible to make an accurate assessment of the results. The massive effort was not rewarded with success, as the bombing was scattered across the city, lacking the concentration vital to an effective attack, and a modest ninety houses were destroyed. F/L Millson was the senior pilot on duty among five crews, who took off for Essen between 00.35 and 00.50 on the night of the 6/7th. They were to be part of an overall force of 157 aircraft, but severe storms and icing conditions on the route out led to all from Bourn returning early, and only a third of those dispatched actually reached the general area of the target to bomb through heavy cloud on estimated positions.

Two nights later, it was the turn of Hamburg to host a new record force of 272 aircraft, of which 101 Squadron provided nine Wellingtons, led again by F/L Millson. They took off either side of 22.00, and headed once more into electrical storms and icing conditions, which prevented over eighty aircraft from reaching the target area. Among these were P/O Gardner and F/Sgt Machin, the former falling foul of the conditions, and the latter engine trouble. The remaining 101 Squadron crews arrived intact, all but one carrying nine SBCs of incendiaries, while Sgt Llewelyn had a 1,000 pounder and six 500 pounders in his bomb bay. They delivered their ordnance through ten-tenths cloud from 19,000 to 20,500 feet, and only one returning crew reported the glow of a fire through the cloud. The local authorities recorded three large fires, but little damage of significance, however, stray incendiaries did cause some useful damage to U-Boots in the Vulkan construction yards at Bremen some fifty-five miles to the south-west. The first of two further large raids on Essen took place on the night of the 10/11th, for which 101 Squadron provided ten Wellingtons in an overall force of 254 aircraft. S/L Watts was the senior pilot on duty as they took off either side of 22.00, having been preceded at 21.20 by Sgt Beecroft and crew heading for Le Havre on their maiden freshman sortie. F/Sgt Raybould and Sgts Chaundy and Diemer returned early with technical issues, but the remainder pressed on to reach the target area, which they identified either visually, through seven to nine-tenths cloud, or by Gee-fix. S/L Watts and three others were part of the flare force, and the others carried nine SBCs of incendiaries, which were delivered from between 16,000 and 18,000 feet. All returned safely, as did Sgt Beecroft and crew, who had dropped their seventeen 250 pounders in two sticks from 13,000 feet across the docks at Le Havre.

The final attempt to hit Essen effectively was mounted on the night of the 12/13th, and involved 251 aircraft, of which, ten Wellingtons represented 101 Squadron. F/L Millson led them away at 22.00, and all were safely outbound to the Ruhr by 22.50. Sgts Cowley and Diemer returned early with technical problems, leaving the others to continue on to the target, where conditions were favourable for bombing, with clear skies but the

61

expected industrial haze. Five crews flew with the flare force, while the others were carrying incendiaries, and these were dropped onto the target from 18,000 to 20,000 feet in the face of a searchlight and flak response. On return, Sgt Chaundy landed at Waterbeach, where a loose flare fell out and ignited under Z1569, which was consumed by fire after the crew had vacated it. Although some damage had been inflicted upon Essen, and a number of bombs had fallen upon the Krupp works, this was another highly disappointing raid, which scattered bombs across the Ruhr. Harris had now launched eight major operations against this target since early March, involving 1,555 aircraft, 1,006 of whose crews had reported bombing in the target area. The series had cost the Command sixty-four aircraft in return for meagre gains, but Harris would not give up, and the battle would go on.

On the following night, the squadron sent six crews on a mining operation in the Heligoland Bight. S/L Watts was the senior pilot on duty, and there was a maiden sortie for Sgt Nesbitt and crew. They took off between 21.25 and 21.45, but Sgt Cowley returned early with an engine glitch. The others delivered their two 1,500lb mines each into the briefed locations, and returned safely. Having failed to succeed at Essen, Harris turned his attention upon its neighbour, Dortmund, at the eastern end of the Ruhr. Six 101 Squadron Wellingtons took off between 22.30 and 22.55 on the 14th, as part of an overall force of 208 aircraft. F/L Millson was the senior pilot on duty, and, for once, the entire squadron contingent arrived in the target area, where they found clear skies. The four flare-carriers released their twelve bundles each over the city from 18,000 feet, while Sgts Early and Llewelyn dropped their incendiaries from 18,000 and 19,500 feet respectively. The target may have changed, but the outcome had not, and bombs were scattered across a forty-mile stretch of the Ruhr, with little damage of significance where intended. 152 aircraft set off for the same target twenty-four hours later, this time with a contribution from the squadron of five Wellingtons. S/L Watts led them away either side of 23.30, and those reaching the target found thick cloud and icing conditions. S/L Watts was unable to identify the target, and brought his flares home, while Sgt Diemer located it by means of a TR-fix, and Sgt Cowley visually, and they released their flares from 18,000 and 19,000 feet respectively. X3694 failed to return with the freshman crew of Sgt Nesbitt, after crashing just inside the Luxembourg border with Belgium, and killing all on board.

Eight NCO crews and that of P/O Gardner lined up for take-off shortly before 23.30 on the 17th, with W/C Nicholls electing to fly as second pilot with the crew of F/Sgt Raybould. The target for the force of 173 aircraft was Hamburg, and those arriving in the target area found clear skies and favourable bombing conditions. Sgt Llewelyn and crew were in X3653, which developed an overheating starboard engine, causing the sortie to be curtailed. They dropped their bombs on a section of the Kiel Canal from 15,000 feet, before returning safely home. Three others delivered their loads of a single 1,000 pounder and six 500 pounders each from 17,000 to 18,500 feet, while P/O Gardner was at 22,000 feet as he released his, but did not positively identify the target. Two of the squadron's Wellingtons were among the eight missing aircraft, both coming down in the general target area. X3356 crashed at 03.34 some ten miles north-north-west of Hamburg, killing Sgt Cowley and his crew, and X3655 crashed at 03.56 at Lübeck-Taterborn, with fatal consequences for P/O House and three of his crew, including F/Sgt Mason DFM, an observer (navigator) with more than fifty operations to his credit. Two members of the crew survived, and were taken into captivity. Seventy-five fires were started in Hamburg, over thirty of them classed as large, but the damage was in no way commensurate with the effort expended.

F/Sgt Raybould was training Sgt Jackson in X3647 on the 20th, when the Wellington was involved in some kind of minor accident on the runway, which was not damaging to aircraft or crew. Cologne was selected as the target for another attempt to use Gee as a blind bombing device on the night of the 22/23rd. It was an entirely 3 Group show involving sixty-four Wellingtons and five Stirlings, all equipped with the device. 101 Squadron dispatched seven Wellingtons between 21.50 and 22.00, led by S/L Watts. Sgt Llewelyn and crew were back on the ground two hours later, after X3669 had been badly shot up by predicted flak at Ostend, which they crossed at 14,000 feet, and they jettisoned their 1,000 pounder and six 500 pounders into the sea. F/L Millson returned a few minutes later with engine and W/T failure, while P/O Gardner blamed an overheating starboard engine for his failure to complete the operation, and he brought his nine SBCs home. The others reached the target, and delivered their respective loads on Gee-fix from between 14,300 and 16,000 feet, before returning to report three large fires observed through gaps in the five-tenths cloud. The local authorities assessed this as a light raid, based on the small number of high explosives and incendiaries landing within the city.

In an attempt to repeat the success at Lübeck, Harris mounted four raids on consecutive nights against Rostock, another Baltic port, which had the nearby Heinkel aircraft factory as an added attraction. The first of the series was mounted on the night of the 23/24th, for which a force of 161 aircraft was made ready, eighteen of them to aim specifically at the Heinkel works. 101 Squadron contributed seven Wellington, which took off between 22.40 and 23.15, with F/L Millson the senior pilot on duty. They arrived in the target area to find clear skies and excellent bombing conditions, and fires already burning. It is known that three of the Bourn contingent were carrying SBCs and three a 1,000 pounder and four 500 pounders, which were dropped over the target from 12,000 to 16,000 feet, it was believed with great accuracy. The ORB does not state Sgt Chaundy's bomb load, only that he and his crew failed to return in X3701, after crashing at 03.00 near Rendsburg, in the middle of the Schleswig-Holstein peninsular, while on the way home. Sgt Chaundy was the only survivor, and he was soon in enemy hands. Despite the enthusiastic claims by returning crews of heavy damage in the town and at the factory, the bombs from the main element fell between two and six miles from the Altstadt aiming-point, and no hits were scored on the factory.

The operation was repeated on the following night by a force of 125 aircraft, but in the absence of a contribution from 101 Squadron. This time, the town was heavily bombed, while the factory again escaped damage, despite a number of bombs falling onto the site and adjacent airfield. The squadron briefed eight crews for the third raid, on the night of the 25/26th, which was to be by a force of 128 aircraft, again divided between the two aiming-points. This time the Heinkel factory was handed to 5 Group, among which were Manchesters of 106 Squadron, led by the soon-to-be-famous W/C Guy Gibson. The 101 Squadron crews got away between 22.10 and 22.20, led by S/L Watts, and set course for the German coast, skirting the Frisian Islands to the north. X3753 was some twenty miles north of Vlieland at 7,500 feet, when it was attacked at 00.10 by a ME110 night fighter, which inflicted extensive damage and wounded the rear gunner. He returned fire, and claimed the enemy aircraft as damaged, and the Wellington limped home after the bombs were jettisoned. Sgt Early and crew were similarly intercepted over the North Sea at 8,000 feet at 00.30, by what they believed was a JU88, but they shook it off after jettisoning their incendiaries, and then headed home. S/L Watts made his bombing run at the relatively low height of 8,000 feet, before dropping his 1,000 pounder and five 500 pounders into the centre of the town, where he saw them burst. Afterwards, he descended to 4,000 feet, where his starboard engine was damaged by flak. The others released their SBCs or HE from between 8,000 and 15,000 feet, and returned to report many fires burning.

The squadron was not involved in the final raid on Rostock on the night of the 26/27th, but the series was a major success, which destroyed 1,765 buildings, and damaged more than five hundred others. An estimated 60% of the town's built-up area was left devastated, and the Heinkel factory also sustained useful damage. F/L Millson's tour came to an end during the w.e.f. the 28th, and he was posted for duties at 21.O.T.U at

Moreton-in-Marsh. Ninety-seven aircraft took part in a raid on Cologne on the night of the 27/28th, four of them provided by 101 Squadron. They took off at 22.00, with P/O Gardner the senior pilot on duty, and the newly commissioned P/O Callender operating as an officer for the first time. P/O Gardner returned early after an engine caught fire, but the others pressed on, arriving in the target area to find favourable conditions, which they used to their advantage to inflict extensive damage upon residential and industrial property. They each delivered their nine SBCs from 16,500 feet, and returned to report numerous fires burning in the target area. The following night brought a raid on the port of Kiel, for which four crews were briefed as part of an overall force of eighty-eight aircraft. S/L Watts led them away at 22.45, but he returned early after the starboard engine overheated, and the intercom system failed. Sgt Early and P/O Gardner were each carrying nine SBCs, while Sgt Attwood had a 1,000 pounder on board, along with five 500 pounders, and they delivered these in bright moonlight onto the target from 16,500 to 17,500 feet, before returning to report fires in the target area, and a strong flak defence. Post-raid reconnaissance suggested no new destruction, but local reports described damage to housing and all three shipyards.

The final operation of the month involved eighty-eight aircraft, the crews of which were briefed to knock out the Gnome & Rhone aero engine factory at Gennevilliers, an industrial district in the Port-de-Paris, north-west of Paris city centre. 101 Squadron dispatched six Wellingtons either side of 21.45, led by S/L Watts, and most were carrying a load of a single 1,000 pounder, six 500 pounders and one 250 pounder. They arrived in the target area to find cloudless skies and perfect bombing conditions, which provided every opportunity to produce an accurate attack, particularly as the target lay in an easily-identifiable loop in the River Seine. The squadron participants went in at 4,000 to 6,000 feet, but S/L Watts was unable to release his bombs, and took photographs instead. Explosions and fires were reported by returning crews, and confidence was high, that the operation had been a success. In fact, the factory had not been hit, although a number of nearby industrial buildings had sustained damage. F/Sgt Machin's X3754 arrived back with damage to the wings and fuselage after being raked by machine-gun fire as he crossed the French coast at Fecamp, but the Wellington would be repaired and returned to service. F/L Edwards was posted in from 1483 T.T. & G Flight at Newmarket during the final week of the month.

May 1942

The first week of the new month would bring a variety of targets on three nights of operations, beginning at Hamburg on the 3/4th. Eighty-one aircraft were made ready, of which three were provided by 101 Squadron, and flown by NCO crews. They took off at 22.50, but Sgt Llewelyn turned back with wireless failure while over the North Sea. F/Sgt Machin and Sgt Early pressed on with their loads of 810 X 4lb incendiaries, and delivered them through nine to ten-tenths cloud on estimated positions from 19,000 feet at 01.50 and 01.58 respectively. Despite the poor vertical visibility, and the fact that only fifty-four aircraft bombed, over a hundred fires were started, half of which were classed as large. Stuttgart received the first of its three raids on consecutive nights twenty-four hours later, but it was a disappointing failure, which 101 Squadron sat out. The second of the series involved seventy-seven aircraft, including five 101 Squadron Wellingtons, which departed Bourn either side of 22.45, led by P/Os Gardner and Callender. F/Sgt Machin returned early with a propeller problem, leaving the others to push on to the target, which they found obscured by ground haze. They were uncertain as to their precise location during the delivery of their 4lb incendiaries, which were released into the general target area from 15,000 to 17,000 feet between 01.33 and 01.55. They returned with little to report, other than the odd flash observed, and evidence of a dummy fire site twenty miles away, which had attracted some bomb loads. While this operation was in progress, the three freshman crews of F/L Edwards, F/L Harper and F/Sgt Williams went to Nantes in north-western France, presumably to bomb the

64

Wellington crews, May 1942. Back row, left to right: Sgts Skipsey (AG), Rogers (W/AG), Mullin (W/AG), Tracey (AG), Skinner (W/AG), Sundborg (AG), Arnold (W/AG), Mullan (Obs), Downer (Obs), Ferguson (AG). Middle row, left to right: Sgts Matheson (W/AG), Sime (AG), Foxcroft (Pilot), Kilwyn (W/AG), Keen (Pilot), Richards (Pilot), Garland (W/AG), Llewelyn (Pilot), Baker (Obs), Clark (Obs), Calhoune (Obs), Sibbald (W/AG), Sauve (W/AG), F/Sgt Machim (Pilot), Sgts Spooner (AG), Brace (W/AG). Seated, left to right: Sgts Hart (W/AG), Marney (Pilot), Wigham (AG), King-Scott (AG), Ward (W/AG), Menage (Obs), Young (W/AG), Diemer (Pilot), Artham (W/AG), Jones (W/AG), Angelo (AG), Pollock (W/AG), Oakley (W/AG), Cormack (W/AG), Bott (W/AG), Mackay (AG), Early (Pilot), F/Sgt Williams (Pilot), Sgt Tatton (W/AG), F/Sgt Woodgate (W/AG), Sgts Urwin (AG), Pearson (Obs), Charles (AG), Attwood (Pilot), F/Sgt Brown (Pilot), Sgt Murray (AG), F/Sgt Burgess (W/AG), Sgts Jaggers (W/AG), Stewart (W/AG), Wade (AG), Symonds (AG). Wellington X3670 was, tragically, not long for this world as she would be lost without trace with the crew of P/O Gardner on the Thousand Bomber Riad against Cologne on 30th May 1942. (GW)

docks with their seven 500 pounders each. F/S Williams was unable to identify the target, but the other two carried out their attacks in good visibility from 11,000 and 14,800 feet at 01.15.

Mining operations in northern waters occupied eighty aircraft from 3 and 5 Groups on the night of the 7/8th, for which 101 Squadron contributed seven Wellingtons, plus four freshman crews to attack the docks at St Nazaire. The latter element took off first, shortly after 22.00, closely followed by the gardeners between 22.25 and 22.50, led by S/L Watts. Weather conditions in the Kiel region were good, and all from Bourn arrived in good order to identify the briefed locations for their two 1,500lb vegetables (mines). They were dropped from 400 to 800 feet between 01.30 and 02.30, and all returned safely to report a successful night's work. Of the freshmen, P/Os Read and Kennedy failed to identify their target, despite fair conditions, while F/L Edwards and F/Sgt Williams dropped their seventeen 250 pounders each inconclusively from 15,000 feet at 00.50 and 01.15 respectively. Thus far, attacks on Baltic ports under Harris had been an unqualified success, and the next to be put under the spotlight was Warnemünde, situated at the mouth of the Seekanal leading south to Rostock. As had been the case during the series of raids on Rostock, the nearby Heinkel factory was an important objective in a plan that featured a high and low-level element. Six 101 Squadron Wellingtons were made ready on the 8th, and they took off between 22.00 and 22.20, with F/L Harper the senior pilot on duty. F/Sgt Machin became indisposed during the outward flight, and he turned back, leaving the remaining five to press on, with their two 1,000 pounders and two 500 pounders each. P/Os Callender and Gardner and Sgts Attwood and Llewelyn were assigned to the low-level force, briefed to attack the factory with their eleven-second-delayed-action hardware, and they went in between 01.50 and 02.10 at heights ranging from 50 to 1,500 feet, in the face of intense searchlight dazzle from beams laid horizontally. It was impossible to assess the effects of their gallant efforts, and even F/L Harper, operating at 11,000 feet, could only report dropping his bombs north of the target, and observing one large and one small fire. Nineteen aircraft were lost, mostly during the low-level pass, and the operation achieved only modest success. 44 Squadron posted missing four Lancasters, including one captained by its newly-appointed commanding officer.

Another 101 Squadron group photograph taken in May 1942, almost certainly on the same occasion as the photograph on the previous page. Unfortunately, no list of names is available (GW).

Small scale and mining operations occupied the middle of May, and 101 Squadron was called upon to provide four Wellingtons for gardening duties in the western Baltic, probably off Kiel again, on the night of the 15/16th. F/L Harper and Sgts Attwood, Diemer and Early took off either side of 23.00, each with two 1,500lb mines on board. They found good weather conditions in the target area, and made timed runs from pre-selected pinpoints to deliver their mines from 500 feet between 02.12 and 02.30. Four freshman crews took off for Boulogne at 22.45 on the 17th, but were unable to locate the target beneath ten-tenths cloud. P/O Read jettisoned his seventeen 250 pounders when attacked by an enemy fighter, which tore a strip of fabric off a wing. P/O Kennedy and Sgt Williams brought their bombs back, but P/O Tregea jettisoned his.

A force of 197 aircraft took off for Mannheim on the night of the 19/20th, five of the Wellingtons belonging to 101 Squadron. They departed Bourn at 22.55, each carrying nine SBCs of incendiaries, but P/O Callender was the first to turn back with a failed intercom. P/O Gardner was hit by flak at 12,000 feet over Dunkerque, and jettisoned his load onto a built-up area before heading home. W/C Nicholls was flying as second pilot to F/L Harper, and they bombed in fair weather conditions from 17,000 feet at 01.24. As they turned away from the target area, they observed one very large fire, which was confirmed to be emanating from a wood some fifteen miles west of Mannheim. Sgt Attwood bombed from 12,000 feet at 01.15, and also reported the dummy fire. X3472 failed to return with the crew of Sgt Beecroft, after an engine fire had compelled them to force-land near Charleville-Mezieres, on the edge of the Ardennes in France, close to the border with Luxembourg.

66

One member of the crew, Sgt Bradley, lost his life while trying to evade capture, but Sgt Beecroft and one other were successful in that regard, while two became guests of the Reich. It was another disappointing night, and the results were not commensurate with the effort expended and the cost of eleven aircraft. While this operation was in progress, the freshman crews of P/O Kennedy, P/O Tregea and F/Sgt Williams were trying to locate St Nazaire in unfavourable weather conditions and extreme darkness. Having taken off shortly before midnight with a bomb load of seventeen 250 pounders each, they eventually carried out their attacks from 14,000 and 15,000 feet between 02.28 and 03.10, and F/Sgt Williams reported observing his bombs fall from east to west across the target, and starting a goodly-sized, red and orange fire, visible for twenty miles.

A 3 Group mining effort on the night of the 21/22nd was directed at the Biscay ports, 101 Squadron dispatching six crews to the waters off La Rochelle. They were all safely airborne by 22.00, with F/L Edwards the senior pilot on duty as they made their way south in poor weather conditions. F/L Edwards turned back with engine trouble, but the others ploughed on to the target area, where the cloud base was found to be at 100 feet. This prevented any vegetables from being planted, and all crews returned to diversion airfields with their loads intact. The remainder of the month was a time of little activity and much speculation, as Harris began to marshal his forces for his masterstroke, which he hoped would silence the critics hounding his Command since the damning Butt report. On taking up his post as C-in-C, Harris had spoken of the need for four thousand heavy bombers with which to win the war, and whilst there was never a chance of getting them, he needed to ensure that those earmarked for him were not spirited away to what he considered to be less deserving causes. Out of this was born the Thousand Plan, Operation Millennium, the commitment of a thousand aircraft in one night against a major German city, for which Harris pencilled-in Hamburg. Harris did not have a thousand front-line aircraft, and in order to achieve the magic and symbolic figure, he would need the co-operation of other Commands, principally Coastal and Flying Training. This was forthcoming in letters received on the 22nd and 23rd, but, following an intervention from the Admiralty, Coastal Command underwent a change of heart, and withdrew its contribution. Undaunted, Harris, or more likely his able deputy, AM Sir Robert Saundby, scraped together every airframe capable of controlled flight, or something resembling it, and called in the screened crews from their instructional duties. Come the night, not only would the figure of one thousand aircraft be achieved, it would be comfortably surpassed.

Over the ensuing days, aircraft and crews from the training units began to assemble on bomber airfields from County Durham to East Anglia in preparation for Operation Millennium, and the only remaining questions concerned the weather. This was in no mood to play ball, and, as the days ticked by inexorably towards the end of May, a real danger arose that the giant force might draw attention to itself, and compromise security. The time was fast approaching when the operation would either have to take place, or be scrubbed altogether for the time being. It was in this atmosphere of frustration that "morning prayers" began at Harris's HQ at High Wycombe on the 30th. Finally, the chief meteorological adviser, Magnus Spence, declared that the Rhineland was the region of Germany most likely to experience a break in the cloud that night, and provide the possibility of moonlight, while north-western Germany would be completely covered. Thus was Hamburg spared by the weather from hosting the first one thousand bomber raid in history, and the fickle finger of fate pointed instead at Cologne. At briefings crews were told that the enormous force was to be pushed across the aiming-point in just ninety minutes. This was unprecedented, and gave rise to the question of collisions as hundreds of aircraft funnelled towards the aiming-point. The answer was to observe timings and flight levels, and the experts calculated that just two aircraft would collide over the target. It is said, that a wag in every briefing room asked, "Do they know which two?" The operation was to be conducted along the now familiar lines, employing three waves, with the genuine heavy aircraft bringing up the rear.

101 Squadron had been joined at Bourn by five Wellingtons and crews from 23 OTU, and later that night, seventeen aircraft took off as part of a force of 1,047. The twelve 101 Squadron crew captains and aircraft were; S/L Watts in X3654, F/L Harper in X3391, F/L Edwards in X3473, P/O Callender in X3669, P/O Gardner in X3670, P/O Read in Z1612, P/O Kennedy in X3648, F/Sgt Williams in X3657, Sgt Attwood in X3668, Sgt Llewelyn in X3754, Sgt Early in X3694, and Sgt Deimer in X3634. S/L Watts was the first away at 22.55, and the others followed in his wake over the ensuing twenty minutes, closely followed by the O.T.U element. All over eastern England, aircraft continued to take off until well after midnight, some of the older training hacks struggling somewhat reluctantly into the air, lifted more by the enthusiasm of their crews than by the power of their engines. A proportion of these, unable to climb to a respectable height, would fall easy prey to the defences, or drop from the sky through mechanical failure. F/L Edwards was back on the ground by midnight with engine problems, and P/O Kennedy was another to miss out on this momentous occasion, because of an unserviceable rear turret. The others reached the target area, where, true to Magnus Spence's prediction, the moon broke through to cast its light upon the hapless city below. All from 101 Squadron were carrying nine SBCs of incendiaries, and these were let go from 12,000 to 19,000 feet between 00.50 and 01.05. It was, by any standards, an outstandingly successful operation, which destroyed over 3,300 buildings, and damaged nine thousand more to some extent. A new record loss of forty-one aircraft was acceptable in return for the scale of the success, and in the conditions, which were kind to both attackers and defenders alike. 101 Squadron was represented among the missing by two aircraft. X3670 was lost without trace with the crew of P/O Gardner, and Z1612 suffered fuel-feed problems, which led to both engines cutting out during evasive action when a night fighter attacked. P/O Read and crew were forced to take to their parachutes, and all survived to fall into enemy hands, although one crew member required treatment for a fractured leg. This was the final operation of the month, during the course of which, sixty-seven sorties had been dispatched. S/L Freeman arrived from Waterbeach, and would assume the role of flight commander in June.

June 1942

Plans had been afoot since the 5th of May to convert 101 Squadron to Stirlings in line with the rest of 3 Group, and a Conversion Flight was established under S/L Crompton on the 1st of June at Oakington. This was still the home of 7 Squadron, and it was from here that it had introduced the type into operational service in March 1941. Fortunately for 101 Squadron, the Stirling's technical problems and slow rate of production meant that there was insufficient of the type for full conversion to go ahead. Also on the 1st of June, W/C Eaton assumed command of the squadron on the posting out to HQ 1 Group of W/C Nicholls. Harris had been keen to employ the Thousand Force again before it was disbanded, and the old enemy of Essen was selected for the Cologne treatment on the night of the 1/2nd. It was not possible to raise a thousand aircraft for the second time in forty-eight hours, and so it was a slightly depleted, but still impressive force of 956 aircraft, which took to the air that evening. 101 Squadron put up ten Wellingtons, led by S/L Watts, who was first off the ground at 23.15, followed closely by the others, except for P/O Kennedy and F/Sgt Williams, who departed at 23.50 and 00.40 respectively. S/L Watts, F/Ls Edwards and Harper and Sgt Attwood flew with the flare force, and all four found great difficulty in identifying the target through ground haze and possibly a layer of cloud. The first two-mentioned carried out their illuminating brief on ETA from 16,000 feet at 00.53, while the second pair followed suit from 17,000 feet at 01.10. The other squadron participants were carrying incendiaries, which they let go from 16,500 to 19,500, also on ETA between 00.58 and 02.03, before returning to claim a successful attack. Unfortunately, the success of Cologne did not eradicate the difficulties that had always blighted attempts to hit Essen, and bombs were again sprayed all over the Ruhr, with very few falling where intended. The operation was an abject failure, at a cost to the Command of thirty-one aircraft.

After a night off, seven 101 Squadron crews were briefed on the 3rd for an operation to Bremen as part of an overall force of 170 aircraft. W/C Eaton took the opportunity to lead the squadron for the first time as commanding officer, and they all got away safely in close order from 23.15. W/C Eaton and four others were carrying flares and three 500 pounders, while P/O Tregea and F/Sgt Williams had nine SBCs on board. They arrived in the target area to find intense darkness and ground haze, but some detail was visible as they carried out their attacks from 16,000 to 17,500 feet between 01.18 and 01.25. W/C Eaton bombed a main railway junction north of the aiming-point, and Sgt Attwood aimed at the marshalling yards, while Sgt Llewelyn hit the north bank of the River Weser, and F/Sgt Williams thought his incendiaries fell half a mile north-west of the old town. He witnessed a tremendous flash, and then fires in a wood, a factory and in the docks area. F/L Harper and Sgt Attwood reported seeing a large oil-based fire, but no one was certain as to the actual effectiveness of the operation. Local reports revealed it to be the most destructive attack yet at this target, inflicting significant damage to residential property, while a few bombs had also fallen into the shipyards and Focke-Wulf factory. Eleven aircraft failed to return, and among them was X3473, which crashed near the target during evasive action, killing F/L Edwards and two of his crew, and delivering the survivors into enemy hands. F/L Edwards was a New Zealander serving in the RAF, and was deputy B Flight commander. Although he had not been long with the squadron, his presence and experience would be missed.

Like a dog with a bone, Harris could not let Essen rest, and he planned further attempts during the month to deliver a telling blow. The first came on the night of the 5/6th, for which a force of 180 aircraft was prepared. 101 Squadron contributed six Wellingtons, with S/L Watts the senior pilot on duty as they took off between 23.10 and 23.40. S/L Watts and F/L Harper carried flares and three 500 pounders each, and the others nine SBCs, and these were delivered from 12,000 to 18,000 feet between 01.18 and 01.40. They returned to describe the visibility over the target as medium, but, again, none could positively claim to have hit it. It was another failure, and, while Harris pondered that, he sent 233 aircraft to the port of Emden, the coastal location of which would at least provide a firm pinpoint. 101 Squadron dispatched six Wellingtons between 23.05 and 23.30, led by W/C Eaton and S/L Watts, each carrying nine SBCs. They found good weather conditions as they bore down on the target at 14,000 to 17,000 feet, and P/O Tregea was within eight miles of the aiming-point, when the ailerons jammed during a steep right-hand turn. He was unable to continue on, but did arrive safely home. The others carried out their attacks between 01.21 and 01.30, before returning home to report large fires in the town centre visible up to 120 miles away. Post-raid reconnaissance revealed the destruction of around three hundred houses, with damage to many others, and some disruption in the dockyard. Harris returned to Essen on the night of the 8/9th, this time with a force of 170 aircraft, of which five represented 101 Squadron. F/L Harper took the lead as they took off in a ten-minute slot to 23.30, and all reached the general target area to release their flares or incendiaries from 16,000 to 19,000 feet between 01.05 and 01.17. Bomb bursts and scattered fires were observed, but there was no clear point of concentration, and Essen escaped again with only light housing damage. While this operation was in progress, the freshman crew of Sgt Keen was trying and failing to identify Dieppe, and jettisoned eight of seventeen 250 pounders on the way home.

Apart from a few mining and minor operations, the Command remained at home for the next eight nights, until briefings took place on the 16th for another crack at Essen. 106 aircraft were made ready, although none from 101 Squadron, and only sixteen crews reported bombing in the target area, while more than half attacked alternatives. This was the last of five raids on Essen in sixteen nights, involving 1,607 sorties at a cost of eighty-four aircraft and crews. It would be three months before Harris went there again. 101 Squadron returned to operations on the night of the 17/18th, when four freshman crews were sent to St Nazaire, although none positively located it beneath a blanket of cloud, and dropped their seventeen 250 pounders each on estimated position. Mining operations on this night were in the waters off St Nazaire and the Frisians, and it is assumed that the three 101 Squadron participants were over the former. F/Sgts Brown and Roberts dropped their two 1,500lb mines in the correct location from below 1,000 feet at around 00.50, but F/Sgt Foderingham failed to locate his drop site in conditions of haze and generally poor visibility.

Following the success gained at Emden earlier in the month, a series of three further operations was planned, which would take place over a four-night period, beginning on the 19/20th. 194 aircraft were made ready, of which eight represented 101 Squadron, and they took off either side of 23.30, led by F/L Harper. They were each carrying nine SBCs of 4lb incendiaries, on a night when matters would not proceed according to plan. F/Sgt Roberts was fifty miles short of the target when his port engine cut, and he returned to land at Horsham-St-Faith on one engine, after jettisoning his load. The others flew on into nine to ten-tenths cloud, which blotted out ground detail, and most bombed on ETA from 11,000 to 20,000 feet between 01.31 and 01.43. P/O Fahnestock was the only one to bomb visually, and he was among those reporting fires. Some members of the flare-force had erroneously started a raid on Osnabrück, some eighty miles to the south, and, having been unable to locate Emden, F/L Harper bombed there through complete cloud cover from 17,000 feet at 02.02. The raid on Emden was a total failure, and cost nine aircraft, including 101 Squadron's X3669, which disappeared into the sea with the crew of Sgt Keen. Three bodies eventually washed ashore on the Dutch coast, and were buried locally.

185 crews were briefed for Emden again on the following night, eight belonging to 101 Squadron, and they took off either side of 23.30 led again by F/L Harper. P/O Fahnestock turned back early with engine trouble, jettisoning his load just off the Norfolk coast, and F/L Osborn DFC, who had been posted in from 12 O.T.U at Chipping Warden during the previous week, also suffered engine problems at the Dutch coast, which ended his part in the operation. The others pressed on to find four to eight-tenths cloud over the target, and dropped their flares, bombs and incendiaries from 15,000 to 18,000 feet between 01.16 and 01.45. A number of fires were observed by some crews through gaps in the cloud, and by others as a glow or reflection in the clouds. In the event, only a proportion of the force located and attacked the target, causing damage to around one hundred houses. The final raid of the series on Emden was launched on the night of the 22/23rd, for which a force of 227 aircraft was prepared. 101 Squadron's contribution amounted to nine Wellingtons, which took off either side of 23.30, led by S/L Freeman, who was undertaking his maiden sortie with the squadron. Seven aircraft were carrying nine SBCs each, while those of F/L Osborn and W/O Ollier were loaded with seventeen 250 pounders. Unfortunately, the former was forced to turn back over the North Sea because of engine and intercom problems. The others found clear skies over the target, but patches of ground haze, and delivered their respective loads from 12,500 to 17,000 feet between 01.15 and 01.38. Returning crews reported their bombs falling into the target area, and starting fires in the town and docks. Local reports confirm fifty houses destroyed and a hundred damaged, but decoy fire sites drew off a proportion of the effort, and it was another disappointing raid.

The Thousand Force was brought together for the final time on the 25th, when 960 crews were briefed for an operation to Bremen. Ordered this time by Prime Minister Churchill to participate, Coastal Command would also send 102 aircraft, in what was classed as a separate operation, and, as a result, the 1,067 aircraft ultimately taking off, would easily exceed those going to Cologne at the end of May. Ten aircraft types represented Bomber Command, making this the most diverse operation ever, and it would be the swansong for the unpopular Manchester. 101 Squadron put up a record sixteen Wellingtons, led by W/C Eaton, and they took off between 23.15 and 23.35. S/L Freeman was the first to turn back, after his rear turret and intercom became unserviceable, and P/Os Fahnestock and Kennedy were thwarted by engine problems, and all brought their incendiary loads home. The others pressed on to find north-western Germany hidden by ten-tenths cloud at around 5,000 feet, the presence of which had been known, but strong winds had been expected to drive it eastwards before the attack began. The wind strength had decreased, however, and it was left to the Gee-equipped aircraft to start fires, which would leave a glow to attract those following behind. The 101 Squadron crews were over the target at 14,000 to 18,000 feet between 01.30 and 01.55, and delivered mostly incendiaries, but W/Os Ollier and Vautour and P/O Angel carried a 1,000 pounder and six 500 pounders each. W/C Eaton and P/O Tregea were unable to identify the primary target, and dropped their incendiaries on Emden from 18,000 and 17,500 feet at 01.50 and 01.51 respectively, and Sgt Foxcroft brought his home after failing to find a suitable objective. This raid did not mirror the success gained at Cologne, but in destroying 572 houses and damaging some six thousand other, it far surpassed the failure at Essen, although costing a new record of forty-seven aircraft.

The following night brought mining operations off Biscay ports and in the Frisians, for which 101 Squadron briefed seven crews. According to the summary section of the ORB, their target area was off the Frisians, but the daily operations sheet shows St Nazaire. They took off either side of 23.00, with P/Os Angel and Fahnestock the only commissioned pilots on duty. The weather in the target area was almost perfect for gardening, with clear skies and good visibility, and all found their respective drop zones after making timed runs, and dropped their two mines each from 500 to 700 feet between 01.26 and 02.13. A series of three follow-up raids on Bremen had begun on the night of the 27/28th, when some worthwhile industrial damage had been achieved by a force of 144 aircraft. The second one was mounted on the night of the 29/30th, for which 253 aircraft were made ready, among them thirteen Wellingtons provided by 101 Squadron. S/L Freeman was the senior pilot on duty as they took off between 23.15 and 23.40, but F/L Osborn and P/O Angel returned early with engine trouble. The others arrived at the target to find nine-tenths cloud, but bright moonlight above it and visibility estimated at eight miles. W/O Vautour was carrying eight 500 pounders, while all of the others had nine SBCs on board, which were released from 12,000 to 19,000 feet between 01.08 and 01.37. A number of returning crews report fires, one of them visible for thirty miles into the return trip. The Bremen authorities recorded extensive damage to important war-industry factories, including Focke-Wulf, and a U-Boot construction yard was also hit. This was the final operation of a busy month, during which Sgts Attwood, Diemer and Early were posted out to O.T.Us at the end of their tours. The squadron had been involved at fourteen separate targets, and had dispatched 103 sorties for the loss of two aircraft and crews.

July 1942

The final follow-up raid on Bremen took place on the night of the 2/3rd, at the hands of an unusually large force of 325 aircraft, of which, 101 Squadron provided eleven Wellingtons. S/L Freeman was the senior pilot on duty as they took off between 23.05 and 23.30, and headed for the east coast, but Sgt Mahoney returned early with a defective rear turret, and W/O Vautour landed at Horsham-St-Faith a few minutes later with fuel-feed problems. The remainder flew on to find the target area in good visibility, and they delivered their all-incendiary loads from 14,500 to 18,000 feet between 01.42 and 02.01, before returning safely to report what appeared to be a successful outcome. Local authorities reported a thousand houses damaged, and seven ships hit in the port area, one of which sank, but many bomb loads also missed the target. Minor operations occupied the remainder of the first week, and 101 Squadron was next in action, for gardening duties, on the night of the 7/8th. Ten crews were briefed to take part in a large 1 and 3 Group effort around the Frisians involving more than a hundred aircraft, and S/L Freeman led them away between 23.25 and 00.20. There was ten-tenths cloud over the North Sea, but visibility below it in the target area was good, and all successfully delivered their two 1,500lb mines each from heights ranging from 700 to 3,000 feet between 01.26 and 02.20.

Sticking to the month's nautical theme thus far, Wilhelmshaven was selected to host an attack by 285 aircraft on the night of the 8/9th. Eight 101 Squadron Wellingtons lined up for take-off at 23.30, and all were safely airborne by 23.45. W/C Eaton was the senior pilot on duty, ably supported by S/L Watts and F/L Osborn, but the last-mentioned was forced to turn back over the North Sea with starboard engine failure. P/O Angel lost the use of his heating system, and decided to bomb Emden as an alternative target, and dropped his 1,000 pounder and six 500 pounders from 15,000 feet at 01.41. Five others made it all the way to the primary target, where they found clear skies and good visibility, and delivered a total of twelve bundles of three flares, eighteen SBCs of incendiaries, a dozen 500 pounders and a single 1,000 pounder from 16,000 to 18,000 feet between 01.38 and 02.00. X3634 failed to return from this operation, and was lost without trace with the crew of P/O Tregea, who was born in Argentina. A large mining effort involved forty-nine aircraft operating in north German waters on the night of the 11/12th. 101 Squadron contributed eight Wellingtons, which were all airborne by 23.05, bound for the Heligoland and led by S/L Freeman. Visibility in the target area was poor, and only two unnamed crews were able to plant their vegetables, one from 700 feet at 01.20, and the other from 3,000 feet at 01.31. Only one was dropped in the briefed location and the other in an alternative one. Four crews brought their mines home, and two others failed to return. S/L Freeman and crew were lost without trace in Z1751, and P/O Angel and his crew, three of whom were Canadians, also lost their lives, when BJ583 crashed in the sea.

A series of five raids against Duisburg began on the night of the 13/14th, and would span the next four weeks. Sadly, it would turn out to be an echo of the Essen experience, as the Ruhr Valley continued to defy Harris. 194 aircraft were made ready, of which just four Wellingtons represented 101 Squadron. F/L Harper was the senior pilot on duty as they took off either side of 22.00, and the other crews were those of F/Sgts De Bartok and Williams and Sgt Foxcroft. They encountered electrical storms outbound, and reached the target area to find nine-tenths cloud, but delivered their loads anyway, the details of which are not included in the ORB, and returned home safely. The bad weather contributed to a scattered and ineffective attack, but the industrial haze was the real culprit, and only eleven houses were classed as destroyed. The squadron dispatched a single mining sortie on the following night, undertaken by the freshman crew of Sgt Bennee to the "Nectarine" region off the Frisians. They took off at 23.25, and dropped their two mines as briefed from 400 feet at 01.13, before returning safely.

The second raid on Duisburg took place on the night of the 21/22nd, for which 291 aircraft were made ready, including thirteen 101 Squadron Wellingtons. W/C Eaton was the senior pilot on duty as they began taking off at 23.40, and all were safely airborne by midnight. The meteorological section accurately forecast good weather conditions, and these probably assisted the 253 crews, who claimed to have attacked the target as briefed. The ORB does not provide details of bombing heights and timings, and states only, that the ten squadron participants delivered between them three bundles of flares, eighteen SBCs of 4lb incendiaries, 243 x 30lb incendiaries, eighteen 500 pounders and two 4,000lb "cookies", and returned home to report a few fires. One crew bombed a last resort target some fifteen miles west of the primary, and one aircraft failed to return. X3312 disappeared into the sea with the crew of F/Sgt Roberts RCAF, and just three bodies were eventually washed ashore on the Dutch coast for burials locally. The operation produced slightly improved bombing, with almost a hundred buildings destroyed, mostly of a residential nature, and many others damaged, but the results still fell short of what should have been achieved by such a large force.

A night's rest preceded the third raid in the series, which involved 215 aircraft, including nine put up by 101 Squadron, led by F/L Harper. All were safely airborne by 01.00, and reached the target area to find seven to ten-tenths cloud. The target was located and bombed on the basis of TR-fixes without visual confirmation, and the squadron participants carried out their part in the attack from 15,000 to 18,000 feet between 02.24 and 02.38. They dropped three bundles of flares, eighteen SBCs of 4lb incendiaries, 144 x 30lb incendiaries, eighteen 500 pounders and two 4,000 pounders, and observed a few fires, but nothing to get them excited. Housing was the principal victim again, but the scale of destruction was still not commensurate with the effort expended. 313 aircraft took off for the same target on the night of the 25/26th, a dozen of them provided by 101 Squadron led by S/L Watts and S/L Paterson, the latter having been posted in from 1651 Conversion Flight at Waterbeach immediately after the loss of S/L Freeman. They were airborne between midnight and 00.35, but Sgts Beale and Follett returned early for unspecified reasons. The remainder attacked the target through thick cloud, which had them, once more, relying on a TR-fix to establish their position. No details of bomb loads, heights and timings are provided, and the damage inflicted was again only modest.

Harris switched his attention to Hamburg on the night of the 26/27th, thus continuing a pattern of attacks on Germany's second city during the last week of July, begun in 1940, and which would be maintained in 1943 and 1944. 101 Squadron contributed fourteen Wellingtons to an overall force of 403 aircraft, and they took off either side of 23.00 with W/C Eaton the senior pilot on duty. The route out was challenging at times, with ice-bearing cloud, but conditions over the target were clear with good visibility, and thirteen of the 101 Squadron participants are known to have reached it to deliver their incendiary and high-explosive loads from 15,000 to 19,500 feet between 01.10 and 01.55. They returned to report the town area to be a sea of flames, with a pall of smoke rising to 17,000 feet. Post-raid reconnaissance confirmed this as a particularly successful operation, which created over five hundred large fires, and destroyed more than eight hundred houses. It was not a one-sided affair, though, and twenty-nine aircraft failed to return, among them BJ590, which came down in north-western Germany, killing Sgt Raymond and his crew. It is not known whether the crash occurred before or after attacking the target.

Two nights later, 256 aircraft were made ready for another attack on Hamburg, for which the squadron briefed thirteen crews. W/C Eaton led from the front again, supported by S/Ls Watts and Paterson as they departed Bourn either side of 23.00, on what would turn out to be a less-than-satisfactory night. Matters began badly, when X3668 collided with Stirling N6121 of the Conversion Flight from Oakington, while they were climbing out of their respective airfields. The Wellington could not recover and crashed, killing Sgt Teall and his crew, while the Stirling also crashed, but in a controlled manner, and the crew of F/O Butterfield came through the incident shaken, but unscathed. The remaining twelve squadron aircraft continued on in worsening weather conditions, until six decided to turn back, possibly having heard a recall signal for the large number of aircraft put up by the training units. Ultimately, only sixty-eight of the original 256 aircraft bombed the target, starting fifteen large fires. Three 101 Squadron crews delivered eighteen SBCs of incendiaries, a single 1,000 pounder and six 500 pounders on Hamburg from 13,000 to 17,000 feet between 01.22 and 01.54, while three others went for last-resort objectives, including Cuxhaven, but the ORB provides no details concerning individual crews.

The first large-scale raid of the war on Saarbrücken, a city in south-western Germany close to the border with France, was mounted on the night of the 29/30th. 291 aircraft took off, including seven Wellingtons representing 101 Squadron, led by S/L Paterson. They departed Bourn either side of midnight, but F/Sgt De Bartok and, it is believed, F/L Harper turned back with their bombs for unspecified reasons. The remaining five pressed on to find seven to eight-tenths cloud over the target, where the defences were expected to be sparse. For this reason, crews had been urged to bomb from as low as possible to aid accuracy, and the 101 Squadron participants complied by delivering their loads from 5,000 to 11,500 feet between 01.52 and 02.25. In all, they contributed twenty-seven SBCs of 4lb incendiaries, seventy-two 30lb incendiaries, one 1,000 pounder and six 500 pounders to what was a heavy and concentrated assault, which left almost four hundred buildings in ruins in central and north-western districts.

On the last night of the month, a force of over six hundred aircraft, again with a contingent from the training units, set off for Düsseldorf, situated on the south-western edge of the Ruhr. 101 Squadron briefed eleven crews, which were led away by F/L Harper between 00.10 and 01.00. They arrived in the target area under clear skies with good visibility, marred vertically by the expected ground haze, and proceeded on their bombing runs. Most were carrying an all-incendiary load, but two also had on board a 4,000 pounder, which were employed to good effect in a scattered but effective attack, which destroyed over four hundred buildings within the city and at nearby Neuss. A further fifteen thousand buildings were damaged to some extent, and almost a thousand fires had to be dealt with. The cost, at twenty-nine aircraft, was high, and among them was the squadron's BJ841, which was brought down to crash near Mönchengladbach, some fifteen miles from the primary target. This suggests that W/O Vautour RCAF and crew had bombed, and were homebound when the end came with fatal consequences for all on board. This was the final operation of another busy month, during the course of which thirteen operations had been undertaken and 121 sorties dispatched, at the high cost of seven aircraft and crews.

August 1942

The weather conditions at the start of the month were unhelpful, and there was little operational activity until the 6th, when preparations were put in hand for the final raid of the series on Duisburg. Night flying tests (NFTs) were carried out at the participating stations, as a force of 216 aircraft was made ready. Eight NFTs took place at Bourn, during the course of which, Sgts Waterhouse and Brown collided on the runway, and put an end to the circuits and landings exercises in progress. F/L Harper was the senior pilot on duty as the eight 101 Squadron Wellingtons took to the air either side of 01.00, half of them carrying flares and six 500 pounders, and the others an assortment of incendiaries. All reached the target, where cloud conditions ranged from clear to ten-tenths, and this allowed some crews to identify ground detail, while most relied on a TR-fix to establish their position. Visibility was described as poor, and the haze cancelled out the benefits of the flares. They carried out their attacks from 10,000 to 18,000 feet between 02.33 and 03.00, but had little idea of the fall of their hardware. It seems that most of it fell to the west of the city, and the raid was another dismal failure, which showered open country with bombs. During the course of the five raids, the Command had committed 1,229 sorties for the loss of forty-three aircraft, and had destroyed a total of 212 houses.

Osnabrück was selected as the target for what would turn out to be the squadron's last operation from Bourn. Eight Wellingtons were made ready during the 9th, and they were led away by F/L Menzies between 00.05 and 00.20 on a night of good weather conditions, which persisted all the way to the target, where the skies were clear. F/Sgts De Bartok and Brown were carrying flares and 500 pounders, while the others were loaded with incendiaries. Most were able to identify ground detail, and they delivered their ordnance into the town centre from 13,000 to 18,000 feet between 02.10 and 02.28. Returning crews reported the town to be well alight, with fires visible for up to seventy-five miles into the return flight. Post-raid reconnaissance confirmed the effectiveness of the operation, which destroyed over two hundred houses for the loss of just five aircraft. The squadron received orders on the 11th to proceed immediately to Stradishall, where its time would be short, and this occupied that day and the 12th, the day on which S/L Watts was awarded the DSO. The move prevented the squadron from being available to take part in the first of two highly destructive raids on the southern city of Mainz on the nights of the 11/12th.

The first operation to be launched from the squadron's new home took place as the second attack on Mainz was in progress on the night of the 12/13th. Ten crews were briefed for a gardening effort off the island of Juist in the German Frisians. F/Ls Harper and Menzies were the senior pilots on duty as they took off either side of 23.00, and headed into challenging weather conditions. There was nine-tenths cloud in the target area, with a base as low as 500 feet, and this rendered the visibility limited as the crews tried to pick up their pinpoints for the timed runs to the drop locations. Accuracy was essential if the mines were to be laid in an effective chain across the shipping lanes, and, for this reason, each crew was given a precise set of coordinates. Seven crews managed to get beneath the cloud base to deliver their vegetables between 00.58 and 01.18, but three others brought theirs home after the failure of their Gee equipment.

The Pathfinder era began on 15th, when the four founder heavy squadrons, 7, 35, 83 and 156 began to take up residence on 3 Group stations at Oakington, Graveley, Wyton and Warboys, and the Mosquitos of 109 Squadron moved also into Wyton, where the organisation's HQ was to be established. Each heavy squadron would represent a group, respectively, 3 Group, 4 Group, 5 Group and 1 Group, from which it would draw fresh crews. The new force would fall nominally under the control of 3 Group until being granted Group status in its own right in the New Year. Although opposed in principle to the formation of an elite target finding and marking force, a view shared by all but one of his group commanders, Harris was overruled by higher authority, and, in typical fashion, gave it his unstinting support. His choice of the then G/C Don Bennett as its leader, was both controversial and inspired, and ruffled a few feathers. Bennett, a humourless Australian, was an experienced bomber pilot and master navigator, whose knowledge of aviation was unsurpassed. He possessed recent operational experience as the commanding officer of 77 and 10 Squadrons, and had recently returned home from Norway, after being shot down while attacking the Tirpitz, and evading capture. He would develop a strict but fatherly relationship with his crews, and would receive from them utter respect and total loyalty.

On the night of the 15/16th, Düsseldorf was selected as the target for 131 aircraft, for which 101 Squadron made ready nine Wellingtons. They took off either side of 00.30, led by S/Ls Paterson and Watts, three of them carrying a mix of high explosives, while the remainder were loaded with incendiaries. They flew into heavy cloud, which blotted out the ground, and the bombing was carried out on estimated positions from 14,000 to 17,500 feet between 02.15 and 03.00. Sgt Brown and crew were the last to arrive, after X3559 refused to climb and made them thirty minutes late. They actually caught sight of the ground, and bombed visually from 16,000 feet, at which point, an engine cut out, and did not pick up again until they were on their way home at 4,000 feet.

It was planned that Osnabrück would host the first Pathfinder-led raid on the night of the 17/18th, but, in the event, its participation was withdrawn as not yet ready, and a standard operation ensued involving 139 aircraft. 101 Squadron prepared a dozen Wellingtons, which took off between 21.35 and 21.54, led by W/C Eaton and S/L Paterson. Sgt Beale and crew were about ten miles north of Sheringham, when the illness of the rear gunner forced them to turn back. It was a vomiting navigator in Sgt G T Brown's crew, and a surging port engine, that persuaded him to abandon his sortie also when twenty-five miles north-west of Vlieland. The others pressed on to reach the target, where the visibility was clear enough to allow a visual identification of the target. The attacks were delivered from 13,500 to 18,000 feet between 00.21 and 00.35, and the bombs were observed to fall into the built-up area, where fires began to spread. Sgt Spinney and crew were carrying a 4,000lb "cookie", and they cruised in the vicinity of the target for twenty minutes before releasing it, and also identified two dummy fire sites to the west. They watched their bomb fall into the south of the town, and described two lines of fire, one on the western side and the other to the east. X3654 was on its way home with the crew of Sgt E H Brown, when it was shot down by a night fighter flown by Oblt Ludwig Becker of 6/NJG2, and crashed at 02.02 a mile or two south-south east of Harlingen in northern Holland, killing all on board. BJ844 was forced to ditch in the North Sea on return, but Sgt Foderingham RCAF and three of his all-Canadian crew made it into the dinghy, and were rescued on the following morning. The front I, F/Sgt Cobbett, was posted as missing, believed drowned. The operation destroyed seventy-seven houses and a number of military buildings, and caused serious damage to many others, mostly in northern and north-western districts.

The Pathfinders eventually took to the air in anger on the following night, when the port of Flensburg was selected for its coastal location on the eastern side of the Schleswig-Holstein peninsular, close to the Danish frontier. A force of 118 aircraft included thirty-one Pathfinders, but no representatives from 101 Squadron. The winds turned out to be not as forecast, and the force was pushed a little further north than intended, leading to an ignominious failure to locate the target, and the consequent bombing of a number of towns in Denmark. Things would get better as the crews got to grips with the requirements of their exacting role, but it would take time. 101 Squadron was not called into action again until the 23rd, when six crews were invited to commit suicide by undertaking one of the infamous "moling" daylight operations. Their target was the Dollart docks at Emden, which was home to the Kriegsmarine rather than merchant shipping. They took off between 10.15 and 12.15, with W/O Ollier first away, closely followed by Sgt De Bartok. Each was carrying eight 500 pounders, and the latter arrived first to positively identify the town and the docks. He dropped his load from 4,500 feet at 12.08, and watched a stick fall across the dock workers' dwellings, five hundred yards west of the inner harbour. W/O Ollier turned up four minutes later at the same altitude, and saw his bombs hit a red-brick warehouse between the inner and industrial harbours. The remaining four crews abandon their sorties in the face of insufficient cloud cover.

It was time for the Pathfinder Force to venture forth once more, and Frankfurt was selected for its second operation, which was scheduled for the night of the 24/25th. 226 aircraft were made ready, of which a squadron record of eighteen Wellingtons represented 101 Squadron. It took an hour to get them into the air, the last one departing Stradishall at 21.55, but it was not long before the first of four early returns headed homeward. W/O Ollier turned back when off Dunkerque after an engine failed, and he landed at Bradwell Bay at 23.10. P/O Gill lost his oxygen system and Gee, Sgt McFarlane couldn't persuade BJ768 to climb, and Sgt Bennee lost his starboard engine when twenty-four miles south-west of Brussels, but they all made it safely back onto the ground by 00.09. This left fourteen others pushing on to the target area in cloudy conditions, and most identified the city by the glow of fires on ETA, or caught a glimpse of the River Main to use as a pinpoint. They flew across the target at 11,500 to 18,000 between 23.30 and 00.23, and delivered their high explosives and incendiaries into, what they believed, was the main part of the city, but much of the effort was actually deposited in open country. Seventeen large fires were started, and some damage was inflicted, but the operation was another failure at a cost of sixteen aircraft. The night fighter of Hptm Hans Autenrieth of II/NJG1 caught Z1594 over Belgium, and shot it down to crash at 00.18, three miles south-south-west of Liege, killing F/Sgt Elkington RCAF and one of his crew. Three others on board managed to escape by parachute, and they all fell into enemy hands.

It was not until the third Pathfinder-led operation, when Kassel was the target on the night of the 27/28th that the first success came. A force of 306 aircraft was assembled, of which thirteen were provided by 101 Squadron, and they took off between 20.35 and 20.55, led by F/Ls Harper and Menzies, although G/C Boyle, the Stradishall station commander, was the senior pilot on duty, having borrowed the crew of S/L Paterson for the occasion. F/Sgt Williams turned back from fifteen miles off the Suffolk coast when unable to maintain height, and Sgt Waterhouse had travelled maybe ten miles further, when the rear turret doors refused to stay closed. X3649 ditched at 22.40 about fifteen miles off the Suffolk coast, and must have been another early return, probably with engine problems. The crew all managed to vacate the Wellington before it sank, but the dinghy failed to inflate, and they were forced to swim towards the shore. F/Sgt Brown RNZAF and one of his crew failed to keep up, and are believed to have drowned, while a trawler crew spotted the others and picked them up. The remaining squadron participants arrived over Kassel to find clear skies, which enabled them to identify ground detail, particularly the River Fulda, in the light provided by the Pathfinder illuminators. For once, the main force crews exploited the opportunity, the 101 Squadron contingent delivering its high explosives or incendiaries from 9,500 to 17,000 feet between 23.30 and 23.47, and contributing to a goodly amount of industrial and residential damage. It was another night of high losses, however, and among the thirty-one failures to return was 101 Squadron's BJ698, which disappeared without trace, and took with it the crew of P/O Beale. X3657 had been hit be flak, before being shot up by a night fighter, and crash-landed at Martlesham Heath at 02.20, where it was consumed by fire. Sgt Spinney and crew had, by then, walked away from the wreckage, but, sadly, their reprieve would be temporary. During the course of the week, S/L Reddick was posted in from 24 O.T.U.

Two operations were mounted on the night of the 28/29th, the larger by a force of 159 aircraft against Nuremberg, and the other by 113 aircraft against Saarbrücken. 101 Squadron supported both, providing seven Wellingtons for the former, and two for the latter. P/O Gill and Sgt McFarlane took off first for Saarbrücken at 20.45, closely followed over the ensuing thirty minutes by the others. S/L Paterson had claimed his crew back from the station commander, and was the senior pilot on duty, supported by F/L Harper, who was on his sixty-seventh operation. With a shorter distance to travel, the Saarbrücken duo reached their objective first, Sgt McFarlane circling for thirty minutes trying to identify his aiming-point. By the time he dropped his 4,000 pounder from 15,700 feet at 23.40, P/O Gill was already on his way home, having delivered his from 18,500 feet some twenty-five minutes earlier. Both believed their efforts to have been on target, but, in truth, this was another unsatisfactory raid, which inflicted little damage. The Nuremberg main force had been briefed to attack from a slow as low as possible, and followed in the wake of the Pathfinders, who had identified the city centre, and marked it with, for the first time, target indicators, adapted from 250lb bomb casings. Four of the 101 Squadron element went in at 14,000 to 18,000 feet between 00.12 and 00.32, clearly not heeding the instructions about bombing height, but having identified ground detail. F/L Menzies failed to identify Nuremberg, and dropped his incendiaries on, what he believed, to be Munich. Some damage was caused within the city, but bombs were also scattered well beyond its boundaries, and it was a disappointing outcome in view of the effort expended and the loss of twenty-three aircraft. The Wellington brigade fared particularly badly, losing fourteen of their number, a massive 34% of those dispatched. Two of those missing were from 101 Squadron, X3752 crashing at 00.30 near Liege in Belgium, killing Sgt Follett RNZAF and three of his crew. The surviving crew member was being sheltered by a brave Belgian, when he was captured. X3391 crash-landed twenty-five miles north-west of Mannheim as a result of technical problems. The crew scrambled clear before a fire broke out, consuming the aircraft. F/L Harper and four of his crew found themselves on extended leave in a German PoW camp, where one died in June 1943, and one other evaded capture. The loss of someone of F/L Harper's experience was a blow to the squadron, but they would be cheered when the news of his survival came through. The squadron participated in ten operations during the month, dispatching ninety-three sorties for the loss of eight Wellingtons, five complete crews and part of another crew.

September 1942

Nine major operations would take place during the first two weeks of September, and although this would bring an unprecedented run of successful raids, it began inauspiciously for the Pathfinders on the night of the 1/2nd. The intended target was Saarbrücken, for which 101 Squadron briefed nine crews, led by S/L Paterson. They took off between 23.25 and 00.07, as part of a force of 231 aircraft, and headed for the south coast, and the Channel crossing to Belgium. Sgt Spinney got as far as Dungeness on the Kent coast before abandoning his sortie because of defective guns, and jettisoned his 500 pounders safe into the sea. The others pressed on, to find an urban area well marked, roughly where they expected the target to be. Ground features, particularly a loop in the river and railway lines, stood out clearly, and P/O Foxcroft spent ten minutes circling, before releasing his incendiaries. The squadron participants delivered their loads of incendiaries or high explosives from 11,000 to 18,000 feet between 02.01 and 02.38, and returned home to report an accurate attack, which had left the target a sea of flames visible from seventy miles away. Sadly, the Pathfinders had marked an area a dozen miles to the north-west, in which lay the small, non-industrial town of Saarlouis. Much to the chagrin of its inhabitants, the main force produced a rare example of precision bombing, and inflicted extensive damage and casualties.

The Command returned to the same general area of south-western Germany on the following night to attack Karlsruhe, a city further to the south-east on the way to Stuttgart. S/L Paterson was again the senior pilot on duty of seven from the squadron briefed to take part in the operation by an overall force of two hundred aircraft. They departed Stradishall either side of 23.00, and all arrived in the target area to find good visibility, which allowed them to identify the River Rhine and the distinctive "toasting fork" profile of the docks. F/Sgt Williams was carrying eight 500 pounders, and P/O Gill a 4,000lb cookie, while the others were loaded with incendiaries, all of which were delivered from 12,500 to 18,000 feet between 01.44 and 02.10. The squadron contingent returned safely with enthusiastic reports of a successful raid, the fires from which were visible for seventy miles into the return journey. The effectiveness of the operation was confirmed by reconnaissance photos, which showed much residential and some industrial damage.

A night's rest preceded the next major operation, for which a force of 251 aircraft was made ready on the 4th. The target was Bremen, and nine 101 Squadron Wellingtons lined up for take-off at ten minutes to midnight, with F/L Menzies the senior pilot on duty. F/Sgt Williams was twenty miles off the Suffolk coast, when he gave up trying to control BJ961, dumped his bombs and turned for home. Sgt Stancliffe got as far as Deventer in Holland, where he turned back at 02.30 with defective turrets, and jettisoned his bombs off Texel on the way home. The others continued on to the target, where the Pathfinders were employing new tactics, which were to form the basis of all future marking efforts. Illuminators went in first with flares, the light from which enabled the marker crews to identify and mark the aiming-point, while the backers-up followed on at intervals to maintain the marking throughout the duration of the attack. The main force crews were able to identify the River Weser and the built-up area, and the 101 Squadron crews bombed from 14,000 to 18,500 feet between 02.01 and 02.45, before returning to report fires visible from ninety miles away. BJ891 failed to return with the crew of P/O Gill, and no trace of aircraft or crew was ever found. Photo-reconnaissance revealed 460 houses and twenty-one industrial concerns to have been destroyed in Bremen for the loss of twelve aircraft.

With a few successes under his belt, Harris returned to the Ruhr on the night of the 6/7th, sending two hundred aircraft to Duisburg. F/L Menzies was the senior pilot of seven on duty for this operation, and they took off in a fifteen-minute slot from 00.55. Frustratingly for Sgt Spinney and crew, they were just three miles north-west of the target when their port engine cut, and were forced to dump their all-incendiary payload from

17,000 feet, and head for home. The others bombed from 14,000 to 17,000 feet between 02.46 and 03.20, and contributed to the destruction of 114 buildings and damage to over three hundred more, an encouraging result at this notoriously difficult target. The squadron lost another aircraft without trace, BJ769, with the all-RCAF crew of F/Sgt Williams RAF. The crews of Sgts McFarlane and Stancliffe joined a gardening effort in northern waters on the following night, taking off at 21.00, and setting course for the eastern bank at the mouth of the River Ems. The former released his two parachute mines five seconds apart from 2,000 feet at 22.57, and the latter dropped his from 800 feet eight minutes later.

The run of successes was temporarily halted at Frankfurt on the night of the 8/9th, when the squadron contributed nine Wellingtons to an operation involving 249 aircraft. It took more than an hour to dispatch the Stradishall contingent either side of 21.00, and it was not long before the first of three early returns was back in the circuit. Sgt Stancliffe was twenty miles off the French coast when his starboard engine failed, and he dumped his 500 pounders safe. W/O Ollier was mid-Channel as his port engine began to malfunction, and the all-incendiary load also ended up in the sea. P/O De Bartok turned back from fifteen miles off the Suffolk coast because of starboard engine trouble and elevator flutter, and all landed in a twenty-minute slot either side of 23.00. The others pressed on to the target, where, despite being able to pick up pinpoints on the River Main, and identifying the docks and general town area, they mostly missed the target to the south-west. The 101 Squadron crews bombed from 12,000 to 17,500 feet between 23.26 and 23.55, and returned to report an effective attack, which, in reality, had caused little damage.

The squadron sent eight crews on gardening sorties during the course of the evening of the 9th and into the early hours of the 10th. P/O Dabbs and Sgts Perry and Waterhouse took off either side of 20.30 for the Trefoils region, south of Den Helder, and made timed runs from pinpoints on the mainland. They dropped their vegetables in the briefed locations from 2,500 feet, and returned safely. S/L Paterson, F/L Menzies, P/Os De Bartok and Foderingham and W/O Olliers departed Stradishall in an eleven-minute slot either side of midnight, and headed for the Rosemary garden, situated in the south-eastern approaches to Heligoland. They were given a number of pinpoints on the Frisians from which to make their timed runs out to sea, and all succeeding in delivering their mines as briefed from 2,200 to 2,500 feet between 02.13 and 02.48. A particularly effective attack on Düsseldorf on the night of the 10/11th was to provide ample consolation for the disappointment at Frankfurt. For the first time, the Pathfinders were to mark the target with "pink pansies" in converted cookie casings, and the large force of 479 aircraft was made possible by the inclusion of an element from the training units. Seven 101 Squadron Wellingtons took off between 21.10 and 21.30 led by S/L Paterson, each carrying an all-incendiary bomb load. Sgt Perry was an hour out when his intercom failed, and his starboard engine began to overheat, so he turned back. The remainder identified the target by the River Rhine, and by the light of flares and fires, and S/L Paterson believed he was over the intended target as he released his load from 12,000 feet on a due south heading at 23.12. The others attacked from 15,000 to 18,000 feet between 23.01 and 23.15, and had a hand in the destruction of over nine hundred houses in all parts of the city and in neighbouring Neuss. There was also a loss of production at fifty-two war industry factories, and a further fifteen hundred houses sustained serious damage, in what was one of the most destructive raid of the war to date. On the debit side, thirty-three aircraft failed to return, the training units suffering disproportionately high casualties, as they had during the Thousand raids.

The training units were involved again for an operation to Bremen on the night of the 13/14th, as the hectic schedule continued. 101 Squadron contributed eleven crews to the overall force of 446 aircraft, and they would be led for the first time by S/L Reddick. They were all airborne in twenty minutes and on their way eastwards by 00.30, eight of them loaded with incendiaries, and three with a 4,000 pounder each. For once, there were no early returns, and all reached the target area to pinpoint on whatever ground features could be identified. The River Weser was picked up by some, while others bombed on ETA or on fires, and not all were able to observe the fall of their bombs. The 101 Squadron crews attacked from 15,000 to 17,000 feet between 02.31 and 03.10, a number of them spending time over the target to decide on the best approach. All returned safely to report the difficulty in positively identifying the target, and also commented on fires visible from the Dutch coast. Post raid reconnaissance revealed a highly successful outcome, far surpassing the effectiveness of the Thousand raid in June. 848 houses were destroyed, and some important war industry factories, the Focke-Wulf works amongst them, suffered a loss of production, at a cost to the Command of twenty-one aircraft, fifteen of them from training units or flights.

W/C Reddick (seated, centre) and his crew. He led the squadron between January and July 1943 (GW).

Twenty-four hours later, Wilhelmshaven was selected as the target for a force of 202 aircraft, ten of which were provided by 101 Squadron. There were also four 408 Squadron Hampdens, undertaking the type's operational swansong with the Command. S/L Reddick was the senior pilot on duty as the Stradishall contingent took off in a ten-minute slot either side of 19.45. All except Sgt Stancliffe were loaded with incendiaries, while he was carrying a 4,000 pounder, and all reached the target area in good order to begin their attack. Most were able to identify the town and the docks area by the light of the Pathfinder flares, which had been accurately placed. The squadron element delivered its ordnance from 16,000 to 19,000 feet between 22.12 and 22.34, and could clearly see the impact on the ground. As they turned for home, fires were beginning to take hold, and the glow could be seen from eighty miles away. Wilhelmshaven reported its worst raid of the war to date, with residential and town-centre buildings being hardest-hit.

With so much recent success to bolster his confidence, Harris had to go for Essen again, and chose the night of the 16/17th, when a force of 369 aircraft was assembled. The training units were called upon again to add numbers, and 101 Squadron's contribution amounted to a dozen Wellingtons, which took off either side of 20.30, led by S/L Reddick. In view of the recent run of 100% serviceability, a disappointing five aircraft returned early, beginning with S/L Reddick, whose rear gunner suddenly became indisposed when they were twenty-five miles west of The Hague. Sgt McFarlane was at the same location over the North Sea, when the failure of the oxygen system ended his sortie. Sgt Stancliffe was fifteen miles further back from the Dutch coast, when starboard engine failure forced him to dump his cookie and head home. Sgt Bennee was minutes from crossing the coast west of Amsterdam, when he was struck down by illness, and Sgt Gillmore had just crossed the coast south-west of Haarlem only to be thwarted by complete electrical failure. The reminder pressed on to reach the target area by means of ETA confirmed by Gee-fix. Pathfinder flares enabled some crews to pick out occasional ground features, like the river and canals, but it was mostly fires that attracted them, and the delivered their all-incendiary loads from 16,600 to 18,500 feet between 22.15 and 22.29. The defences were formidable on this night, and brought down thirty-nine aircraft, 10.6% of those dispatched. 101 Squadron was represented among them by BJ897, which crashed somewhere in the general target area, killing P/O Grant and his crew. Nineteen of the losses came from the training units, and this would be the last time that they would be called upon to provide aircraft and crews. Reconnaissance showed Essen to have been attacked with greater effectiveness than ever before, with much housing damage, hits on the Krupp works and thirty-three large fires. There was also much evidence of bombs being scattered onto the nearby cities of Bochum and Wuppertal. Never the less, if any period could be said to represent the turning point in Bomber Command's long and tortuous road to becoming a war-winning weapon, then, perhaps, these first sixteen nights of September were it. It can be no coincidence, that the emergence of the Pathfinders from an uncertain start, and the evolution of tactics, came together at this time, and, although failures would still substantially outnumber successes for some time to come, the encouraging signs were there.

Two targets were selected for the night of the 19/20th, Saarbrücken and Munich, and it was for the former, that thirteen 101 Squadron crews were briefed. They began taking off shortly after 20.00, led by the flight commanders, S/Ls Paterson and Reddick, but, it is believed, that P/O Carter was unable to continue for an undisclosed reason, and landed at Middle Wallop. The others continued on to reach the target area shortly before 23.00. Identification was based largely on ETA confirmed by a Gee-fix, but some ground detail was picked up by a few, despite the presence of ground haze. Most crews carried all-incendiary loads, but there were also two cookies and eight 500 pounders, and the squadron participants carried out their work predominantly from 14,000 to 15,000 feet, although Sgt Hawkins was at 8,100 feet when he dropped his incendiaries. They were over the target from 23.00 to 23.55, and all but one returned safely home. The absentee was P/O De Bartok DFC, RCAF and his crew, who all lost their lives, when BJ689 came down in north-eastern France on the edge of the Ardennes between Rethel and the Belgian frontier. Sadly, the operation was not a success, and the target escaped with superficial damage.

Seventeen aircraft were sent gardening on the night of the 21/22nd, of which eight were provided by 101 squadron. They were all airborne by 19.55, and heading either for the Heligoland approaches, or the Kiel Bay region of the Baltic, with S/L Paterson the senior pilot on duty. P/O Foderingham turned back early with a burst tyre and other technical issues, but five others reached their respective target areas to deliver their vegetables between 22.40 and 23.07, after making timed runs from predetermined pinpoints. X3815 failed to arrive home after falling to the guns of a night fighter while outbound at 4,000 feet, and crashing into the sea. It was a truly cosmopolitan crew containing S/L Paterson DFC and one other member of the RAF, along with representatives of the RCAF, RAAF and RNZAF. S/L Paterson and two others lost their lives, and were recovered for burial on Danish soil, while the two survivors were taken into captivity. Also failing to return was X3457, which was lost without trace with the crew of F/Sgt Rimmer, and these would be the final casualties sustained by the squadron as a Wellington unit.

A change of home, Group and aircraft beckoned in the very near future, but, first, six crews undertook the squadron's final operation from Stradishall. It was another mining effort, this time in the Silverthorne region of the Kattegat, between Denmark and Sweden. They took off between 20.15 and 20.30, with F/L Menzies the senior pilot on duty, and headed for the western coast of Denmark. A general recall signal was sent out at 21.00, which was only picked up by W/O Ollier and Sgt McFarlane, who responded and turned back from a position close to landfall. Having travelled so far, group would ultimately count both sorties as completed operations. The others pressed on, and Sgt Ralph and crew reported seventeen E-Boots at 21.24, travelling fast in three lines on a north-west heading. There was some cloud in the target area, but moonlight helped with identification of pinpoints, and the mines were laid in the briefed locations from 700 to 900 feet between

23.53 and 00.06. On the following day, orders came through to prepare for the move to the 1 Group station at Holme-on-Spalding-Moor and conversion to Lancasters. An advance party set out on the 28th, and the main move took place on the 29th, with the departure from Stradishall of sixteen Wellingtons and crews. On the following day, ten crews were packed off to 1654 HCU at Wigsley to begin training on Lancasters. During the course of the month the squadron operated fourteen time, dispatched 118 sorties and lost six Wellingtons and crews.

October 1942

The Stirling Conversion Flight was absorbed into 1657 HCU on the 1st, the day on which 125 bicycles were issued to the squadron, creating an absolute nightmare for the adjutant, F/L Eagleton. Also on this day, the experienced F/L T.D. Misselbrook was posted in from 22 O.T.U at Wellesbourne. The squadron was not to be screened from operations during the working up period, and would continue to go to war in Wellingtons for the time being. The first operation of the month took place on the night of the 2/3rd, when the squadron contributed four Wellingtons to an overall force of 188 to attack Krefeld in the Ruhr. They took off either side of 19.00 led by S/L Reddick, and headed for the target in unfavourable weather conditions, each loaded with incendiaries. The Pathfinders were late, and hampered by poor vertical visibility, which led to a scattered raid. The 101 Squadron crews carried out their part from 12,500 to 15,000 feet between 20.56 and 21.12, and returned safely with little to report. Aachen was the target for a force of 257 aircraft on the night of the 5/6th, of which five Wellingtons belonged to 101 Squadron. They took off at around 18.45 with S/L Reddick again taking the lead, and all loaded with incendiaries. Sgt Fussell and crew encountered severe icing on the way out, and decided to turn back, leaving the others to press on to the target, where there was little evidence of Pathfinder marking. They delivered the contents of their bomb bays from 10,000 to 14,000 feet between 21.50 and 22.00, and returned to report many fires, and much enemy night fighter activity. Most of the bombing missed the target, and some fell onto the small Dutch town of Lutterade, some fifteen miles to the north-west. This, as will be described at the appropriate juncture, would have short-term consequences in the development of the Oboe blind-bombing device, which was to transform operations over the Ruhr in the coming spring.

Osnabrück was the target for 237 aircraft on the night of the 6/7th, for which five 101 Squadron crews were briefed. W/O Ollier was the senior pilot on duty as they began taking off at 19.00, loaded with incendiaries, but Sgt Bowyer was forced to turn back with a failed oxygen system. The Pathfinders located the target and marked its centre accurately, and when the main force followed up, they had little difficulty in dropping their bombs into the central and southern districts. The 101 Squadron crews carried out their attacks from 12,000 to 14,800 feet between 21.30 and 21.40, and returned to report many fires visible from more than a hundred miles away, and considerable searchlight activity. Enemy night fighters were also evident, and a number of aircraft were reported falling in flames. When Lancaster R5482 arrived on the 11th, the squadron became the twelfth operational unit to receive the type. Just five days earlier, 460 Squadron RAAF had taken its first Lancaster on charge, to become the first in 1 Group to do so. It was thus saved from operating the Halifax, the type which had been planned for the Group, and which was, in fact, operating at this time in the hands of a disgruntled 103 Squadron at Elsham Wolds.

The night of the 11/12th was devoted to mining operations, for which the squadron made ready six Wellingtons, five for the Forget-me-not region, and one for Wallflowers in the Kiel Canal and Kiel Bay areas respectively of the western Baltic. They took off at 18.45, and set course for the target areas, where Sgt Atwood failed to pick up a pinpoint on Denmark's western coast, and abandoned his sortie. This left the others to continue on to the Kiel Canal, where they encountered scattered cloud but good visibility, and also had to contend with searchlights, along with flak from ships off the coast. They delivered their mines from 800 to 1,000 feet between 21.38 and 21.57, before embarking on the homeward journey. Sgt Hazard was at 5,000 feet, when an enemy aircraft with a searchlight in its nose crossed his path half a mile ahead at 22.33, and continued on its way. On the following night, six 101 Squadron Wellingtons took off at around 17.30, four to mine the waters in the Wallflower area of Kiel Bay, and two for Hawthorne, the approaches to Esbjerg. Sgt Campbell turned back with an inoperable front turret, leaving the others to push on in unfavourable weather conditions, which thwarted two of Wallflower element, preventing them from finding a pinpoint by which to navigate, and persuading them to abandon their sorties. Sgt Hazard seemed to be a magnet for enemy night fighters with searchlights, and attracted two more, which were evaded. Sgt Fussell, alone of his quartet, found the briefed drop zone, and delivered his two mines from 1,000 feet at 20.10. The weather conditions near Esbjerg were not as difficult, and Sgts Bowyer and Atwood dropped their stores from 700 and 800 feet at 19.52 and 19.53 respectively. On the way home, some twenty minutes later, a twin-engine enemy aircraft turned towards Sgt Bowyer from three hundred yards ahead, but the Wellington escaped into cloud, and was not troubled again, other than by searchlights and flak at a number of locations.

A major operation was mounted against Kiel on the night of the 13/14th, involving 288 aircraft, but none from 101 Squadron. Half of the bomb loads were drawn away by a decoy fire site, but the remainder fell into the general area of the town and caused damage to residential, utility and public buildings. Five 101 Squadron Wellingtons were the only aircraft operating on the night of the 14/15th, and they were tasked with planting mines in the Nectarines region off the Frisians. They were all safely airborne by 18.30, with W/O Ollier the senior pilot on duty. The weather was fine at first, but deteriorated in the target area, and he and Sgts Bowyer and Harrower were unable to pick up their pinpoints from which to make timed runs. Sgt Bowyer was at 800 feet over what he believed to be over Simonszand, between the islands of Schiermonnikoog and Rottumerplaat, when two searchlights and six light flak guns opened up. The rear gunner fired three-second bursts down one of the beams, and the light was extinguished. Sgts Campbell and Hazard overcame the adverse weather conditions to deliver their two mines each from 700 and 800 feet at 20.21 and 20.18 respectively. The squadron's final Wellington operation took place on the night of the 15/16th, when Cologne was the destination for a force of 289 aircraft. Six 101 Squadron crews were briefed, and took off between 18.45 and 18.55, with W/O Ollier again the senior pilot on duty, and undertaking the final sortie of his tour. All were carrying an incendiary load, and W/O Ollier also had on board the station commander, G/C "Bobby" Blucke. They all reached the target to bomb from 13,000 to 14,000 feet between 20.45 and 21.03, and returned to report many scattered fires, and bombs clearly falling outside of the target area. They also commented upon the intense searchlight and flak activity, and the presence of many night fighters, some with searchlights in the nose. A number of aircraft were seen to be shot down in the target area, and Sgt Harrower and crew saw, what they believed, was a torch in the sea. Despite descending to 800 feet to investigate, they were unable to establish what it was. They landed at 00.45, and thus had the honour of completing the last of more than 1,250 Wellington sorties in 101 Squadron service.

Over the ensuing days, the Wellingtons were ferried out to new homes, while Lancasters continued to arrive in ones and twos. The converted crews returned on the 19th, full of praise for the Lancaster, and eager to demonstrate to Hitler what it could do in 101 Squadron hands. Sgt Ralph carried out the first test-flight in SR-A on the 24th, and, by the end of the month, fourteen Lancasters had been taken on charge. A new campaign against Italian cities began with an attack on Genoa by a 5 Group and Pathfinder force on the night of the 22/23rd. This was in support of Operation Torch, the Allied landings in North Africa, and coincided with the start of Montgomery's El Alamein offensive, which would end in victory over Rommel. Before the end of the month, Genoa was attacked again, and Milan twice, as Germany was left in peace and minor operations held sway. During the course of the month the squadron carried out nine operations (counting each garden as a separate operation), and dispatched thirty-seven sorties without loss.

November 1942

The new month began with training, and G/C Blucke flew a Lancaster on a local jaunt on the 2nd. The tour-expired W/O Ollier was posted to 1656 Conversion Unit at Lindholme on the 4th, and further aircrew movements took place to and from the squadron, as day and night cross-countries and loading tests were carried out, along with practice bombing. W4784 was in the middle of a flap run, when its undercarriage was retracted, and the ORB records it as sitting at its dispersal looking like a flying boat. The crews were unhappy, because it spoiled their unblemished record on the type. Worse was to come, however, as the training programme continued on the 15th and into the 16th. Five crews carried out training exercises on the 15th, two on formation practice, two on bombing and one on air-sea firing, until fog swept in during the evening to ground them. It lifted later on, and Sgt Spinney and crew took off in W4236 at 01.00 on the 16th for a cross-country, bombing and photography exercise. The Lancaster fell out of a clear sky from 12,000 feet, and crashed at Dolwen Hill, Llanerfyl, near Montgomery in North Wales, killing all on board. It will be recalled, that Sgt Spinney RCAF and his crew had survived the crash-landing at Martlesham Heath on return from Kassel in late August. The tragedy cast a shadow of gloom over the entire squadron, as there seemed to be no explanation for the loss. It was eventually believed, that the photo-flash had exploded, and caused structural failure to the rear fuselage. Training continued, and three crews flew over the crash site to search for bodies, as, thus far, only two had been recovered, lending weight to the belief that the aircraft had broken up in the air. F/L Manahan DFC was posted in during the last week of the month, and was promoted immediately to squadron leader rank, to assume the role of flight commander.

Despite being the second squadron in the Group to equip with Lancasters, 101 Squadron was actually the first to operate, doing so on the on the night of the 20/21st. W/C Eaton was in W4321, leading a squadron contingent of eight, as part of a force of over two hundred assorted aircraft sent to attack Turin. The other crews and aircraft on this momentous occasion were those of S/L Reddick in W4782, F/L Misselbrook in W4309, P/O Dabbs in W4276, F/Sgt Waterhouse in R5482, and Sgts Gillmore in W4322, Ralph in W4275, and Wiltshire in W4319. They took off either side of 18.30, and all reached the target area to find clear skies and bright moonlight, although smoke was already rising and adding to the cloak of ground haze. The Rivers Po and Lanzo were clearly visible, however, and the squadron crews delivered their incendiaries and two 1,000 pounders each on and around the aiming-point from 9,000 to 12,400 feet between 22.10 and 22.48. As they retreated, they could see fires joining up to create larger ones, and all returned safely to report a successful first Lancaster outing. Seven crews were briefed for Stuttgart on the 22nd, the occasion of 460 Squadron's first Lancaster operation. They were part of an overall force of 222 aircraft, and S/Ls Reddick and Manahan were the senior pilots on duty as they departed Holme either side of 18.30, again carrying incendiaries and two 1,000 pounders each. They all reached the target area, where a thin layer of cloud combined with ground haze to cause problems for the Pathfinders. They failed to mark the centre of the city, and the main weight of bombs fell into the south-western and southern districts. The 101 Squadron crews all reported poor visibility over the target, but were able to identify the River Neckar and the marshalling yards. They bombed from 5,000 (F/L Misselbrook) to 12,000 feet between 22.01 and 22.30, and returned to report another successful trip. It was established later that a modest eighty-eight houses had been destroyed.

Mining operations dominated for the remainder of the month, until the night of the 28/29th, when another attack on Turin was scheduled. 101 Squadron supported it with six aircraft, led by F/L Misselbrook, and they took off between 18.35 and 18.51, four carrying a load of 1,260 x 4lb incendiaries, and two a cookie each and two 1,000 pounders. The target was identified by the rivers, picked out in the light of Pathfinder flares, and by fires already burning. The squadron crews bombed from 9,500 to 11,000 feet between 22.24 and 22.45, and all returned safely, confident in the quality of their work. There seemed to be some kind of sickness on the station at this time, as both flight commanders were among a number of aircrew spending time undergoing medical treatment, S/L Reddick in station sick quarters, and S/L Manahan in York Military Hospital. There is no mention of any kind of accident, so one must assume a bug of some description. During the course of the month the squadron operated three times, and dispatched twenty-one sorties, losing one Lancaster and crew to the training accident.

December 1942

The new month began with a raid on Frankfurt by a modest 112 aircraft, for which 101 Squadron provided five Lancasters. They took off between 01.35 and 01.50, led by F/L Misselbrook, carrying incendiaries and three 1,000 pounders each, and reached the target to find clear skies and thick ground haze, which proved difficult for the Pathfinders to overcome. They failed to identify the city, and this led to most of the bombs falling into open country to the south-west. The 101 Squadron crews eventually identified sections of the River Main, and four of the crews released their loads from 10,000 to 14,000 feet between 04.26 and 04.50. On arrival at the target at 04.30, P/O Dabbs found the bomb release mechanism to be inoperable through freezing up. He was forced to bring the bomb load back, and did so with a failed starboard-inner engine and an unserviceable starboard fuel tank, probably as the result of being hit by flak in the Mainz area. A few days hence, in recognition of his fortitude on this night, he would be awarded an immediate DFC, but, sadly, would not live to receive the news. The operation was a complete failure, for which a decoy fire site may have been partially responsible. There was much celebration on the 5th, as awards of the DFC were announced to W/C Eaton, and to the now tour-expired F/L Menzies, P/Os De Bartok and Foderingham and W/O Olliers.

Inevitably, the first operational loss of a 101 Squadron Lancaster would come, and it did so on the night of the 6/7th, when Mannheim was the target for 272 aircraft, including five representing the squadron. F/L Misselbrook led them away at 17.30, each carrying a 4,000 pounder and ten SBCs loaded with ninety 4lb incendiaries. Sgt Fussell and crew made it all the way to Strasbourg on the Franco/German frontier, only for their starboard-outer engine to cut out and force them to turn back. The others reached the target area to find ten-tenths cloud with tops at 7,000 feet, and could only bomb on estimated position. This they did from 8,500 to 12,000 feet between 20.16 and 21.00, and three returned safely to report their doubts about the effectiveness of the attack. P/O Dabbs and crew did not return, and were posted missing. News began to filter through later in the day, that ED322 had crashed in Carmarthen Bay, off Tenby in South Wales, and P/O Dabbs and his crew had lost their lives. At the time of recording the event in the ORB, two bodies had been washed ashore, and, in time, P/O Dabbs and three others would be recovered for burial. This "first class captain and crew" had been allotted Lancaster W4312 SR-H, but had been forced to switch to another when it became unserviceable, and had chosen a new aircraft, ED322 SR-T. Whether or not they reached and bombed the target has not been established, and why they crashed where they did is also a mystery. F/Sgt Smith was an experience navigator with an excellent reputation, but no one knows what went on inside the Lancaster. The simple explanation is that they lost their way after crossing the French coast homebound, and ran out of fuel within sight of land. The fact that F/L Misselbrook had to land at Thorney Island on the south coast, because of a fuel shortage, lends weight to this theory, but it is pure speculation. Whatever the cause, the loss was keenly felt by the whole squadron.

German soldiers inspect the wreckage of W4782, SR-J which was shot down near Esbjerg with the loss of pilot Sgt Quinn and two of his crew. The remainder were captured (GW).

Two nights later, six crews took off between 17.25 and 17.47 to mine the waters of the Great Belt between Denmark and Sweden. F/L Misselbrook was the senior pilot on duty as they headed for the west coast of Denmark loaded with six mines each. F/Sgt Waterhouse returned early with hydraulics failure, and Sgt Ralph failed to pick up his final turning point because of extreme darkness and poor visibility, and brought his load back. Three of the others located their pinpoints, and made timed runs, dropping the mines at ten-second intervals from 800 to 900 feet between 20.11 and 20.27. W4782 was hit by flak at the Danish coast, and crashed at 20.30 a couple of miles east of Esbjerg, killing Sgt Quinn and two of his mixed RAF, RAAF and RCAF crew, while the survivors fell into enemy hands. The main operation on this night had been the first of three in four nights against Turin, and 101 Squadron made ready six Lancasters for the second one on the night of the 9/10. They got away from Holme either side of 17.30, led by S/L Reddick, and joined the other 221 participating aircraft heading for the south coast. Sgt Wiltshire had crossed the French coast five miles north-west of Beauvais, when a component detonated in the RDF equipment, rendering it unserviceable, and temporarily blinding the navigator. It was decided to turn back, and the cookie was jettisoned off the French coast, while the incendiaries came home. The others arrived over the target to find haze and smoke obscuring ground detail, and not a lot of help from the Pathfinders. Even so, they were able to focus on the aiming-point, and deliver their loads of high explosives and incendiaries from 9,000 to 12,000 feet between 21.52 and 22.10.

Sgt Ralph and crew were tasked with making a special report of the raid, and they remained over the target from 21.54 to 22.15, and saw; "many fires over the whole target area, especially aiming-point and marshalling yards. Sticks of incendiaries seen to burst near aiming-point, and HEs on marshalling yards and centre of town". All from the squadron returned safely to echo Sgt Ralph's sentiments, although it was difficult to assess how much new damage had actually been inflicted.

The third Turin raid took place after a night's rest, and involved seven 101 Squadron Lancasters in an overall force of eighty-two aircraft drawn from 1, 4 and 5 Groups and the Pathfinders. S/L Reddick was the senior pilot on duty, as they took off in a thirty-minute slot from 16.55. The weather conditions outbound were highly challenging, with ten-tenths cloud all the way to the target, soaring in places to 23,000 feet, and half of the force turned back because of severe icing before crossing the Alps. F/L Misselbrook was among them, after three engines cut out simultaneously for about ten seconds, and he found it impossible to maintain sufficient height to cross the Alps. Sgt Ralph initially estimated that he had dropped his bombs fifteen miles west of the target from 18,000 feet at 21.45, but the navigator re-plotted their position, and decided they had fallen close to Lake Annecy, on the French side of the Alps, some ninety miles short. Sgt MacFarlane reported releasing his bombs at 21.19 from 21,000 feet at a position some forty miles south of Lake Annecy, and claimed that the conditions were the worst he had ever experienced. The others believed they were in the target area when they carried out their attacks from 10,000 to 18,000 feet between 21.26 and 21.58, and all made it home to the congratulations of the station commander on their navigation.

The weather curtailed operational activity for a few nights, until Sgt Fussell and crew managed to get away in W4319 early on the evening of the 17th to carry out a gardening sortie. The ORB does not provide details of drop zone and timing, but their return over the north-east coast shortly after 22.00 suggests the Frisians or the Baltic as their target area. The Lancaster was fired upon by a friendly anti-aircraft battery, and crashed at 22.10 at Grangetown, between Redcar and Middlesbrough on Teesside, killing all on board. The ORB describes them as "a new but promising crew", which contained three New Zealanders and a Canadian. It was at this time that acting S/L Ollason became attached to the squadron from 1520 BAT Flight, and assumed command of B Flight. The night of the 20/21st was one of great significance for the Command, and not because of the main operation to Duisburg, which involved six 101 Squadron Lancasters, led by F/L Misselbrook. They took off in a twenty-minute slot from 18.05, as part of an overall force of 232 aircraft. Sgt Harrower was over the Wash when he turned back with four overheating engines, and he was fired upon by trigger-happy coastal flak, despite sending out the correct IFF signal. Fortunately, they missed! The others were greeted by a thin layer of cloud over the western Ruhr, but visibility was good, and it was possible to pick out ground detail, such as the docks. Searchlight dazzle concealed the aiming-point from most, but it made little difference, and the bombing was carried out from 13,000 to 15,000 feet between 19.56 and 20.23. The 101 Squadron element returned intact, and claimed a successful operation, although there was no confirmation either by post-raid reconnaissance or German reports. While this operation was in progress, a force of six Mosquitos from 109 Squadron, led by its commanding officer, W/C Hal Bufton, dropped the first Oboe-aimed bombs on a coking plant at Lutterade in Holland. The operation was a calibration test to gauge the device's margin of error, and the target had been chosen as one previously unsullied by bomb craters. Sadly, stray bombs from the earlier-mentioned attack on Aachen in early October had pitted the ground, and it was not possible to identify the Oboe bombs. However, further trials would be carried out over the ensuing weeks, and the magnificent pioneering work of 109 Squadron, in marrying Oboe to the Mosquito after joining the Pathfinders in August, would pay massive dividends in the coming year, and transform the bombing of the Ruhr.

Munich provided the target for 137 aircraft from 1 and 5 Groups and the Pathfinders on the night of the 21/22nd, for which 101 Squadron provided nine Lancasters. They were led by F/L Misselbrook, and took off between 17.08 and 17.35, but Sgt Gumbrell turned back early after the rear gunner collapsed with oxygen starvation over Cambridge. The others arrived in the target area after pinpointing on a lake in brilliant moonlight, but found the city to be obscured by cloud. According to the compass headings recorded in the ORB, bombing runs were carried out in a variety of directions from west to east, east to west and south-east to north-west, and from altitudes ranging from 10,500 to 13,000 feet between 21.09 and 21.33. Despite the apparent chaos, the Holme contingent made it home safely, although W4311 was attacked by a ME110, which shot away the trailing edge of its port tailplane and severely damaged the mid-upper and rear turrets. Most of the electrical circuitry was also knocked out, and a tyre riddled, despite which, Sgt Wiltshire put the Lancaster on the ground in very challenging weather conditions. ED379 was also attacked on the way home, at 23.20 when flying at 11,000 feet ten miles south of Brussels. The assailant was a JU88, which inflicted some damage before being shaken off, and the Lancaster landed safely at Marston Moor in the hands of Sgt Harrower. The consensus of returning crews was of a successful attack, which left large fires burning and much smoke rising, but their photos revealed later, that most of the bombing had fallen into open country.

Eight crews carried out NFTs on the evening of the 23rd in adverse weather conditions, and W4312 crashed on landing after making several attempts to get down, and ended up beyond the runway among trees and entangled in barbed wire. Sgt Gillmore and crew emerged bruised and shaken, but otherwise intact. There were no further operations for the squadron before the close of the year, and the mood of the Command was in marked contrast to that of twelve months earlier, when the very existence of an independent bomber force had hung in the balance. The next twelve months would bring some outstanding successes, but no answer to the burgeoning effectiveness of the enemy night fighter force. During the course of December the squadron undertook eight operations, launching forty-five sorties for the loss of four Lancasters and three crews.

January 1943

The year would begin with a continuation of the Oboe trials programme, involving Mosquitos of 109 Squadron and small, gradually increasing forces of Lancasters from 1 and 5 Groups. Essen was to be the principal objective, and would host seven raids during the first two weeks, while Duisburg would receive just one. 6 Group came into existence on New Year's Day, and the first batch of Canadian squadrons was transferred to it, along with any 4 Group stations occupied by them. A few RCAF units would remain for the time-being with their original Groups, but, ultimately, all would transfer. New Year's Day itself was beset with fog, keeping the Command on the ground, and it would be the second half of the month before large numbers of aircraft were committed to operations. In the meantime, the Oboe trials programme got under way on the night of the 3/4th, with the first of the Essen raids, carried out by three Pathfinder Mosquitos and nineteen Lancasters of 5 Group. The plan was for the high-level Mosquitos to drop target markers by Oboe, and for the Pathfinders to use these as a reference to deliver skymarkers for the bombing element. Teething troubles would beset the Oboe equipment in the Mosquitos throughout the series, but this was a necessary and, to some extent, anticipated stage in the development of the device.

101 Squadron also ventured forth on this night, sending eight Lancasters to lay mines in the Gironde Estuary on France's Biscay coast. F/L Misselbrook led them away at 16.30, with Sgt Ralph bringing up the rear at 17.05. F/Sgt Waterhouse suffered the frustrating experience of almost reaching the target area, only for engine failure to force him to jettison a few of his six mines and return home. F/L Misselbrook pinpointed on Pointe-Coubre, before carrying out a timed run, covering seven miles to the drop site, where he delivered his mines from 800 feet at 19.41. Sgts Ralph, MacFarlane and Wiltshire used the same pinpoints from which to make their runs, and delivered their stores from 800 and 1,000 feet at 19.42 and 19.25 respectively. F/Sgt Bowyer and Sgt Gillmore selected a pinpoint on Lake Hourtin (Carcans) as their starting point, and dropped their mines as briefed from 800 and 650 feet at 19.26 and 19.33 respectively. Sgt Hazard and crew apparently also took part in this operation, but there are no details of their sortie, and they may have been scrubbed before take-off.

The second of the Essen raids took place on the night of the 4/5th, for which 101 Squadron contributed eight NCO-captained Lancasters to a 1 Group effort of thirty-one aircraft, which were to join forces with others from 5 Group. F/Sgt Waterhouse was the senior pilot on duty as they took off between 17.20 and 17.50, but Sgts Campbell and Gumbrell were soon on their way back with rear turret and various other technical issues. The others pressed on to find the target lying under five to eight-tenths cloud, with tops, in places, as high as 15,000 feet, and this would prevent an accurate assessment of the outcome. Sgt Hazard dropped his bombs in the Mönchengladbach area from 24,000 feet, but the others were guided by the Pathfinder markers, and delivered their cookie and incendiaries each from 20,000 to 21,500 feet at around 19.45. It is not known whether F/Sgt Waterhouse RNZAF and crew reached the target to bomb, as they failed to return, and disappeared without trace in W4796. They were a skilled and popular crew, whose loss could be ill-afforded by the Squadron, and the navigator, P/O Brodie, was considered to be among the best of his trade.

The Pathfinders finally achieved group status as 8 Group on the 8th, and, for the purpose of this book, both titles are valid and interchangeable. A number of squadron crews participated in altitude tests on the 8th, one reaching 28,100 feet with a full fuel load. The Oboe trials continued at Duisburg on this night, while 1 Group planned a large mining effort in the Baltic, around the Frisians and off the west coast of France. A number of 101 Squadron Lancasters were ready to take-off, when their participation was scrubbed because of a forecast of extremely adverse weather conditions. Four crews were briefed for the next attack on Essen on the night of the 9/10th, and they were all safely airborne by 17.00, but F/O Tuckwell and F/Sgt Bowyer returned early with technical issues. P/Os Duffill and Harrower continued on, and found the target under clear skies and in good visibility. The operation was another test of the "Wanganui" skymarking system, employing parachute flares, and, other than being a minute late in being released, they allowed the main force to bomb with a degree of accuracy. P/O Duffill dropped his cookie and incendiaries from 22,200 feet at 19.24, and P/O Harrower followed suit twelve minutes later from 20,000 feet.

Seven 101 Squadron aircraft took off between 16.35 and 17.00 on the 11th, for the latest attack on Essen. A total of seventy-two 1 and 5 Group Lancasters were involved, but few, if any, found the target on this night. P/O Duffill and F/Sgt Bowyer returned early, leaving the others to press on to find the target concealed beneath ten-tenths cloud. The Pathfinder skymarkers failed to materialize, and bombing took place on ETA, which rarely produced satisfying results. The squadron element attacked from 21,000 to 22,000 feet between 19.30 and 19.45, and returned with little to report, other than the glow of a few fires reflected in the clouds. The same target was posted for the following night, and it was approaching 03.00 on the 12th, when eleven 101 Squadron Lancasters snaked their way along the peri-track from dispersal pan to runway threshold. F/O Tuckwell, P/O Harrower and Sgt Ralph took off without incident, before F/Sgt Bowyer put a wheel off the concrete and became bogged down, blocking the entrance to the runway, and forcing the cancellation of the remaining sorties. The airborne 101 Squadron trio all reached the target, and bombed on Pathfinder flares through ten-tenths cloud from 20,500 to 22,000 feet between 06.17 and 06.20, before returning to report only reflections of bomb bursts. The night of the 13/14th brought more of the same, this time with sixty-six Lancasters from 1, 5 and 8 Groups. 101 Squadron provided eight aircraft, which took off between 16.35 and 17.00, but F/Sgt Bowyer, who was experiencing a spell of ill-fortune, returned early with engine failure, and, after landing, ran off the runway and became bogged down again! F/Sgt Campbell returned with instrument failure, and P/O Duffill's cabin heating broke down, leaving the others to push on to the target, which they found under eight to ten-tenths cloud. The Oboe system broke down slightly again, and enemy aircraft laid decoy flares to distract the bombers, despite which, enough bombs found their way into Essen to destroy fifty-two buildings. The 101 Squadron crews bombed from 20,000 to 22,000 feet between 19.27 and 19.39 in the face of intense and accurate flak, and returned home bearing the scars and reporting the glow of fires.

A new Air Ministry directive was issued on the 14th, which called for the area bombing of the French ports providing bases and support facilities for U-Boots. The list was headed by Lorient, with St Nazaire, Brest and La Pallice included. That night, Lorient received the first of its eight raids over the ensuing four weeks, but the attack by over a hundred aircraft was, perhaps, the least effective of the series, as "wild" bombing hit mostly the town, rather than naval facilities, and destroyed 120 buildings. 101 Squadron was not invited to take part, and sat out the second one also, which took place twenty-four hours later, and destroyed eight hundred buildings.

Berlin, which would feature heavily during the second half of the year, received attention on consecutive nights in mid-month. The first operation took place on the 16/17th, for which 101 Squadron made ready fourteen Lancasters, to join forces with 176 others and eleven Halifaxes drawn from 1, 4, 5 and 8 Groups. The Pathfinders were to employ genuine target indicators for the first time, but would do so without the benefit of Oboe, which was affected by the curvature of the earth, and did not have the range to reach Berlin. The Holme contingent took off between 16.30 and 17.05, with F/L Misselbrook the senior pilot on duty, but three returned early with technical issues and a fourth through illness. Sgt Thompson lost his starboard-inner engine, and turned back when eighty miles out from the Yorkshire coast, and F/O Duffill was sixty miles off the northern coast of Denmark, well north of track, and realised that he would arrive at the target too late to take part in the attack. Sgt Hazard and crew were some sixty miles off southern Denmark when one of the gunners reported a problem with his equipment, and that was enough to persuade them to turn back. P/O Harrower was taken ill on the way out, and his landing time suggests, that he must have been close to the target when he felt unable to continue. The others pushed on in thick cloud, but found the target under largely clear skies and in good visibility. The Pathfinder flares were late, and only a third of the force, including most of the 101 Squadron crews, saw them, and bombed from 18,000 to 21,500 feet between 20.23 and 20.41. The bombing was scattered across the southern part of the city, and the raid failed to produce the hoped-for outcome. There was one notable scalp, however, and this was the complete destruction of the huge 10,000-seater Deutschlandhalle, the largest covered venue in Europe. The evening performance of the annual circus was in progress as the attack started, and the sell-out crowd, with all of the animals, were successfully evacuated to nearby open ground and parks. Also on the credit side, only one Lancaster failed to return from this operation.

Ten 101 Squadron crews were called to arms for Berlin on the following night, as part of an overall force of 170 Lancasters and seventeen Halifaxes. F/L Misselbrook led them away again between 16.30 and 17.00, and F/Sgt Bowyer had flown beyond the mid-point of the North Sea crossing, when the intercom to the rear turret failed. F/Sgt MacFarlane was just about to cross Rømø Island at the Danish coast, when his navigator collapsed, forcing them to turn back. The ORB states; "Reports that this was due to his bomb-aimer having told him he was dead on track, are untrue, as his subsequent medical board found him unfit for flying". The

W4321, SR-P 'Pluto', was lost without trace on the Berlin raid of 17/18th January 1943 (GW).

conditions outbound were more favourable than twenty-four hours earlier, with bright moonlight and little cloud, but the white stuff began to build as the target approached, and covered it for the first half of the attack, before thinning and then moving in again. The 101 Squadron crews bombed on Pathfinder markers, visual pinpoints or on ETA from 18,000 to 21,000 feet between 20.43 and 21.08, and returned with little of use to report. F/L Misselbrook found ten-tenths cloud as he ran in to deliver his all-incendiary load, and decided not to waste it in the vain hope of hitting something. He opted to look for a Baltic port as an alternative target, but ran into a ME110 night fighter, which attacked three times, setting fire to the starboard-outer engine, and holing a petrol tank. The rear half of the fuselage also sustained damage, and both turrets were put out of action, but not before their occupants had shot down the assailant in flames. The bombs were jettisoned, and a safe return made, upon which, F/L Misselbrook received the immediate award of the DFC, and his rear gunner, Sgt Harrison, a DFM. The operation was a complete failure, which failed to destroy a single building, and among the twenty-two missing aircraft was the squadron's W4321, which disappeared without trace with the crew of P/O Duffill.

The Oboe trials continued at Essen on the night of the 21/22nd, for which a heavy force of seventy-nine Lancasters was made ready, including ten at Holme-on-Spalding-Moor. They took off either side of 17.00, with F/L Misselbrook once more the senior pilot on duty, but he was one of two early returns on a night of challenging weather conditions. He lost the use of his rear turret, and turned back just a couple of minutes before crossing the Dutch coast south of Ijmuiden. Sgt Hazard was at the mid-point of the North Sea crossing much further north, heading directly for Texel, when a frozen ASI and an engine problem curtailed his sortie. The others reached the target to find varying amounts of cloud, and poor vertical visibility, and bombed either on the Pathfinder warning flares or on ETA. The 101 Squadron crews were mostly over the target at 18,000 to 20,000 feet, either side of 19.45, but F/O Vane let his load go from 14,000 feet while trying to evade searchlights and flak. On the way home, F/Sgt MacFarlane was attacked by two or three enemy night fighters over the Zuider Zee, and the mid-upper gunner, Sgt Singleton, was killed, while the rear gunner, Sgt O'Brien, sustained wounds. F/Sgt MacFarlane brought W4833 to a landing at East Wretham, and received an immediate DFM for his airmanship. ED443 failed to return, after crashing near Dortmund, and there were no survivors from the crew of Sgt Wiltshire RNZAF.

Lorient was attacked again on the night of the 23/24th, while eighty Lancaster of 1, 5 and 8 Groups carried out an Oboe trials attack on Düsseldorf. The ever-present F/L Misselbrook was the senior pilot on duty of seven crews, which got away at 17.15, but four turned back early, two because of technical issues, and two because wrongly-forecast winds would have made them late on target. F/L Misselbrook, P/O Harrower and Sgt Gillmore pressed on in bright moonlight and good visibility over ten-tenths cloud, and bombed on Pathfinder flares or ETA from 20,000 feet between 19.52 and 19.59. W/C Eaton was posted to HQ 1 Group on the 26th at the conclusion of a highly successful tour in command, which had seen the squadron through a conversion programme and two changes of address. His presence would be missed, but his operational career was not over, and he would return in a year's time to command 156 Squadron of the Pathfinders. Sadly, this popular and respected officer would lose his life while leading his crews into battle, and this is dealt with in the excellent book by Michael Wadsworth, They Led the Way. The blow of his departure from 101 Squadron was softened by the promotion from within and appointment of S/L Reddick as his successor. That night, Lorient received further attention, while 101 Squadron stayed at home.

S/L Fisher became W/C Reddick's successor as A Flight commander on the 27th, and would take over his crew, but was not included on the Order of Battle for that night's attack on Düsseldorf, which was to add a further component to Pathfinding techniques. For the first time, the Mosquito element was to carry out "ground marking", the delivery of target indicators to burst and cascade at around 3,000 feet as a reference for the Pathfinder heavy brigade. A larger force than of late, consisting of 157 heavies and five Mosquitos, reflected the importance of the occasion, for which 101 Squadron contributed six Lancasters, led by F/Ls Misselbrook and Tuckwell. They took off in the minutes before 18.00, and adopted the southern approach to the Ruhr, via the French coast between Calais and Boulogne, and into Germany through the Mönchengladbach/Cologne corridor. Sgt Gumbrell had just crossed the French coast when he became indisposed, and had to turn back. The others pushed on over nine to ten-tenths cloud in good visibility, and bombed from 16,500 to 20,000 feet between 20.04 and 20.11, the earlier arrivals on ETA, and the later ones on Pathfinder markers. The new technique undoubtedly contributed to the destruction of, or serious damage to, over four hundred houses, and it portended well for the future.

The final operation of the month was directed at Hamburg on the night of the 30/31st, for which 1, 5 and 8 Groups made ready 148 heavy aircraft, of which, eight Lancasters belonged to 101 Squadron. Hamburg lay beyond the range of Oboe, but the new ground-mapping H2S device had become available, and would be carried into battle for the first time by 8 Group Stirlings and Halifaxes. The radar, contained in a cupola beneath the rear fuselage, scanned the terrain, and cast a primitive image onto a cathode-ray tube in the navigator's compartment, which the H2S operator had to interpret to pinpoint the aircraft's location. It was a difficult task to identify the shape of an urban area amongst the jumble of black and white information on the screen, particularly with the Mk I device, but practice and technical advancements would, in time, turn it into a useful blind-bombing aid. The 101 Squadron element began to take off shortly after midnight, led by the flight commanders, S/Ls Fisher and Ollason. Sgt Ralph turned back early with icing issues having reached the Ijsselmeer, while S/L Fisher lost his starboard-outer engine, and bombed Vechta aerodrome from 19,500 feet at 02.37 before heading home. Cloud conditions in the target area ranged from little to ten-tenths, but visibility above was good, and the remaining squadron crews attacked from 19,000 to 22,000 feet between 03.06 and 03.18. F/Sgt Campbell RCAF and crew failed to return in ED447, having been brought down by marine flak at the Dutch coast, south of Amsterdam, with the loss of all on board. It had been a sobering start to the year for 101 Squadron, with four crews posted missing from a dozen operations and ninety-two sorties, and, although it was not known at the time, there was not a single survivor among them.

February 1943

The February account was opened at Cologne on the night of the 2/3rd, for which a force of 161 aircraft was made ready, including eight representing 101 Squadron. The plan of attack called for Oboe marking by Mosquitos, along with H2S by Pathfinder heavies in the continuing quest to improve techniques and tactics. Take-off from Holme began at 18.40 with the departure of S/L Ollason, and continued until 17.00, when S/L Fisher was the last to leave the ground. There were no early returns, and the outward flight took place in good conditions, which persisted over the target, where three to six-tenths patchy cloud was encountered, along with ground haze. A small number of crews gained a visual reference, but the majority bombed on Pathfinder markers, the 101 Squadron element doing so from 17,500 to 19,000 feet between 21.05 and 21.12. Returning crews reported many fires, well concentrated around the markers, and the general impression was of a successful attack. This was not supported by a local assessment, however, which reported scattered bombing right across the city, the destruction of sixty-five houses and blast damage to fifteen hundred more, caused by just fifteen cookies.

On the following night, it was the weather that was to provide most of the problems for the force of 263 aircraft setting off for Hamburg. 101 Squadron briefed six crews, who took off either side of 18.00 led by S/L

Fisher, and headed into the kind of heavy, ice-bearing cloud, that would persuade many crews to turn back. Sgt Gillmore was the first of the 101 Squadron contingent to do so, after his oxygen system failed as he approached the Wash. S/L Fisher and F/Sgt Bowyer got as far as Egmond on the Dutch coast, before icing forced them to abandon their sorties. The cloud persisted all the way to the target, where the Pathfinders were unable to provide sustained and concentrated marking by H2S. The three remaining 101 Squadron participants, F/L Tuckwell, P/O Harrower and Sgt Riley, delivered their cookie and twelve SBCs each from 20,000 to 21,000 feet between 21.04 and 21.09, and contributed to the creation of over forty large fires, but the result was not commensurate with the effort expended and the loss of sixteen aircraft. The assault on the port of Lorient continued on the night of the 4/5th, while 188 aircraft set off to cross the Alps and attack Turin. Just four 101 Squadron crews took part, and they took off at 17.45, led by F/L Misselbrook. There were no early returns, and weather conditions remained excellent throughout, with clear skies over the target. Bombing took place visually and on markers from 12,000 to 16,000 feet between 21.39 and 21.42, and all returned safely to report an accurate and concentrated attack, for which, bombing photographs provided confirmation of the severe and widespread damage.

The latest and largest yet attack on Lorient took place in two phases on the night of the 7/8th at the hands of more than three hundred aircraft, and it was the first time that Lancasters had been committed to this target in numbers. 101 Squadron was not involved, but would have gone to Wilhelmshaven twenty-four hours later, had the operation not been cancelled just before take-off because of adverse weather conditions. The same thing happened on the evening of the 9th, after the crews had endured the tensions of being briefed for Wilhelmshaven again, eating their pre-operation meal, donning their flying gear, being conveyed to their aircraft on their dispersal pans, settling in to the aircraft, starting engines and taxiing to the runway, only to be told that it was off. It was this that stretched the nerves, and was far more of a "bind" to the crews than the operation itself. The only consolation was that the early departure time left the rest of the evening free for a pint or two in the mess or local pubs. It happened again on the following night, but Wilhelmshaven could not rely on the weather to protect it indefinitely, and, finally, on the night of the 11/12th, 177 aircraft departed their stations and headed for northern Germany. 101 Squadron dispatched a dozen Lancasters led by S/Ls Fisher and Ollason, which all got away in a ten-minute slot from 17.30, and headed into heavy, ice-bearing cloud. S/L Ollason abandoned his sortie while climbing out, after his instrument panel failed, and P/O Bennee turned back from a few miles east of Spurn Head in the Humber Estuary because of icing. F/Sgt Bowyer had covered more than a hundred miles, and was deep into the North Sea crossing, when icing forced him to turn back also. The others pressed on in the unfavourable conditions to the target on the north-eastern coast of Jade Bay, where the Pathfinders' least reliable H2S-based skymarking technique was to guide them to the aiming-point beneath the cloud. Against all the odds, the marking and main force bombing hit the mark, the 101 Squadron crews carrying out their attacks from 12,000 to 15,500 feet between 20.02 and 20.17. Returning crews were happy with the outcome, and described a huge explosion on the ground, the glow from which lingered for almost ten minutes. It would be established later, that a naval ammunition dump at Mariensiel had been hit, to the west of the dockland, and the resultant explosion had laid waste to a vast area of it and the southern town area. Only three aircraft failed to return, and among them was the squadron's W4313, which was lost without trace with the new, but promising crew of Sgt Hiley RAAF.

The night of the 13/14th was devoted to the largest assault yet on Lorient, for which a force of 466 aircraft was made ready. Thirteen Lancasters lined up for take-off at Holme-on-Spalding-Moor, and they began to roll at 17.30, with the station commander, G/C Blucke, the senior pilot on duty, ably supported by both flight commanders. There were no early returns, and clear skies ensured the accurate delivery, for the first time, of more than a thousand tons of bombs. The 101 Squadron crews dropped their 1,000 pounders and incendiaries from 9,500 to 15,000 feet between 20.34 and 20.50, and contributed to a highly effective and destructive raid, confirmed by three aiming-point photos. While other elements of the Command concentrated on Cologne on the night of the 14/15th, 1, 5 and 8 Groups sent 140 Lancasters across the Alps to Milan, of which twelve were provided by 101 Squadron. They took off between 18.30 and 18.58, with W/C Reddick the senior pilot on duty, and all but two would reach the target. Sgt Miller was thirty miles short of the French coast when an engine-driven pump failed, and P/O Bennee lost the use of all compasses. The weather conditions were perfect, with clear skies and bright moonlight, and most crews were able to identify the target visually. The 101 Squadron contingent bombed from 10,000 to 13,000 feet between 21.38 and 21.54, and returned to report fires visible from a hundred miles into the return trip. Shortly after leaving the target, ED377 was attacked by an Italian Fiat CR42 Falco biplane fighter, which damaged the starboard-outer engine and rear turret, and set fire to the central fuselage, burning out the mid-upper turret, and causing burn wounds to its occupant. The rear gunner also sustained wounds, but the pair managed to shoot down their assailant, before receiving assistance from their crew colleagues. Sgt Hazard warned the crew to prepare to bail out, and the bomb-aimer, P/O Moffatt, mistook it as a firm order, and went out through the front hatch. The port engine caught fire, and Sgt Hazard dived down to 800 feet to successfully extinguish the flames, while the uninjured crew members dealt with the internal fire and assisted their pilot to get the aircraft back to a landing at Tangmere. W/C Reddick recommended Sgt Ivan Hazard and F/Sgt George Dove for a VC, which was supported by the A-O-C 1 Group. Ultimately Harris denied the recommendation, and authorised the award of a CGM, on the basis that they were on their way home after bombing, and had, thus, completed the important part of the operation. Had they been outbound at the time of the incident, a VC may have been granted. The other officer in the crew, wireless operator P/O Gates, was award an immediate DSO, while the NCOs each received the highly-valued and relatively rare CGM.

Sgt Ivan Hazard (centre), his wireless operator, P/O Gates (left) and F/Sgt George Dove, mid-upper gunner (right, with his wife Christine at the investiture ceremony for the awards of DSO and CGMs). Along with the rest of their crew they suffered a torrid op to Milan, bringing back their crippled and burning Lancaster to a landing at Tangmere. Their experience was soon over, unlike the ordeal of the bomb aimer, P/O Moffatt, who mistakenly baled out. The crew was lost the following month when they crashed near Hornsea, East Yorkshire, on a training flight (GW).

The fourth raid of the month on Lorient, and eighth in all, took place on the night of the 16/17th, to bring the campaign to an end. The force of 377 aircraft included twelve Lancasters from 101 Squadron, which took off in an impressive eight-minute slot from 18.30, led by W/C Reddick and both flight commanders. There were no early returns, and the squadron contingent arrived at the target to find clear skies and good bombing conditions. They were each carrying a cookie and twelve SBCs, which were delivered from 6,500 to 13,000 feet between 20.46 and 20.58. They turned for home, leaving a deserted ruin, where once had been a vibrant town and port. The single squadron casualty resulting from this operation was ED374, which had sustained flak damage to the control surfaces, and came down just short of the runway, before bursting into flames. Six of the crew scrambled clear unaided, but the flight engineer had to be pulled clear by S/L Fisher and his air and ground crew, who were in a nearby dispersal. Wilhelmshaven continued to attract attention, and, after a night's rest for the Command, received the first of three more visits within a week. 195 crews were briefed on the 18th, and set off that night for what should have been a routine attack on a familiar target. Twelve 101 Squadron Lancasters took off in a fifteen-minute slot from 18.15, with S/L Ollason the senior pilot on duty, but Sgt Bell's port-outer engine failed immediately, and that was the end of his sortie. The others pushed on, and found the skies over Wilhelmshaven to be clear, allowing the Pathfinders to carry out what they believed to be accurate marking. The 101 Squadron crews bombed from 15,000 to 19,200 feet between 20.33 and 20.41, and returned safely to report a very concentrated and successful attack. Sadly, most of the bombing photos showed the main weight of the raid to have fallen on open country to the west of the town, and the effort was a dismal failure.

A force of 338 aircraft returned to Wilhelmshaven twenty-four hours later, while 101 Squadron stayed at home, and delivered another wasted effort, upon which, it was discovered, that the Pathfinders were employing out-of-date maps. W/C Reddick and S/L Fisher were both in acting ranks, and not paid accordingly, and they received the good news on the 20th, that they were to be remunerated at a level commensurate with their responsibilities! The squadron contributed ten Lancasters to a force of 143 aircraft prepared for an operation to Bremen on the night of the 21/22nd. S/L Ollason was the senior pilot on duty as they began taking off at 18.30, and all reached the target to find it, as forecast by the meteorological brains, hidden by ten-tenths cloud. The 101 Squadron aircraft were carrying a cookie each and twelve SBCs of 30 or 40lb incendiaries, which were dropped onto Pathfinder skymarkers from 15,000 to 19,000 feet between 20.49 and 21.02. All returned safely to Holme-on-Spalding-Moor with little to report other than the glow of fires beneath the clouds. The last of the series of raids on Wilhelmshaven was carried out by elements of 6 and 8 Groups on the night of the 24/25th, and was another dismal failure. 1 Group had received orders to attack Hamburg on that night, and 101 Squadron crews were briefed, but the operation was cancelled because of the weather.

When orders came through on the 25th, they announced a large-scale attack on Nuremberg, for which a force of 337 aircraft was prepared. This would be a first visit to the birthplace of Nazism for 1 Group Lancasters, of which there would be forty-five, a dozen of them representing 101 Squadron. They took off either side of 19.30, with S/L Ollason the senior pilot on duty, and flew out in clear skies that persisted all the way to the target area, where industrial haze, and later, smoke, hindered visual identification. The Pathfinders were late in opening the attack, some reports suggesting by fifteen minutes, but the subsequent marking and bombing were said to be concentrated. The 101 Squadron crews delivered their loads of a cookie and incendiaries from 12,000 to 19,000 feet between 23.19 to 23.38, and all returned safely, with varying ideas as to the outcome. Local reports show the attack to have fallen on the northern fringes of the city and on the neighbouring town of Fürth and beyond, causing damage to around three hundred buildings.

The penultimate operation of the month was directed at Cologne, for which 101 Squadron made ready eleven Lancasters in an overall force of 427 aircraft. The ORB does not provide details of the operation, other than it was led by S/L Fisher, and all returned safely. The weather outbound and over the target was clear, and visibility was only compromised by ground haze. The Pathfinders were again late in opening the attack, but once in progress, it appeared to be accurate and concentrated. In fact, only about 25% of the bomb loads fell into the city, in its south-western corner, and there was damage to residential, commercial, historic and public buildings, but nothing substantial and meaningful. Having dealt with Lorient under the current directive, Harris now turned his attention upon St Nazaire, and sent a force of 427 aircraft there on the last night of the month. 101 Squadron supported the operation with eleven Lancasters led by S/L Fisher. They took off either side of 18.15, and headed south in excellent weather conditions of clear skies and good visibility. The target was easily identified visually and by Pathfinder markers, and the squadron participants bombed from 8,500 to 16,000 feet between 21.12 and 21.31, before returning to report a highly successful raid. For some undisclosed reason, Sgt Bell landed at Dumfries, half an hour after the last arrival at Holme, and one must assume that some kind of navigational error was responsible. The operation was confirmed as an outstanding success, which destroyed an estimated 60% of the town, as well as causing extensive damage to the docks area. The squadron bade farewell to two of its experienced crews, as those of Sgt Ralph and F/Sgt Gillmore finished their tours, and were packed off to do a stint at a training unit. They had earned their rest, but their presence would be missed. During the course of the month the squadron operated eleven time, and dispatched 110 sorties for the loss of two Lancasters and one crew.

March 1943

March would bring the opening rounds in the first major campaign of the year, and the first of the war for which the Command was genuinely equipped and prepared. Before that, however, there would be the small matter of trips to Berlin and Hamburg to negotiate, and preparations were made on the 1st for the former. A force of 302 aircraft included nine Lancasters from 101 Squadron in a 1 Group contribution of forty-two of the type. S/L Fisher was the senior pilot on duty as they took off either side of 18.50, and headed into fine weather conditions of clear skies and good visibility, which would persist throughout the operation. The limitations of H2S over a massive urban sprawl became apparent, as the Pathfinders failed to concentrate the marking over the intended aiming-point. The result was a scattering of bombs over an area of a hundred square miles, with the main emphasis in the south-western districts. Some of the 101 Squadron crews were able to make a visual identification, while the others were guided by the markers, and delivered their cookie and incendiaries each from 15,500 to 18,300 feet between 22.07 and 22.21. They all returned safely, some with flak damage, and reported a highly concentrated and accurate attack, which had left fires burning that were visible from 150 miles away. The reality was that, despite lacking concentration, the raid had, indeed, caused more damage than any previous one, destroying 875 buildings, and inflicting useful damage on war industry factories and railway workshops.

Eleven 101 Squadron Lancasters were made ready for Hamburg on the 3rd, and they were to join 406 other aircraft for the assault on Germany's second city that night. S/L Ollason was the senior pilot on duty as they began departing Holme at 18.30, and only Sgt Smitheringale and crew turned back when thirty miles out from the Yorkshire coast, after the starboard-inner engine began to vibrate excessively. The others made it to the target area, where clear skies provided the opportunity for a successful attack. Unfortunately, and possibly because of relying on H2S, the Pathfinders marked an area to the west of Hamburg, perhaps mistaking the low-tide profile of mud banks on the River Elbe for Hamburg's dockland. Much of the main force element followed up to bomb the town of Wedel, thirteen miles downstream from Hamburg's centre, causing severe

A frost-coated Lancaster, SR-X, sits at dispersal (GW).

damage. Even so, enough bombs fell onto the intended target to start a hundred fires, and these had to be dealt with before assistance could be lent to the neighbouring town. The 101 Squadron crews bombed from 14,500 to 19,000 feet between 21.20 and 21.33, and returned safely, with enthusiastic reports of a successful operation.

Now came the time for Harris to focus upon the Ruhr, and, with the aid of Oboe and a predominantly four-engine bomber force, banish the frustrations of the previous year's efforts to destroy Essen, Duisburg and Düsseldorf. The Ruhr campaign would begin at Essen, home of the Krupp works, on the night of the 5/6th, and a force of 442 aircraft was made ready. 101 Squadron contributed eleven Lancasters to this momentous night, its contingent led by S/L Fisher in ED442. The other Lancasters and crew captains were; ED375 F/L Bigelow, ED372 F/L Misselbrook, ED373 F/L Tuckwell, ED552 P/O Bennee, W4833 F/Sgt Bowyer, ED382 F/Sgt Steele, W4888 Sgt Bell, W4324 Sgt Miller, ED479 Sgt Smitheringale, and W4863 Sgt Stancliffe. They began taking off at 19.00, but S/L Fisher's sortie was over almost before it began, after the port-inner engine failed. Sgt Smitheringale turned back from twenty miles off Lowestoft because of an unserviceable rear turret, and these two were among an unusually high number of early returns, which combined with the bombing of alternative targets to reduce the number of aircraft reaching Essen to 362. These found clear skies and good visibility, and, because of Oboe's ability to "see" through the cloak of industrial haze, the city had lost its protection. The 101 Squadron crews delivered their cookie and SBCs each from 17,000 to 18,600 feet between 21.20 and 21.27, with the exception, that is, of Sgt Stancliffe, who let his go slightly early, when two miles north of the target, after becoming coned by searchlights and stalked by a single-engine enemy fighter. All returned safely, and were of one mind, that they had been part of an outstandingly successful assault on Essen, and had left fires burning that produced a glow in the sky visible from 150 miles away. Post-raid reconnaissance confirmed the destruction of over three thousand houses, with 2,100 others seriously damaged, and revealed also that fifty-three buildings had been hit within the Krupp complex, at a cost to the Command of fourteen aircraft.

It would be a full week before Harris returned to the Ruhr, and, in the meantime, he turned his attention to southern Germany, planning three raids on major cities, beginning with Nuremberg on the night of the 8/9th. A force of 335 aircraft was assembled, of which ten Lancasters were provided by 101 Squadron. They took off between 19.30 and 20.10, but last-away, Sgt Stancliffe, returned immediately with a coolant leak. The others pressed on in good conditions on a moonless night with clear skies, but found ground haze limiting vertical visibility. The Pathfinders marked either visually or by H2S, but failed to achieve concentration, the markers falling along the line of approach up to ten miles short of the city centre. This led to half of the bomb loads falling outside of the city boundaries, although this was not appreciated at the time by the crews. The 101 Squadron crews bombed from 12,000 to 15,000 feet between 23.21 and 23.41, and all returned safely to report on the scattered nature of the markers. In the event, the attack had been delivered with sufficient precision to destroy six hundred buildings, and a number of important war-industry factories sustained damage.

On the following night it was the turn of Munich to host a force that, at take-off, consisted of 264 aircraft, of which eleven Lancasters were provided by 101 Squadron. W/C Reddick was the senior pilot on duty as they began to take-off at 20.00 on another night of favourable weather conditions. F/Sgt Steele and crew reached Dungeness on the Kent coast, before turning back with rear turret oxygen problems, and Sgt Stancliffe was at 16,000 feet, fifteen miles short of the French coast, when his port-outer engine began to overheat. There was only a little high cloud over Munich, and none below bombing altitude, and haze was the only impediment to the visibility. A strong wind drove the marking towards the western half of the city, and the 101 Squadron crews picked these up to bomb from 12,000 to 16,000 feet between 00.11 and 00.25. All returned safely to report many fires and much smoke, and one very large, red explosion. The local authorities confirmed an extensive catalogue of damage to housing, public and military buildings, and industrial concerns, including the BMW factory, where the aero-engine assembly plant was put out of action for six weeks.

After a night's rest, Stuttgart was selected to face a force of 314 aircraft, of which ten Lancasters belonged to 101 Squadron. W/C Reddick again led from the front as they took off either side of 19.45 as part of a 1 Group effort of forty-one aircraft. P/O Kee lost power to his rear turret while still over Holme, and was forced to abandon his sortie. The weather remained good, and the others found the target under clear skies, with just ground haze to impair visibility. The Pathfinders were a little late in opening the attack, and decoy target indicators were employed by the enemy for the first time, but as far as the crews were concerned, it appeared to be an accurate attack. The 101 Squadron crews bombed from 14,000 to 15,000 feet between 23.10 and 23.19, and returned safely to report their impressions. It was established later, that the main weight of the attack had fallen into open country, and that a modest 118 buildings, mostly houses, had been destroyed in two south-western suburbs.

It was now time to resume the Ruhr offensive, and it was to be Essen again on the night of the 12/13th, for which a force of 457 aircraft was made ready. Nine 101 Squadron Lancasters took off in a five-minute slot from 19.15, with S/L Ollason taking the lead. F/Sgt Bowyer turned back from ten miles off Lowestoft with an overheating starboard-outer engine, leaving the others to press on to the target, which was found under clear skies and accurately marked by the Pathfinders. The squadron crews bombed from 15,000 to 18,000 feet between 21.31 and 21.39, and all but one returned safely to report a highly accurate and concentrated raid. Absent from debriefing was the crew of P/O Kee RCAF, whose W4862 had crashed in the target area, killing all on board. Although a new crew, they had shown much promise, and their loss was regretted at Holme-on-Spalding-Moor. Post-raid reconnaissance confirmed this as another highly successful tilt at the old enemy, and whilst substantially fewer buildings were destroyed, the Krupp complex was in the centre of the bombing area, and incurred 30% more damage than a week earlier. It had been a hectic first two weeks of March, and there would be a nine-night stand-down now for the heavy squadrons as the weather changed, and planned operations were cancelled. Despite the lack of operations, the squadron lost a crew to a flying accident on the 20th. ED446 crashed at 11.00 at Atwick, three miles north of Hornsea on the Yorkshire coast, during an air-test being carried out by Sgt Hazard and his crew, plus an eighth man attached to the squadron from Training Command. They were apparently engaged in low-level flying at the time, and all eight men lost their lives.

Support for the hard-pressed merchant seamen continued with the next attack on St Nazaire, which took place on the night of the 22/23rd. 101 Squadron contributed eight Lancasters to the overall force of 357 aircraft, which was reduced, when fifty-five of sixty-three Stirlings picked up a recall signal from 3 Group. S/L Fisher was the senior pilot on duty as they departed Holme-on-Spalding-Moor either side of 18.45, carrying ten 1,000 pounders each, one of which contained a delayed action fuse. There were no early returns, and all reached the target to find clear skies and moderate visibility. The squadron crews bombed from 13,200 to 16,000 feet between 21.38 and 21.49, and contributed to a punishing attack on the port. Just one aircraft was lost, and that was ED375 of 101 Squadron, which crashed in the target area, killing Sgt Lewis and his crew, who were on their first operation. A return to the Ruhr on the night of the 26/27th would be directed at Duisburg, for which a force of 455 aircraft was prepared. 101 Squadron put up ten Lancasters, which took off either side of 19.30, led by S/L Fisher. F/Sgt Steel lost his starboard-outer engine as he climbed out, and had to abandon his sortie, leaving the others to continue on to find the target hidden beneath ten-tenths cloud. One of the Oboe Mosquitos was lost on the way out, and five others returned early with technical issues, thus reducing the effectiveness of the marking. The 101 Squadron participants bombed on Pathfinder skymarkers from 16,000 to 20,000 feet between 22.10 and 22.23, and returned to report the glow of fires through the cloud, but little else. Duisburg had, in fact, escaped with superficial damage amounting to fifteen houses destroyed and seventy damaged, and its charmed life would continue for a further seven weeks.

The following night brought another attack on Berlin, for which a force of 396 aircraft was assembled, which included a contribution of ten Lancasters from 101 Squadron. They departed Holme either side of 20.00, and set off to climb through ten-tenths cloud, which would persist until twenty miles from the German Capital. Sgt Smitheringale was forty miles off Scarborough when he became indisposed, and had to turn back, while F/Sgt Steel was forty miles north-east of Sheringham, when his wireless operator reported an eye problem that forced them to abandon their sortie. The others benefitted from the clear skies over Berlin as they approached from the south, but the Pathfinders missed the opportunity to exploit the conditions, and established two areas of marking, both short of the city. The squadron crews bombed from 16,000 to 18,200 feet between 22.45 to 23.08, and all but one returned with a variety of impressions concerning the effectiveness of the attack, ranging from very concentrated to scattered over a six-mile radius. The latter was the more accurate, the majority of the bombs having fallen seven to seventeen miles from the city centre, and causing no significant damage. W4322 was one of nine missing aircraft, and had crashed at Wunstorf, west of Hannover, with no survivors from the crew of Sgt Bell.

The squadron sat out the latest raid on St Nazaire on the night of the 28/29th, but had two crews out training. P/O Hobday and his freshman crew had taken off in ED522 at 03.31 for a cross-country exercise, and, on return to the Holme-on-Spalding-Moor circuit, had collided with trees at South Cliffe, four miles south-east of the airfield, and crashed, killing all but the rear gunner. That night, the squadron was scheduled to participate in a return to Berlin, but a last-minute change of runway caused so much confusion, that it was cancelled. In the event, adverse weather conditions contributed to another disappointing outcome at the Capital. F/L Misselbrook and P/O Bennee were declared tour-expired at the end of the month, and were posted to a training unit at Blyton for a well-earned rest. The squadron operated ten times during the month, and launched ninety-nine sorties for the loss of six aircraft and crews.

April 1943

April would prove to be the least rewarding month of the Ruhr period, but this was largely because of the number of operations mounted to targets in other regions of Germany, beyond the range of Oboe. 101 Squadron introduced a third or C Flight at the start of the month, in keeping with the Command's expansion programme that saw many squadrons take on additional aircraft and crews. In most cases the C Flight would be hived off as the nucleus in the formation of an entirely new squadron, usually occupying the same station, initially at least. Ten crews were called to briefing on the 2nd, and were assigned to one of three operations planned for that night. Five would be part of the final raid of the series against Lorient, while the freshman crew of F/Sgt Gray would be the sole squadron representatives on the final attack on Lorient, both under the January directive, from which the Command was about to be released. At the same time, four others were to carry out mining duties at the southern end of the French Biscay coast off Biarritz. They were airborne for their respective target areas between 19.30 and 20.40, with S/L Fisher leading the gardeners, each of which was carrying five parachute mines. They reached the target area after a flight lasting around three and a half hours, and found ten-tenths cloud with a base at 1,000 feet. They pinpointed on the River Adour, before making their timed runs, and delivering their vegetables from 900 to 1,100 feet between 22.59 and 23.12. Sgt Gray dropped his bombs out of clear skies onto St Nazaire from 15,000 feet at 22.27, and reported a well-concentrated attack and very satisfactory trip. A similar sentiment was expressed by the crews returning from Lorient, where they had bombed from 14,000 to 16,000 feet between 23.13 and 23.20.

Above Left: Robert "Bob" Quarterman, an American (centre), joined the squadron as a sergeant pilot in spring of 1943, and by the end of his tour in August 1943 had risen to Warrant Officer. Right: Quarterman's ground crew (GW).

The Ruhr campaign continued promisingly at Essen on the night of the 3/4th, for which the squadron contributed a record seventeen crews, six each from A and B Flights and five from C Flight. They took off between 19.30 and 20.00 with S/L Ollason the senior pilot on duty. P/O Nelson lost his starboard-outer engine during the climb out, F/Sgt Steel was approaching the Lincolnshire coast north of Skegness, when his port-outer engine failed, and Sgt Quarterman was twenty-five miles off Lowestoft, when he finally gave up on an oil pressure problem afflicting his port-inner engine. The alarm bells had started ringing at 20.45, but he had pressed on for a further thirty minutes in the vain hope that it would rectify itself. The others reached the target, where clear skies and good visibility offered another chance to pound this important city. The defences had other ideas, however, and the flak barrage was described by returning crews as the most intense ever. The squadron crews bombed from 15,000 to 20,000 feet between 22.04 and 22.18, Sgt Hamilton suffering an engine failure over the target, but returning safely on three from what was the crew's maiden operation. S/L Ollason was homebound over the Amsterdam area, when a flak shell exploded nearby, badly damaging the Lancaster, killing the mid-upper gunner, Sgt Gadd, and seriously wounding the rear gunner, Sgt Foy. The remaining crew members nursed the Lancaster home, where the sad news of the casualties was compounded by the failure to return of F/O Johnson and crew, who were all killed, when ED736 crashed in the Bocholt-Borkum area north of the Ruhr.

The largest non-1,000 force to date, of 577 aircraft, was made ready on the 4th for an operation that night to the naval port of Kiel. 101 Squadron contributed twelve Lancasters, which took off either side of 18.30, led by S/L Fisher. The cloud thickened as the crews made their way eastwards over the North Sea, relying on their instruments to keep them on an even keel and get them to the target. Sgt Stancliffe was the first of three early returns, and was fifty miles east of Flamborough Head when he became too ill to continue. F/L Manahan was some eighty miles short of the Schleswig-Holstein coast when he turned back, complaining that W4833 had become unmanageable and impossible to fly on instruments. Sgt Gray had strayed over northern Germany, and was fifty miles south-west of Hamburg, when his starboard-inner engine failed and forced him to give up. The others found the target hidden under ten-tenths cloud with tops at 14,000 feet and above, and, with no ground reference, the success of the operation relied entirely upon the accuracy of the Pathfinders, whose task was made more difficult by strong winds. The 101 Squadron crews bombed on the Pathfinder skymarkers from 16,000 to 19,000 feet between 23.04 and 23.29, and returned to report a satisfactory trip. The operation was a complete failure that missed the target almost entirely, for which the glow of decoy fire sites may have been partly responsible. This demonstrated again, that attacks beyond the range of Oboe were still something of a lottery.

392 aircraft were made ready for Duisburg on the 8th, ten of the Lancasters provided by 101 Squadron, and they began departing Holme at 21.05, with F/Ls Bigelow, Manahan and Tuckwell the senior pilots on duty. Ten-tenths cloud built up from the Dutch coast to the target with tops at 20,000 feet, and no Pathfinder flares were seen, forcing the crews to bomb on ETA. The 101 Squadron participants delivered their cookie and incendiaries each from 16,000 to 21,000 feet between 23.29 and 23.45, and returned to report mostly an unsatisfactory effort. Local reports listed forty buildings destroyed and seventy-two seriously damaged, which represented a result clearly not commensurate with the commitment of such a large force. Harris tried again at the same target on the following night, this time with a reduced all-Lancaster heavy force of 104 aircraft. 101 Squadron briefed eight crews, led again by the same trio of flight lieutenants, and they took off at 20.20 on another cloudy night. F/L Manahan and F/Sgt Bowyer were beyond the mid-point of the North Sea crossing, and in close proximity, when both suffered port-inner engine failures, and had to turn back. ED618 had crossed the Dutch coast near Haarlem, and was making its way inland, when it was attacked at 22.45 by a night fighter flown by Lt Oskar Köstler of IV/NJG1. The Lancaster exploded with such force, that debris

struck the enemy aircraft and killed the pilot, before the rest of the remains of the bomber fell at Doornswijk, just south of Elburg. There were no survivors from the crew of F/Sgt Steel RCAF, and the loss of this experienced crew would not be the only one suffered by the squadron on this night. ED608 was hit by flak at 21,000 feet over the target, and went down with both gunners still on board. P/O Nelson RAAF and four others in this predominantly RAAF crew, had occupied the front section of the aircraft, and escaped by parachute to fall into the arms of their captors. The target was concealed by a thin layer of ten-tenths cloud, and bombing by the squadron element was aimed at Pathfinder release-point flares and ground markers. They delivered their cookie and incendiaries each from 19,400 to 21,000 feet between 23.07 and 23.16, and returned home to report a satisfactory trip, but no revealing impressions of the outcome. It had been another scattered attack, which destroyed a modest fifty houses, a poor return for the loss of eight Lancasters and crews.

There was a late take-off for nine 101 Squadron crews on the night of the 10/11th, who were bound for Frankfurt as part of a force of five hundred aircraft, which, remarkably, for this stage of the war, still featured more Wellingtons than any other type. They departed Holme-on-Spalding-Moor either side of midnight, led by W/C Reddick, and flew into cloud, above which, the visibility was excellent. F/Sgt Gray turned back with engine and turret issues, leaving the others to push on to the target, where ten-tenths cloud between 6,000 and 10,000 feet concealed the ground. The Pathfinders employed a mixture of sky and ground marking techniques, which disappeared into the cloud and became scattered, providing the main force crews with a confusing choice of aiming-points. The 101 Squadron bombing took place from 16,000 to 18,000 feet between 02.44 and 03.06, and all returned safely with no clue as to the outcome. Sadly, it had been another wasted effort, which almost entirely missed the city.

A force of 208 Lancasters and three Halifaxes took off for Italy on the evening of the 13th, to bomb the docks at La Spezia on the north-western coast. 101 Squadron dispatched a record nineteen Lancasters, which were all safely airborne by 20.15, led by W/C Reddick. Sgt Fee and crew were undertaking their first operation, and lost their port-outer engine as they climbed out. They jettisoned the bomb load off Flamborough Head, and returned to base, where ED807 crashed without survivors on the south-western side of the airfield. Sgt Hamilton and crew were over the Channel some thirty miles south of Worthing, when both outer engines cut, and forced them to turn back. They flew slowly to a point fifty miles east of Flamborough Head to jettison the bombs safe at 23.33, and landed at Holme at 00.45. The others pressed on to the target, where they were greeted by clear skies and good visibility, with only ground haze and smoke screens to hamper visibility. The Pathfinder marking was accurate and concentrated, and the main force exploited the opportunity to cause heavy damage. The 101 Squadron crews were each carrying five 1,000 pounders and incendiaries, and delivered them from 6,000 to 11,000 feet between 01.37 and 02.23, before returning home or to diversion airfields to report a successful raid, which was confirmed by aiming-point photos. Stuttgart was the target for the night of the 14/15th, for which a force of 462 aircraft was made ready. 101 Squadron contributed the crew of Sgt Hamilton, who all lost their lives when W4951 crashed in north-eastern France, close to the Belgian border. The operation achieved some useful damage to war-industry factories in the Bad-Canstatt district in the north of the city, and in neighbouring areas, where a total of 393 buildings were destroyed at a cost to the Command of twenty-three aircraft. Earlier in the day, F/L Craig had been officially appointed as C Flight commander, and news had been received, that S/L Sturgess was on his way from 30 O.T.U to take over B Flight.

Harris divided his forces on the night of the 16/17th, so that he could target the important Skoda armaments works at Pilsen in Czechoslovakia, and distract the enemy defences by attacking Mannheim as a diversion. A force of 327 Lancasters and Halifaxes was made ready for the former, while 271 Wellingtons, Stirlings and

Halifax crews were briefed for the latter. The plan of attack at Pilsen was, in many ways, one which invited chaos because of its departure from standard practice. The Pathfinders were not to mark the target, but lay route markers seven miles away as a guide to the main force crews, who were to locate the factory visually, and attack it from low level. 101 Squadron provided fifteen Lancasters, which took off in a half-hour slot from 20.50. Sgt Cunningham abandoned his sortie when east of Peterborough, after his port-inner engine failed, and F/O Stanford had just passed Dartford in Kent when his starboard-inner stopped. Both jettisoned their bombs over the sea before returning safely. Sgt Brook and crew lost oil pressure in their starboard-inner engine, and dropped their bombs on Saarbrücken from 8,000 feet at 00.02, before heading home. Sgt Wilkins and crew were coned by searchlights and picked up fifteen holes courtesy of flak, which persuaded them to bomb Karlsruhe from 3,000 feet at 00.29. Sgt Sloper and crew were falling behind schedule as they crossed into Germany, and, realising they would be too late to attack the primary target, also dropped their bombs on Saarbrücken, in their case from 6,000 feet at 01.01. F/Sgt Kelly and crew were coned by searchlights between Mannheim and Karlsruhe, and then hit by flak, which damaged the starboard mainplane. All thoughts of attacking the primary target were abandoned, and the bombs were dropped on Karlsruhe from 3,000 feet instead.

The others continued on, crossing the known fighter belt at low level, and reaching the target area under clear skies and bright moonlight. The Pathfinders dropped their route markers as planned, and some of the early arrivals among the main force decided to bomb them, creating confusion for those following on behind, and smoke to obscure the ground. The 101 Squadron crews carried out their attacks from 6,000 to 9,000 feet between 01.41 and 02.06, and all but one returned to claim a very satisfactory trip. F/L Bigelow commented, that if the PFF markers were accurate, then so was the attack, and that encapsulated the entire problem. The markers were not intended to identify the target, but just the final turning point. Despite claims by a proportion of returning crews that the factory complex had sustained heavy damage, it had, in fact, not received any bombs, and, it was an asylum building seven miles away that had attracted them. The disappointment, once discovered, was compounded by the loss of thirty-six aircraft, divided evenly between the two types, and among them was ED379, which crashed in southern Germany, killing F/Sgt Menzies RAAF and all but one of his crew, who became a PoW. A further eighteen aircraft were lost from the diversion, which did, at least, inflict considerable damage on Mannheim, and this brought the night's total of missing aircraft to a new record of fifty-four.

A return to La Spezia on the night of the 18/19th involved fifteen 101 Squadron Lancasters in an overall force of 178 aircraft. W/C Reddick was the senior pilot on duty, and flying with him in ED608, on his "second-dickie" trip, was the recently-arrived S/L St John. They took off either side of 21.00, and F/L Bigelow was almost within sight of Bury St Edmunds when his intercom failed, ending his part in the proceedings. F/Sgt Gray was approaching the French coast north-east of Caen, when an oil leak forced him to shut down the port-inner engine. He dropped his bombs from 15,000 feet onto a flak position on or just off the coast at 00.15, and hoped they had hit something of value. The others arrived at the target to find clear skies and excellent visibility, and delivered their five 1,000 pounders and incendiaries each from 5,500 to 8,500 feet between 01.50 and 02.10, before returning safely to report a very successful trip. Reconnaissance showed that the main weight of the attack had fallen north-west of the docks, hitting the main railway station and many public buildings.

Stettin provided the next long-range destination, and involved a roughly 1,500-mile round trip to the eastern end of Germany's Baltic coast. A force of 339 aircraft was made ready on the 20th, of which sixteen Lancasters were provided by 101 Squadron. There were no senior officers on duty as they began taking off at 21.25, and

Crews pose for a publicity photo in briefing before the Stettin raid on 20th April 1943. Sixteen crews took part from 101 Sqn, one turning back with engine problems and another sustaining flak damage. Ultimately, however, all returned to base (Crown copyright).

it was left to F/Ls Bigelow, McCullough and Manahan to lead the way. Sgt Smith was a hundred miles out from Flamborough Head when his starboard-inner engine failed, and he dumped his cookie and incendiaries into the North Sea at 22.42. The weather conditions were excellent for the operation, with clear skies and bright moonlight, and this aided navigation as the force made its way at low level across Denmark, before climbing to bombing height at the German coast. It was while approaching landfall over Germany at 5,000 feet, that ED422 was hit by flak, probably fired from one of the many flak ships moored off the coast. The port-outer engine was set on fire, the mid-upper turret was put out of action, and a fuel tank was holed, forcing F/Sgt Gray to jettison the bomb load at 00.32, and head back home. The others from the squadron reached the target after climbing to 12,000 feet, although, when the time came to deliver their bombs, the altitudes ranged from 10,000 to 14,000 feet. They dropped their hardware on Pathfinder markers or by visual identification of the aiming-point between 01.08 and 01.25, and contributed to an outstandingly concentrated attack, which devastated the centre of the town, destroying 380 houses and thirteen industrial premises.

Harris returned to the Ruhr on the night of the 26/27th, to take another swipe at Duisburg. 101 Squadron prepared sixteen Lancasters as part of an overall force of 561 aircraft, and they took off either side of midnight, led by W/C Reddick and S/L St John, who was operating with the squadron as crew captain for the first time. W/C Reddick's navigator was S/L Greig, who had recently arrived on the squadron, and would shortly be

The Quarterman crew with their Lancaster SR-F (GW)

confirmed as C Flight commander. F/Sgt Gray's luck deserted him again, as his port-inner engine failed soon after take-off, and he proceeded out to sea to jettison his load. Sgt Margerum was twenty miles out from the Dutch coast at Haarlem when his instruments failed, and he was the only other squadron participant to turn back. The remainder continued on to the target over a layer of ten-tenths cloud, which cleared as the target drew near, and allowed good general visibility, while the industrial haze obscured ground detail. The squadron crews delivered their cookie and incendiaries each from 17,000 to 19,500 feet between 02.21 and 02.45, and W/C Reddick reported fires visible from 150 miles away. The consensus was that, if the Pathfinder markers had been accurate, then so had been the attack. Post-raid reconnaissance showed the marking to have been to the north-east of the city, but, even so, the operation was partially successful, and resulted in the destruction of three hundred buildings.

The largest mining effort to date took place in French and Dutch coastal waters on the night of the 27/28th, for which 101 Squadron briefed five crews. They took off shortly after 21.30 for the waters off south Biscay, and F/Sgt Gray's ill-luck continued, as he again returned early with a failed engine after reaching the Sussex coast at Selsey Bill. The remainder all reached the target area, where, in contrast to the other gardens, they encountered clear skies, but extreme darkness and poor visibility. They picked up their visual pinpoints and made timed runs to the drop zones, where they delivered five mines each from 800 and 900 feet between 01.37 and 01.59. Only one aircraft was missing from the 160 taking part on this night, and that was 101 Squadron's ED728, which contained the crew of Sgt Margerum. A returning crew reported observing an aircraft being held in searchlights in the target area, and being shot down by light flak. An even larger mine-laying force of 207 aircraft was sent to northern waters on the following night, and incurred the heaviest loss to date from this type of operation. Twenty-two aircraft failed to return, but the number of mines laid, 593, was also a new record for a single night.

The month closed with another attack on Essen, for which 101 Squadron put up fourteen Lancasters, as part of an overall force of 305 aircraft. They were led for the first time by S/L St John, and took off either side of 23.30 for what was planned to be a blind-bombing operation in conditions of ten-tenths cloud. Undertaking his first operation with the squadron on this night as second pilot to Sgt Brook was F/O Scrimgeour-

Wedderburn, and there was not an adjutant in the world prepared to write up the full name every time he operated. For this reason, during his long association with the squadron spanning two tours, he would always be referred to in the ORB as 'F/L S-Wedderburn'. F/S Foran lost his port-outer engine soon after take-off, but he was the only early return, and the others pressed on to find cloud as forecast, with tops as high as 17,000 feet. The 101 Squadron crews were carrying the usual cookie and incendiary loads, which they delivered from 19,000 to 22,000 feet between 02.36 and 02.48, and returned to report observing nothing of interest. The cloud prevented any bombing photos from being taken, but local reports showed fresh damage across the city, and the destruction of 189 buildings, with further hits on the Krupp works, as well as on other Ruhr locations. During the course of this busy month, the squadron operated against sixteen targets, including mining locations, and dispatched 167 sorties for the loss of seven Lancasters and crews.

W4995, SR-N (N-Nuts) was frequently flown by F/L Scrimgeour-Wedderburn and crew, who are believed to be shown in the photo (left) along with members of ground crew. N-Nuts survived her time with 101 Sqn, being eventually passed on to 625 Sqn. Below: Bombing up Lancaster SR-I, date and target not known. (GW).

May 1943

May would bring a return to winning ways with some spectacular successes, but it began with operations called and then cancelled on the first three nights. A new record non-1,000 force of 596 aircraft was made ready on the 4th to continue the Ruhr offensive at Dortmund. 101 Squadron put up eighteen Lancasters, which departed Holme-on-Spalding-Moor between 21.25 and 22.10, led for the first time by S/L Sturgess, and with F/O S-Wedderburn operating as crew captain for the first time. It was to be a night to forget for the squadron, which began with F/O Hull losing his port-outer engine during the climb-out, and jettisoning his bombs before returning home. F/L Bigelow's port-inner engine let go some fifty miles east of Mablethorpe, while S/L Sturgess was in sight of Texel, when his port-outer engine caught fire, and they were forced to abandon their sorties also. The others found the target under clear skies, with only ground haze to impair visibility, and they delivered their standard mixed loads of high explosives and incendiaries onto Pathfinder markers from 20,000 to 22,000 feet between 01.03 and 01.48. On return, W4863 crashed at Scorton, east-south-east of Richmond in Yorkshire, killing Sgt Browning RNZAF, and three of his crew, and injuring the others. ED776 crashed short of the runway at 03.20, and ran into a radar hut, but F/Sgt Kelly and crew emerged unscathed. ED835 returned with severe flak damage, and crashed ten miles south-west of Beverley at 03.42, killing F/Sgt Hough and two of his crew, and injuring the others on board. ED830 struck trees and crashed three miles south-west of Linton-on-Ouse airfield at 04.30, but Sgt Smith and crew walked away with only bruises to show for their experience. W4784 disappeared without trace with the crew of Sgt Nicholson, who were operating for the

F/L Bigelow and crew (GW)

108

first time, and W4888 was shot down by Oblt Lothar Linke of IV/NJG1, and crashed at 01.40 at Workum, on the north-eastern shore of the Ijsselmeer, killing F/O Stanford and all but his navigator, who became a PoW. The wireless operator, P/O Lewis DFM, RCAF, was a very popular member of the squadron, who had just returned for a second tour. Despite decoy fires attracting a proportion of the bombing, central and northern districts of Dortmund were hit extremely hard, and over twelve hundred buildings were destroyed, while two thousand others, some of an important industrial nature, sustained serious damage. However, the loss of thirty-one aircraft was the highest from a Ruhr target thus far during the campaign, and it would set something of a trend as the defenders geared up for the continuing fight.

A lull in main force activity preceded the next major operation, which was mounted against Duisburg on the night of the 12/13th. A force of 572 aircraft was assembled, of which just five represented 101 Squadron. Eighteen had been detailed, but one became bogged down while taxiing, and prevented thirteen others from taking off. Those able to reach the threshold became airborne between 22.45 and 23.35, with F/L McCullough the senior pilot on duty. F/Sgt Gray's bad luck returned to him, as he became a victim of the severe icing conditions in the cloud over base, and could not continue. By the time the target hove into view, the skies had cleared to provide good visibility, and the aircraft of the first wave, which included the squadron's F/O Hull, were each carrying an all HE load of three 2,000 and six 1,000 pounders. They dropped these onto the concentrated Pathfinder markers, and, by 02.15, fifteen minutes after zero-hour, large fires had taken hold. The squadron crews bombed from 18,500 to 20,000 feet between 02.05 and 02.33, and returned full of enthusiasm for the quality of the raid. This time there had been no escape for Germany's largest inland port, and more than sixteen hundred buildings were left in ruins, while sixty thousand tons of shipping was sunk or seriously damaged. On the debit side, the thirty-four missing bombers represented a new record for the campaign.

While 5 Group set off to attempt to rectify the recent failure at Pilsen on the night of the 13/14th, Bochum was selected to host the latest round in the Ruhr campaign, A force of 442 aircraft included seventeen 101 Squadron Lancasters, which took off either side of midnight led by S/Ls St John and Sturgess. A new route into the Ruhr was tested on this night, a "back door" entry over Mönchengladbach and between Düsseldorf to the north and Cologne to the south, which, it was believed at the time, would provide a corridor through the flak belt. This proved not to be the case, and some crews experienced a torrid time crossing the Rhine. Sgt Cunningham turned back thirty miles before reaching the Belgian coast because of rising temperatures in both port engines, but the remainder carried on in good weather conditions, and approached Bochum from the south under clear skies and with good visibility. The 101 Squadron aircraft were carrying either a cookie and incendiaries each or three 2,000 and six 1,000 pounders, and these were dropped onto red target indicators (TIs) from 18,000 to 21,000 feet in the face of a spirited flak defence between 02.06 and 02.40. The usual large explosions were observed, and one in particular sent a pall of black smoke skyward, suggesting that someone had "struck oil". The effects of the raid were visible from the Dutch coast, and all of the 101 Squadron crews returned very satisfied with their night's work. It was established later, that decoy markers had drawn off a proportion of the bombing, but the attack had destroyed 394 buildings, and seriously damaged a further seven hundred, at a cost to the Command of twenty-four aircraft.

During the ensuing nine-day break in main force operations, 617 Squadron wrote its name into history with its epic attack on the Möhne, Eder and Sorpe dams on the night of the 16/17th, an operation which remains to this day, the greatest feat of arms in aviation history. On the following night, 101 Squadron sent two crews mining in the Furze region between Biarritz and the Spanish frontier. Sgts Quarterman and Groome took off at 21.50, and dropped their six vegetables each from 800 and 1,000 feet between 01.53 and 01.50 respectively, after making timed runs of forty-nine and fifty-eight seconds from pre-selected pinpoints. Four crews set off to return to the same area at 21.55 on the night of the 20/21st, and all arrived safely, but Sgt Cunningham abandoned his sortie at 01.46 because of low cloud. The others carried out timed runs from Pointe de Biarritz, and delivered their mines as briefed from 1,000 to 2,000 feet between 01.57 and 02.06.

Thereafter, it was back to work for the rest of the Command on the night of the 23/24th. For the second time in the month, Dortmund was to host a new record non-1,000 force, this time of 826 aircraft. This was 230 aircraft more than the previous record, and was made possible by the previously-mentioned rampant expansion going on within the Command. 1 Group put up a record 180 Lancasters, topped by 103 Squadron with a massive twenty-seven, closely followed by 101 Squadron, which launched twenty-five Lancasters between 21.40 and 22.30. The senior pilot on duty was S/L Sturgess, and the vast majority of crews were captained by NCO pilots. There was bound to be some fallout from such a large effort, and S/L Sturgess, F/Sgt Foran and Sgt Quarterman all abandoned their sorties over base because of engine and other technical problems. Sgt Fry had made landfall on the eastern shore of the Ijsselmeer when first the starboard-inner engine, and then the outer failed, and the cookie was dropped from 18,000 feet into the inland sea at 01.34. They headed home with an engine on fire, and, while attempting to land at Coltishall in Norfolk, ED775 crashed at 02.50 near North Walsham, causing injuries to the navigator, Sgt Leedham, to which he would succumb. The other crew members were able to walk away from the wreckage, apparently unscathed. The remainder pressed on in clear weather conditions, which persisted all the way to the target, and assisted the Pathfinder crews in identifying the aiming-point. The 101 Squadron crews bombed from 17,000 to 22,500 feet between 01.06 and 01.49, and all but one returned safely to report a highly concentrated and successful attack, the fires from which were still visible as a glow from a hundred miles away. The defenders fought back, and claimed yet another record haul for the campaign, this time of thirty-eight aircraft, and 101 Squadron was represented among them by W4919, which was shot down by a night fighter, and crashed at 02.33 on the east bank of the River Maas at Bergen, just inside Holland's border with Germany. There were no survivors from the new but promising crew of F/S Hayes RAAF. Post-raid reconnaissance revealed that the attack had devastated large areas of the city, destroying almost two thousand buildings, and inflicting damage upon important war-industry factories. This was the final operation of F/L Bigelow's tour, and, after an appropriate amount of beer had flowed, he would be packed off to 1667 Conversion Unit on the 9th of June to begin his stint as an instructor.

A force of 759 aircraft was assembled on the 25th to attack Düsseldorf that night, and 101 Squadron contributed twenty-three Lancasters. They took off between 22.30 and 23.55, depending upon their scheduled spot in the attack, and S/L Sturgess was the senior pilot on duty. Sgt Shattock and crew turned back when half way across the North Sea with a malfunctioning mid-upper turret and IFF system, but the others continued on to approach the target from the north. The weather conditions on this night were less favourable, and eight to ten-tenths cloud in two layers awaited the crews' arrival over the Ruhr. This created difficulties for the Pathfinders, who failed to achieve any concentration, and decoy fire sites may also have contributed to what developed into a widely scattered attack. No more than a hundred buildings were destroyed in return for the loss of twenty-seven bombers, among which was 101 Squadron's ED660. The Lancaster was shot down by a night fighter, and crashed a dozen miles north-west of Eindhoven in southern Holland at 01.53, with no survivors from the crew of Sgt Tindale.

Yet another attack on Essen was scheduled for the night of the 27/28th, for which 101 Squadron contributed twenty-one Lancasters to an overall force of 518 aircraft. F/Ls McCullough and Wedderburn were the senior pilots on duty as the squadron departed Holme-on-Spalding-Moor between 22.05 and 22.45, and headed into

Joe for King, SR-K², DV299, photographed at Holme-on-Spalding Moor in May / June 1943. She was lost without trace on 16/17th December 1943 along with the crew of F/Sgt Head. The motto on the shield reads 'Man of Steel' whilst the ops tally is designated by crossed Soviet and British flags (GW).

cloudy skies. The conditions had been anticipated, and a skymarking plan prepared, which the Pathfinders carried out with apparent accuracy, attracting praise from the main force crews on their return. There were no early returns among the 101 Squadron contingent, and they bombed from 19,000 to 22,000 feet between 00.52 and 01.34, before returning safely to report observing fires, one of which was large and issuing black smoke. It was established later, that the attack had undershot somewhat, and had been scattered largely across the northern districts, where almost five hundred buildings were destroyed. In the context of the campaign, the loss of twenty-three aircraft could be considered relatively modest.

Although not all the Ruhr operations to date had been outstanding successes, and a good proportion of the bombing had fallen wide of the mark, every now and then the plan worked perfectly, and total devastation was inflicted upon the target town or city. Wuppertal, a previously untouched conurbation consisting of the towns of Barmen and Elberfeld, nestles in a valley at the south-eastern end of the Ruhr, and was the next in line to host Harris's legions. A force of 719 aircraft was made ready on the 29th, of which twenty-two belonged to 101 Squadron. The target on this night was the Barmen half, for which the 101 Squadron participants took off between 21.50 and 22.40, with S/L St John the senior pilot on duty. Sgt Johnson had just entered southern Holland via the western Scheldt, when his port-outer engine failed, forcing him to turn back from a dozen miles west of Antwerp. The others pressed on to the target through the supposed gap in the defences between Düsseldorf and Cologne, and those that survived would confirm that no such gap existed. The conditions over the target were clear, with only ground haze, and later smoke, to hamper the vertical visibility. The Pathfinders produced accurate and concentrated marking, which the main force element exploited to devastating effect. The 101 Squadron crews bombed from 19,000 to 22,000 feet between 00.41 and 01.35, and contributed to one of the most destructive raids of the campaign. Almost four thousand houses were reduced to rubble, along with five large and over two hundred smaller factories, and approximately 80% of the built-up area was wiped out by fire. The inhabitants also underwent a terrible ordeal, and the death toll was estimated at around 3,400 people. The defenders had their say, however, and thirty-three bombers were hacked down, although 101 Squadron came through unscathed, and this brought the month's proceedings to an end. 137 sorties were dispatched during the month on nine operations, which had resulted in the loss of nine Lancasters, four complete crews and isolated members of other crews.

June 1943

No major operations took place during the first ten nights of the new month, and squadrons took the opportunity to put the less experienced crews through as much training as possible. At 101 Squadron, fighter affiliation, bombing practice, air-firing and cross-country exercises took priority, and, as there were "Wings for Victory" celebrations going on around the country, W/C Reddick led a trio from the squadron in a pass over York on the 5th and again on the 7th. A number of operations were announced and then cancelled, until the 11th, when a force of 783 aircraft was put together to attack Düsseldorf. 101 Squadron detailed a record twenty-six Lancasters, but, at start-up, F/Sgt Naffin's aircraft was found to be unserviceable, as was the spare, and, ultimately, it was a record-equalling twenty-five Lancasters that departed Holme-on-Spalding-Moor between 22.20 and 23.20, led by S/L Sturgess. They climbed into ice-bearing cloud, which would cause

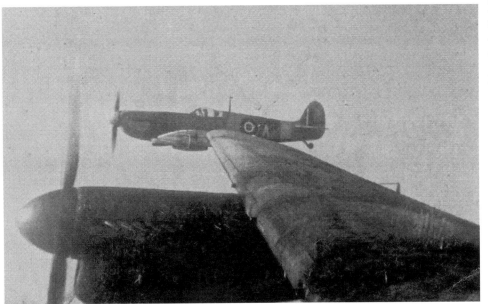

problems for a number of crews, but it was a fainting wireless operator that forced P/O Day to turn back just after midnight. Sgt Athey had dragged W4966 to 20,000 feet over the North Sea, but was unable to coax more than 135 mph out of her, and turned back from twenty miles off the Suffolk coast. F/Sgt Gray lost his port-inner engine a dozen miles north-west of Antwerp, and also had to call it a night. The others pressed on south-eastwards in decreasing cloud, and reached the target it to find it relatively clear and Pathfinder markers already outlining the aiming-point.

Better with us, than against us... A Spitfire flies alongside a 101 Sqn Lancaster. Fighter affiliation was a vital part of the training programme. In reality, the Luftwaffe was much harder to see and evade (GW).

The 101 Squadron crews bombed from 19,500 to 22,000 feet between 01.22 and 02.18, and returned to report a concentrated raid, which had left many fires burning. An Oboe Mosquito probably drew off some of the bomb loads, after inadvertently releasing TIs fourteen miles north-east of the target, but the majority landed where intended, and reconnaissance photos revealed 130 acres of devastation in central districts. Local reports told of almost nine thousand fires in an area measuring 8 x 5 kilometres, dozens of war industry factories losing vital production, eight ships being sunk or damaged, and 140,000 people being rendered homeless. The cost to the Command was again high, at thirty-eight aircraft, which matched the record loss at Dortmund in early May. The fearsome reputation of "Happy Valley" was now set for all time.

A month after its first heavy raid, Bochum was scheduled for a further visit on the night of the 12/13th, for which a force of 503 aircraft was made ready. 101 Squadron detailed twenty-three Lancasters and crews, with S/L Sturgess again the senior pilot on duty. They took off between 22.20 and 23.30 for what would be the final time from Holme-on-Spalding-Moor, and headed for the Dutch coast for a northerly approach to the Ruhr. F/O Frazer-Hollins and crew were at 20,000 feet over central Holland, east of Elburg, when ED325 was attacked twice by night fighters at 01.37. The assailants were shaken off, and the bombs jettisoned over the Ijsselmeer as the sortie was abandoned. The others pressed on to find the target, a city associated with the oil and coal industries, under a thin layer of eight to ten-tenths cloud. The raid planners had known about this, and gambled that ground markers would be visible through it. This proved to be the case, and the initial bombing was accurate and concentrated, until, it was thought, dummy TIs appeared, and the later stages of the attack became scattered. The 101 Squadron crews carried out their part in the plan from 19,000 to 23,000 feet between 01.18 and 02.11, and all but one returned home to report a successful raid, but not on the same scale as Düsseldorf. Twenty-four aircraft failed to return, and the squadron posted missing Sgt Claydon and his crew in ED987, which was lost without trace. A local report listed 449 buildings in Bochum as totally destroyed.

Two nights later, it was the turn of Duisburg's near neighbour, Oberhausen, to wilt under the bombs of a modest heavy force of under two hundred Lancasters. 101 Squadron remained at home on this night, preparing for the move to Ludford Magna, a new airfield built by George Wimpy on a 650-acre site on what had been High Fields Farm, situated in the Lincolnshire Wolds east of Market Rasen. At 428 feet above sea level, it would be the highest bomber airfield in England, and cost £803,000 to build. After heavy rains it would become a sea of mud, and would soon be given the alternative name of "Mudford-Magna. Thirty-one Lancasters were involved in the move on the 15th, and all ranks pulled together to ensure a smooth and speedy settling-in process. The ORB commented, that, "The incorrigibles, of course, operated the first night. A very low-level attack was staged on Louth, the Mason's Arms being the target." On the night of the 16/17th, while the squadron was still off the Order of Battle, two hundred aircraft from 1, 5 and 8 Groups delivered the first of four raids on Cologne over a three-week period, and this was moderately effective, and destroyed four hundred houses. The first training and familiarization flights by 101 Squadron crews took place on the 17th, and all three flights had most of their crews on local flying on the 20th.

A flurry of four major operations in the space of five nights began at Krefeld on the 21st, by which time the squadron was ready to resume offensive activity. A force of 705 aircraft included a record twenty-six Lancasters put up by 101 Squadron, and they took off between 22.45 and 23.45, led by S/Ls St John and Sturgess. Sgt Groome lost his starboard-outer engine while over base, but the others headed out in perfect weather conditions to reach what was a virgin target. S/L Sturgess's starboard-outer engine gave up some forty miles before the target, but he took advantage of the situation to get in some useful three-engine practice, and was among those from the squadron bombing from 18,000 to 19,500 feet between 01.22 and 02.27. All but one returned to report an excellent performance by the Pathfinders, whose marking was accurate and concentrated over the city centre, and five crews brought back aiming-point photos. The attack was an outstanding success, which destroyed five and a half thousand houses, killed a thousand people, and erased by fire the entire centre of the town. The losses continued to rise, and a new record of forty-four aircraft failed to return on this night, including the squadron's ED650, which crashed near Mönchengladbach, killing Sgt Brook and his crew. The wireless operator was F/L Sibbald DFC, RCAF, who was the squadron's signals leader, and a popular long-serving member of the squadron.

The following night brought Mülheim into the bomb sights, a mining town lying in the south-eastern shadow of Duisburg. Stray bombs would undoubtedly have fallen within its boundaries before, but this would the first occasion on which it was specifically targeted. A force of 557 aircraft was made ready, of which twenty-four Lancasters represented 101 Squadron. The senior pilots on duty were W/C Reddick and S/Ls St John and Sturgess as they took to the air in a forty-minute slot either side of 23.00. W/C Reddick's Gee aerial was reportedly removed by another aircraft as they circled the airfield gaining height. F/Sgt Foran's sortie ended over base with the failure of the navigator's oxygen supply, and Sgt Quarterman turned back from the mid-point of the North Sea crossing with pneumatics problems. Sgt Cunningham was also over the North Sea when his starboard-outer engine began to overheat, and Sgt Lane became ensnared by searchlights when at 19,000 feet just north of Amsterdam. He was compelled to take evasive action, and, ultimately, jettisoned his bomb load and turned for home. S/L St John was attacked by two night fighters over Holland, which shot away most of the tail unit, holed petrol tanks and knocked out the starboard-outer engine. He jettisoned his bombs safe at 01.06, when at 20,000 feet east of Tilburg, and, with the aid of his crew, nursed the badly-damaged EE137 back home on three engines. The others pushed on in favourable weather conditions, and reached the target to find two to five-tenths thin low cloud, through which the Pathfinder ground markers were clearly visible. The 101 Squadron crews delivered their bombs from 16,000 to 20,000 feet between 01.21 and 01.56 in the face of a considerable flak defence in barrage form, and S/L Sturgess's rear gunner was wounded. All but one returned to claim a highly successful attack, which had left the target well alight. Sgt Waterhouse and crew failed to return, one of thirty-five missing crews, and had been shot down by Oblt Werner Baake of I/NJG1, to crash a couple of miles from Nijmegen at 01.38. Only the bomb-aimer survived, and he fell into enemy hands. Reconnaissance showed the central and northern districts of Mülheim to have been devastated, and some of the bombing had spilled over into the eastern side of Oberhausen. More than eleven hundred houses were destroyed, while 12,000 others sustained some kind of damage, and it was another demonstration of the burgeoning power of Bomber Command.

After a night's rest, the Elberfeld half of Wuppertal was earmarked for attention at the hands of a force numbering 630 aircraft, of which twenty-one Lancasters would represent 101 Squadron. S/L St John was the senior pilot on duty as they departed Ludford Magna between 22.20 and 23.25, and headed for the southern route to the Ruhr via the now discredited "gap" in the defences in the Mönchengladbach area between Düsseldorf and Cologne. S/L St John was twenty-six minutes later in taking-off, after his bomb-aimer reported sick. He was then attacked over the North Sea by two night fighters, which forced him down to 4,000 feet before he shook them off. By the time he reached the Belgian coast, he had not regained sufficient altitude to continue safely, and jettisoned his bomb load from 9,000 feet at 00.54, before returning home. The others reached the target area, after fighting their way through the already-mentioned searchlight and flak belt, and found the target under clear skies, but partially hidden by industrial haze. The Pathfinders dropped TIs accurately onto the Mosquito-laid Oboe markers, and the main force followed up with great precision. The 101 Squadron crews bombed from 14,500 to 21,600 feet between 01.05 and 01.46, and all but one made it safely home to report another outstanding attack. The raid was recorded by 2nd Lt Berger of the Photographic

Unit, who was flying with F/L Hull. W4311 was one of thirty-four aircraft to fail to return, and became another victim of the night fighters stalking the skies over Holland. Major Günther Radusch of I/NJG1 shot the Lancaster down to crash three miles north-north-west of Venlo at 01.40, and Sgt Lane and his crew were all killed. Elberfeld sustained catastrophic damage to the tune of three thousand houses destroyed, along with 171 industrial premises, and many more houses and factories seriously damaged, and a post-war survey would estimate a 90% destruction of the built-up area on this night.

The run of successes would be brought to an end at Gelsenkirchen on the night of the 25/26th, a target always difficult to hit, possibly because of its north-central location in the Ruhr, where town and city boundaries almost overlapped. As a site of synthetic oil production, Gelsenkirchen's importance to the German war effort was beyond question, and it was always well-defended. A force of 473 aircraft was made ready to attack it, of which seventeen Lancasters were provided by 101 Squadron. They took off between 22.40 and 23.40, with S/L Sturgess the senior pilot on duty, but F/Sgt Smith turned back at 16,000 feet over Sheringham after an engine failed and caught fire. F/O Austin was within ten miles of the Dutch coast at Haarlem, when he lost a starboard engine at 18,000 feet, and had to return. The others reached the target, where the tops of the forecast ten-tenths cloud reached 12,000 feet, and, under normal circumstances, the effects of this would have been negated by Oboe. However, five of the twelve Oboe Mosquitos suffered equipment failure on the way out, and the others failed to provide sufficient reference for the heavy Pathfinder crews to deliver concentrated skymarkers. In an echo of the past, bombs were sprayed around the Ruhr, and even Düsseldorf, thirty miles to the south-west, reported buildings destroyed and damaged. The 101 Squadron crews bombed from 18,500 to 21,600 feet between 01.25 and 01.58, and those who returned commented on the attack opening late, strong winds driving the marker flares across the target, the glow of cookies bursting, and a generally disappointing effort. Two of the squadron's crews were not at debriefing, and were among thirty to fail to return. LM318 came down near Lüdinghausen, a few miles from the northern rim of the eastern Ruhr, and there were no survivors from the crew of Sgt Hay. ED373 was abandoned by its crew over the Dutch coast, after being intercepted by a night fighter, but, tragically, F/Sgt Banks RAAF and five of his crew landed in the sea and were drowned. The bomb-aimer landed on or close to the dunes, and was captured, while the bodies of his crew mates eventually came ashore in the Zandvoort area, initially, for a local burial.

On the night of the 27/28th, the squadron sent six freshman crews to plant vegetables in the Cinnamon region off La Rochelle. They took off shortly before 23.00 carrying six mines each, and arrived in the target area to find clear skies but haze. They each had a pinpoint from which to make a timed run, La Sables, Ile d'Oleron and Pointe L'Aigville among them, and the mines were dropped as briefed from 3,500 to 5,000 feet between 01.28 and 01.40. ED377 was homebound at 15,000 feet, when shot down by a night fighter to crash near Cande in north-western France. F/O Buck RCAF and crew were on their first operational sortie, and only the bomb-aimer was able to save himself, and, ultimately, evade capture. A series of three raids on Cologne would span the turn of the month, and the first was mounted on the night of the 28/29th, for which a force of 608 aircraft was assembled. 101 Squadron briefed sixteen crews, of which, those of W/C Reddick and S/L St John were the most senior. They took off between 22.40 and 23.25, and there were no early returns to reduce the squadron's effort. The Pathfinders had prepared for both sky and ground marking, on the basis that there may be breaks in the forecast cloud cover. In the event, it was necessary to employ the least reliable method of skymarking, which had to be based on the performance of just six of the twelve Oboe Mosquitos that had originally set out. The marking was seven minutes late and intermittent, meaning that the first two waves had nothing to aim at, and had to release their loads on ETA. The omens for a successful operation were not promising as the 101 Squadron crews arrived to find the cloud tops to be at 5,000 to 10,000 feet. They delivered their cookies and incendiaries from 19,000 to 22,000 feet between 01.40 and 02.16, and all returned home to report being unable to assess the outcome. The consensus was of a concentrated raid despite the problems, and, in fact, it became this city's most crushing assault of the war, resulting in the destruction of 6,400 buildings, with a further fifteen thousand damaged to some extent. More than 4,300 people lost their lives, and 230,000 were bombed out of their homes, at a cost to the Command of twenty-five aircraft. The squadron dispatched 158 sorties on eight operations at a cost of seven Lancasters and crews.

July 1943

Having closed the June account, it fell to Cologne to open that of July on the night of the 3/4th. A force of 653 aircraft was made ready, of which twenty-one Lancasters were provided by 101 Squadron. It was on this night that the Luftwaffe introduced its Wilde Sau (Wild Boar) night fighter system, which involved single-engine day fighters of the newly-formed Stab JG300 operating over the target, picking out bombers silhouetted against the fires on the ground. Oberstleutnant (later, Major) Hans-Joachim (Hajo) Hermann was the commander of the new unit, which had been formed at Deelen on the 26th of June with borrowed FW190 and BF109G aircraft, to explore the potential of employing experienced former bomber pilots and instructors against Bomber Command. The tactic smacked of desperation in the face of the mounting destruction of Germany's industrial heartland, and would expose the pilots to extreme danger from friendly ground fire. The 101 Squadron crews departed Ludford Magna between 22.20 and 23.00, led by W/C Reddick, but F/Sgt Jefferies abandoned his sortie over base because of instrument and engine problems. The others all reached the target carrying a mixture of high explosives and incendiaries, and bombed on Pathfinder ground markers from 18,000 to 22,000 feet between 01.16 and 01.59. W/O Quarterman lost his port-inner engine immediately after bombing, but made it home safely on three. The aiming-point had been in the industrialized section of the city on the eastern bank of the Rhine, and it was another devastating blow, which reduced to rubble twenty industrial premises, 2,200 houses, and rendered homeless 72,000 people. Twelve of the thirty missing aircraft fell in the target area, victims of both fighter and flak activity.

S/L St John was awarded the DFC on the 6th in recognition of his airmanship following the Mülheim raid in June, and, that night, three freshman crews were sent mining off La Rochelle. F/Sgt Walker and P/O Ager were unable to find their pinpoints in conditions of eight to ten-tenths cloud with a base below 1,000 feet, but, somewhat surprisingly, F/L MacKay found clear skies, although poor visibility, and dropped his six mines into the briefed location from 5,000 feet at 02.29. The final raid on Cologne took place at the hands of a 282-strong all-Lancaster heavy force from 1, 5 and 8 Groups on the night of the 8/9th, and involved twenty-one representatives from 101 Squadron. It had been intended to include 1 Group's remaining Wellingtons in this operation, but poor weather conditions led to their participation being cancelled. The 101 Squadron element took off between 22.20 and 23.00 led by S/Ls St John and Sturgess, but W/O Quarterman abandoned his sortie over base because of engine problems, and F/Sgt Walker turned back just short of the enemy coast with a sick navigator, who was probably suffering from oxygen starvation. The others reached the target area to encounter ten-tenths cloud with tops at 12,000 to 14,000 feet, and this required the Pathfinders to employ skymarking. They squadron crews delivered their mix of HE and incendiaries from 19,500 to 23,000 feet between 01.14 and 01.25, and all but two returned home, some to report the glow of fires and explosions, and others with little to say. Only seven Lancasters were lost from this operation, among which was ED697, which was heard by F/Sgt Naffin's crew asking for navigational assistance at 00.45, when they were fixed near the mid-point of the Channel between Eastbourne and Dieppe. The timing suggests that it was returning early with technical problems when it crashed into the sea, taking with it F/L Fleming RAAF and crew, who were on their second tour with the squadron. W4275 was shot down from around 18,000 feet by a night fighter, and crashed at Marly-Gomont in France, close to the Belgian border while homebound. P/O Ager and crew were on just their second operation, and four of them lost their lives, while the pilot, rear gunner and bomb-aimer survived, the last-mentioned ultimately evading capture. Sgt De Loire's name suggests he may have been of French origin, and, possibly fluent in the language, which would have aided his escape. The flight engineer, Sgt Lloyd, was just seventeen years of age at the time of his death, and had joined the RAF in around September 1941. When the dust had settled at Cologne, the authorities were able to assess the cost of the three-raid series at eleven thousand buildings destroyed, five and a half thousand people killed, and 350,000 others rendered homeless.

Another attempt to deliver a telling blow on Gelsenkirchen was mounted on the night of the 9/10th, for which 418 aircraft were detailed, fourteen of the Lancasters provided by 101 Squadron. They took off between 22.30 and 23.15 with F/Ls Austin, Hull and Wedderburn the senior pilots on duty. F/O Mahoney lost his starboard-outer engine a few miles out from the Norfolk coast, and F/Sgt Jeffries was at the mid-point of the North Sea crossing between Sheringham and Den Helder when he turned back with navigation-aid failure. Half of the Oboe Mosquitos experienced equipment failure on this night, and another dropped skymarkers ten miles north of the target in error. The 101 Squadron crews arrived to encounter ten-tenths cloud with tops ranging from 15,000 to 22,500 feet, and had to rely on the skymarkers to identify the aiming-point. They carried out their attacks from 18,500 to 22,000 feet between 01.15 and 01.38, and returned home to report the glow of fires and general satisfaction with the night's work. The opinion was that the attack had been concentrated on the markers, and the success depended, therefore, on their accuracy. Sadly, this was lacking, and, although the Scholven synthetic oil plant was hit, along with a number of other industrial premises, damage was not serious, and the neighbouring towns of Bochum and Wattenscheid received more bombs that Gelsenkirchen. Although two more operations to the Ruhr region would take place at the end of the month, the offensive was now effectively over, and Harris could look back over the past five months with genuine pride at the performance of his crews, and take particular satisfaction from the success of Oboe. It was true, that losses had been grievously high, but the Empire Training Scheme and the factories were more than keeping pace with the rate of attrition, and replacement crews and aircraft were readily available to fill the gaps.

There was a welcome change of scenery for nineteen 101 Squadron crews on the night of the 12/13th, as they joined 276 others from 1, 5 and 8 Groups for an all-Lancaster attack on Turin. S/L Sturgess was the senior pilot on duty as they took off either side of 22.30, and headed south to encounter difficult weather conditions over France, which included electrical storms and icing. W/O Cunningham was at 16,000 feet, twenty miles north of Lake Bourget, when icing forced him to jettison his bomb load at 01.30. On return, he and his crew would learn that the sortie would still count towards their tour. The weather was much better on the eastern side of the Alps, and Turin lay under clear skies and visibility so good, that crews were able to identify the aiming-point visually. The Ludford Magna brigade bombed from 15,000 to 18,100 feet, between 01.53 and 02.25, and returned home to report a successful outcome, backed up by ten plottable photos. Reconnaissance confirmed that severe damage had been inflicted on north-central districts, and local reports put the death toll at almost eight hundred people. One particularly sad loss on this night was that of W/C Nettleton VC and crew of 44 Squadron. Nettleton had famously earned his award for the epic daylight raid on the M.A.N diesel engine works at Augsburg in April 1942.

Harris now sought to mount a knockout blow against a major German city under Operation Gomorrah, a short, sharp series of heavy raids until the job was done. Hamburg had been spared by the weather from hosting the first one-thousand-bomber raid in May 1942, but now, Germany's second city held the necessary political status to serve as a suitable sacrificial lamb, the destruction of which, would, it was rather optimistically hoped, crush Germany's will to continue the fight. Other considerations also confirmed it as the ideal target for Harris's purposes. Its importance as a centre of war production was undeniable, and its close proximity to

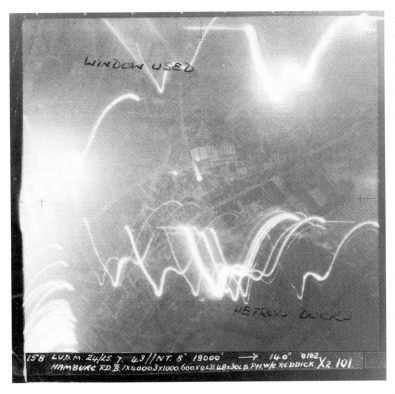

the bomber stations enabled it to be reached in the few hours of darkness afforded by mid-summer, with access from the sea reducing the time spent over enemy territory. Additionally, the wide River Elbe would provide good H2S returns in the absence of Oboe, which did not have the range. Bomber Command always went to Hamburg in the last week of July, and 1943 would be no exception. After ten nights on the ground for the main force Lancaster squadrons, a force of 791 aircraft was assembled on the 24th and made ready for that night's operation. 101 Squadron had twenty-three Lancasters lined up for take-off, and they became airborne between 22.20 and 23.15, led by W/C Reddick. In addition to their mixed HE and incendiary loads, the entire force carried with them for the first time, a new weapon in the electronics war. "Window" consisted of tinfoil-backed strips of paper, which, when released, would drift slowly to earth in massed clouds, and swamp the enemy night fighter, searchlight and gun laying radar with false returns, rendering it effectively blind. The

Aiming point photo from W/C Reddick's Lancaster, SR-X2, 19,000 feet over Hamburg on 24/25th July. Note the handwritten comments, including the mention of 'Window' (GW).

device had been available for a year, but its use had been vetoed for fear of it being copied by the enemy. The Germans already had their own counterpart, called "Düppel", which had been withheld from use for the same reason.

S/L St John was lucky to get off the ground and climb away without crashing, as engine trouble struck at a critical moment. Fortunately, he was able to jettison the HE part of his load safe, and land without difficulty. The others pressed on in excellent weather conditions, and, at a predetermined point over the North Sea, the designated member in each crew began to feed the Window out into the air stream, where its effectiveness was made manifest by the relatively few combats taking place. Over the target, there was an absence of the usually efficient co-ordination between the searchlight and gun batteries, and an opportunity was there under clear skies to exploit the situation and deliver a telling first blow. In the event, the H2S and visual marking was slightly misplaced, and an extensive creep-back developed, which cut a swathe of destruction from the city centre, across the north-western districts along the line of approach, and out into open country. The 101 Squadron crews were over the target at 15,000 to 22,500 feet between 01.02 and 01.56, and all returned safely to report at least one large explosion, many fires, and black smoke rising up to 22,000 feet. A modest twelve aircraft failed to return, and much of the credit for this belonged to Window, which, at a stroke, had rendered ineffective the entire Luftwaffe defensive organisation.

It would be only a transitory advantage, however, and within weeks the Luftwaffe would emerge from the body-blow of Window, a leaner, fitter, more efficient and much deadlier adversary than before. Harris decided against an immediate return to Hamburg, probably because of the volume of smoke still hanging over it and obscuring the ground. Instead, he took advantage of the confusion created by Window, to attack Essen again, and a force of 705 aircraft was made ready. 101 Squadron contributed twenty-one Lancasters, led for the final time by W/C Reddick, who was about to be posted. The squadron took off between 22.00 and 22.35, but F/Sgt Jeffries succumbed to engine trouble, and turned back when twenty miles east of Skegness. Shortly afterwards, W/O Cunningham abandoned his sortie when some forty miles out from Sheringham, also because of overheating in the engine department. The others all reached the Ruhr to find good visibility with the usual ground haze, but, as W/O Quarterman made his way eastwards, the bomb release circuit became active, and the bombs dropped live onto Oberhausen from 20,000 feet at 00.35, with Essen in sight. The others released their loads from 18,500 to 23,000 feet between 00.31 and 01.11, and contributed to the destruction of 2,852 houses and fifty-one industrial buildings, and also to the Krupp works suffering its worst night of the war. It is said, that Dr Gustav Krupp, the founder, suffered a stroke on the following morning, from which he never fully recovered.

W/C Reddick, who had a long association with the squadron, joining it first as a sergeant pilot back in 1932, was posted as station commander to Lindholme on the 27th. He had served as a flight commander, before taking over from W/C Eaton, and leading the squadron with distinction through its early days as a Lancaster unit, and maintaining the standards of his predecessor. He was succeeded by W/C Carey-Foster, who had arrived as commanding officer-elect from 1656 Conversion Unit on the 23rd. He presided over his first operation on the night of his appointment, which, following a night's rest, was to be the second raid on Hamburg. A force of 787 aircraft was made ready, of which twenty-four represented 101 Squadron. S/L St John was the senior pilot on duty as they took off between 22.20 and 23.05, and headed for the Schleswig-Holstein peninsular to approach the target from the north. F/Sgt Sexton was fifty miles off Germany's northern coast, when turret and compass failure persuaded him to turn back at 00.54. Having crossed the western coast of the peninsular, Sgt Jeffries' port-outer engine caught fire, and he opted to bomb a searchlight and flak concentration eight miles south-west of Rendsburg from 20,000 feet at 01.15. His starboard-outer overheated on the way home, and also had to be shut down, and the sea crossing was made at 5,000 feet after everything moveable had been thrown out to save weight. F/O Turner lost his communications at the same time, and bombed the same searchlight and flak concentration from 18,000 feet.

The others made it to the target, and, what followed their arrival over the city, was both unprecedented and unforeseeable, and resulted from a conspiracy of circumstances. A period of unusually hot and dry weather had left tinderbox conditions within parts of the city, and the first sparks to ignite it came with the Pathfinder markers. These fell two miles east of the planned aiming-point, but with unaccustomed concentration into the densely populated working-class districts of Hamm, Hammerbrook and Borgfeld. The main force followed up also with unusual accuracy and scarcely any creep-back, and deposited much of its 2,300 tons of bombs into this relatively compact area. The individual fires joined together to form one giant conflagration, which sucked in oxygen from surrounding districts at hurricane velocity to feed its voracious appetite. Such was the force of this meteorological event that trees were uprooted and flung bodily into the inferno, along with debris and people, and the temperatures at its seat exceeded one thousand degrees Celsius. The flames only died down once all the combustible material had been consumed, by which time there was no-one left to rescue. Forty thousand people lost their lives on this one night alone in the first recorded example of a firestorm, and these were added to the fifteen hundred killed three nights earlier. Daylight brought the beginning of a mass evacuation, which would eventually number 1.1 million people. Again, losses among the bombers were acceptably modest, seventeen in all, but that figure included 101 Squadron's JA863, which, it is believed, was shot down over the target by the BF109 of the previously-mentioned commander of Stab JG300, Major Hajo Hermann, and there were no survivors from the crew of F/Sgt Hurst.

Forty-eight hours later, a force of 777 aircraft took off again for beleaguered Hamburg, among them twenty-three 101 Squadron Lancasters. They took off between 22.20 and 23.05 led by S/L St John, and there were no early returns to Ludford Magna as the bomber stream made its way to a turning point over the North Sea, from where it headed for the Schleswig-Holstein coast. After passing over Heide, the final turning point came near Hohenwestedt, with a direct run then on the target from a little west of due north. The intention this time was to hit the northern and north-eastern districts, but the Pathfinders approach took them two miles to the east of their intended track, and the markers fell south of the firestorm area. The initial bombing stirred the embers here, before a four-mile-long creep-back extended across the residential districts of Wandsbek, Barmbek, Uhlenhorst and Winterhude. In all, another 2,300 tons of bombs inflicted further devastation on the city, which was still burning from the firestorm raid. The 101 Squadron crews bombed from 17,000 to 24,000 feet between 00.41 and 01.31, and returned safely to report another huge success, but an increase in searchlight and flak activity. This was made manifest by the increased loss of twenty-eight aircraft, as the Luftwaffe continued its recovery from the shock of Window.

The final curtain on the Ruhr campaign came down on the night of the 30/31st, when a force of 264 Halifaxes, Stirlings and Lancasters was sent with Mosquito support to attack the town of Remscheid. Situated on the southern rim of the Ruhr, about eight miles south of Wuppertal, the town was known for its mechanical engineering and tool-making factories, and would be facing Bomber Command for the first time. 101 Squadron detailed twenty-three crews, but seventeen were cancelled because of doubts about the weather, and just six Lancasters took off from Ludford Magna either side of 22.30, with F/Ls Frazer-Hollins and Hall the senior pilots on duty. They all reached the target to find clear skies and good visibility, and bombed on the Pathfinder ground markers from 18,000 to 20,000 feet between 01.06 and 01.14. Fires were beginning to take hold as they turned away, and all returned safely to report a successful night's work. Post-raid reconnaissance confirmed the devastating effects of the raid, which produced a small firestorm, and destroyed more than three thousand houses and a hundred industrial buildings, amounting to 83% of the town's built-up area. 1,120 people lost their lives, and 6,700 were injured, while the local industry lost three months' production, and never fully recovered. During the course of the month the squadron participated in ten operations, and dispatched 175 sorties for the loss of three Lancasters and crews.

August 1943

Harris had intended to attack Hamburg again on the night of the 31st, but heavy thunderstorms hit the bomber stations shortly before take-off time, and the operation was scrubbed. The weather also kept them on the ground on the night of the 1/2nd, and thus the conclusion of the Hamburg offensive was delayed until the night of the 2/3rd. It was known that storms were active over northern Germany, but the expectation was, that the raid could slip in between them. 101 Squadron contributed twenty-two Lancasters to the overall force of 740 aircraft, and they took off between 23.05 and 00.05, with S/Ls St John and Sturgess the senior pilots on duty. F/L MacKay lost his starboard inner engine on take-off, while F/L Day was north-west of the Frisians, when he turned back with an unserviceable rear turret. The cloud-covered outward route took them to a turning point over the North Sea, from where a starboard change of course would lead them to a landfall south of the Elbe, for a south to north bombing-run right over the centre of the city. As they approached the coast, great flashes of light lit up a huge cloud mass towering above them, at least to 25,000 feet, through which they would have to pass to reach the target. This persuaded many crews to abandon their sorties, and bomb alternative targets, or jettison their bombs over the sea. S/L Sturgess, W/O Syme, F/Sgts Gray, Naffin and Shattock and Sgt Slater bombed in the region of Wesermünde, north of Bremen, while W/O Johnson dropped his a little further east over Zeven. W/O Walker chose a site near Oldesloe, north-east of Hamburg, Sgt Sexton found the little town of Fintel, some twenty miles south-west of the centre of Hamburg, and S/L St John relieved himself over Bremervörde, between Bremerhaven and Hamburg. The others believed themselves to be over the primary target as they bombed in ten-tenths cloud from 17,000 to 20,500 feet between 02.00 and 02.51. They returned home to report the worst conditions they had ever experienced, no doubt relieved to find all of their colleagues had made it back. Little further damage was inflicted upon Hamburg, but the damage had been done. Thirty aircraft failed to return on this night, some falling victim to the conditions. Over the four raids on Hamburg, 101 Squadron despatched ninety-two sorties, eighty-five of which reached and bombed the primary target, and only one crew was lost. (The Battle of Hamburg. Martin Middlebrook).

Italy was now teetering on the brink of capitulation, and a series of operations against its cities in the first half of August was intended to nudge it over the edge. Genoa, Milan and Turin were selected for attention on the night of the 7/8th, for which 197 Lancasters of 1, 5 and 8 Groups were made ready. 101 Squadron put up seventeen aircraft for Turin, an operation which was to benefit from the use of a Master Bomber, a senior officer, who would control the attack by VHF, as Gibson had done during Operation Chastise. G/C John Searby of 83 Squadron was appointed to the role, which was something of a test of the procedure, with a view to its employment for a very important operation in ten days' time. W/C Carey-Foster took the opportunity to lead the squadron for the first time, and all were safely airborne by 21.05. There were no early returns, and all arrived in the target area to find clear skies and good visibility. They were carrying either a cookie or four 1,000 pounders each, along with incendiaries, which they delivered onto green TIs from 16,500 to 21,000 feet between 00.59 and 01.11. Fires were taking hold as they turned for home, and a pall of black smoke was beginning to rise, but, it seems that no post-raid reconnaissance was carried out to provide an assessment.

Harris returned temporarily to Germany for two operations, beginning with Mannheim on the night of the 9/10th. 101 Squadron contributed twenty-three Lancasters to the force of 457 aircraft, and they took off between 21.55 and 23.05, led by S/L St John. F/Sgt Edis turned back from a dozen miles short of the French coast after he lost his starboard-outer engine, and F/Sgt Foran had to feather his starboard-inner engine over France, as a result of which, he was unable to maintain speed and altitude. He reached Trier, some seventy-five miles short of Mannheim, and dropped his bomb load there from 13,500 feet at 01.43. The others all reached the primary target to find eight to ten-tenths cloud, with tops ranging from 5,000 to 10,000 feet, and bombed on the Pathfinder markers from 17,000 to 21,000 feet between 01.34 and 02.05. All returned safely to report numerous fires and a large orange explosion reflected on the cloud at 01.36. There were varying opinions as to the degree of concentration, but local authorities listed 1,316 buildings as destroyed or seriously damaged, and a loss of production at forty-two factories, at a cost to the Command of nine aircraft.

The following night would bring Nuremberg into the bomb sights of an initial force of 653 aircraft, of which nineteen Lancasters were provided by 101 Squadron. They took off between 21.25 and 22.05 led by the station commander, G/C "Bobby" Blucke, with S/Ls St John and Sturgess in support. W/O Bond was just ten miles south-east of Peterborough, when his starboard-inner engine caught fire to put an end to his sortie. F/Sgt Kelly and F/O Rowland both turned back at Beachy Head, the former after losing his starboard-outer engine, and the latter with an overheating starboard-inner engine and unserviceable artificial horizon. The remainder continued on to reach the target, which lay under nine to ten-tenths cloud. Despite this, the Pathfinders dropped green TIs to mark the ground, which, against the odds, remained visible, and the main force delivered their bombs accordingly, many of them falling into central and southern districts. The 101 Squadron crews bombed from 15,000 to 21,000 feet between 01.04 and 01.50, and those catching a glimpse of the ground through occasional gaps in the cloud, observed fires taking hold. A large orange glow in the cloud could be seen from 150 miles into the return journey, and suggested that the target was burning fiercely. The general opinion on

W/O Ray Bond (front row, centre), and his crew (GW)

return was that the raid had been scattered with a lot of undershooting, and the expectation of success was muted. Local reports told a different story, one of widespread destruction of residential and industrial property, and the deaths of 577 people.

It was back to Italy on the night of the 12/13th, with simultaneous attacks on Milan and Turin, by forces of 504 and 152 aircraft respectively. The latter was a 3 and 8 Group show, while the former involved twenty 101 Squadron Lancasters, which took off between 21.10 and 21.35, led by S/Ls St John and Sturgess. All reached the target to find excellent weather conditions, with small amounts of cloud, and a Master Bomber to keep the bombing on track. They delivered their cookie and incendiaries each on Pathfinder ground markers from 18,000 to 20,800 feet between 01.16 and 01.48, and all returned safely to report a concentrated attack. Preparations were made on the 14th for a further attack on Milan by 140 Lancasters of 1, 5 and 8 Groups. A section of the force was assigned specifically to attack the Breda works, and six of the eleven participating 101 Squadron crews were among these. They departed Ludford Magna at 21.00, led by W/C Carey-Foster, who was to attack the special objective with F/Ls McCulough and Wedderburn, F/O Mahoney, W/O Quarterman and Sgt Slater. F/O Mahoney lost his starboard-outer engine on take-off, and abandoned his sortie, but the others made it to the target, where they found clear skies, but considerable ground haze, and visibility was assessed as two miles only. The Pathfinders dropped white flares over the Breda works, which enabled to crews to pick out the buildings and deliver their four 1,000 pounders and incendiaries each visually. This they did from 6,200 to 7,500 feet between 01.18 and 01.28, and W/O Quarterman and crew watched their bombs explode on a shed and start fires. On return they would declare it as "the best trip ever - a bomb-aimer's prayer". The others dropped their cookies and incendiaries onto green TIs from around 18,500 feet, although S/L St John came down to 7,000 feet to carry out his attack, and all returned safely to report a successful operation. There was to be no rest for the inhabitants of Milan, as another 199 Lancasters took off on the following night to continue their torment. Eleven 101 Squadron Lancasters became airborne by 20.10, led by S/L Sturgess, but F/Sgt Kelly abandoned his sortie almost immediately after a flexible hydraulics line to the rear turret burst. The others pressed on to reach the target in fine weather conditions, and bombed from 18,000 to 20,700 between 00.02 and 00.15, before returning to report many fires in the city, and smoke rising to 10,000 feet. The Bomber Command campaign against Italy, which had begun in June 1940, concluded on the night of the 16/17th, with a 3 and 8 Group attack on Turin.

Since the outbreak of war, intelligence had been filtering through concerning German research into rocketry. It was ultimately discovered that the centre for this activity was at Peenemünde, on the island of Usedom on the Baltic coast. Aerial reconnaissance of the area was carried out, and the photographic interpreters at Medmenham eventually found the "Peenemünde 20", the V-1 flying bomb. Through "Ultra", the reading of German Enigma codes, the brilliant scientist, Dr R V Jones, was able to monitor the trials of the V-1 over the

Baltic, and learn much about its capabilities, which would be put to good use when it was unleashed upon London in the summer of 1944. Churchill's chief scientific adviser, Professor Lindemann, or Lord Cherwell as he became, steadfastly refused to give credence to rocket weaponry, and, even when confronted with a photograph of a V-2 taken by a PRU Mosquito in June 1943, maintained his stubborn stance. It took the combined urgings of Duncan Sandys and Dr Jones, to persuade Churchill to act, and a decision was at last taken to attack the site at the first available opportunity. This arose on the night of the 17/18th of August, by which time a plan had been carefully prepared to try to ensure the target's destruction at the first attempt. A Master of Ceremonies (Master Bomber) was to direct the attack, and G/C Searby of 83 Squadron was selected, having used the Turin raid on the 7/8th as a not-entirely-successful test run.

The plan for Operation Hydra called for the attack to be conducted in three waves, each assigned to a specific aiming-point, with the Pathfinder squadrons bearing the responsibility of shifting the point of aim accordingly. The first wave, consisting of 3 and 4 Group aircraft, were to attack the workers' and scientists' housing estate, the second wave, 1 Group, the rocket assembly sheds, and the third wave, 5 and 6 Groups, the experimental site. G/C Searby would orbit the target area for as long as the raid and his fuel lasted, directing the bombing and exhorting the crews to press home their attacks, all the time within range of what was expected to be a formidable flak defence. It was hoped that a feint by eight Mosquitos of 139 Squadron at Berlin, led by the former 49 Squadron commanding officer, G/C Len Slee, would be successful in keeping night fighters away from the scene. 597 aircraft departed their stations in mid-evening, the numbers somewhat depleted by the late return from Italy the night before of a proportion of the Stirling force, which had been diverted, and could not be made ready in time. 101 Squadron contributed twenty Lancasters and crews as follows; F/Ls Day, McCulloch, Mackay and Wedderburn in EE137, W5009, ED372 and W4995 respectively, F/Os Carpenter, Robertson and Rowlands in ED328, EE192 and ED382, P/O Leeder in ED422, W/Os Bond, Cunningham and Walker in W4923, W4993 and ED951, F/Sgts McConnell, Marsh, Rays, Sexton, Shattock and Tucker in ED370, DV194, W4966, JA926, W4997 and ED659, and Sgts Fawcett, Naffin and Skipper in ED317, ED327 and ED809. It was somewhat surprising, on a night when many squadron and flight commanders included themselves on the Order of Battle for such an important operation, that this was not the case at 101 Squadron.

They all became safely airborne from Ludford Magna between 21.15 and 21.35, but not all would reach the target. F/Sgt McConnell was fifty miles out from Sheringham when a variety of malfunctions terminated his sortie at 22.15, while F/Ls McCullough and Mackay turned back an hour later from around eighty miles off the Schleswig-Holstein coast. The former's navigator became unconscious and could not be brought round, and the latter lost his port-outer engine. The others pressed on across Denmark in fine weather conditions, which held firm all the way to the target, bright moonlight negating to some extent the presence of thin cloud. The Pathfinders found the target area without difficulty, and the conditions provided them with the opportunity to carry out visual marking. The initial marking of the housing estate went somewhat awry, and some target indicators fell onto the forced workers camp at Trassenheide, more than a mile beyond the intended aiming-point. Inevitably, these attracted a proportion of the 3 and 4 Group bombs, and heavy casualties were inflicted on the friendly foreign nationals, who were trapped inside their wooden barracks. Once rectified, the operation proceeded more or less according to plan, but, by the time the seventeen-strong 101 Squadron contingent arrived, an effective smoke screen had obliterated ground detail. The green TIs remained visible, however, and they bombed as planned in the second wave from 5,800 to 9,000 feet between 00.27 and 00.40. A strong crosswind drove a number of bomb loads across the narrow neck of land into the dunes and sea to the east, but returning crews were generally satisfied with their work, and most praised the performance of the Master Bomber. The Berlin feint was initially successful, but night fighter crews observed the fierce activity a hundred miles to the north, and took it upon themselves to head in that direction. They arrived during the later stages of the attack, and, once on the scene, took a heavy toll of bombers, both in the skies around Peenemünde, and on the route home towards Denmark. Forty aircraft were shot down, twenty-nine of them from the 5 and 6 Group final wave attacking the experimental site. Some fell victim to the new Schräge Musik upward firing cannon, which were being used by the Luftwaffe for the first time. Whilst not entirely successful, the operation caused sufficient damage to delay development of the weapons for a few weeks. It also forced the Germans to move the manufacturing site to caves at Nordhausen, east of the Ruhr, where brutal slave labour would be utilized, while the testing programme went to Poland, out of range of Harris's bombers.

Harris had long believed that Berlin held the key to ultimate victory. As the symbol and the seat of Nazi government, its destruction would rock the foundations of national morale, and, hopefully, bring about the downfall of the Nazi regime. Having witnessed at first hand the carnage of a protracted and bloody land campaign during the Great War, he hoped to save Allied lives by avoiding something similar this time round. There is some question among historians as to whether the Berlin offensive began in August or in November. A number of ORBs answer that question emphatically, by referring to the "so-called Battle of Berlin" beginning on the night of the 23/24th. First, however, an attack was planned on the Ruhr city of Leverkusen, which was home to an I.G Farben factory, and was known to be employing slave labour. A force of 462 aircraft was assembled, which included a contribution from 101 Squadron of twenty-one Lancasters. They took off between 21.00 and 21.35, led by W/C Carey-Foster with S/Ls St John and Sturgess in support. F/O Mahoney dropped out immediately with a split exhaust stub, but the others all managed to reach the target area, where thick cloud obscured the ground, and a problem with the Oboe ground stations caused a partial failure of the signals. The Pathfinders, which were supposed to use the I.G Farben factory as the aiming-point, were unable to achieve any concentration, and bombs were distributed liberally around the Ruhr, particularly on Düsseldorf a dozen or so miles to the north. The 101 Squadron crews mostly reported the belief that they had attacked the primary target, doing so from 16,500 to 20,000 feet between 00.03 and 00.37, but, in truth, they had little idea where their bombs fell.

Berlin had been attacked many times before, on occasions to good effect, but never had there been a concerted effort to bring about its ruin. During the course of the 23rd, a force of 727 aircraft was made ready for the opening salvo, in what would be the longest and most hard-fought campaign of Bomber Command's war. 101 Squadron contributed twenty Lancasters to the operation, which took off between 20.00 and 20.35 carrying a cookie each, with a 1,000 pounder and incendiaries. S/Ls St John and Sturgess were the senior pilots on duty as they headed out across the North Sea to enter enemy territory north of Haarlem, before continuing on eastwards to pass north of Hannover and approach Berlin from the south-east. There were no early returns among the Ludford Magna brigade, as they made their way to the target in conditions of little cloud, and it is believed that all of them arrived to deliver their bombs. The attack was aided by the use, once more, of a Master Bomber, which, on this night, was the tough Canadian commander of 405 (Vancouver) Squadron RCAF, G/C Johnny Fauquier. The skies over Berlin were clear, and the moon cast its light onto the streets below, enabling the crews to identify ground detail. Despite this, the Pathfinders, employing H2S, marked the south-western corner of the city rather than the centre. The main force, which was a little late in arriving, failed to pass south of the city to approach from the south-east, as planned, but came in directly from the south-west. This caused the main weight of bombs to fall into these already damaged districts and onto outlying communities and open country. The 101 Squadron crews bombed on red and green TIs from 18,000 to 21,500 feet between 23.52 and 00.25, and all but two returned home to report a concentrated attack, most giving a special mention in praise of the performance of the Master Bomber. The defences were very active, particularly the Nachtjagd, and a record fifty-six aircraft failed to return, two of them from 101 Squadron. ED328 crashed at Lanke, north-east of Berlin, clearly having bombed, and F/Sgt Naffin RAAF and his crew all lost their lives. The fate of EE192 and the crew of F/O Mahoney has never been established, and the likely scenario is, that it crashed into the North Sea on the way home as the result of battle damage. Although this was the most successful attack of the war to date on the Capital, destroying or seriously damaging 2,600 buildings of a residential, industrial and public nature, it could have been many times more effective had it fallen on the city centre as intended.

S/L Dilworth arrived from 1662 Conversion Unit on the 23rd, to ultimately assume command of C Flight, while S/L Moody came in from 1667 Conversion Unit on the 27th. Both were on the Order of Battle for the night of the 27/28th, when Nuremberg was the target for 674 aircraft, of which nineteen Lancasters were provided by 101 Squadron. W/C Carey-Foster was the senior pilot on duty as they took off either side of 21.00, and the only one to turn back was F/Sgt Sexton, whose compass failed twenty miles south-east of Arras. The others found Nuremberg to be free of cloud, but obscured by extreme darkness, and, had many of the Pathfinders not experienced problems with their H2S sets, the outcome might have been better. The initial marking was accurate, but a creep-back developed, which the Master Bomber could not arrest, and, although some of the bombing was scattered across south-eastern districts, much of it fell into open country to the south-west. The 101 Squadron participants delivered their cookies and incendiaries from 18,500 to 21,000 feet between 00.32 and 01.09, and all returned with mixed opinions as to the quality of the raid. F/O Robertson had just crossed the Rhine on the way home, when both starboard engines caught fire, and he issued a warning order to his crew to prepare to abandon the aircraft. The port-inner engine then packed-up, and they rapidly lost height from 18,000 feet. As they passed through 12,000 feet, the pilot ordered all moveable equipment to be dumped to save weight, at which point it was discovered that the bomb-aimer, wireless operator and both gunners had jumped without even saying goodbye! By the time they reached 6,000 feet, the fires had been extinguished and the starboard-inner engine shut down, leaving them to limp home on the outer engines. F/O Robertson praised the part played by the flight engineer and navigator in helping to get the wounded W5009 home.

The target on the night of the 30/31st lay much closer to home, and would require a round trip of around five hours or less. The twin towns of Mönchengladbach and Rheydt acted as a gateway to the Ruhr on its south-western rim, and the 1 Group ORB describes it as the "sole surviving built-up area in the Ruhr". A force of 660 aircraft was made ready, of which twenty-two Lancasters represented 101 Squadron, and they took off either side of midnight, led by S/Ls Dilworth, Moody and Sturgess. W/O Cunningham lost his port-outer engine over base, and F/Sgt Ray's starboard-outer gave up shortly after he had crossed the Belgian coast. The others arrived at the target to find unexpected ten-tenths cloud, which, fortunately, was thin enough for the TIs to remain visible. Bombing by the squadron took place from 18,000 to 21,000 feet between 02.03 and 02.50, and all returned home to report a concentrated attack with many fires, the glow from which could be seen from the enemy coast. It was, indeed, a highly effective raid, which produced massive damage at both targets, and around 50% of the built-up area of each was destroyed. In terms of buildings, this amounted to over 2,300 destroyed at the two locations, of which 171 in Mönchengladbach were industrial.

The final operation of the month saw a force of 622 aircraft take off, and set out for Berlin. 101 Squadron put up twenty Lancasters, which departed Ludford Magna either side of 20.00, with S/L Dilworth the senior pilot on duty. F/O Rowland and F/Sgt Sexton turned back at Mablethorpe, the former with an unserviceable rear turret, and the latter with an indisposed bomb-aimer. F/Sgt Foran lost his port-outer engine a few miles out over the North Sea, while Sgt Evans was midway between Norfolk and Texel when his starboard-outer engine let go. The outward route passed between Texel and Vlieland, and continued on a south-easterly heading to pass south of Hannover as if heading for Leipzig, before turning again to the north-west, to bypass Berlin to

Sgt Pat Evans (right) and friends (GW)

the south, and then swing sharply to run in on the city centre from the south-east. The return route would be via Kassel and south of Cologne for an exit over the French coast. There was cloud in the target area, estimated at between three and nine-tenths with tops at around 10,000 feet, and this combined with continuing problems with H2S to cause the Pathfinders to mark an area well short of the city centre. This was exacerbated by the almost inevitable creep-back, which left a trail of bomb craters up to thirty miles back along the line of approach. The 101 Squadron crews delivered their hardware onto green TIs from 19,000 to 22,000 feet between 23.38 and 00.08, and all but one returned to make their reports. The cloud had made an accurate assessment impossible, but the consensus was of a successful attack, if the Pathfinder marking had been accurate. Forty-seven aircraft failed to return, among them JB150, which disappeared without trace with the crew of F/Sgt Edis RAAF. The 1 Group ORB describes this operation as "misfiring by a rather disturbing distance". The squadron participated in thirteen operations during the month, and dispatched a record 245 sorties for the loss of three Lancasters and crews.

September 1943

Preparations for the third and final Berlin operation in the current phase took place on the 3rd, and affected only the Lancaster stations, upon which a force of 316 of the type was made ready. The use of an all-Lancaster force may well have reflected the disproportionately high and unsustainable losses suffered by the Halifaxes and Stirlings in recent operations. 101 Squadron provided twenty-one Lancasters, which took off between 19.30 and 19.55, led by W/C Carey-Foster. F/Sgt Foran abandoned his sortie over base because of engine failure, and W/O Cunningham turned back from south of Norwich for the same reason. The others pressed on, adopting an outward route that took the bomber stream in a straight line across the Den Helder peninsular and northern shore of the Ijsselmeer, all the way to Brandenburg, thirty-five miles from the city centre, from where the Pathfinders were to plot their way to the aiming-point via a series of lakes. The thick cloud that had been present all the way from the Dutch coast cleared almost miraculously at the target, allowing the Pathfinders to ground mark, rather than employ parachute flares. The first TIs were dropped accurately onto the planned aiming-point, but the remainder fell between two and five miles back along the line of approach. The 101 Squadron crews bombed from 18,000 to 21,500 feet between 23.25 and 23.38, before heading north for the elongated return journey, which intentionally violated Swedish airspace, and skirted the northern tip of Denmark. The consensus at debriefing was of a well-concentrated and successful attack, the first part of which was borne out in a post-raid assessment. Fortunately, the planners had allowed a bombing window of just eleven minutes, too short a time to allow a massive creep-back to develop, and most of the bombs had fallen within the built-up area of the city, mostly across the residential districts of Wedding, Moabit and Charlottenburg, and the industrial district of Siemensstadt. Twenty-two aircraft failed to return, and three of these belonged to 101 Squadron, which represented the heaviest loss since its conversion to Lancasters. ED410 crashed at Suttrup in Germany's Münsterland on the way out, killing F/O Carpenter and five of his crew, with just the bomb-aimer surviving to fall into enemy hands. There were no survivors from W/O Tucker's ED659, which went down somewhere near the target, and only F/Sgt Hammond and his bomb-aimer survived the destruction by a night fighter of JB149, possibly after both gunners had been killed during the engagement.

A total of 125 aircraft and crews had been lost from the three Berlin operations of this first phase, and this may have influenced Harris's decision to call a halt at this point, until the long, dark, cloudy nights of winter could provide better protection for his bombers. There were, however, plenty of other targets to occupy the attention of his force, and after one night's rest, 605 aircraft were made ready on the 5th to raid the twin cities of Mannheim and Ludwigshafen, sitting astride the Rhine in southern Germany. The plan was to exploit the creep-back phenomenon, by selecting an aiming-point in the eastern half of Mannheim, to allow the bombing to spread back along the line of approach from the west, and spill into Ludwigshafen. 101 Squadron detailed nineteen Lancasters, which took off between 19.05 and 19.37 with no senior officers on duty, other than the station commander, G/C Blucke. There were no early returns, and all reached the target to find clear skies and good visibility, although haze, and later, smoke, obscured ground detail to an extent, except for the river. This was not critical, as the Pathfinders maintained a constant supply of cascading green TIs, which the squadron crews aimed at from 18,000 to 20,000 feet between 23.03 and 23.42. All but one returned home to describe a well-concentrated attack, that produced many fires, the glow from which was visible a hundred miles into the return journey. Local reports confirmed the devastating effects of the raid, Mannheim describing a catastrophe, and Ludwigshafen detailing 1,080 houses destroyed, and many industrial premises, including an I.G. Farben factory, damaged. Thirty-four aircraft failed to return, and the squadron's run of missing crews continued. A night fighter accounted for JA926 between the Luxembourg frontier and the target, and, unusually for a 101 Squadron crew, F/O Graham and five others survived to join the ever-swelling ranks of Bomber Command airmen on extended leave in PoW camps.

The original plan for the night of the 5/6th had been to attack Munich, and this operation was reinstated for the following night, for which a force of 404 aircraft was made ready. S/L St John was posted to 1667 Conversion Unit during the course of the day, at the conclusion of his tour, and his flight commander role passed to S/L Moody. It is believed that he moved again to 1656 Conversion Unit, from where he would return to the operational scene in May 1944, as the commanding officer of 103 Squadron at Elsham Wolds. 101 Squadron briefed sixteen crews for the night's work, and they took off between 19.20 and 19.35 led by S/L Dilworth. F/O Kelly was unable to coax ED809 above 13,000 feet, and turned back from near Poix, some fifty miles inland from Caen, but the other pushed on to the target area, where the cloud cover was assessed as somewhere between three and eight-tenths. On ETA., red and green TIs were in evidence, and the 101 Squadron crews bombed on these from 19,000 to 21,000 feet between 23.37 and 23.56. Returning crews were of mixed opinions as to the effectiveness of the attack and where the bombs fell, but the general opinion was that it had begun in scattered fashion before becoming more concentrated in the later stages. Some crews made timed runs from the Ammersee, a lake twenty-one miles south-west of the city, but there is no mention of 101 Squadron crews doing so. It was established later, that the bombs hitting the city had fallen mostly into southern and western districts.

Acting S/L Greig DFC, the navigator who had been in charge of C Flight, was posted to 2 PDC during the second week of the month, and S/L Sturgess was awarded a DFC at the same time. Over the course of a four-week period, Hannover would be targeted four times, the first operation being scheduled for the night of the 22/23rd. 101 Squadron would use the occasion for the first small-scale operational use of ABC, when JA977 lined up with F/L Austin at the controls, among nineteen Lancasters from the squadron as part of an overall force of 711 aircraft. They took off either side of 18.30, led by S/Ls Dilworth, Moody and Sturgess, and there were no early returns. Conditions in the target area were ideal, with clear skies and good visibility, and there was only a stronger-than-forecast wind to cause a problem. The 101 Squadron crews bombed on cascading green TIs from 18,000 to 21,500 feet between 21.30 and 21.50, and all but one returned home to report a highly concentrated attack, which set off explosions, and spread fire across the city, the glow from which could be seen from the Dutch coast, two hundred miles away. F/L Austin and crew described it as, "Excellent attack – should be the end of Hannover". Twenty-six aircraft failed to return, and among them was the squadron's W4324, which crashed on the northern outskirts of Bremerhaven, killing Sgt Green and his crew. Exactly what did happen at Hannover is something of a mystery, because it seems, that the main weight of the attack fell between two and five miles south-east of the city centre, and, according to Martin Middlebrook in Bomber Command War Diaries, it was unlikely to have caused serious damage. The main force crews were unanimous in their assessment that it was among the most destructive attacks that they had experienced, although the 8 Group ORB admits to a hugely disappointing performance by the Pathfinders. That said, fires visible from a distance of two hundred miles are not produced by a dummy or decoy fire site, so something significant was burning. It is also suspicious, that only one of the four raids on Hannover was described as successful (to be dealt with at the appropriate juncture), and caused such disproportionately massive damage to be unusual for a single attack. It is my opinion that the damage to Hannover was not achieved in one night, but was accumulative, and spread over the entire series.

The following night brought a return to Mannheim, which was still reeling from the blow earlier in the month. A force of 628 aircraft included a contribution from 101 Squadron of eighteen Lancasters, not one of them captained by a senior officer. They took off either side of 18.30, and made their way to the target in good weather conditions, which persisted all the way. The target was identified by the Pathfinder red, yellow and green TIs, although the visibility allowed crews to identify the river and built-up area of the city visually. They bombed from 18,000 to 21,000 feet between 21.52 and 22.14, and all but one returned to report a successful operation, describing concentrated bombing in the north, but some scattering to the south, a number of large explosions, much smoke and many fires visible from 130 miles into the return journey. Thirty-two aircraft were missing, including 101 Squadron's only participating ABC Lancaster, JA977, which was damaged by enemy action, before exploding and crashing near Metz in north-eastern France. F/O Turner and five of his crew lost their lives, but the flight engineer and bomb-aimer survived as PoWs. The flight engineer and special equipment operator were both holders of the DFM. W4923 landed at 03.35 in the hands of F/O McManus and crew, and, following an inspection, would be struck off charge on the 12th of October. Mannheim had suffered heavily again on this night, registering the destruction of more than nine hundred houses before the bombing spread across the Rhine into Ludwigshafen.

Preparations took place on the 27th for the second raid on Hannover, for which a force of 678 aircraft was assembled and included seventeen Lancasters from 101 Squadron. The senior officers remained at home as the squadron element began taking off at 19.15, and headed for the target, where conditions were similar to those attending the earlier raid. The problem on this night was an inaccurate wind forecast, which allowed the Pathfinder markers to drift towards the northern edge of the city, where a concentrated attack took place. The 101 Squadron crews bombed from 18,800 to 21,000 feet between 22.02 and 22.24, except, that is, for W/O Walker and crew, whose LM364 was coned by searchlights and hit by flak five miles short of the target. They dropped the bombs at 21.59, and established that the bomb doors and underside of the aircraft had been severely damaged. A fire broke out, which was only extinguished through a huge effort by the flight engineer, assisted by other members of the crew. P/O Skipper called base at 01.10 to ask permission to land, but was diverted to Lindholme, and, ten minutes later, JA965 was shot down by an intruder near Wickenby, and all eight crew members were killed. This was the second ABC Lancaster to be lost. The operation was another failure, which deposited most of the bombs in open country and onto outlying communities five miles north of the city centre.

The squadron carried out its final operation of the month on the night of the 29/30th, when supporting a raid on Bochum by 352 aircraft. They had been briefed for Hannover, but the forecast weather conditions were deemed to be unfavourable, and the target was switched to the Ruhr. A dozen 101 Squadron Lancasters took off either side of 18.30, again without the presence of a senior officer, and headed eastwards for the Dutch coast. F/L Frazer-Hollins was half-way into the North Sea crossing when an engine on each side gave cause for concern, while F/Sgt Fawcett was approaching Texel when his port-outer engine began to fail, and both were forced to turn back. The others pressed on to find good conditions over the target, and accurate Pathfinder marking in progress. They bombed on green TIs from 18,000 to 21,000 feet between 20.57 and 21.10, and all returned safely to report a concentrated attack, which created many fires and produced large amounts of smoke. The effectiveness of the operation was confirmed by post-raid reconnaissance, which showed over five hundred houses to have been destroyed, with a further seven hundred seriously damaged. During the course of the month the squadron undertook seven operations, launching 122 sorties for the loss of seven aircraft and crews.

W/O Walker and crew, at the time the most decorated crew in Bomber Command. On 26/27th November 1943, P/O Walker, as he then was, and his crew failed to return from Berlin (GW).

101 Squadron's Secret Equipment: 'Airborne Cigar'

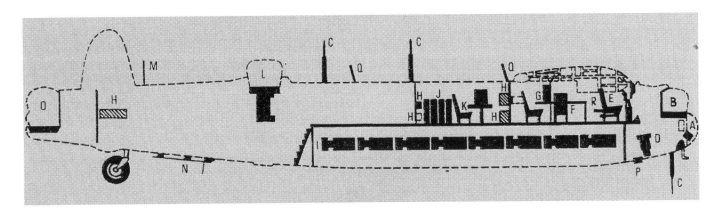

Above: The layout of an ABC-equipped Lancaster of 101 Sqn. (Rusty Waughman)

A: Bomb Aimer
B: Front turret
C: ABC transmitter aerials
D: Camera
E: Pilot
F: Navigator

G: Wireless Operator
H: Main (front) and tail (rear) spars
I: Bomb bay
J: ABC transmitters and receiver (port side of aircraft)
K: Special Equipment Operator
L: Mid-upper turret

M: ABC receiver aerial
N: Beam approach aerial
O: Rear turret
P: 'Window' / flare chute
Q: Standard fit wireless aerial
R: Flight engineer

Above left: A crude attempt has been made to censor this photo of LL774, SR-U, in an apparent effort to delete the three ABC aerials and the squadron designator. The aircraft was lost without trace on 14th October 1944 with P/O Hunt and his crew, attacking Duisburg on the second raid of that day (GW).

Above right: Rusty Waughman's Lancaster LL757, SR-W 'Oor Wullie', being serviced at her dispersal in May 1944. Rusty is in the cockpit; the figure kneeling on the wing is Willie 'Jock' Steadman, the ground crew NCO. Photographs of ABC-equipped aircraft were strictly forbidden, and this one was taken surreptitiously by Ted Manners, the crew's Special Duties Operator. Two of the three ABC transmitter aerials can clearly be seen on top of the fuselage and the third can just be made out under the nose (Rusty Waughman).

This is the only known picture of the secret ABC radio transmitter / receiver equipment, fitted to 101 Sqn Lancasters from late 1943 onwards. The black boxes (centre) were the transmitters. Leads go to the aerials which were the distinguishing feature of ABC-equipped aircraft (Rusty Waughman / GW)

One of the most fascinating aspects of the bomber war was in the field of electronics, where every measure to gain advantage over the enemy was met by a countermeasure. Now that the efficacy of Window was waning, it was decided to equip a squadron with frequency jamming apparatus, and 100 Squadron was earmarked to be the recipient of the device, code-named "Jostle". There was also to be a phased introduction of H2S to non-Pathfinder aircraft as standard issue, and, as 101 Squadron was not included in the first phase of conversions, while 100 Squadron was, it was to Ludford Magna that the equipment was delivered. The device provided an opportunity to jam three frequencies simultaneously with engine noise, with the aim of interfering with ground to air night fighter communications. An extra crew member was required to operate Jostle, renamed Airborne Cigar, or ABC in 101 Squadron aircraft. The job of broadcasting spurious instructions was already being handled by a special ground unit in England, and would prove to be effective.

A number of trials took place in a squadron aircraft in early September, overseen by a radar specialist, F/L Collins, who was on secondment from Bomber Command. A trials flight actually approached to within ten miles of the enemy coast on the 8th, and F/L Austin was the pilot selected for all proving flights. The first two ABC-equipped Lancasters, JA965 and JA977, arrived on the squadron via the Signals Intelligence Unit, and were easily identifiable by the three seven-foot long aerials sprouting from the fuselage. However, a full bomb load would also be carried, the only concession being a reduction of around 1,000lbs to compensate for the weight of the extra equipment at 605lbs, and the operator. The intention was, that once the ABC Flight became operational, a minimum of eight of its aircraft would accompany every major Bomber Command operation, spread through the stream, not more than ten miles apart, and this would happen whether or not the rest of 1 Group was operating. To accommodate the increased activity, the complement of aircraft on charge would exceed thirty, and, at one time, would reach forty-two, including reserves.

The application and use of ABC is described in Ted Manner's biography, 'Carried on the Wind' (Woodfield Publishing, 2010) by Sean Feast and is reproduced with his permission:

"ABC is designed for use on bombing raids over enemy territory to interrupt enemy communications by jamming particular frequencies on which radio messages are being sent to night fighters from ground control stations. It comprises three 50-watt transmitters, each capable of sending out frequency-modulated jamming signals covering narrow frequency bands selected within the 38.3 to 42.5 Mhz range by means of manual tuning controls. A 'panoramic' receiver provides means of locating enemy transmissions in this range of frequencies, and setting jamming signals accurately upon them.

The total weight of the equipment is 604¾ lbs. When the equipment is switched on, all three transmitters are suppressed simultaneously while the panoramic receiver sweeps over the 38.3 to 42.5 Mhz band 25 times each second. Any signals picked up are displayed on a three-inch diameter cathode ray tube. Here the frequencies are represented as a horizontal line, and any signals picked up are shown as vertical 'blips' which grow out of the base. When a 'blip' appears, the operator sets a bright strobe spot to mark it and 'throws' a switch which stops the panoramic sweep of the receiver; he tunes it to the single frequency marked by the strobe and brings his earphones into the receiver circuit so that he can listen to the incoming signal. Having identified this as an enemy ground transmission, he may then switch on a transmitter and tune the tuning control until the jamming signal, as displayed on the cathode ray tube, covers the marker spot. The enemy signal is then completely obliterated in his earphones by the output of the jamming transmitter.

Whenever desirable, the operator may suppress the transmitter in order to determine whether the enemy has changed to a new frequency, and if so, re-adjust the jamming signal. Three transmitters are provided so that three communications channels in the enemy Ground Control Intercept (GCI) band may be simultaneously jammed."

Rather than being a German speaker, the Special Duties Operator needed only to recognise genuine German broadcasts, as opposed to Czech, Dutch or other European languages. The operators quickly learned key operational and technical words and phrases which confirmed that the communications were, indeed, intended for night fighters.

October 1943

There would be a much-reduced effort from 101 Squadron during the early part of the new month, as the Jostle equipment was installed into its Lancasters and the crews underwent training for their Radio Countermeasures (RCM) role. There would be a hectic round of operations for the Lancaster squadrons generally during the first eight nights, beginning on the 1/2nd with Hagen, a steel and coal-producing town south of Dortmund at the eastern end of the Ruhr. The all-Lancaster heavy force of 243 aircraft included ten from 101 Squadron, led by F/L MacKay, which were airborne from Ludford Magna by 18.20. Rather than adopt the usual route out across the Lincolnshire coast, they headed down to Dungeness to cross the Channel and approach the target via the French coast and the Mönchengladbach area. F/O Humphries developed starboard engine problems, and abandoned his sortie over base. He was joined by F/Sgt Page, whose rear turret became inoperable. The others continued on to find the target covered by thin cloud, and identified it by the red and green TIs seen cascading down. The initial Oboe skymarking had been spot-on, and the ground markers could be seen clearly by the main force crews. The 101 Squadron contingent bombed from 15,500 to 21,000 feet between 21.00 and 21.11, and contributed to the delivery of a major blow against the town's industry. Included in the industrial damage was a factory producing accumulator batteries for U-Boots, and this had a serious effect on production of the vessels.

The following night brought Munich into the bomb sights of an initial force of 294 Lancasters from 1, 5 and 8 Groups. Among them were nine representing 101 Squadron, led by F/L Robertson. They began taking off at 18.30, but F/Sgt Sexton turned back at the Belgian coast when his navigator complained of a lack of oxygen. F/Sgt Marsh was at 20,000 feet between Amiens and Reims when a starboard engine cut, and he also turned back. The others found clear skies over the target, and, whilst such conditions were beneficial for the marking process, they were also of assistance to the many night fighters appearing on the scene. The initial marking was scattered, but the 101 Squadron crews were able to identify the built-up area, and bombed on the markers from 19,500 to 21,000 feet between 22.33 and 22.45. They all returned safely to report a pall of smoke from the many fires that were visible a hundred miles into the return journey. Post-raid reconnaissance revealed that heavy bombing had taken place over the southern and south-eastern districts of the city, before a creep-back, largely by 5 Group, developed up to fifteen miles out along the line of approach. 339 buildings were destroyed, but it could have been many more had the Pathfinder markers been concentrated over the intended aiming-point, and 5 Group had not employed its "time-and-distance" bombing method.

The Lancaster brigade was joined by Halifaxes and Stirlings on the night of the 3/4th, when Kassel was selected as the target for an overall force of 547 aircraft. Just eight crews were briefed at Ludford Magna, and they took off between 18.25 and 19.10, before heading for the Lincolnshire coast and an exit between Mablethorpe and Skegness. F/O Leeder was forty miles north-east of Sheringham bound for the northern tip of Texel, when his rear turret failed, and W/O Cunningham was also over the North Sea as his port-outer engine caught fire, and forced him to abandon his sortie. The night's early returns were completed when a surging starboard-inner engine ended W/O Groome's participation. The five remaining squadron crews reached the target, where the Pathfinder blind markers (H2S) overshot the aiming-point, and thick ground haze prevented the visual markers from being able to correct the situation. This caused the main weight of bombs to fall into the western half of the city and beyond into outlying communities, but the district of Wolfsanger, east of the city centre was devastated, possibly because a stray bomb caused an ammunition dump in nearby Ihringshausen to detonate and attract more bomb loads. Among the damage were fires at the Henschel and Fieseler aircraft factories. The 101 Squadron crews played their part from 18,000 to 20,400 feet between 21.18 and 21.38, and returned safely to report a successful operation, with a number of large explosions and a pall of black smoke rising to 10,000 feet. Twenty-four aircraft failed to return, but there were only four Lancasters in that figure.

The squadron briefed a further eight crews on the 4th, for an operation that night to Frankfurt by an overall mixed force of 406 aircraft. A spoof raid was also laid on at Ludwigshafen, where the I.G Farben works was to be the aiming-point. The 101 Squadron crews took off in a fifteen-minute slot from 18.30, led by F/Ls MacKay and Robertson, and all made it to the target, where good weather conditions prevailed. The Pathfinders marked the aiming-point accurately with red and green TIs, and the main force exploited the opportunity to deliver the first really effective blow on this important city. The 101 Squadron crews bombed from 18,500 to 20,000 feet between 21.32 and 22.00, and returned with tales of large explosions, many fires and smoke drifting upwards to 10,000 feet and beyond. Post-raid reconnaissance confirmed the accuracy of the attack, which left the eastern districts and docks area a "sea of flames".

The crew of F/Sgt Nightingale with an unidentified Lancaster (GW).

By the 6th, over half of the squadron's Lancasters had been fitted with Jostle, and the first full use of ABC came during an operation to Stuttgart on the night of the 7/8th. A force of 343 Lancaster was drawn from 1, 3, 5, 6 and 8 Groups, of which nineteen represented 101 Squadron, and it is believed that ten of them were equipped with Jostle. W/C Carey-Foster was the senior pilot on duty, backed up by S/L Dilworth, and they took off either side of 20.30, before flying south to exit the English coast at Beachy Head. F/Sgt Nightingale abandoned his sortie over base with a failed port-inner engine, and W/O Cunningham did likewise when the gremlins knocked out his compass, Gee and Jostle equipment. Finally, Sgt Evans turned back because of a coolant leak, having reached the midpoint of the Channel. The others pressed on in clear skies until fifty miles from the target, where the cloud built up and hid the ground from view. The Pathfinder markers identified two distinct areas, but bombs fell in various parts of the city. The 101 Squadron crews bombed from 19,000 to 21,000 feet between 00.09 and 00.21, and contributed to the destruction of 344 buildings, and damage to 4,500 others. Whether it was Jostle, the diversionary operations or a combination of both that were responsible for the light losses on this night is not known, but only four aircraft failed to return.

The third Hanover raid followed on the night of the 8/9th, for which 504 aircraft were made ready, including the last twenty-six Wellingtons to take part in a Bomber Command operation as bombers. 101 Squadron contributed fifteen Lancasters, which took off between 22.35 and 22.50, led by S/L Dilworth, but F/O McManus abandoned his sortie over base with oxygen failure, and Sgt Daye turned back from Skegness with an engine problem. The others continued on, adopting the usual route for central Germany, via Texel, and began to arrive in the target area shortly after 01.30 to find clear skies and an abundance of night fighters. The Pathfinders marked the centre of the city for the first time, and the main force followed up with concentrated bombing that crept back no more than two miles within the built-up area. The 101 Squadron crews delivered their mixed loads of HE and incendiaries from 18,000 to 21,000 feet between 01.30 and 01.43, and returned with enthusiastic reports of a successful operation. This time, post-raid reconnaissance provided good news, and confirmed the crews' accounts. Severe damage resulted in central and most other districts, and 3,932 buildings were completely destroyed, with thirty thousand others damaged to some extent.

There would now be a lull in main force operations until the night of the 18/19th, when the final operation against Hannover was scheduled. It was to be an all-Lancaster affair, for which 360 aircraft were made ready, of which fifteen belonged to 101 Squadron. They took off between 17.05 and 17.25, led by S/Ls Moody and Sturgess, and there were no early returns. They arrived at the target to find eight to ten-tenths cloud, and scattered Pathfinder marking, and bombed from 19,500 to 20,500 between 20.18 and 20.32, before returning home with pessimistic reports of the outcome. The raid was, indeed, a failure, which fell mostly upon open country to the north and north-west. Among the eighteen missing aircraft were two from 101 Squadron, ending a recent run of loss-free operations. DV230 was shot down by a night fighter, and crashed a dozen miles north-north-west of the target, killing F/O Humphries and the other eight men on board, while DV266 crashed about seven miles south-west of Hannover at 20.30, with fatal consequences for Sgt Daye and six of his eight-man crew. As frequently happened, the bomb-aimer was the only survivor, as he lay literally on top of his escape hatch, and he became a PoW.

The first major raid of the war on Leipzig was mounted on the night of the 20/21st. An all-Lancaster force of 358 aircraft from 1, 5, 6 and 8 Groups was assembled, and sixteen of them were provided by 101 Squadron. There were no senior officers present as they took off from Ludford Magna between 17.15 and 17.45, and headed into appalling weather conditions, which included severe icing. F/O Todd lost his port-inner engine on take-off, and P/O Adamson had his Gee equipment catch fire while climbing over base. Sgt Bruce lost the use of his port-outer engine when twenty-five miles short of Texel, and Sgt Evans was in the same area when a variety of problems ended his part in the operation. At the target there was almost complete cloud cover, with tops at 10,000 feet and a second layer at 20,000 feet. Flak was negligible, but searchlights were active and lit up the clouds brilliantly. There were some night fighters in evidence, but a spoof raid on Berlin by Mosquitos may have drawn the majority away. The Pathfinders employed both sky and ground markers, but the attack was scattered and ineffective. The 101 Squadron contingent began to arrive soon after 21.00, and they bombed either on ETA., or on the markers from 19,000 and 23,000 feet between 21.02 and 21.10. Returning crews were not optimistic about the outcome, and some described the operation as a wasted effort. S/L Sturgess concluded his tour at this point, and was posted to 1662 Conversion Unit.

In contrast, to the above, the second raid of the month on Kassel, on the 22/23rd, would be one of the outstanding successes of the year. A force of 569 aircraft included a contribution from 101 Squadron of fourteen Lancasters, which took off either side of 18.00 led by S/Ls Dilworth and Moody, to form up over the station before heading south to pass out over Dungeness. F/Sgt Matthews lost his port-outer engine two-thirds of the way to the Scheldt Estuary, and turned back at 19.47, while the others pressed on, and arrived at the target about an hour and a quarter later to find clear skies. The blind marking overshot the aiming-point, but the visual marker crews rescued the operation by correctly identifying the centre of the city and delivered their markers there. The main force followed up with extreme accuracy, and despite a decoy site, perhaps, drawing off a few bomb loads, the majority found the mark and an outstandingly successful raid was the result. The 101 Squadron crews bombed from 19,000 to 21,000 feet between 21.01 and 21.28, and observed a large concentration of fires, and smoke rising to 15,000 feet. In some ways, the raid progressed along the lines of the firestorm raid on Hamburg, and, while it was by no means as extensive a conflagration, more than 3,500 individual fires had to be dealt with, and 4,349 apartment blocks were completely destroyed, with a further 6,700 damaged. This amounted to 63% of the city's living accommodation. 155 industrial buildings were also destroyed, along with many of a public nature, and in excess of six thousand people lost their lives. It was not a one-sided contest, however, and a successful night fighter operation contributed to the loss of forty-three aircraft. This was the first occasion on which all 101 Squadron participants carried ABC. The month brought nine operations, 114 sorties and the loss of two Lancasters and crews.

November 1943

Harris sent a letter to Prime Minister Churchill on the 3rd, in which he stated, that if supported by the UK based American 8th bomber force, he could "wreck Berlin from end to end", and obtain a victory without the need for the kind of protracted and costly land campaigns which he had personally witnessed during the Great War. He also predicted that it would cost around five hundred aircraft between them. The Americans, however, were committed to victory on land, where the cameras could capture the action for the folks back home, and there was never the slightest chance of enlisting their help. It should also be remembered, that it was the United States Army Air Force, and unlike the independent RAF, it did not have the authority to determine its own actions. In typically bullish fashion, Harris would go to Berlin with or without the Americans, and laid plans for a resumption of the campaign later in the month.

In the meantime, Düsseldorf was selected as the target for the first operation of the month, for which 589 Lancasters and Halifaxes were made ready during the course of the 3rd. Twenty-six Lancasters lined up for take-off at Ludford Magna, of which eighteen were ABC aircraft, and they got away without incident between 16.55 and 17.25. The most senior pilots were of flight lieutenant rank, but the senior officer on duty was S/L Rosevear, a navigator who had been posted in from 27 O.T.U back in early October, and, when operating, would fly with the crew of P/O Kelly. While F/L Robertson was abandoning his sortie over base with technical problems, the others flew out over the Norfolk coast, and began to arrive in the target area at about 19.40 to find clear skies and plenty of searchlights. They bombed on green TIs from 15,000 to 23,000 feet between 19.44 and 20.00, and returning crews were confident that they had dealt a severe blow. Eighteen aircraft failed to return, and among these were two from 101 Squadron. DV265 was intercepted over the target by a night fighter, the cannon shells from which started a fire in the fuselage, trapping the four crew members aft of the navigator's compartment. These and the pilot, Sgt Evans, were still on board when the Lancaster crashed on the north-eastern edge of the city, and the three survivors fell into enemy hands. LM365 crashed in the Mönchengladbach area, which suggests that it was homebound at the time, and F/Sgt Cummings died alongside his seven crew mates. Post-raid reconnaissance revealed that the main weight of the attack had fallen into central and southern districts, and created much further damage to housing and industry.

Also present among the bomber force on this night were Lancaster IIs of 3 and 6 Groups, which were conducting the first large-scale test of the G-H blind bombing device. This was based on a G-H leader bombing on a broadcast signal, much like Oboe. The release of his bombs acted as the signal to the aircraft in the following gaggle to let their bombs go also, and the system could be employed by night and day. On this occasion, equipment failure caused the test to be inconclusive, and it would be the autumn of 1944 before the system was put fully and effectively into service with 3 Group, and used extensively in the campaigns against Germany's oil industry and railway network.

A number of operations were planned during the ensuing week, but all were cancelled because of concerns about the weather. A high volume of postings in and out occurred during the month, and among those arriving from 1662 Conversion Unit was S/L Robertson DFC. Briefings took place on the morning of the 10th for ABC crews to accompany a 5 Group attack on the port of Königsberg, situated at the eastern end of Germany's

Baltic coast. (Now known as Kaliningrad in Russia). This required a round-trip of 1,870 miles, which decreed a heavy fuel and light bomb load. At midday, a change of target came through, and the armourers had to toil throughout the afternoon bombing up twenty Lancasters to join 293 others from 1, 5 and 8 Groups to attack the marshalling yards at the mouth of the Mont Cenis railway tunnel at Modane, on the main line between southern France and Italy. They took off between 20.30 and 20.50, led by S/Ls Dilworth, Moody and Rosevear, the last-mentioned shown in the ORB as crew captain, thus recognising his status as B Flight commander, despite being navigator to P/O Kelly. P/O Fawcett abandoned his sortie over base, after his navigational equipment and ASI failed, leaving the remaining squadron participants to fly out over Selsey Bill, and make landfall on the French coast at Cabourg, before heading for the target area. They began to arrive at around 01.00 in bright moonlight, to find Pathfinder ground markers clearly visible but slightly beyond the planned aiming-point. They bombed from 18,000 to 21,000 feet between 01.00 and 01.24, and contributed to the severe damage inflicted upon the railway installations. They all returned safely to report large explosions, some scattering of bombs, but, generally, satisfaction for a successful night's work.

Minor operations occupied most of the heavy squadrons through to the resumption of the Berlin offensive, a period which would see the Command reach its lowest ebb. The long and exceedingly rocky road to Berlin was re-joined on the night of the 18/19th, for which an all-Lancaster heavy force of 440 aircraft was prepared. While this operation was in progress, a diversion by 395 aircraft of 3, 4, 6 and 8 Groups would take place at Mannheim and Ludwigshafen, to hopefully fool, or at least, split the defences. 101 Squadron contributed twenty-three aircraft to the Berlin raid, and they took off between 17.00 and 17.40, with W/C Carey-Foster the senior pilot on duty. The route out took them over the Lincolnshire coast to rendezvous with the rest of the force over the North Sea. From there they were to adopt a fairly direct course, a little south of east, passing north of Hanover to attack Berlin from west to east. The return journey routed them south of the Ruhr, across Belgium, to depart Fortress Europe over the French coast. P/O Slater abandoned his sortie over base because of an unserviceable rear turret, and Sgt Bodger was twenty-five miles out from Skegness when he turned back for an unspecified reason. F/L Frazer-Hollins was within sight of the gap between Den Helder and Texel, when he lost the use of both turrets, and P/O Walker found a petrol cock frozen solid, denying him access to 500 gallons, and this persuaded him to bomb Nienburg from 22,000 feet at 20.06 as an alternative. The others pressed on to find that the forecast clear weather had failed to materialize, and the outward leg had to be undertaken over thick cloud. The winds were also not as forecast, which upset the timings, and the single aircraft equipped with the new, improved Mk III H2S equipment had to turn back early. Almost three-quarters of the blind markers using the old H2S sets either suffered malfunctions, or failed to identify Brandenburg, from where they were to make a timed run to the flare release-point. The flares that were dropped quickly disappeared into the cloud, and the result was a scattered and largely ineffective raid. The 101 Squadron crews began to arrive shortly before 21.00, and bombed on ETA or on the glow of TIs beneath the cloud from 20,000 to 23,000 feet between 20.58 and 21.18. Nine Lancasters failed to return, and among them was the squadron's LM370, which crashed while outbound at Schoonebeek in Holland, close to the frontier with Germany, killing P/O McManus and the other seven men on board. The Mannheim diversion did help to reduce losses among the Berlin contingent, but lost twenty-three aircraft itself.

The weather closed in for the next two days, before a call for a maximum effort on Berlin on the 22nd was answered by 101 Squadron with twenty-six Lancasters, in an overall force of 764 aircraft. The route was as for the previous occasion, with a reciprocal return, and no diversion was planned. An early take-off had the Ludford Magna crews transported to their aircraft before 16.00, for departure either side of 17.00, led for the first time by S/L Robertson. DV291 swung as it raced along the runway, and was written off in the subsequent crash and fire, but no injuries were reported among the crew of P/O Wallis. W/O Nightingale was just off

137

Skegness when his port-inner engine failed and ended his interest in the night's proceedings. F/Sgt Laurens had just crossed the frontier into Germany when his instruments iced-up, and he, too, turned back. The others began to arrive over the target shortly after 20.00, and found ten-tenths cloud, above which the parachute flares drifted at the behest of the wind. It was impossible for the crews to determine precisely where they were above the city, and the 101 Squadron crews aimed at the Wanganui flares (skymarkers) from 19,000 to 22,000 feet between 20.05 and 20.31. In fact, the H2S operators had done their job perfectly, and the main weight of bombs fell squarely into the central area of the city and westwards. They hit residential and industrial districts alike, causing major fires, a number of which developed along the lines of a firestorm. The catalogue of destruction included three thousand houses and twenty-three industrial premises, and many more buildings suffered damage. Around 175,000 people lost their homes, but these were the fortunate ones, as two thousand others lost their lives. This would prove to be the most destructive raid of the war on Germany's capital city. 1 Group came through this operation without a single loss from its 169 participants, but twenty-six other aircraft failed to return. Stirling casualty figures had been causing concern for months, and, following this operation, the type was withdrawn from further activity over Germany.

The crews were back at Ludford Magna around midnight, and were able to spend a night in bed, before awaking to find the station a hive of activity after orders came through to prepare for another raid on Berlin that night. A 375-strong heavy force, consisting predominantly of Lancasters, was made ready, of which nineteen represented 101 Squadron, and they took off between 17.00 and 17.25, led again by S/L Robertson. They were to follow the same route as twenty-four hours earlier, but a total of forty-six aircraft returned early, a massive 12% of those dispatched, and among these were five from 101 Squadron. F/O Todd and F/Sgt Zanchi abandoned their sorties over base, the former with malfunctioning Gee and Jostle, and the latter for an undisclosed reason, while F/Sgt Bruce was fifty miles north-east of Sheringham when one of his gunners became indisposed. F/Sgt Trotter and Sgt Langford were both deep into the North Sea crossing, and turned back with icing and engine problems respectively. The remaining 101 Squadron participants began to arrive over the cloud-covered city shortly after 20.00, and found skymarkers drifting over the aiming-point. Some crews bombed these, while others aimed at the glow of fires still burning from the night before. They carried out their attacks from 19,000 to 22,000 feet between 20.02 and 20.29, and contributed to another outstandingly accurate and destructive attack, which left a further two thousand houses in ruins, along with eight industrial premises, while fourteen hundred people lost their lives. The German night fighter controllers correctly identified Berlin as the target, but their running commentary instructions were hampered by spurious instructions being broadcast from England. Never the less, twenty Lancasters failed to return, 5.2% of the force.

The Lancaster crews were rested on the night of the 24/25th, while elements of 4, 6 and 8 Groups carried out a modestly effective raid on Frankfurt. On the 25th, 576 Squadron was formed at Elsham Wold from C Flight of 103 Squadron, which became the new squadron's A Flight. B Flight initially consisted of four crews posted over from 101 Squadron, including those of S/L Dilworth, and Sgts Alan Bodger and Roy Whalley. Bodger, who would be a very popular member of his new unit, and would survive the war, had arrived at 101 Squadron in October, and operated for the first time against Kassel on the 22/23rd. Whalley had been posted to 101 Squadron from 1656 Conversion Unit on the 23rd of October, and had undertaken his maiden sortie against Modane on the night of the 10/11th of November. Sadly, he would lose his life during the Mailly-le-Camp raid in May 1944.

Briefings took place on the 26th for the fourth Berlin operation since the resumption, and twenty-two Lancasters were made ready at Ludford Magna. It was to be another all-Lancaster effort of 443 aircraft, and

'Paul Zanchi (left) and his crew shared a Nissen hut with mine at No. 1662 HCU at Blyton from 30th September to 28th November 1943. We became very close companions. Paul joined 101 Sqn just before I did, but sadly was shot down on 26th November 1943, just before I joined 101 Sqn. Paul's navigator, John Jossa (centre), survived their crash from over 20,000 feet. Paul and the rest of his crew were all killed. Curly Ormerod, his flight engineer, and John 'Gats' Wetton, his wireless operator, did not fly with Paul that night because of illness. My own flight engineer could not cope on operations and had to leave. I took over Curly who was then a 'spare bod' – Rusty Waughman.

the planners prepared a diversion and change of route to confuse the enemy defences. While the main operation was in progress, 178 aircraft, predominantly Halifaxes, were to carry out an attack on Stuttgart. The two forces were to exit over Beachy Head, before making for the French coast, and then head east across Belgium to a point north-east of Frankfurt, where they would diverge, one due south and the other to the north-east. The bombing run at Berlin would be roughly west to east across the city, followed by a 180 degree turn and a direct flight home between Hannover and Bremen, exiting the Dutch coast near Egmond. Sixteen of the 101 Squadron aircraft were assigned to the main operation, and six to provide RCM cover for the Stuttgart force. They began to take off at 17.00, and were all safely airborne within thirty minutes, with S/L Rosevear the senior officer on duty. Sgt Rowe and F/Sgt Head each turned back shortly after crossing the French coast, the former after electrical circuitry to vital parts of the aircraft failed, and the latter because of a sick navigator, but the others pressed on to their respective targets, and, those heading for Berlin, arrived to find the skies clear. They bombed the markers from 20,000 to 22,000 feet between 21.13 and 21.33, but the marking on this night was inaccurate, and concentrated many miles to the north-west of the intended aiming-point. Despite this, the bombing still fell within the city boundaries, and, by a stroke of luck, found the industrial suburbs of Siemensstadt and Tegel, where thirty-eight war industry factories were destroyed, and many more damaged. Night fighters got amongst the bombers on the way home, and twenty-eight Lancasters failed to return, of which two belonged to 101 Squadron. DV268, SR-O2, crashed from 20,000 feet with only the navigator, Sgt John Jossa, survived as a PoW, from the seven-man crew of Sgt Paul Zanchi. The aircraft came down crashed somewhere in northern Germany, with the six dead crewmen buried in Sage Cemetery. The fortunate navigator was captured, and was repatriated in February 1945.

There is a discrepancy concerning the loss of the second crew from the Berlin operation, and another which failed to return from Stuttgart. The Squadron ORB records F/Sgt Bennett RCAF and crew as assigned to Berlin, and P/O Walker and crew to Stuttgart in DV289 and DV285 respectively. However, in Bomber Command Losses for 1943, Bill Chorley states that F/Sgt Bennett and five of his crew rest in Dürnbach cemetery in Bavaria, which suggests strongly, that they had been assigned to Stuttgart. Two members of the crew survived to fall into enemy hands, but the Jostle operator died on the 21st of July 1944 in a camp at Vogelsang, which is near Berlin, and is buried in the Berlin War Cemetery. This may account for the confusion. P/O Walker and crew were shot down by Hptm Eckart-Wilhelm von Bonin of II/NJG1 en-route to Berlin, and crashed south-west of Verviers in Belgium, killing five of the occupants. The pilot and wireless operator were taken into captivity, while the navigator managed to evade a similar fate. This was a very experienced crew, containing holders of the CGM, the DFC and two DFMs. During the course of the month the squadron operated on six occasions, dispatched 136 sorties, losing in the process seven Lancasters and six crews.

Sgt Roy Whalley and crew went on to serve with 576 Sqn, but were lost on the Mailly-le-Camp raid in May 1944. They were on their 26th op with the unit and were flying in the aircraft in this photograph, ME586, UL-B. Back row: Sgt Scott, Roy Whalley, Fred Burgess, Jeremiah McCool. Front row - Cyril Van de Velde, Sgt Ward and Stanley Barr. (David Fell).

'We lit a fire under Les's bed! Some of my, and Paul's crew. 2nd left is Harry Nunn, my rear gunner. On the right is Norman Westby, my bomb aimer.' – Rusty Waughman.

In February 1944 snows descended on the Lincolnshire Wolds. Ludford Magna was isolated by 3 ft. of snow and 16 ft. snowdrifts. Everyone, ground and air crew, with the aid of a rum ration, cleared the runway and its approaches. The camp was operational again in a few days. A newspaper caption read 'Even heavy snow did not break their business appointment with Germany'. This is Tommy, Norman, Curly and Taffy.' – Rusty Waughman.

'Paul Zanchi, his engineer Curly Ormerod and my engineer, Les Reeves.' – Rusty Waughman. NB. This would have been taken at 1662 HCU before the crews were posted to 101 Sqn.

'Curly, myself inside and ground crew Nobby Stiles.' – Rusty Waughman.

'Curly and Ted returning after the morning Daily Inspection.' – Rusty Waughman.

A selection of photos inside and around Rusty Waughman's Lancaster.

'Top left: The engineer's view of the Lancaster's cockpit. Top right: Jock (William) Steadman working on an engine.

Above left: Looking forward from the Nav's position on the left. Flight engineer's panel and his strap seat on the right. Norman, the bomb aimer, at his control panel, in the nose.

Above right: Looking back from mid-fuselage to the rear turret. The Elsan toilet and flare chute can be seen. The main door is on the left.

Left: 'Bomb doors open.' 101 Sqn Lancs had the identification letter SR. Aircraft were given a letter of the alphabet; mine was W, hence the markings SR-W.' – Rusty Waughman

December 1943

The new month began for 101 Squadron as the old one had ended, with the red ribbon on the wall map in the briefing room on the 2nd terminating at Berlin. It also showed that it was to be a straight-in-straight-out route with no feints or diversions. An all-Lancaster main force of 378 aircraft would have eighty Lancasters, fifteen Halifaxes and eighteen Mosquitos of 8 Group leading the way and marking the target. 101 Squadron prepared twenty-one Lancasters, which took off between 16.40 and 17.00, led away by W/C Carey-Foster. P/O Syme abandoned his sortie over base after his starboard-inner engine failed, leaving the others to fly out over the sandy shoreline between Mablethorpe and Skegness, and set course for the Dutch coast near Egmond for the three-and-a-quarter-hour outward flight. Sgt Shearer was fifty miles out from Mablethorpe when both outer engines began to overheat, and he was forced to turn back. P/O Adamson was off track and became coned by searchlights and accurately engaged by flak ten miles north of Magdeburg, and dropped his bomb load there at 20.10. P/O Slater was twenty minutes behind schedule, and also bombed a searchlight and flak concentration at Magdeburg from 19,000 feet at 20.22. Those reaching the target area found a thin layer of cloud, but the ground markers were clearly visible, and bombing took place from 18,000 to 21,500 feet between 20.16.and 20.38. The Pathfinders had experienced difficulty in establishing their position, and the bombing was scattered mostly across southern districts and open country, although some useful damage was inflicted upon war industry factories in eastern and western districts. Night fighter flares were much in evidence, which boded ill for the returning bombers, particularly as wrongly forecast winds began to spread them out. Forty aircraft failed to return, and it was another sobering night for 101 Squadron, which posted missing three crews for the second operation running. The one bright spot was the survival of S/L Robertson and his seven crew members from the demise of JB128, but their colleagues in LM363 and LM364 had no such luck. The former crashed near Diepholz, probably on the way home, and the latter came down at Rehfelde, some twenty miles east of Berlin, which suggests that it had been damaged during the bombing run and had struggled on. All sixteen men in the crews of F/L Frazer-Hollins DFC and F/Sgt Murrell respectively lost their lives.

On the following night, 527 aircraft took off to attack Leipzig, which had been saved by foul weather back in October. 101 Squadron dispatched fifteen Lancasters from 00.01, in what was a very late take-off for the time of year. They headed out over the Lincolnshire coast to rendezvous with the gathering bomber stream, before setting a direct course for Berlin as a feint. F/Sgt Trotter abandoned his sortie a dozen miles north of Sheringham because of intercom problems and an ailing mid-upper gunner, and F/Sgt Laurens's starboard-outer engine failed as he approached Texel, so he dropped his bombs onto a searchlight and flak concentration on the island from 13,000 feet at 02.01, and had the satisfaction of extinguishing the lights. Assuming the Capital to be the target, the enemy night fighter controller was able to intercept the bomber stream, but lost it as it turned unexpectedly south for Leipzig. The 101 Squadron crews arrived at the target shortly before 04.00 to find cloud, which largely concealed the ground markers. Skymarkers were also in use, however, and these provided a reference point for the main force, among which, the first five 101 Squadron crews to arrive bombed from 18,000 to 21,000 at 04.01, and the last at 04.12. They contributed to a highly effective attack, which turned out to be the most damaging of the war on this city. There were few combats in the target area, but many aircraft stumbled into the Frankfurt defence zone during the long southern withdrawal route, and many of the missing twenty-four aircraft were lost here. 101 Squadron welcomed all of its crews home, but loss was never far away, and DV270 crashed a few miles from Ludford Magna while training on the evening of the 5th. Witnesses watched it emerge from low cloud and hit the ground at 20.28, killing F/O Oliver and his crew. The bomb-aimer, Sgt Anderson, was a former sprinter, who had competed for Great Britain in the 440 yards race in an international athletics meet against France in 1935.

After Leipzig, the main force stayed on the ground until mid-month, during which lull, F/L Marshall was posted in to replace the recently-departed S/L Dilworth as A Flight commander, and the acting rank of squadron leader was bestowed upon him. It was not until the night of the 16/17th that the Command ventured forth again in numbers, when an all-Lancaster heavy force of 483 aircraft was made ready for the next assault on Berlin. 101 Squadron dispatched twenty-one aircraft between 16.05 and 16.25, led by S/L Marshall, but F/O Leeder turned back with an overheating engine when forty miles off Sheringham, and P/O Dickinson was at the midpoint between the Norfolk and Dutch coasts when the oxygen system failed. The others joined the bomber stream, which adopted the now familiar direct route across Holland to the target, but, this time, with a planned withdrawal to the north-west over the Baltic and across southern Denmark to the North Sea. The German night fighter controller correctly guessed the target, and introduced elements of his force into the bomber stream very early on. F/L Robertson's DV307 was hit by flak six miles north of Hannover, and the bomb doors could not be opened to jettison the bombs. A course was set for the Baltic coast at Rostock, and, having manually opened the bomb doors, the 4,000 pounder was unloaded onto the town. Once at Berlin the Pathfinders employed skymarkers in the face of thick cloud, while five Oboe Mosquitos delivered spoof night fighter flares twenty-five miles from the target. The 101 Squadron contingent arrived in the target area on time, shortly before 20.00, and delivered their bombs onto red and green parachute flares from 17,500 to 22,000 feet between 20.00 and 20.13. The attack lacked concentration, but much of the bombing fell into central and eastern districts, where residential property sustained the most damage.

This photo is believed to be of F/O Lazenby (prior to commissioning) and his crew, who had to leave DV283 to her fate when diabolical weather conditions wrought havoc with bomber crews returning from Berlin on 16/17th December 1943 (GW).

As the tired crews crossed the English coast homebound, those from 1, 6 and 8 Groups, in particular, found a blanket of low cloud, which some described as fog, enveloping their airfields. Most did not have sufficient reserves of fuel to undertake the long diversion to Scotland or the south-west, and, consequently, stumbled around in the murk, desperately seeking somewhere to land. Others gave up, and abandoned their aircraft, and they probably made the sensible decision. For an hour before midnight, and a few hours afterwards, reports came in of downed aircraft all over eastern England, and, it was eventually established, that twenty-nine Lancasters had crashed or been abandoned by their crews. It took time to evaluate the information coming in, but, in the cold light of day, it was learned that almost 150 airmen had lost their lives when so close to safety. Losses to enemy action were inescapably part and parcel of the job, but, to have to battle the weather on return to base at the end of an exhausting seven or eight-hour slog, was asking too much. Two 101 Squadron crews were involved in the problems over England, one incident having a happy ending, the other not. DV283 arrived back short of fuel, and in the absence of a suitable landing place, was successfully abandoned by F/O Lazenby and his crew at 00.14 near Ingham. LM389 crashed into a hillside ten miles east-south-east of Selby in Yorkshire at 00.27, and only the two gunners survived with injuries from the crew of Sgt Cooper. Once all of the returning aircraft had been accounted for, it was possible to confirm that twenty-five were missing from Berlin, and two of these belonged to 101 Squadron. DV299 was lost without trace with the eight-man crew of F/Sgt Head, and DV300 fell victim to a night fighter flown by Oblt Heinz-Wolfgang Schnaufer of IV/NJG1, while outbound over the Dutch coast. The ABC Lancaster exploded near Lemmer on the northern shore of the Ijsselmeer at 18.15, and there were no survivors from the eight-man crew of F/L MacFarlane DFM, a long-standing and popular member of the squadron.

There were no operations during the ensuing three nights, and it was the 20th when orders came through to prepare for a major attack on Frankfurt. 650 aircraft were detailed, and sixteen crews briefed at Ludford Magna. It was becoming routine for the enemy night fighter controllers to plot Berlin as the destination for large bomber fleets, and, perhaps, that is why Harris selected Frankfurt. A southerly approach to Berlin would take the force past Frankfurt to the north, as had been the case with the recent operation, when Stuttgart had been used as a diversion. The intention was to keep the enemy guessing as to the final destination, Stuttgart, Munich, Mannheim or Frankfurt in the south, or Kassel, Hanover or Berlin to the north. If not deceiving the enemy entirely, the ploy might dilute the strength of the night fighter numbers brought to bear. On this night a small 8 Group diversionary raid was to take place at Mannheim, but it would not succeed in its purpose. The 101 Squadron Lancasters took off in a fifteen-minute slot from 17.15, with S/Ls Marshall and Rosevear the senior officers on duty, and, there would be no early returns. After climbing out, they made for the Norfolk coast, where the bomber stream was immediately picked up by the German controllers, who correctly guessed Frankfurt as the target. They fed night fighters into the stream all the way out, and many combats took place, although returning Lancaster crews described fighter activity as not great. Perhaps that was because of the beating the Halifax brigade was suffering a few thousand feet below. Clear skies had been forecast, and the Pathfinders had planned to employ ground markers, but they arrived at the target to find five to eight-tenths cloud, and resorted to skymarking, which became scattered. The 101 Squadron crews bombed from 18,500 to 20,500 feet between 19.37 and 19.56, and returned to report large explosions at 19.43, 19.45 and 20.15, and the glow of fires visible from 180 miles away. There were dummy target indicators and a decoy fire to create confusion, and some of the bombing was lured away as a result. The operation was rescued by the fact that some of the bombing did fall within the city, and destroyed 466 houses there and in neighbouring communities, and seriously damaged almost two thousand more. Many cultural, historical and public buildings were also hit, and 23,000 people were rendered homeless.

Preparations were put in hand on the 23rd for the seventh attack on Berlin since the resumption. A heavy force of 371 aircraft included a contribution from 101 Squadron of seventeen Lancasters, and the senior officer on duty would be the C Flight commander, S/L Rosevear, flying as navigator to P/O Kelly. F/L Rowland was first off the ground at 23.59, and F/Sgt Langford was last up at 00.35. This was the first operation for F/Sgt Waughman and crew, who had arrived from 1662 Conversion Unit in November, right in the middle of the Berlin offensive, at what surely was the worst possible time to embark on a first tour. According to the map reference in the ORB, they abandoned their sortie ten miles short of the Suffolk coast after losing navigational equipment and failing to coax DV307 above 16,000 feet. P/O Nightingale was within sight of the Scheldt Estuary when he lost an engine on each wing, and he turned back, leaving the others to push on to the Belgian/German frontier, then due east to a position south of Frankfurt, where a Mosquito element peeled off to carry out a diversionary raid on Leipzig. Berlin would be approached from the south-west, and, after bombing, the crews were to continue to the north, before turning sharply west for the direct route home across Holland. The weather outbound was not helpful to the enemy night fighters, and the Mosquito feint helped to draw them off. The target area was largely cloud-covered, and a proportion of the Pathfinder force experienced technical problems with their H2S sets. Marking was consequently scattered and sparse for the 101 Squadron crews to aim at, and they delivered their cookie and incendiaries each onto red and green TIs from 19,000 to

145

22,000 feet between 04.01 and 04.16, before returning safely to report what appeared to be an effective attack. In fact, only two districts in the south-east of the city had sustained meaningful damage in return for the loss of sixteen Lancasters.

Ludford Magna celebrates Christmas 1943 with the obligatory dance band (GW).

The fifth wartime Christmas came and went, and the final operation of the year was again directed at Berlin on the night of the 29/30th. This was to be the first of an unprecedented series of three raids in the space of five nights against the Capital spanning the turn of the year, for which 101 Squadron made ready seventeen Lancasters as part of an overall force of 712 aircraft. The route would take the bomber stream out over Texel on a long, straight leg aimed at Leipzig, where Mosquitos were to peel off to carry out spoof raids on that city and Magdeburg, while another spoof took place many miles to the west over the Ruhr. They took off between 16.55 and 17.15, with S/L Marshall the senior pilot on duty, and only F/Sgt Corkhill returned early from thirty miles off Sheringham, when his Gee and rear turret failed. The others pressed on in generally poor weather conditions to find Berlin lying beneath thick cloud. They bombed on red and green parachute flares from 19,000 to 21,500 feet between 20.06 and 20.24, before returning home south of Bremen and out over the Frisians. As often was the case, skymarking could lead to a lack of concentration, and, on this night, it caused most of the bombs to fall into southern and south-eastern districts and outlying communities, where 388 houses and other buildings were destroyed. Twenty aircraft failed to return, including the squadron's LM371, which crashed near Burgdorf, north-east of Hannover, after F/Sgt Shearer and six of his seven-man crew had parachuted into enemy hands. This was the second sortie for the Waughman crew, who had been in DV292, and described the target as "pretty hot". They reported being attacked three times by enemy fighters at the Dutch coast, and twice over the target by a JU88 and a FW190. The squadron operated six times during the month, and dispatched 107 sorties for the loss of nine Lancasters and eight crews.

It had been a hard year for all squadrons, but on balance a highly successful one, and many German cities bore the scars of battle. Their residents must have known that the coming year would only bring more of the same. An identical thought must have dominated the minds of the bomber crews, particularly those who started their tour just as the Berlin campaign resumed, and the first three months of 1944 would pit them against the Luftwaffe's Nachtjagd at its most lethal.

January 1944

One can assume with some degree of certainty, that the beleaguered residents of Berlin, and the hard-pressed crews of Bomber Command, shared a common hope for the coming year, that Germany's Capital would cease to be the focus of Harris's attention. Proud to be Berliners first and Germans second, they were a hardy breed, and just like their counterparts in London under the blitz of 1940, they bore their trials with fortitude and humour. During this, their "winter of discontent," they paraded banners in the streets, which proclaimed, "You may break our walls, but not our hearts", and the melodic song, *Nach jedem Dezember kommt immer ein Mai* (After every December comes always a May), was played endlessly over the air waves, hinting at a change of fortunes with the onset of spring. Both camps would have to endure for some time yet, however, and before New Year's Day was over, a force of 421 Lancasters would be winging its way towards the Capital, most of them to arrive overhead in the very early hours of the 2nd.

101 Squadron made ready sixteen aircraft, with S/L Marshall the senior pilot on duty, backed up by the newly-promoted S/L Robertson (not to be confused with the S/L Robertson recently posted missing). The original outward route, given to the crews at briefing, crossed the enemy coast over Denmark, and withdrew south of Leipzig to cross Belgium, and exit enemy territory at the French coast. Doubts about the weather led to a delay in take-off time, however, and this reduced the hours of darkness available to carry out the operation. It became necessary to shorten the flight time, and this was achieved by adopting the frequently used direct route to the target over Holland. As the stream passed south of Hamburg, a spoof raid by 8 Group Mosquitos would take place on that city to draw off the night fighters and keep the controller guessing. The 101 Squadron crews became airborne from Ludford Magna either side of midnight, and headed eastwards to the Dutch coast, where cloud began to increase. F/Sgt Waughman had just crossed the Dutch/German frontier in DV246, when his starboard-outer engine failed, and he turned back. He would write in his diary that all was not well with the flight engineer, who was deaf, and would have to be replaced. The other 101 Squadron participants pressed on, and, by the time they arrived in the target area shortly after 03.00, the cloud had built to ten-tenths with tops at 10,000 to 12,000 feet. The Pathfinders were using red flares with green stars, and the 101 Squadron crews bombed on their approximate position from 19,000 to 21,000 feet between 03.10 and 03.25. Unfortunately, the skymarking had soon lost accuracy and cohesion, and this led to a scattered raid that fell largely into wooded and open country. It was a disappointing outcome for the huge effort involved and the loss of twenty-eight Lancasters, including two from 101 Squadron. DV307 was lost without trace with the crew of S/L Robertson DFC, which contained two other holders of the DFC and one of the DFM, and the ABC operator wore the ribbons of both. The rear gunner was T/Sgt Jones of the USAAF. DV308 crashed in Belgium, killing four of the crew, but P/O Bell and two others survived to fall into enemy hands, while the navigator evaded a similar fate.

Snow was on the ground as the crews tumbled out of bed during the afternoon of the 2nd, still tired after their eight-hour slog to Berlin. In the briefing room they were incredulous to learn that they were being sent back there, and rumblings of discontent could be heard. There were some fresh crews available, of course, but many who had returned from Germany at breakfast time would have to go again, and it would be another late take-off. A predominantly Lancaster heavy force of 383 aircraft was prepared, to which 101 Squadron contributed a dozen, with S/L Marshall again leading from the front. The outward flight was routed directly across Holland to a point south of Bremen, where a dogleg would take the bombers to a final turning point north-west of Berlin. On the way home they would pass south of Hanover and north of the Ruhr to exit at the entry point on the Dutch coast. The 101 Squadron crews took off in the minutes before midnight, and F/Sgt Murphy was about fifty miles short of the Dutch coast when he picked up a message to land at Exeter. The instruction was intended for the Group's Wellington mining force, but fifteen Lancasters returned early as a result. The others arrived in the target area shortly before 03.00, to find ten-tenths cloud and skymarking in progress. They bombed on the Wanganui flares from 18,000 to 22,000 feet between 02.45 and 03.02, all but one returned safely to claim that the marking and bombing had been concentrated, and explosions had been observed reflecting on the clouds. In reality, the raid had been scattered and ineffective, and another expensive failure. Twenty-seven Lancasters were lost, including DV269, which was shot down by a night fighter south-west of Berlin on the way home. On board was the crew of the recently-promoted F/L Lazenby, who had, perhaps, already used up most of their ration of good fortune after taking to their parachutes on return from Berlin in mid-December. On this occasion, the pilot and three others perished, and the four survivors fell into enemy hands.

It had been a punishing round of operations, but Berlin would now be spared a visit from Harris's heavy brigade for almost three weeks. To compensate, however, he would send regular Mosquito nuisance raids to rob the inhabitants of their sleep. After two nights at home, a dozen 101 Squadron crews were called to briefing on the 5th to be told that they had another long-range operation ahead of them. Not only that, it would also be another of those unpopular late take-offs that would have them flying through the night and in bed during daylight. At least the target on this occasion was not Berlin, but the port of Stettin at the eastern end of Germany's Baltic coast, which had last been attacked to devastating effect in April. There were no senior pilots on duty as they departed Ludford Magna either side of midnight, and flew out over the Lincolnshire coast to rendezvous with the rest of the force, comprising 336 Lancasters and ten Halifaxes. Sgt Forsythe was a hundred miles east of Scarborough when the oxygen to the rear turret failed, and he was forced to turn back, while Sgt Clegg was a hundred miles further out over the North Sea when he lost the use of his starboard-inner engine and mid-upper turret. The others pushed on, and all were doubtless hopeful that the Mosquito diversion at Berlin would draw off the night fighters. Complete cloud cover all the way to the target helped to conceal the bomber stream from prying eyes, and then the cloud dispersed somewhat over the target, to enable the Pathfinders to employ both sky and ground markers. These were clearly visible to the 101 Squadron crews, who bombed from 20,000 to 22,000 feet shortly before 04.00. There was clear evidence on the ground of a successful attack, with huge fires in central districts and one very large explosion, despite the bombing drifting westwards in the later stages. Local reports stated that over five hundred houses and twenty industrial premises had been destroyed, with a further eleven hundred houses and twenty-nine industrial buildings sustaining serious damage. Harbour installations had also been hit, and eight ships sunk in the harbour. The Berlin diversion was successful in keeping most of the enemy fighters away, but sixteen Lancasters were lost. This was the fourth sortie for "Rusty" Waughman and crew, who were pleased to have acquired a new flight engineer in the shape of Sgt "Curly" Ormerod. He had formerly flown with Rusty's good and now departed friend, Sgt Zanchi. DV389 had carried them to Stettin on this night, and brought them most of the way home on three engines. They landed at 09.00, short of fuel after a round-trip of nine hours and five minutes.

The arrival of the moon period allowed further respite from operations, and batches of crews were given a forty-eight-hour pass over the ensuing week. Snowfalls and freezing conditions made life difficult for ground personnel, but they were able to keep Lancasters flying for training purposes. It was during this period, on the 11th, that S/L Morton and crew were posted in from 550 Squadron, he to assume the role of flight commander. Lancaster crews were next called to briefings on the 14th, and there must have been a degree of relief when the curtains were drawn back on the wall maps in briefing rooms all over eastern England. The red tape terminated about 125 miles short of Berlin, at Brunswick, an historic city fifty miles east of Hannover, and virtually virgin territory as far as Bomber Command was concerned. A force of 494 Lancasters was made ready, of which twenty were provided by 101 Squadron, and they would be joined by two Halifaxes. The

Ludford Magna contingent took off between 16.30 and 17.10, and, after climbing out, headed for the Lincolnshire coast and a rendezvous with the rest of the bomber stream over the North Sea. F/Sgt Holland was forty miles off Sheringham when an overheating engine persuaded him to turn back, but this was the only early return. Night fighters began to pick up the bombers shortly after they crossed the German coast near Bremen, and would remain in contact all the way to the target and back to the Dutch coast. The 101 Squadron crews reached the target area to find the Pathfinder ground markers masked by the cloud, and had to bomb on skymarkers, which, initially, were scattered and spasmodic. They delivered their cookie and incendiaries each from 20,000 to 22,000 feet between 19.15 and 19.30, and those returning home were unable to provide an assessment of the outcome. In fact, this operation was a total failure, which deposited its main effort onto outlying communities to the south. The disappointment was compounded by the loss of thirty-eight aircraft, eleven of them Pathfinders, and it was another bad night for 101 Squadron, which posted missing two eight-man crews and one of nine. The last mentioned was that of P/O Slater in DV287, which was shot down by the ace, Oblt Martin Drewes of IV/NJG1, while outbound over Holland, and crashed at Klazienaveen, southeast of Emmen and close to the border with Germany. The sole survivor was the navigator, who ultimately evaded capture. LM367 also fell to a night fighter, only this time over Germany at Lautenthal, south-west of Brunswick, on the way home, and there were no survivors from the crew of F/L Rowland DFC. Finally, F/S Bruce and his crew were all killed when ME566 crashed in Germany. This was the fifth sortie for the Waughman crew, who now had their own dedicated Lancaster, ME565, SR-W, which carried "A Wing and a Prayer" nose art.

The two Berlin operations and Brunswick had been a disaster for the Command, claiming ninety-three Lancasters in just two weeks for no worthwhile gain. 156 Squadron, which drew its fresh crews from 1 Group squadrons, had suffered unbelievably severely with the loss of fourteen aircraft during this period, and that was equivalent almost to the front-line strength of a standard two-flight squadron. Fog persisted from the 15th onwards, and a thaw set in on the 17th to ease conditions, but hardly any flying took place until air-tests on the 20th in preparation for that night's operation. On the 18th, 101 Squadron bade farewell to W/C Carey-Foster, who was posted to Bomber Command HQ, and welcomed his successor, W/C Alexander, who arrived from 550 Squadron, where he had been a flight commander.

He presided over his first operation on the night of the 20/21st, a maximum effort return to Berlin involving 769 aircraft, of which twenty Lancasters were provided by 101 Squadron. They took off either side of 16.30 led for the first time by S/L Morton, who had W/C Alexander alongside him as second pilot, and there were no early returns. Recent heavy losses had pointed to the need to adopt diversionary tactics, and abandon the straight-in straight-out routing. The plan

January 1944 saw the arrival of a new squadron commander, Wing Commander Alexander (GW)

for this night was to enter German airspace near Bremen, and approach Berlin from the north-west, while small Mosquito feints at Kiel and Hannover, hopefully, caused confusion in the mind of the night fighter controller. This did not happen, and night fighters infiltrated the bomber stream south of Kiel. They were employing new tactics, Sahme Sau, or tame boar, based on night fighters assembling around radio beacons and being directed to the bombers by running commentary. LM319 was attacked by a night fighter over Bitterfeld, some eighty miles short of the Capital at 19.31, and both gunners were killed in the engagement, while the ABC operator received a shoulder wound. Despite the damage to aircraft and crew, F/O Knights pressed on to the target to carry out his brief. Both sky and ground markers were used by the Pathfinders, but complete cloud cover forced all but two of the 101 Squadron crews to aim for the former, and they delivered their loads from 19,000 to 21,000 feet between 19.35 and 19.55, before turning south-west to a point north of Leipzig. From here they headed due west, with the night fighters still very much in evidence until south of Brunswick, where most peeled off. North-east of the Ruhr they turned to the north-west to cross northern Holland and exit enemy territory over Terschelling. By this time, twenty-two Halifaxes and thirteen Lancasters had been brought down, including the squadron's LM387, which was lost without trace with the eight-man crew of F/O Perry RCAF. Returning crews were unable to provide an assessment of their efforts, but, it was established later, that much of the bombing had fallen into the hitherto less-severely damaged eastern districts.

On the following night, 648 aircraft were made ready for the first major operation against Magdeburg, a city situated between Brunswick and Berlin. A simultaneous small-scale operation against Berlin by twenty-two 5 Group Lancasters and a dozen 8 Group Mosquitos would take place as a diversion. 101 Squadron detailed fifteen Lancasters, and they departed Ludford Magna between 19.55 and 20.20, with S/L Marshall the senior pilot on duty. They headed out over the Lincolnshire coast for the three-hour flight to the target, which was undertaken over thick cloud that prevented sight of the spot-fire route markers. Conditions improved as Magdeburg hove into sight, and the cloud thinned to three to six-tenths with tops up to 6,000 feet. Some main force crews, who were now in Lancasters equipped with H2S, arrived ahead of the Pathfinders because of stronger than forecast winds, and, rather than wait for zero hour, began to bomb. The fires caused by this, along with very effective enemy decoy markers, compromised the Pathfinder efforts to achieve concentration after their initial red target indicators went down at 22.50. The first 101 Squadron participants arrived just before 23.00, to find both sky and ground markers in use, and all but one bombed those on the ground from 17,500 to 24,000 feet between 23.00 and 23.23. F/Sgt Langford and crew were attacked by a night fighter during the bombing run, and jettisoned the HE and incendiaries live over the target. On return, they would report much overshooting caused by aircraft attacking from all points of the compass. F/Sgt Irving and crew were unable to see markers of any kind over Magdeburg at 23.09, and dropped their bombs on Brunswick from 22,000 feet, while on the way home at 23.30. Sadly, the operation was a complete failure, and very little, if any, damage was achieved. In contrast, the German defenders enjoyed their best night to date, with a haul of fifty-seven aircraft, thirty-five of them Halifaxes, 15.6% of those dispatched.

101 Squadron suffered no losses on this night, but an unprecedented three Berlin raids in the space of four nights awaited them at the end of the month, in the final concerted attempt to destroy the German Capital. The first of these was briefed on the 27th, when the crews learned, that they were to be operating in an all-Lancaster heavy force of 515 aircraft. 101 Squadron contributed sixteen aircraft, which took off either side of 17.30, led by S/Ls Marshall and Morton, and none returned early. There was a complex plan in place, which involved following a small mining diversion towards the German Bight, before turning south-east towards central Germany, to hint at a possible attack on Hannover, Brunswick, Magdeburg or Leipzig. At a predetermined point the stream swung to the north-east to run in on Berlin, while a Mosquito element

maintained the original course and dropped dummy route markers. The ruses worked to an extent, and fewer fighters infiltrated the stream than of late. Berlin was cloud-covered, and the Pathfinders employed skymarkers, which were bombed by the 101 Squadron crews from 19,000 to 22,000 feet between 20.34 and 20.47. Returning crews reported the marking to be well-concentrated, and fires were reported beneath the clouds, the glow from which, according to S/L Morton, was visible from two hundred miles away. It was established later, that the bombing had been scattered over a wide area, much of it falling into outlying communities, something which was a feature of the entire campaign. Never the less, some fresh industrial and residential damage was caused within the city, and a further substantial number of residents were deprived of their homes. Part of the night fighter force had been lured away by the mining diversion, but sufficient remained to contribute to thirty-three missing bombers. The squadron posted missing the eight-man crew of F/Sgt Sandford in DV231, which was shot down by a combination of flak and a night fighter, and crashed near Northeim, some forty miles south-west of Brunswick. The flight engineer survived in enemy hands, until being repatriated in February 1945.

A caricature of S/L Geoffrey Fisher, who became a flight commander on 27th January 1944 (GW).

Halifaxes joined the Lancasters on the following night to create a force of 677 aircraft, of which fourteen were provided by 101 Squadron, led for the first time by W/C Alexander, supported by S/L Marshall. It was a late take-off, the first crew departing Ludford Magna at 00.05, and the last twenty minutes later. This time the bomber stream was routed in and out over Denmark on a more-or-less reciprocal course, and its departure had been preceded by various spoof and diversionary efforts earlier in the evening, including a Mosquito attack on Berlin, gardening in Kiel Bay and a spoof attack on Hannover. One feature of this operation was the high rate of early returns, amounting to sixty-six aircraft, or almost 10% of those dispatched, and this tended to be the consequence of back-to-back long-range trips. Among them was W/C Alexander, who was still a hundred miles short of the Danish coast when his Gee equipment failed. The night fighter controller concentrated his forces over Berlin, where the 101 Squadron crews began to arrive shortly after 03.00 to find cloud cover and the employment of skymarkers. These were bombed by all but one of the squadron from 19,000 and 22,000 feet between 03.16 and 03.31, but P/O Marsh was attacked by a JU88 during the bombing run, and, with a searchlight and flak concentration in his bombsight, dropped his load from 15,000 feet. Large explosions were witnessed at 03.14, 03.16, 03.19, 03.21, 03.25, 03.29 and 03.32, and the glow of fires was visible from Rostock on the return journey. At debriefing, the crews were convinced that they had delivered a telling blow, and this was partially borne out by local reports, which identified the western and southern districts as the hardest hit, but dozens of outlying communities also found themselves under the bombs. 180,000 people were rendered homeless, and they may have been cheered to know that forty-six of their tormentors had failed to make it home, twenty-six of them Halifaxes, and more than half were brought down in the target area. The Waughman crew made it safely home from their sixth sortie, despite facing attacks by a JU88, a FW190 and an unidentified enemy aircraft. ME565 had a hole in the cockpit Perspex to show for it, along with a missing mid-upper hatch, the loss of which had caused the temperature on board to plummet.

151

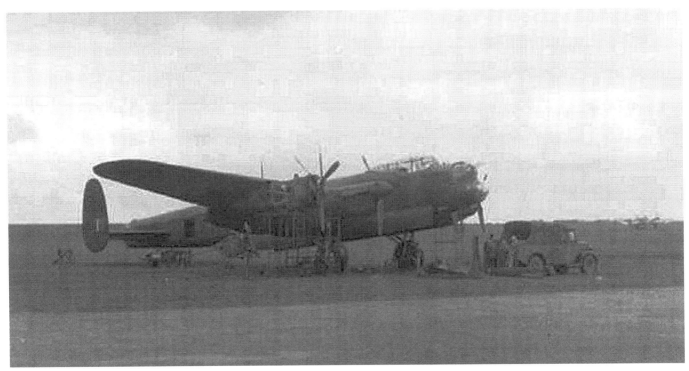

An ABC-equipped Lancaster at dispersal (GW)

After a night's rest 534 aircraft were called into action for yet another tilt at the "Big City", and 440 of these were Lancasters. 101 Squadron dispatched fifteen Lancasters between 17.00 and 17.23, led by S/Ls Marshall and Morton. They joined up with the others to cross the Schleswig-Holstein peninsular and approach the target from the north-west, with a planned withdrawal south of Brunswick, and a dash for the Dutch coast via the northern tip of the Ijsselmeer. There were no early returns among the 101 Squadron contingent, which arrived in the target area to find complete cloud cover and skymarkers in use. They bombed on these from 19,000 to 21,000 feet between 20.19 and 20.32, and a large explosion was observed at 20.25. Returning crews reported the glow of fires reflected in the clouds, and the consensus was of a concentrated and effective attack. Many parts of Berlin and outlying communities had, indeed, received bombs, but it was the central and south-western districts that sustained the heaviest damage, and around a thousand people lost their lives. Thirty-two Lancasters and a single Halifax failed to return, and there was a single 101 Squadron representative among them. DV303 had fallen to the cannons of a night fighter near the target, and had crashed at Tetow, some ten miles south-west of the centre of Berlin. Sgt Froggatt and four of his crew lost their lives, and the three survivors fell into enemy hands. This was the seventh sortie for the Waughman crew, who had now emerged from the "dangerous" first phase of their tour. Once past the freshman first six operations, the odds of survival improved until the mid-twenties, when they shortened again.

There is no question that this three-raid series had seriously hurt Berlin, but it remained a functioning city and the seat of government, and nowhere were there signs of imminent collapse. As had been demonstrated in the heavily-bombed British cities, the population would cope, and resolve would harden, rather than lead to a breakdown of morale. During the course of the month the squadron operated on nine nights, launched 140 sorties and lost nine Lancasters and crews.

'Good-bye Berlin. The First Pictures of Daylight Take-off by Night Bombers'.
Illustrated Magazine Feature

The Berlin raid of 20/21st January 1944 was the subject of a photo feature in *Illustrated* magazine. A selection of photos from the article shows preparations for the raid, crews preparing for departure, with all but one crew eventually returning for the obligatory debrief. The article was published on 19th February 1944. Photos courtesy of Gary Weightman and Rusty Waughman.

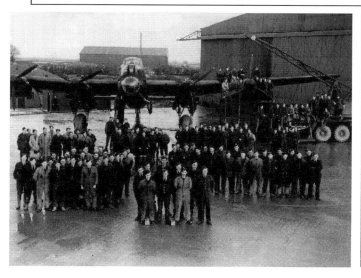

Above left: An illustration of the number of ground crew required to keep a Lancaster in the air. Right: The bomb train for the raid. The bomb load comprises a typical mixture of 8,000 lb 'Blockbusters' and Small Bomb Containers filled with incendiaries. The prevalent tactic was to break buildings open with high explosive and set fire to the ruins with the incendiaries (GW). Below: In the crew room, after the main briefing, waiting for the 'off'. Right: The Gunnery Leader, Flt Lt Hill, helping a rear gunner, 'Ackers', into his heated suit (Rusty Waughman).

Rusty Waughman comments:

(Above) Filling our thermos flasks in the crew room after our main briefing for a raid on Berlin. I am directly behind the urn with a fag and a flask. To my left are my Nunn and navigator, 18-year-old Alec Cowan, who had lied about his age and joined up at 16 years of age. The blanked-out part of the picture was a map of Europe, eliminated for security reasons.

(Left) Catering staff prepare our rations.

(Below) Cover of Illustrated magazine, 19th February 1944.

'Kitted-up crews on their way to the crew buses. You can see why the station was called 'Mudford' Magna! In the top photo, Norman, my bomb aimer, is second from the left.' – Rusty Waughman.

Lancasters 'G' and 'P' are waved off by ground crews as they take off for Berlin. An ABC aerial is visible under the nose of 'G' (top); the censors apparently did not notice it when removing the aerials from the top of the fuselage. It would have been much more apparent in the lower photo, assuming that 'P' was equipped with ABC. There is a suggestion that the lower photo has similarly been censored (GW).

'De-briefing after the raid on Berlin. Above: Flt Lt Henderson, the Intelligence Officer, debriefs P/O RA Nightingale (pilot), Sgt KF Scott (navigator), Sgt JF Muldfowney (rear gunner), P/O A McCartney (bomb aimer) and Sgt L Ley (flight engineer). Left: The Navigation Leader, Sqn Leader Fitch, interrogating Flt Lt Andy Wallis and crew. Left: Bombing Leader, Flt Lt Knute Brydon with the Laurens crew, debriefing bomb aimers. Norman, my bomb aimer is top left. Behind him, with glasses, is F/O Stan Horrocks, the Met Officer. Top right, with fag, is F/O Arthur, Deputy Squadron Engineering Officer. Note the cups of hot chocolate or coffee, laced with rum to help you to talk!' – Rusty Waughman. NB both crews shown here appear to have survived the war.

157

February 1944

Bad weather brought a welcome rest for the crews for the first two weeks of February, as the main force stayed at home, and it gave the squadrons time to draw breath and replenish. It was during the first week that W/O Evans and F/Sgt Rusty Waughman cast off their NCO tag and became pilot officers. Gunner P/O "Jack" Whymark was posted in from 11 Base on the 14th to join the Evans crew for the remainder of their tour, after which he would join the crew of P/O Holland. He was a man with a remarkable career to date, having served in France with the British Expeditionary Force, before joining the RAF as aircrew in 1940. His first tour of forty operations began with the Wellingtons of 149 Squadron in December 1940, whereafter he was posted to North Africa and Malta to serve with 148 Squadron, also on Wellingtons. On his return to the UK he was posted to 106 Squadron, with which he would have flown in Hampdens, and was eventually screened in

P/O Jack Whymark (GW).

November 1942. He was posted then to the Central Gunnery School at Sutton Bridge in Lincolnshire as an instructor, before his return to operations now in 1944 with 101 Squadron, with which he would complete twenty sorties in three months, earning the DFC in the process. A fairly brief spell at the 1687 Bomber Defence Training Flight during the summer would culminate with a posting to 103 Squadron at Elsham Wolds in September, where he would serve as Gunnery Leader in the rank of flight lieutenant. He would end the war with a confirmed eighty-nine sorties in his logbook, although, it is believed, he may have completed as many as ninety-seven. He would be recommended for a DSO shortly before war's end, but never receive it. Tragically, he would lose his life on the 4th of October 1945, after taking off from Elsham Wolds as a member of the crew of F/L Taylor for a flight to Italy in PA278, to deliver two nurses and seventeen members of the Auxiliary Territorial Service (ATS). Adverse weather over southern France and the Mediterranean is believed to have brought the Lancaster down with fatal consequences.

When the bombers next took to the air, on the night of the 15/16th, it would be for a record-breaking effort, and would turn out to be the penultimate raid of the war by Bomber Command heavy aircraft on Berlin. The largest non-1,000 force to date of 891 aircraft was made ready, of which twenty-two Lancasters represented 101 Squadron. It would be the first time that more than five hundred Lancasters and three hundred Halifaxes had operated together, and they would be carrying a record weight of bombs, which, had a massive seventy-five aircraft not returned early, would easily have exceeded three thousand tons. The outward leg was routed across southern Denmark, before a turn to the south-east led directly to the target. A mining operation would already have taken place in Kiel Bay before the giant fleet passed over the region, and there would also have been a spoof attack by Mosquitos on Berlin and Frankfurt-an-Oder further to the east. The return route was to be almost direct from a point south of Berlin, with a slight dogleg to pass south of Bremen and out over the North Sea via Egmond. The attack was timed to begin at 21.13, and the 101 Squadron aircraft took off either side of 17.30, with W/C Alexander the senior pilot on duty, and S/L Rosevear flying as navigator to F/L Todd. There were no early returns among the Ludford Magna brigade, and all reached the target area to find ten-tenths cloud with tops at around 8,000 feet. The Pathfinders opened the attack a little early with ground markers, which soon became obscured by the cloud, and early arrivals aimed at release point flares. P/O Nightingale was the first from 101 Squadron to arrive, and he bombed the flares, red with green stars, at 21.17 from 21,500 feet. The others followed up to bomb from 20,000 to 23,000 between 21.18 and 21.37, and, on return, could report little other than an occasional explosion and the glow of fires. Forty-three aircraft failed to return home, and among them was 101 Squadron's DV236, which was shot down from 17,000 feet over the target by a night fighter, killing P/O McConnell DFC and both gunners. The five surviving crew members all fell into enemy hands. It was established later that much of the 2,640 tons had been delivered to good effect within the Capital's built-up area, particularly in central and south-western districts, and a thousand houses had been destroyed, along with five hundred temporary wooden barracks. Some important industrial buildings were hit, and the emergency services had to deal with over eleven hundred fires. This was the eighth trip for "Rusty" Waughman and crew, and despite a hot reception from night fighters over the target, it was a fairly regulation affair.

Serious though the losses were from this operation, they would pale into insignificance compared with what was about to befall the Command. Preparations were made for operations on each of the ensuing three days, but each was cancelled. The potential for disaster attended every major Bomber Command operation, and, on three occasions before the end of the winter campaign it would be realized in horrific fashion. The crews were called to briefings on the 19th, and informed that the target for the night was Leipzig, for which 823 aircraft were made ready, including twenty-one Lancasters by 101 Squadron. A route was planned that took the bomber stream across the Dutch coast, while a mining diversion was carried out in Kiel Bay to hopefully draw off the night fighters. S/L Marshall was the senior pilot on duty as they took off between 23.35 and 00.05, and

DV267, SR-K and the crew of W/O Jack Laurens DFM. They were shot down on the Leipzig raid of 19/20th February 1944 (GW).

there were no early returns. To get to Leipzig, they had to run the gauntlet of enemy night fighters, which met the bomber stream at the Dutch coast and stayed in contact all the way. Broken cloud was encountered as far as Hannover, at which point it became ten-tenths with tops at 7,000 to 10,000 feet. The anticipated head-winds were lighter than forecast, and this brought the bomber stream to the target ahead of schedule. Some crews doglegged to waste time, while others orbited the target to await the arrival of the Pathfinders, and around twenty of these were shot down by the local flak. Four others were involved in collisions and crashed as a result. The Waughman crew, who were on their ninth sortie, were among those arriving very early, and had to lose twenty minutes.

The Pathfinders opened the attack two or three minutes early, employing both ground and skymarkers, and the H2S-equipped main force crews were able to confirm their positions and the accuracy of the marking. W/O Rowe and crew were the first from 101 Squadron to arrive, before any markers went down, and they bombed on ETA on a searchlight and flak concentration from 22,000 feet at 03.53. The others from the squadron followed up from 19,000 to 23,000 feet between 04.00 and 04.28, mostly aiming at green release-point flares with red stars, but a few also caught a glimpse of glowing green TIs on the ground. It was impossible to assess the results of the attack because of the cloud cover, and no photo-reconnaissance was possible before an American raid took place. When all of the returning aircraft had been accounted for, there was a massive shortfall of seventy-eight, the heaviest loss to date by a clear twenty-one aircraft, and there was a 13.3% loss-rate among the Halifaxes, which would prove to be the final straw as far as Harris was concerned, and the Mk II and V variants were withdrawn from future operations over Germany. 101 Squadron could probably count itself fortunate, that only one of its Lancasters figured among the missing. DV267 was the aircraft in question, and W/O Laurens DFM and two of his crew lost their lives when it crashed at Tolbert, a few miles west of Groningen in northern Holland. Five members of the crew managed to parachute from the stricken aircraft, and they were taken into captivity.

Despite the losses, 598 aircraft were made ready on the following day for a raid on Stuttgart, which would prove to be the first of three major assaults on this industrialized southern city over a three-week period. 101 Squadron briefed twenty crews, with S/L Rosevear the senior officer on duty, flying again with F/L Todd. They took off between 23.35 and 00.05, and headed for the Channel, which they crossed over broken cloud. A large exercise over the North Sea by aircraft predominantly from the training units, and a Mosquito diversion at Munich, successfully drew up many night fighters two hours before the main raid made landfall over France, where the cloud built up to five to ten-tenths and remained thus all the way to the target. The lack of night fighters allowed the attack to proceed unmolested, and the 101 Squadron crews bombed from 20,000 to 23,500 feet between 04.00 and 04.18, having aimed mostly at a combination of release-point flares and TIs. Returning crews spoke of fairly concentrated marking, large fires visible 150 miles away, and a column of smoke rising to 21,000 feet. Local reports confirmed heavy damage in central and northern districts from west to east, and an important Bosch factory was severely damaged. A very modest nine aircraft failed to return, and there were no absentees from among the 101 Squadron contingent. This was the tenth sortie for Rusty Waughman and crew, who enjoyed a quiet trip, and would not be required to operate again for three weeks.

A new tactic was tried out over the next two operations, in an attempt to reduce the prohibitive losses suffered since the turn of the year. The plan was to split the bomber force in two, and separate them by two hours, in the hope of catching the enemy night fighter force on the ground as the second wave passed through. The ball-bearing centre of Schweinfurt was selected as the target on the night of the 24/25th, and a force of 734 aircraft made ready, 392 in the first wave, and 342 in the second. 101 Squadron contributed twenty-two aircraft, seven in the first wave, taking off between 18.17 and 18.25, led by W/C Alexander, and fifteen in the second wave departing between 20.10 and 20.35. They flew south to exit England over the Sussex coast, and all but one reached the French coast, from where they encountered five to seven-tenths cloud for the next seventy miles. F/Sgt Thomas had been forced to turn back a few miles short of the French coast after failing to climb above 14,500 feet. The cloud had cleared by the time the others reached the target, and the crews were able to visually identify ground detail. The Pathfinders were a little late in opening the attack, but accurate and concentrated TIs were soon attracting the bomb loads, and all seemed to be proceeding as planned. The 101 Squadron crews bombed from 20,500 to 22,300 feet between 23.11 and 23.23, and returned to report what appeared to be a successful operation. The second wave lost P/O Clegg shortly before crossing the French coast, after his port-outer engine failed. F/L Knights got as far as Peronne in north-eastern France, before turning back with a suspected fuel leak, and he dropped his cookie and incendiaries on Abbeville aerodrome from 15,500 feet at 23.07. The same weather conditions persisted as earlier, and the crews were guided to the target by the fires burning from the first phase attack, which could be seen from 150 miles on approach. The 101 Squadron crews bombed from 20,000 to 22,000 feet between 01.07 and 01.24, and confirmed the impressions of the earlier wave, although there was a reference to undershooting by both the Pathfinders and the main force. Despite the operation being less successful than first appeared, the second phase force lost 50% fewer aircraft than the first, in an overall casualty figure of thirty-three, and this suggested some merit in the tactic. The sad new filtered through later from 100 Squadron at Grimsby that W/C Dilworth had failed to return from this operation, and his death would ultimately be confirmed.

On the following night the target was Augsburg, the beautiful and historic city deep in southern Germany, which will be remembered for the epic daylight raid on the M.A.N diesel engine factory there in April 1942, for which the late and previously-mentioned S/L Nettleton had earned a VC. This operation involved 594 aircraft, again divided into two waves, and 101 Squadron provided twelve Lancasters for the first and seven for the second. The first-wave participants took off between 18.05 and 18.30, and headed for the exit point at Beachy Head to join up with the rest of the force. Sgt Davidson and F/Sgt Corkill abandoned their sorties shortly afterwards, the former with Gee failure and the latter with engine problems. This left the others to push on in five to six-tenths cloud until

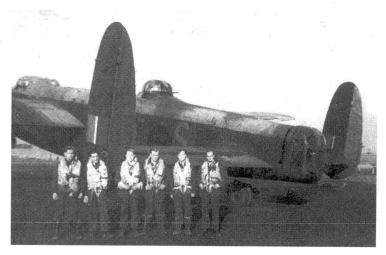

Sgt Corkill and crew whilst at RAF Blyton, in 1943, either at No. 1662 HCU or No. 1 Lancaster Finishing School. Left to right: Joe Welsh, rear gunner; Dick Gundy, bomb aimer; Ken Corkill, pilot; 'Keith', navigator; Les Swales, MU gunner; Charlie Manser, wireless operator/air gunner (GW).

6˚E, when it began to clear, and the target was found to be under cloudless skies. The Pathfinders took advantage of the excellent conditions to deliver accurate and concentrated ground markers, and it was one of those rare occasions, when all facets of the plan came together in perfect harmony, to demonstrate the Command at its most lethal. The 101 Squadron crews bombed from 19,000 to 22,000 feet between 22.45 and 23.01, and all returned safely, although F/L Leeder lost his port-outer engine twenty miles into the return trip, and came home at 16,000 feet. The second phase crews took off between 21.15 and 21.30, but F/L Dickenson abandoned his sortie over base with a failing electrical system. The others enjoyed similar weather conditions as they traversed France, and could see the glow of Augsburg burning from as far away as Saarbrücken, just across the German frontier, a distance of two hundred miles. They carried out their attacks from 20,000 to

161

22,000 feet between 01.15 and 01.19, and contributed further to the destruction of this old city. Its heart was ripped out, devastated by a fire that destroyed for ever centuries of history and cultural treasure. A total of 2,920 houses was destroyed, and five thousand others were damaged to some extent, while few of the important public and cultural buildings remained intact. This concluded a relatively light month of operations for the squadron, which operated on just five occasions, dispatching 104 sorties for the loss of two Lancasters and crews.

March 1944

The main activity at the start of the new month was snow clearance. Six crews were sent over to Wickenby to operate from there, while all other aircrew personnel toiled with shovel in hand. Stuttgart was chosen to open the March account on the night of the 1/2nd, for which a force of 557 aircraft was made ready. F/Ls Dickinson and Knights were the senior pilots on duty as they took off from Wickenby among their 12 and 626 Squadron counterparts between 22.55 and 23.30. There was little cloud on the way out until they were south of Paris, from where it built to ten-tenths all the way to southern Germany and over the target, with tops at 10,000 to 15,000 feet. The Pathfinders dropped TIs, but these, having cascaded above the cloud, disappeared into it and became lost from sight, forcing the crews to aim at release-point flares. The 101 Squadron crews bombed from 20,500 to 22,000 feet between 03.07 and 03.21, and returned to report a scattered attack, with poor Pathfinder marking, and little evidence of fires. In contrast, P/O Batten-Smith reported the glow of fires visible from a hundred miles away. In fact, it had been a very effective raid, which caused much fresh damage in central, western and northern districts, and was achieved for the remarkably low loss of just four aircraft.

Thereafter, most of the Lancaster squadrons remained at home until mid-month, during which period began a new campaign of interdiction. The French and Belgian railway systems were to be dismantled by bombing, to prevent their use by the Germans to defend the coming invasion of Europe. It provided an opportunity to gainfully employ the Stirlings and Halifaxes in the role for which they had been designed, following their withdrawal from the front line, and it was the Halifaxes of 4 and 6 Groups that successfully opened the campaign against the marshalling yards at Trappes on the night of the 6/7th. On the following night the yards at Le Mans sustained heavy damage, and the same target was attacked again on the night of the 13/14th. S/L Marshall had now completed his tour as flight commander, and he was posted to the RAF Staff College on the 13th.

The Lancasters and Mk III Halifaxes had to wait until the night of the 15/16th, when Stuttgart was once more the destination, this time for a maximum effort raid by 863 aircraft. 101 Squadron contributed twenty-five Lancasters, which took off either side of 17.00 led by S/L Morton, and headed south over Reading to Selsey Bill, before making for the French coast. W/O Drew turned back from somewhere deep inside France after losing his port-inner engine, leaving the others to press on over thin, broken cloud, which thickened to seven to ten-tenths as the target approached. The Pathfinders were late in arriving, and dropped TIs, which most crews were able to pick out as the cloud drifted across the city. The 101 Squadron crews bombed either on these or on green release-point flares with red stars from 20,000 to 23,000 feet between 23.16 and 23.34, and all but one returned safely to report scattered marking, some undershooting, fires taking hold, one or two large explosions, and the glow of fires visible for a hundred miles. ME558 was one of thirty-seven failures to return, and was shot down by a night fighter over France five miles from the German frontier, without survivors from the eight-man crew of P/O Clegg GM. The Waughman crew was back in harness for this one, their eleventh sortie, and had to dogleg to waste time until the Pathfinders opened the attack. It was established later, that this operation was less successful than the one of two weeks earlier, possibly because of the stronger-than-forecast winds, and, although some of the early bombing did hit the city centre, much of the effort had fallen short and into open country to the south-west.

The first of two attacks on Frankfurt was planned for the night of the 18/19th, for which a force of 846 aircraft was made ready. 101 Squadron detailed twenty-five Lancasters, which took off between 19.00 and 19.30, led again by S/L Morton. They headed south to cross the Kent coast at Orfordness, where thin layer cloud accompanied them, until thinning over France to leave clear skies. F/Sgt Fillingham abandoned his sortie over base with intercom failure, and the navigator in the crew of Sgt Harnish spent so much time synchronising his DR compass, that he forgot to keep a regular check on position, and they had to turn back from somewhere deep in France. The others pressed on, and arrived in the target area under cloudless skies, but hampered by dense ground haze and poor visibility. The initial, slightly scattered Pathfinder marking was soon corrected, and the ground markers first became grouped and then concentrated within the city. There was a decoy fire site six miles north of the target, but crews were able to employ their own H2S to confirm their position and the accuracy of the marking. The 101 Squadron crews swept across the aiming-point at 19,000 to 22,000 feet between 22.00 and 22.13, and contributed to a swathe of destruction that spread from east to west across the central districts. Many returning crews commented on two massive explosions at 22.03 and 22.04, and a dense column of smoke rising to a great height, which promoted confidence all round that it had been a very effective attack. They were correct, and it was learned that five and a half thousand houses had been either destroyed or seriously damaged, along with ninety-nine industrial firms, and many other business premises and public buildings had also been hit. Twenty-two aircraft failed to return, but all from 101 Squadron made it back to home airspace. It was after crossing the Suffolk coast that LM464 crashed between Brockford and Needham, east-north-east of Diss, and close to the Suffolk/Norfolk border. A few miles to the west of Bury St Edmunds, F/Sgt Carson and crew clearly heard P/O Dixon's wireless operator broadcast their call sign at 00.14, but nothing further was heard. It is believed that total engine failure was the cause of the crash, which tragically claimed the lives of P/O Dixon DFM and the seven members of his crew. P/O Waughman and crew completed their twelfth sortie without incident, and could now consider themselves to be an experienced outfit.

816 aircraft were detailed for the same target on the night of the 22/23rd, for which 101 Squadron provided twenty-six Lancasters. Take-off from Ludford Magna took place between 18.25 and 18.50, led by S/L Morton, and the force headed for the Dutch coast in a departure from the normal routine for a target in southern Germany. Sgt Harnish lost his starboard-inner engine over the sea, and had to turn back, leaving the others to continue on to the target, which they found under five-tenths thin cloud with tops at 8,000 to 10,000 feet. The Pathfinders opened the attack with skymarkers, and the early arrivals bombed on these, but, once delivered, the ground markers were clearly visible, and they became the focus. The 101 Squadron participants began to run in on the aiming-point in the minutes before 22.00, and bombed from 20,000 to 22,000 feet between 21.52 and 22.10. Returning crews described an outstandingly concentrated attack, and spoke of the glow of fires being visible from two hundred miles into the return journey. The level of destruction was even greater than that inflicted four days earlier, and half of the city would now be left without electricity, gas and water for an extended period. At 948 people the death toll on the ground was more than twice that of the earlier raid. Thirty-three aircraft failed to return, but 101 Squadron came through unscathed.

The nineteenth and final operation of the campaign against Berlin was scheduled for the night of the 24/25th, for which a force of 811 aircraft was made ready. This would also be the final time that RAF heavy bombers attacked Germany's capital city, although Mosquitos of 8 Group's Light Night Striking Force would continue to harass the residents right up to the moment that Soviet troops arrived in the suburbs in April 1945. At Ludford Magna, 101 Squadron briefed twenty-five crews, who would be led by W/C Alexander, backed up by S/L Morton. The force was routed out over southern Denmark and the Baltic to aim for a point north-east of Berlin, before turning to approach the city from north-east to south-west. After running across the city they were to carry out two doglegs to starboard to take them north of Magdeburg and south of Hanover, and then a shallow turn to port to cross Holland and gain the North Sea via Egmond. The 101 Squadron crews began to take-off at 18.25, and all were airborne by 19.00, before climbing out and heading for the North Sea via the Lincolnshire coast. W/O Drew was halfway across the North Sea when oxygen-system failure forced him to turn back, and F/Sgt McHattie was seventy miles short of the Schleswig-Holstein coast when an engine problem ended his sortie. The others pressed on flying over ten-tenths cloud, which would clear once they reached Denmark, and remain thus until the German coast, when a thin layer would begin to build up and reach six to eight-tenths in the target area.

While still over the North Sea, some crews began to realise, that all was not proceeding according to plan. H2S told them that they were thirty miles south of the intended track and over the southern end of Sylt. The wind had been correctly forecast as coming from the north, but the strength had been massively underestimated, and was, in fact, blowing at an unprecedented speed. The windfinder system was activated, in which selected crews ascertained the strength of the wind, and communicated the findings back to group, for re-broadcast to the force as a whole. By this method, the navigators should be able to adjust their course and speed accordingly, and remain on track. The windfinders doubtless did their best to remain on top of the situation, but they were facing wind speeds in excess of one hundred miles an hour, which had not been encountered before. They would ultimately be referred to as jetstreams, but, in 1944, their existence was not understood. The result was, that the bomber stream became scattered, and many crews believing themselves to be over Denmark, were, in fact, already over Germany. After fifty-three aircraft had turned back early for a variety of reasons, the majority of the remainder somehow navigated their way to the target, in what was now a scattered and elongated bomber stream. The first 101 Squadron crews arrived shortly before 22.30 to find the release-point flares being driven across the city towards the south-west. They were able to pick out the red and green TIs cascading and then twinkling on the ground, and bombed on these from 17,500 (Sgt Harnish) to 23,300 feet between 22.28 and 22.55. Sgt Harnish had lost his starboard-outer engine over Denmark, and had jettisoned his incendiaries into the Baltic to maintain height. F/O Davies was unable to identify the primary target, and dropped his bombs on an aerodrome north-west of Leipzig, and F/O McKenna bombed Halberstadt, south-west of Magdeburg, after also failing to find Berlin. Aircraft continued to be driven off course on the way home, and many strayed over the heavily defended Ruhr, providing the flak batteries with their best bag of the war. Seventy-two aircraft failed to return, the second heaviest loss of the war, and this, just a month after the Leipzig disaster. Amazingly, 101 Squadron came through unscathed, but its own blackest night lay just six days in the future. Including a small diversionary raid by 5 Group on the night of the Magdeburg debacle, twenty operations had been directed at Berlin between the 23rd of August and the 24th of March. 101 Squadron was present on all but the diversion, despatching 363 sorties, the second highest number in the Command. The campaign cost it twenty-two aircraft and 133 men killed, with a further forty-two languishing in PoW camps. (The Berlin Raids. Martin Middlebrook).

P/O Evans DFC had now completed his tour, and was posted to 1667 Conversion unit on the 26th. As already mentioned, his gunner, F/O Whymark, now joined the crew of P/O Holland. What became known as the Battle of Berlin period, or more accurately, the winter campaign, still had a week to run, and two more major operations for the crews to negotiate. First for 101 Squadron, however, was its maiden involvement in the Transportation Plan, when four crews joined a mixed force of 192 aircraft to provide ABC cover for an attack on the marshalling yards at Aulnoye in north-eastern France. The senior pilot on duty was the Senior Air Staff Officer (SASO) of 13 Base, Air Commodore Cozens, and he was supported by P/O Lander, W/O Drew and

F/Sgt McHattie and their crews. They were airborne by 19.20, each loaded with twelve 1,000 and four 500 pounders, and bombed from 6,300 to 9,500 feet either side of 22.00. Unfortunately, the marking on this night was not accurate, and, despite a large explosion and much smoke, it seems that most of the bombs fell wide of the mark.

When crews assembled in briefing rooms on the 26th, it was to learn that Essen was to be their target that night, something probably not anticipated by them or by the enemy. A force of 705 aircraft was assembled, which included twenty Lancasters provided by 101 Squadron. The senior pilots on duty were F/Ls Bertlesen and Todd, who took off with the other squadron participants either side of 19.30, and climbed away into clear skies. There was ten-tenths cloud from the Dutch coast to the target, and crews commented on the complete lack of a response from the enemy flak defences as they continued on unmolested. With the benefit of Oboe, the Pathfinders were able to deliver their skymarkers accurately, and the 101 Squadron contingent bombed them from 19,500 to 22,000 feet between 22.01 and 22.15, before returning safely home. It was an outstandingly successful raid, which destroyed a further seventeen hundred houses in this already battered city, and inflicted more hurt on important war industry factories. Thus was continued the remarkable run of effective attacks against this once elusive target since the introduction of Oboe to main force operations twelve months earlier. Rusty Waughman and crew completed their thirteenth sortie without incident, and appreciated a rare short-range trip.

Among those posted to the squadron on the 29th was the previously-mentioned F/L Scrymgeour-Wedderburn, who arrived from 1656 Conversion Unit to begin his second tour. Two days later, S/L Thompson arrived from 1662 Conversion Unit to assume the role of flight commander. The final operation of the long, bitterly-fought and costly winter campaign was directed at Nuremberg on the night of the 30/31st. This was to be a standard deep-penetration operation for which 795 aircraft were made ready. The plan was based on the belief that a layer of high cloud would protect the bomber stream from the moonlight, but, that the target area would be clear. The usual planning meeting took place, at which a 5 Group-inspired direct route was offered, which would involve a 250-mile straight leg across Germany to a point fifty miles north of Nuremberg, from where the final run-in would begin. The A-O-Cs of the Lancaster-equipped groups were happy with the plan, but Roddy Carr of 4 Group was less enamoured about the prospects for his Halifaxes, even though they were the new Hercules-powered Mk III version. Under normal circumstances the operation would be planned by 8 Group, and would incorporate feints, diversions and a circuitous route to the target to keep the enemy controllers guessing. AVM Bennett, the 8 Group A-O-C, was incandescent with raged when he was told of the plan agreed by the others, and, it is said, predicted a disaster.

101 Squadron provided twenty-six Lancasters, and S/L Morton was to be the senior pilot on duty. A report from a Meteorological Flight Mosquito cast doubt on the weather forecast, particularly the amount and altitude of the cloud, and many expected the operation to be scrubbed. It was not, and, between 21.35 and 22.15, the 101 Squadron crews took to the air, and after climbing to around 12,000 feet over base, headed for Southwold and then Selsey Bill to join what was planned as a sixty-eight-mile-long bomber stream, which would pass across the aiming-point in seventeen minutes. It was not long before the crews began to notice some unusual, unsettling and, perhaps, even freak features about the conditions, which included uncharacteristically bright moonlight. This created crystal-clear visibility, which enabled the crews to see other aircraft around them, something to which they were not accustomed. Often, they would feel totally alone all the way to the target, and only as they funnelled towards the aiming-point would they become aware of the presence of other aircraft. They also noted the fact that the forecast high cloud was absent, and instead, a layer of white cloud

Above L: Sgt Brinkhurst (left) was mid-upper gunner in P/O Adamson's crew. The photo was taken whilst he was evading capture in Belgium, from where he managed to reach England. He went on to complete a further twenty ops. R: P/O Adamson DFC and members of his crew. Tragically they were shot down by an overeager gunner in a Halifax, on the penultimate op of their tour (GW).

below them acted as a backdrop to silhouette them like flies on a table cloth. The two final insults were the formation of condensation trails to further advertise their presence in the hostile skies, and the close proximity of the route to two night fighter beacons. All of these features served to hand the bomber stream on a plate to the waiting night fighters, and the route to the target could be traced by the burning wreckage on the ground of Lancasters and Halifaxes.

The carnage began at Charleroi in Belgium, and, continued all the way to the target, and at least eighty aircraft were lost during the outward leg. The same jetstream winds that had so adversely affected the Berlin raid in the previous week, were also present, only this time from the south, and those crews who either failed to notice, or refused to believe the evidence, were driven up to fifty miles north of the planned route. The windfinders did not believe their findings, and modified them before broadcasting them to group. In turn group refused to believe the modified data, and modified it still further before re-broadcasting it to the outbound force. The result was that many crews turned towards Nuremberg from a false position, and when they came across Schweinfurt, and found some Pathfinder markers, they believed it to be the target. These and the losses reduced dramatically the numbers bombing at Nuremberg, and the city escaped serious damage. The 101 Squadron participants bombed from 19,000 to 22,000 feet between 01.13 and 01.28, aiming at either release-point flares or TIs on the ground. F/L Todd bombed a searchlight and flak concentration from 22,000 feet at 01.15, after seeing no markers, and noted many other aircraft attacking the same target. It was only as he turned away, that red TIs could be seen twenty or thirty miles away to port. The disaster of Leipzig, nearly six weeks earlier, was eclipsed by the failure to return of ninety-five bombers, with more being written off in crashes on return or with battle damage too severe to repair. 101 Squadron was one of many squadrons to suffer grievously, with seven Lancasters failing to return to Ludford Magna, each containing an eight-man crew. With the aid of Martin Middlebrook's account in his magnificent book, The Nuremberg Raid, we can chart the fall of the Squadron's aircraft.

DV264 was the seventh loss of the operation, and was shot down by a Halifax, to crash near the small town of Gemünd, situated right on the Belgian/German frontier. P/O Adamson DFC and four of his crew were killed, and this was particularly tragic, not only for the "friendly fire" incident, but because it was also the

166

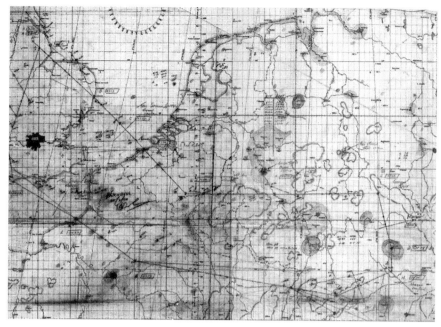

A route map for the Nuremberg raid, from an unknown crew. The 'long leg' across Germany on the outbound route is all too clear (GW).

twenty-ninth and penultimate operation of their tour. Two members of the crew were taken into captivity, while the mid-upper gunner evaded a similar fate, and would eventually return to the squadron to complete a further twenty operations. LL832 was the seventeenth casualty, and was one of the few victims of flak. It was brought down while approaching Coblenz, and crashed at 00.15 two miles west-north-west of the town. F/Sgt Tivey and his crew were all killed on what was their tenth operation. LM463 became the thirty-first loss after being caught by a night fighter at 18,000 feet, and exploding near Dillenburg, a dozen miles or so south-east of Siegen. Only the pilot, P/O Lander RNZAF, and one other escaped by parachute to fall into enemy hands. It was just their second operation. LL861 was intercepted by a BF110 flown by Hptm Gustav Tham of IV/NJG5, and exploded with great force to fall in pieces in the area of Lauterbach, twenty miles east of Giessen. There were no survivors from the predominantly Australian crew of P/O Irving RAAF, who were on their ninth operation and became the sixty-second victim of the night. ME618 was approaching the final turning point, when it crossed paths with Lt Wilhelm Seuss of IV/NJG5 in his BF110. It crashed near the town of Hilders, some seventy-five miles north-west of the target, killing Sgt Harnish RCAF and two other members of his predominantly Canadian crew, and another succumbed to his injuries within hours. The four survivors were taken into captivity. They were on their sixth operation, and were the sixty-seventh loss of the raid. P/O Batten-Smith's DV276 was among the last to be shot down before reaching the target, and fell to the guns of Oblt Helmut Schulte of II/NJG5 as the eighty-fourth victim. The Lancaster crashed at 01.25 at Röthenbach, about ten miles east-north-east of the centre of Nuremberg, killing P/O Jimmy Batten-Smith DFC and the rest of his crew on their twenty-second sortie. Finally, DV290 was one of numerous other aircraft to be written off in crashes in England, in this case near the USAAF base at Welford in Berkshire at 05.03. There were no survivors from the crew of F/Sgt Thomas, who were on their fifth operation, and were the night's 101st casualty. The Waughman crew, who were on their fourteenth sortie, reported seeing at least sixteen aircraft shot down in almost daylight conditions. The diary entry sums up their reaction to the squadron's casualties. "All pretty tired and shaken! Never the less, we must press-on regardless." During the course of the month the squadron took part in eight operations, dispatching 157 sorties for the loss of eight Lancasters and crews.

167

April 1944

That now facing the crews was in marked contrast to what had been endured over the autumn and winter months. In place of the long slog to Germany on dark, often dirty nights, shorter range hops to France and Belgium would become the order of the day. These, however, would prove to be equally demanding in their way, and would require of the crews a greater commitment to accuracy to avoid casualties among friendly civilians. The only fly in the ointment was a decree from on high, which determined that most such operations were worthy of counting as just one third of a sortie towards the completion of a tour, and until this flawed policy was rescinded, an air of mutiny would pervade the crew rooms. The Transportation Plan had been prosecuted since early March, largely by elements of 3 and 4 Groups employing aircraft withdrawn from the main battle, but now, the campaign could get into full swing with the availability of the entire bomber force. Despite the prohibitive losses of the winter, the Command was in remarkably fine fettle to face its new challenge, and Harris was in the enviable position of being able to achieve what had eluded his predecessor. This was, to attack multiple targets simultaneously, with forces large enough to make an impact, and he could now assign targets to individual groups, to groups in tandem or to the Command as a whole, as dictated by operational requirements.

The railway yards at Trappes, Le Mans, Amiens, Laon and Aulnoye had all received attention, and would continue to do so for as long as the campaign endured. Of course, while Harris was at the helm, his preferred policy of city-busting would never be shelved entirely in favour of other considerations, but for the time being at least, Germany would largely be left to the Mosquitos of 8 Group's Light Night Striking Force. The new campaign began in earnest on the night of the 9/10th, when railway installations were attacked at the Lille-Delivrance yards by elements of 3, 4, 6 and 8 Groups, while elements from all Groups went to Villeneuve-St-Georges on the outskirts of Paris. 101 Squadron supported the latter operation with seven Lancasters in a total force of 225 aircraft, while 239 were assigned to Lille. Taking off either side of 21.00, they headed for the south coast, where the skies cleared and remained cloud-free all the way to the target. This was the first operation of his second tour for F/L S-Wedderburn, who found the target bathed in bright moonlight, and well-marked by the Pathfinders. The 101 Squadron participants bombed on the centre of a cluster of red and green TIs from 12,000 to 14,000 feet between 23.55 and 23.59, and observed two large explosions immediately after midnight. Post-raid reconnaissance suggested a successful outcome, but four hundred houses were also destroyed or damaged, and ninety-three civilians were killed. At Lille the attack destroyed more than 2,100 items of rolling stock, and caused damage to buildings and installations, but also flattened or damaged five thousand houses, and killed 456 civilians. The problem of collateral damage would never find a satisfactory solution.

Briefings took place on the 10th for attacks on four railway targets in France and one in Belgium. 1 Group was assigned to Aulnoye in north-eastern France, and detailed 130 Lancasters, of which nineteen were provided by 101 Squadron. They took off either side of 23.30, with F/Ls Keard and Nimmo the senior pilots on duty, but F/Sgt Fillingham lost his starboard-outer engine on take-off, and was back on the ground within ninety minutes. The others headed into ten-tenths cloud, which dispersed gradually over the Channel to leave clear skies over France, until the target was reached. Here, thin cloud combined with thick haze, to obscure ground detail, although Oboe was able to negate the disadvantage. 1 Group provided its own Master Bomber and Deputy for the first time on this night, whose role was to assess the accuracy of the Mosquito-laid Oboe markers, and correct them if necessary. The 101 squadron crews delivered their twelve 1,000 and four 500 pounders each from 8,000 to 10,000 feet between 02.22 and 02.46, on the instructions of the

P/O Ken Fillingham and crew, their car bearing various nicknames and their aircraft code (GW).

Master Bomber, which some crews later described as vague, and reported confusion around the red and green markers. On the way home, French coastal defences and night fighters made their presence felt, and seven Lancasters failed to return home. Among them was DV288, which was shot down from 22,000 feet by a night fighter in the Amiens area. F/L Nimmo and three of his crew survived to evade capture, but the wireless operator and both gunners lost their lives. Most of the crew were on their seventeenth operation, but the gunners had each flown thirty-four. All but one of the night's targets suffered severe damage, and, while some bombing at Aulnoye missed the mark and destroyed or damaged 340 houses, the engine shed was hit, and thirty locomotives put out of action.

Aachen was a major railway hub, with marshalling yards at each end of the town, but the attack planned for it on the night of the 11/12th was intended for the town itself. 341 Lancasters from 1, 3, 5 and 8 Groups were to provide the heavy element, with eleven representing 101 Squadron led by S/L Morton. The recently-arrived S/L Thompson was undertaking his first operation with the squadron, and flying as second pilot to F/L Knights. They took off between 20.15 and 20.30 under the threat of thunderstorms, which were hanging over Elsham Wolds twenty miles to the north. There were no early returns, and all reached the target to find six to eight-tenths thin cloud, through which the TIs were clearly visible. The squadron crews bombed from 18,000 to 21,000 feet on red and green TIs that were either cascading or already on the ground, and were all on their way home by 22.52. Post-raid reconnaissance revealed massive damage in central and southern districts, and local reports put the death toll at 1,525 people. Aachen would be attacked in the future, but never again with

169

Lancaster DV288, seen here wearing her initial code of SR-D, was lost on the Aulnoye raid of 10/11th April. The crew shown is that of F/L Rodgers, who were not flying DV288 when she was shot down (GW)

the ferocity experienced on this night. Officially from the 14th, Bomber Command became subject to the requirements of the Supreme HQ Allied Expeditionary Force (SHAEF), and would remain thus shackled until the Allied armies were sweeping towards the German frontier at the end of the summer. 1 Group's Special Duties Flight was officially formed on the 18th, and would operate out of Binbrook as the group's own target marking force. It would remain small, and draw crews from within the Group, and among the founder members was that of F/L Hull from 101 Squadron.

Four more railway yards were earmarked for destruction on the night of the 18/19th, and 1 Group provided 140 of the 273 assigned to those at Rouen, while 3 and 8 Groups put up the others. S/L Thompson was the senior pilot on duty for the first time, but it was P/O "Rusty" Waughman and his crew, on their fifteenth sortie, (officially fourteen and a third), who led the twenty-three squadron participants away between 21.35 and 22.05. They climbed into clear skies, and crossed the English coast at Selsey Bill still in excellent conditions and clear visibility, which extended all the way to the target. There were no early returns among the Ludford Magna brigade, and they bombed from 6,000 to 10,500 feet between 00.20 and 00.31, with little flak opposition and no searchlights to hamper their efforts, and all arrived home safely to report a concentrated attack. The Waughman crew observed German raiders over London on the way home, and also intruders in the Ludford circuit at 1,000 feet. A ME110 was spotted, but no contact was made.

5 Group had been developing its own low-level marking system since the turn of the year, and, so successful was it, that its former stalwarts, 83 and 97 Squadrons, had been posted back on permanent loan from the Pathfinders to act as heavy marker squadrons, along with 627 Squadron to provide the Mosquito element pioneered by 617 Squadron. The first full-scale trial by the "Independent Air Force", or "Lincolnshire Poachers" as 5 Group would be referred to disparagingly in 8 Group circles, came at the railway yards at La Chapelle on the night of the 20/21st, while the still "pressed" airmen of 1, 3, 6 and 8 Groups were briefed to attack Cologne. A force of 379 Lancasters was put together, of which 196 were provided by 1 Group. 101 Squadron managed to offer a record twenty-nine aircraft, which took off between 23.15 and 00.05, led by W/C Alexander. Enemy intruders were active in the area, and crews were advised to find alternative routes to the departure point at Southwold. F/Sgt Hingley was a mile off the Kent coast at Reculver when instrument failure ended his sortie, and P/O Welsby was twenty miles inland from the Belgian coast when navigational problems persuaded him to abandon his sortie. P/O Arnold was much deeper into Belgian territory, when his starboard-outer engine caught fire and forced him to turn back. The others pressed on to find nine to ten-tenths cloud over the target, where the attack opened nine minutes late on release-point flares. The squadron crews bombed from 19,000 to 21,000 feet between 02.03 and 02.21, and turned for home with the reflection of bomb flashes and the glow of large fires showing in the cloud. F/O McKenna brought LL779 back with holes between the engines in the starboard wing, courtesy of a JU88 on the way home, but, otherwise it was a fairly routine trip. What they had been unable to see through the cloud, was Cologne experiencing a torrid time, with bombs falling predominantly to the north and west of the city centre into partly industrial districts. Over eighteen hundred dwelling units were destroyed and twenty thousand others damaged, along with 192 industrial premises. Many public, administrative and transport-related buildings were also hit, and there were almost 1,300 separate fires to deal with. Defence was described as negligible, and only four Lancasters failed to return on another loss-free night for Ludford Magna. The Waughman crew's sixteenth sortie went according to plan, although they were the last from the squadron to bomb and the last home.

The squadron briefed twenty-six crews on the 22nd, sixteen for the night's main operation to Düsseldorf in company with 580 others of the heavy brigade from 1, 3, 4, 6 and 8 Groups, and ten for the 5 Group raid on Brunswick. The latter was to be a trial for the low-level marking system at a heavily defended German urban target, having proved its effectiveness against precision targets in France. Take-off at Ludford Magna was a protracted affair, which began at 22.27 and ended at 23.45, the Lancasters climbing away into cloudless skies before setting course for their respective targets. P/O Waughman was half way across the North Sea bound for Brunswick, when his DR compass failed, and he was forced to turn back on what was the crew's seventeenth sortie. There were no other early returns, and the Düsseldorf force arrived over the city to find thin cloud at high level, which would provide no hindrance to the progress of the attack. The first markers went down at 01.14, after which, a constant supply of red and green TIs maintained the aiming-point throughout the raid. The 101 Squadron crews bombed from 17,500 to 21,800 feet between 01.21 and 01.34, and all but one returned to report explosions and massive fires in what was an echo of the experiences of a year earlier. In the meantime, the Ruhr had lost none of its ability to defend itself with flak and night fighters, and twenty-nine aircraft failed to return. ME619 was hit by flak at 20,000 feet while flying close to Krefeld, and P/O McDowell lost his life along with the ABC operator and both gunners. The four surviving crew members were taken into captivity. Post-raid reconnaissance revealed a massively successful operation, which fell largely into northern districts, where two thousand houses were destroyed or seriously damaged, and fifty-six large industrial premises were hit.

While this operation was in progress, the Brunswick force reached its destination, and encountered thin cirrus cloud at 20,000 feet, which was added to by contrails. Despite this, the markers were clearly visible, and the

101 Squadron crews bombed from 15,000 to 21,000 feet either side of 02.00, aiming mostly at five red Mosquito-laid spotfires burning on the ground. They all returned safely to report many fires all over the target, and an apparently successful attack, which was not borne out by post-raid reconnaissance. The early bombing had hit the city centre, but some H2S-laid reserve markers had also been dropped well to the south, and had attracted much of the bombing. The situation was exacerbated by confusion arising between the various controllers, and, it is unlikely that the operation achieved more than modest success.

The main operation on the night of the 24/25th was to be against Karlsruhe in southern Germany, while 5 Group tested its marking method again at Munich, one of the most heavily defended cities in the Reich, boasting a reputed two hundred flak guns. 101 Squadron briefed seventeen crews for the former and ten for the latter, and, with further to travel, the Munich element took off first, between 20.45 and 21.00, with F/L Knights and Reade the senior pilots on duty. They were part of an overall heavy force of 234 Lancasters, for which 617 Squadron Mosquitos were to carry out the marking for the final time, before handing the job over to 627 Squadron. A force of 637 aircraft was assembled for Karlsruhe, and the 101 Squadron Lancasters took off between 21.20 and 21.45 led by F/Ls Keard and Todd. They flew into light medium cloud as far as 6°E, after which, a band of cirrus between 18,000 and 23,000 feet caused icing problems for some crews. There was variable cloud over the target, but not enough to obscure the ground markers, and the 101 Squadron crews bombed on them from 15,500 and 22,000 feet between 00.40 and 00.57. All then returned safely home to describe what appeared to them to be a fairly concentrated raid, which produced many fires. Local reports reveal a highly scattered attack covering a wide area to the north, well beyond the city, but also the destruction of or serious damage to nine hundred houses. At Munich, there was no cloud below bombing height, and crews easily picked out the red spotfires delivered by the Mosquito force, chief among which was W/C Cheshire, the 617 Squadron commanding officer. The 101 Squadron element bombed from 18,000 to 20,000 feet between 01.48 and 01.58, and bombing photos would ultimately reveal the accuracy of the attack, and the severe damage inflicted upon the centre of the city, where eleven hundred buildings were destroyed. Rusty Waughman's diary entry for this, his eighteenth sortie, makes interesting reading. "Ops Munich, via Italy, Austria, Switzerland and France. Crossed the Alps twice. Mt Blanc. Heavy flak and searchlights, 60 per cone….Best prang yet…10¼ hour trip…carried petrol for 9.35 hours. Curly did a grand job."

Twenty 101 Squadron Lancasters were made ready for operations on the night of the 26/27th, eleven of them as part of a heavy force of 475 Lancasters and Halifaxes assigned to Essen, while nine others supported a 5 Group attack on Schweinfurt. The latter took off first, between 21.15 and 21.30, led by F/L Todd, with S/L Rosevear flying as his regular navigator. Conditions outbound were fine, and only two to four-tenths cloud was present over the target, where the low-level marking was being carried out for the first time by Mosquitos of 627 Squadron. The 101 Squadron crews bombed on red or green spotfires from 15,000 to 18,000 feet between 02.29 and 02.44, and observed large fires developing around the markers as they turned away. Twenty-one Lancasters failed to return, a hefty nine percent of the force, and among them was LL860, which is believed to have crashed south-west of Paris. F/O Rowe DFC was killed with the other seven members of his crew, all of whom had been decorated with the DFM. The Essen contingent departed Ludford Magna between 23.15 and 23.30 for the shorter trip to the Ruhr, and enjoyed clear skies all the way out and over the target, where some arrived ahead of time, and had to wait for the Pathfinders to open the attack at 01.24. The ground defences were much stronger than on recent visits to the Ruhr, and the main force had to run the gauntlet of flak to deliver their bombs onto the red and green TIs. The 101 Squadron crews attacked from 19,800 to 21,500 feet between 01.23 and 01.37, and all returned safely to report explosions, many fires and much smoke rising to meet them. Rusty Waughman described the target as "hot" after having to endure the longest route through the Ruhr defences, but a short round-trip of four hours and five minutes was a pleasing way to complete his nineteenth sortie.

On the following night an audacious attack was scheduled on the relatively small but highly industrialized town of Friedrichshafen, situated in south-western Germany on the shore of Lake Constance close to the Swiss frontier. It was a centre for tank engine and gearbox production, but presented a small target that needed the help of moonlight. It was only a month since those conditions had brought about the disaster of Nuremberg, and so a number of diversions and feints were incorporated into the plan. The force of 322 Lancasters of 1, 3, 6 and 8 Groups included seventeen from 101 Squadron led by S/L Morton. They departed Ludford Magna in perfect weather conditions between 21.35 and 22.10, and exited England over the Sussex coast. F/Sgt Askew turned back twenty-five miles short of Dieppe because of instrument failure, leaving the others to press on to the target. The night fighter controller was confused by the diversions, and the force remained largely unmolested during the outward leg. The exception was LM493, which was intercepted and shot down by a night fighter at 17,000 feet, and crashed near Elzach, some eighty miles short of the target. F/L Dickinson and the four crew members in the front section of the aircraft survived to fall into enemy hands, but the ABC operator and both gunners lost their lives. The others found the target under clear skies and well-marked by the Pathfinders, and delivered 1,234 tons of bombs to very good effect. The 101 Squadron contingent bombed from 18,500 to 20,000 feet between 02.03 and 02.19, and played their part in hitting all of the important targets, and destroying an estimated ninety-nine acres of the town, or 67% of its built-up area. It was while the attack was in progress that the night fighters appeared on the scene in numbers, and, once in contact, they scored steadily, bringing down eighteen aircraft. W/O Noble, who had twice been "Mentioned in Dispatches", was five minutes into the homeward flight, when LL750 was attacked by a night fighter flown by Hptm Gerhard Friedrich of I/NJG6, and sent spiralling out of control. At 02.10, while falling between 11,000 and 9,000 feet, an explosion threw the pilot and bomb-aimer clear, and they landed in deep snow a hundred yards from the wreckage of their Lancaster on the Swiss side of the frontier. After a brief period of internment, they crossed into France, and, presumably returned home. This was the twentieth sortie for Rusty Waughman and crew, and they brought back an aiming-point photo. A post-war survey would reveal this to be the most damaging setback to Germany's tank production of the war.

The night of the 30th was devoted to attacks on two railway yards, and a bomb and ammunition dump hidden in a wood at Maintenon, north-west of Chartres. The last-mentioned was assigned to 116 Lancasters of 1 Group, of which fourteen represented 101 Squadron. This would be the first time that the Special Duties Flight (SDF) had to find and mark a target for the group on its own. S/L Morton led the 101 Squadron element off at 21.35, with a G/C King acting as second pilot, and they were all safely on their way by 21.50. The outward flight was undertaken in clear conditions, and all from the squadron arrived in the target area to find the dump clearly identified and marked by the SDF. Although the Master Bomber's voice was indistinct, they could make out his instructions to bomb the fires, and they carried out their attacks from 6,500 to 7,800 feet either side of midnight, and a number of very large explosions confirmed the attack to be an outstanding success. This was the twenty-first sortie for the Waughman crew, who had their regular rear gunner, F/Sgt Harry Nunn, back after missing five operations through illness. The squadron took part in thirteen operations during the month, and dispatched 193 sorties for the loss of six Lancasters and crews.

May 1944

The main focus for the new month would be the paving of the way for the coming invasion by targeting enemy defences, resources and communications. It began with six small-scale operations over France on the night of the 1/2nd, three directed at railway targets and three at specific factories. The target for seventy-five Lancasters of 1 Group, six of them from the SDF, was the Berliet motor works at Lyons, for which 101 Squadron provided eight aircraft led by F/Ls Knights and Keard. Conditions were excellent as they departed Ludford Magna around 21.30 and made for Selsey Bill and then Cabourg on the French coast. The fine conditions persisted all the way to the target, where the marking began at 00.47. The Master Bomber, S/L Breakspear of the SDF, appeared to be struggling to maintain control over his support crews, and one group of target indicators was judged to be wide of the mark. This was soon corrected, however, and the first phase of the main force was called in at 01.02, followed by the second at 01.07. The 101 Squadron crews bombed from 8,500 to 10,500 feet between 01.05 and 01.17, those of the first phase having a clear view of the target, while those in the second were troubled by smoke. Even so, the target was well plastered, and the force suffered no losses.

One of the most controversial operations of the war took place on the night of the 3/4th, when the target was a Panzer transport depot and training camp at Mailly-le-Camp in north-central France. It was an important target because of its potential to impact the Allied invasion, now just a month away, and 346 Lancasters of 1 and 5 Groups represented the main force tasked with taking it apart. 101 Squadron provided twenty aircraft and crews led by F/Ls Keard, Knights, Swanston and Todd, and they departed Ludford Magna in excellent conditions either side of 22.00, before pointing their noses towards Beachy Head on the Sussex coast. F/Sgt Hingley didn't get that far, having abandoned his sortie over base after the mid-upper gunner collapsed. The others pressed on towards what should have been a straight-forward affair, but, instead, turned into a disaster for 1 Group. Master Bomber for the operation was G/C Deane of 83 Squadron, with W/C Leonard Cheshire of 617 Squadron controlling the Mosquito markers. Each had attended a separate briefing, and this was something that may have contributed to the later confusion. Neither seems to have been fully aware, either, of the part to be played by 1 Group's SDF, which was assigned to mark a specific target of its own, the tank repair depot, for a section of 1 Group aircraft. The plan was for 617 Squadron Mosquitos to mark two aiming-points, one for each group, and for Cheshire to hand proceedings over to Deane at the appropriate junctures.

Cheshire and S/L David Shannon were in position before midnight, and, as soon as the illuminating flares went down from the 83 and 97 Squadron Lancasters, Cheshire released two red spotfires onto the first aiming-point from fifteen hundred feet at 00.00½, which Shannon backed up from four hundred feet thirty seconds later. As far as Cheshire was concerned, the operation was now bang on schedule, and he called up Deane to bring in the 5 Group first phase of the main force. It was at this stage that communications problems prevented Deane from being able to pass on the necessary instructions, and it seems that some crews, noticing the red markers burning clearly on the ground, decided to go in and bomb. These were predominantly 5 Group crews, who, according to the plan, should have completed their part in the operation by 00.16, leaving the way clear for the second pair of 617 Squadron Mosquitos to mark the camp for the 1 Group element of 140 Lancasters. In the event, 5 Group bombs were still falling, and Cheshire asked for a pause in the bombing to allow the marking to take place. Eventually, Deane's deputy, S/L Sparks of 83 Squadron, found a clear channel and called for a halt, but chaos reigned and bombs were still falling as the 617 Squadron Mosquitos flew across the target to mark the aiming-points at 00.23 and 00.25. At two thousand feet they were lucky to survive the blast from the cookies going off below them. Their efforts were backed up by a stick of markers from a 97 Squadron Lancaster, and Sparks was at last able to call 1 Group in to bomb. It would be discovered later, that

174

interference from an American Forces broadcasting station, and a wrongly tuned VHF transmitter, prevented the original instructions from getting through.

Four SDF aircraft, led by F/L Hull, formerly of 101 Squadron, were specifically tasked with marking Target "B", the tank repair depot to the east of the main camp. The initial green spot flare was judged by Hull to have overshot by a thousand yards, and a second was misplaced by five hundred yards. The deputy marker leader laid a third marker, which was judged to be accurate, and, at 00.11, the first dozen of twenty-nine Lancasters from 460 and 625 Squadrons followed up with accurate bombing, before the target became obscured by smoke. As a result of this, and the fact that the 5 Group attack had commenced close by, the remaining seventeen 1 Group aircraft assigned to the "special target" were diverted to assist in that.

Three views of the German Panzer depot at Mailly-le-Camp, before (top left), during (right) and after the fateful attack on the facility. Note the stricken Lancaster in the aiming point photo, which appears to be missing her port inner engine and part of her tailplane (GW).

P/O Drew and crew, FTR Mailly-le-Camp 3/4.5.44.

During the ten-minute delay caused by the communications difficulties, enemy night fighters took advantage of the bright, moonlit and cloud-free conditions to get amongst the bombers as they circled a fighter beacon just a few miles from the target. They began to pick off Lancasters with impunity, Hptm Helmut Bergmann alone downing no fewer than six bombers in thirty minutes. As burning Lancasters were seen to fall out of the sky in large numbers, some crews succumbed to their anxiety and frustration, and a number of uncomplimentary comments were broadcast in a rare breakdown of R/T discipline. Once under way, the bombing was accurate, and much damage was inflicted on barracks and transport sheds, and thirty-seven tanks were among the hundred vehicles destroyed. The 101 Squadron crews bombed from 6,500 to 7,500 feet between 00.25 and 00.44, and reported a fairly concentrated attack, and a number commented on the "back-chat", but made no mention of seeing night fighters and rockets, as reported by some other squadrons. This was the twenty-second sortie for Rusty Waughman and crew, who described it in the diary as quite a good prang. "¾ moon all the trip. Fighters everywhere, saw several aircraft shot down….Scarecrow burst underneath us over target, and blew us into a 300+ mph dive. Kite dented but no real damage." The reference to a scarecrow is common, and refers to the belief among crews that the Germans employed a heavy flak shall, which was designed to resemble a bomber exploding in the air, to affect the morale of any witnessing crews. The Air Ministry encouraged such a belief, but the truth is that a scarecrow shell never existed, and what resembled a bomber blowing up, was, in fact, a bomber blowing up with a full bomb load. Remarkably, in the light of what transpired, this operation counted as just one third of a sortie.

Forty-two Lancasters were shot down, twenty-eight of them from the 1 Group second phase, and 101 Squadron posted missing four crews. LM419 was among the first to be shot down, and crashed at Dravegny, west of Reims while outbound, killing P/O Drew and all but his bomb-aimer, who fell into enemy hands. DV275 was hit by flak from the north-eastern corner of the camp and crashed almost immediately, killing F/O Baker and the other seven occupants. LM467 had turned for home when it was brought down to crash just south of the target, with fatal consequences for F/O Muir and his seven crew mates. ME564 crashed close by, and only the rear gunner survived from the crew of F/L Keard. Thus, only two of the thirty-two men involved escaped with their lives. The sad news came through from Binbrook later that F/L Hull and his crew were among the missing, and their deaths would be confirmed some weeks hence. Afterwards, many accusations were unjustly directed at W/C Cheshire, particularly by members of 1 Group, and, even today, Mailly-le-Camp remains an open wound. It is understandable that they needed someone to blame, just as the survivors from Nuremberg claimed that the Germans had been forewarned of that attack and were lying in wait. Both were, of course, the result of the fortunes of war, and every operation held the potential for disaster.

An ammunition dump at Aubigne Racan was selected as the target for fifty-two Lancasters of 1 Group on the night of the 6/7th. 101 Squadron detailed six aircraft led by F/L Reade, and they took off between 00.25 and 00.45 in excellent weather conditions, which persisted all the way to the target. The marking was accurate, as was the ensuing bombing, which the 101 Squadron crews carried out from 7,000 feet either side of 02.45. The individual loads of nine 1,000 and four 500 pounders blasted the target indicators, and within eight minutes of the attack opening, a column of smoke had reached 10,000 feet. This was the twenty-third trip for the Waughman crew, who made a point in the diary of the fact that they took off at 00.30 on a SUNDAY! They had a second pilot on board for experience, P/O Allen, and, as it was twenty-four hours short of a full moon, the opinion was that they might as well have gone in daylight! "Explosions in target put Vesuvius in the shade, flames up to 6,000 feet approx., smoke up to 10,000 feet. Bombed at 7,000 feet, almost went up with the target!"

The following night brought further attacks on ammunition dumps, coastal defences and airfields, and fifty-five Lancasters of 1 Group were assigned to the airfield at Rennes in north-western France. 101 Squadron contributed ten aircraft, which were all safely airborne in a fifteen-minute slot just before 22.00, led by S/L Morton. Having climbed out, they headed for the Devon coast in fine weather conditions, which remained constant for the entire operation. The target was found under bright moonlight with a little ground haze, and the first red spot fire going down at 00.11 was assessed as being very close to the aiming-point between the runways. The main force was called in, and the bombing began at 00.14, falling accurately onto the central aiming-point, where fires were started in the hangars. The fuel storage depot was also hit, creating a large volume of oily smoke, and then someone landed a bomb on the ammunition dump, causing a massive explosion. The 101 Squadron aircraft bombed from 10,000 to 12,000 feet between 00.15 and 00.35, the earlier arrivals bothered for two minutes by searchlights, and the later ones finding the markers obscured by smoke.

The night of the 9/10th was devoted largely to operations against coastal batteries in the Pas-de-Calais, involving over four hundred aircraft. The purpose of such attacks was to maintain the deception, and the German belief that the invasion would come ashore in the Calais area, rather than on the Normandy beaches. 101 Squadron committed eleven Lancasters to a battery at Mardyck, west of Dunkerque, as part of an overall 1 Group effort of fifty-three aircraft. They took off between 22.45 and 23.00, led by F/Ls Knights and Todd, and headed into clear conditions, which held firm all the way to the target. The target area was bathed in bright moonlight, and the accurate and compact marking provided an ideal aiming-point for the 101 Squadron crews, who bombed on the red TIs from 11,800 to 14,000 feet between 00.09 and 00.14, before returning home to confirm an accurate attack.

The night of the 10/11th brought a return to railway targets at five locations, which 101 Squadron sat out at home. Six operations were briefed on the 11th, four against railway targets, a fifth by 4 Group on a gun position, and the largest effort, by 5 Group, against a military camp at Bourg Leopold in eastern Belgium. 101 Squadron made ready eighteen aircraft for an attack by 105 Lancasters of 1 Group on the marshalling yards at Hasselt, situated about ten miles south of the 5 Group target. They took off between 21.45 and 22.05, led by F/Ls Knights and Reade, and set course in good weather conditions, which held firm during the flight out. Before reaching the target, some heard the Master Bomber abandon the operation, and order the crews to take their bombs home. He had noticed that, in the hazy conditions, bombs were falling outside of the target area, and completely missing the railway installations, putting civilian lives at risk. Six 101 Squadron crews either failed to pick up the broadcast, or declined to comply with it, and were among thirty-nine to deliver their

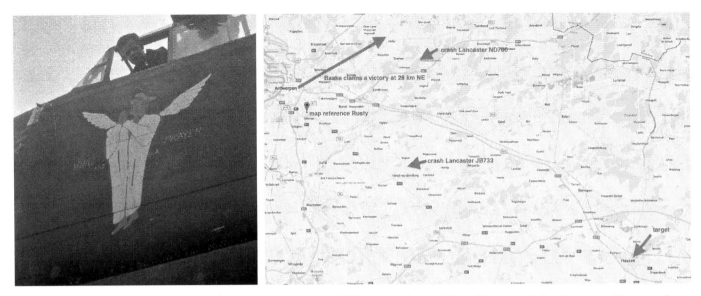

Left: Flight engineer 'Curly' Ormerod in the cockpit of ME565, SR-W 'Wing and a Prayer', Rusty Waughman's first Lancaster. The aircraft was written off despite having flown home following a mid-air collision with another bomber. This is believed to be a 103 Sqn Lancaster JB733, flown by P/O Whitley, which crashed near Antwerp with the loss of all on board (Rusty Waughman). Right: Key locations relating to the collision between ME565 and the Lancaster believed to be JB733. Baake's claim was much closer to where another Lancaster, ND700 of 103 Sqn, crashed whereas ME565's collision was very close to the crash site of JB733 (Wim Govaerts).

bombs from 10,000 to 12,000 feet between 23.54 and 00.09. A number of crews from other squadrons picked up a transmission from the Master Bomber at a different target, almost certainly at Bourg Leopold, telling the crews to bomb the red T.Is. Immediately thereafter, another message was received from group confirming the recall, which they took to be an enemy trick, and decided to add their bombs to the 5 Group effort. This, too, was abandoned by the Master Bomber after half of the force had bombed, and both targets would have to be revisited.

This was the twenty-fourth, and almost the last, sortie for the Waughman crew, who were at 12,000 feet some ten minutes short of the target at 23.50, when another Lancaster rose to meet them and made heavy contact with their underside. A propeller sliced through the bomb-aimer's compartment just missing the occupant, and the offending Lancaster had its canopy and mid-upper turret wiped off. Rusty Waughman felt his controls go slack as his Lancaster rested on the one beneath, but, in seconds, they separated, and the controls responded again. Some members of the crew watched the other Lancaster fall away and break up, while Waughman, realising he still had full control, carried on to the target, where the bombs were delivered from 12,000 feet at 00.01. They returned home to land on one and a bit wheels, and slewed off the runway before coming to a halt. The damage to the bomb doors, both inner engine nacelles, the tailplane and the undercarriage was very significant, and ME565 was taken off charge. This meant a new Lancaster for the crew, and LL757 SR-W became their new mount, and was christened "Oor Wullie". The other Lancaster involved in this tragic incident was almost certainly JB733 of 103 Squadron, which distributed itself over a wide area south-east of Antwerp, and on a line within a few miles of the area of the map reference given by the Waughman crew as the location of the collision. There were no survivors from the crew of P/O Whitley, the loss of whom, in Bomber Command Losses 1944, is attributed to the night fighter of Oblt Werner Baake of 1/NJG1. The crash site given, north-east of Antwerp, is actually that of 103 Squadron's ND700, which contained the crew of the recently appointed commanding officer, W/C Hubert Goodman, who was leading the squadron into battle for the first time. He had borrowed the highly experienced and popular crew of the "Mad Belgian", S/L van Rolleghem, who was in hospital at the time, and was understandably angry and distraught on learning of the loss, which would also be keenly felt by everyone at Elsham Wolds.

On the 12th, the former 101 Squadron flight commander, S/L St John, was promoted and posted from 1656 Conversion Unit to Elsham Wolds to take command of 103 Squadron. Eight operations of varying sizes were mounted on the night of the 19/20th, five of them against railway yards, and the other two against coastal defences. 101 Squadron contributed sixteen Lancasters to an overall 1 and 8 Group heavy force of 118 aircraft bound for the marshalling yards at Orleans in north-central France. S/Ls Morton and Thompson were the senior pilots on duty as they took off between 22.00 and 22.30 to climb into low cloud and drizzle before pointing their noses towards Beachy Head. Twenty miles from the target the weather cleared, allowing the accurately-placed markers to be clearly visible, and the 101 Squadron crews bombed mostly from 9,000 feet, although a minority selected other heights from 7,000 to 10,000 feet. They were over the target between 00.42 and 00.58, during which, at 00.46, a huge orange-red explosion sent smoke rising to 5,000 feet, and the resultant fire totally obscured the TIs. The Master Bomber instructed the remaining crews to bomb the centre of the fire, and, this done, they returned safely home to report a highly successful operation. This was the twenty-fifth operation for the Waughman crew, and the first in their new Lancaster, which, apart from an unserviceable bomb-sight, performed admirably, and, bomb-sight or not, the bombs still landed on the aiming-point.

In a complete change of objective on the night of the 21/22nd, Duisburg was selected to host its first major attack for a year. A heavy force of 510 Lancasters was drawn from 1, 3, 5 and 8 Groups, of which twenty-four represented 101 Squadron. W/C Alexander was the senior pilot on duty, supported by S/L Morton, as they all got away safely either side of 22.30. P/O Brown abandoned his sortie over base after his intercom and Gee failed, but his was the only early return, and the others took the well-trodden path out over the Lincolnshire coast in poor weather conditions, which persisted all the way to the cloud-covered Ruhr. The early arrivals among the 101 Squadron contingent bombed either on ETA or on red release-point flares with yellow stars, but, eventually, it was necessary to rely on their glow beneath the clouds. With the

F/L Goeres and his crew. On this occasion, Goeres, in the sidecar, is happy to let someone else drive.

exception of F/L Goeres, who saw nothing through the cloud and brought his entire bomb load back, the others delivered their cookie and incendiaries each from a uniform 21,000 feet between 01.08 and 01.38, and returned safely to report what they believed to be a scattered attack. In fact, it had been a successful raid, during which the main weight of bombs had fallen into southern districts of the city, destroying 350 buildings and severely damaging 665 others. The Waughman crew were in DV302 for this, their twenty-sixth sortie, and enjoyed a fairly quiet and routine trip in Ruhr terms.

Twenty-four hours later, it was the turn of Dortmund to face its first large-scale attack since the Ruhr offensive. A force of 361 Lancasters from 1, 3, 6 and 8 Groups included a contribution from 101 Squadron of eighteen, which would be led by S/Ls Morton and Thompson, while five others supported a 5 Group return to Brunswick. They took off together between 22.00 and 22.50, and climbed into five to ten-tenths cloud which persisted over the North Sea, but dispersed from the Dutch coast to leave Dortmund free of cloud. This allowed the crews to clearly see the red and green Oboe markers cascading and burning on the ground, and they delivered their payloads from 20,000 to 22,000 feet between 00.48 and 00.53. Returning crews commented on many fires and large explosions, while F/Sgt Sullock reported a combat with a FW190 at 20,000 feet at 00.50, with resultant damage to the front turret, starboard wing and inner engine. The crews' confidence in the effectiveness of the raid was confirmed by post-raid reconnaissance, which revealed the main weight of the attack to have fallen into south-eastern districts, where 850 houses were destroyed along with six industrial buildings, and almost eight hundred other houses were seriously damaged. Eighteen Lancasters paid the price for the success, and among them was the squadron's LM395, which was brought down by a combination of flak and a night fighter after bombing, and crashed at Hagen, some ten miles south of the target. P/O Davidson RNZAF and two of his crew survived in enemy hands, but the other five crew members died in the wreckage. Rusty Waughman and crew were still in DV302 SR-H for this, their twenty-seventh sortie, and faced the full fury of the searchlight, flak and fighter defences, but still described the five-hour trip as "a wizard prang".

Meanwhile, the five 101 Squadron crews on duty with the "Independent Air Force" had encountered patches of ten-tenths cloud over Germany on their way to Brunswick, but this had reduced to a thin layer of four-tenths over the target, with tops at 5,000 feet. On arrival, they found a complete absence of marking, and bombed on ETA, aiming at incendiary fires from 20,000 feet between 01.20 and 01.25. As F/O Davies was about to release his load, a green TI appeared, and he was able to aim for that. There was considerable interference over R/T communications, and, although the Master Bomber could be heard in discussions with his deputies, no instructions were received from him, and the attack lacked cohesion. Post-raid reconnaissance confirmed that most of the bombing had fallen onto outlying communities[1].

A popular comic character from The Sunday Post from the late 30s onwards, this image of 'Oor Wullie' adorned Rusty Waughman's second Lancaster after the demise of 'Wing and a Prayer' (Rusty Waughman).

Two marshalling yards in Aachen were selected for attention on the night of the 24/25th, for which a force of 442 Lancasters and Halifaxes was prepared. 218 aircraft, including 107 Lancasters from 1 Group, were to attack those at the western end of the town, Aachen West, while 214 others, including nine from 1 Group, attacked those at Rothe Erde at the eastern end. The squadron and group ORBs do not specify how the nineteen 101 Squadron crews were assigned, but their bombing times and altitudes paint a fairly clear picture of events. The operation took place in two distinct phases, and nine 101 Squadron crews took off between 22.45 and 22.55, led by S/L Thompson, to attack the eastern yards. They adopted a northerly route across the North Sea, and encountered patches of cumulus cloud, which decreased to three-tenths thin stratus at 10,000 feet in the target area, and combined with haze to largely obscure ground detail. However, the marking began punctually, and the red markers were backed up by greens to provide a clear

---

[1] *There was a belief in the area at the time, that the Command was deliberately targeting the villages, in order to drive the residents into the city before carrying out a major raid upon it.*

aiming-point, which the 101 Squadron crews bombed from 16,000 to 17,000 feet between 00.56 and 01.00. F/Sgt Sullock and crew failed to return home, one of twenty-five crews to go missing from the combined operation, and it was established later that DV389 had crashed at Olzheim, some forty miles south-east of Aachen, presumably after bombing, and there were no survivors among the eight men on board. The Waughman crew were back in Oor Wullie for this one, their twenty-eighth sortie, and had P/O Arnell RCAF on board as second pilot. Sadly, he and the previously-mentioned second pilot, P/O Allen, would be lost with their crews early in their tours. The ten second phase crews took off from Ludford Magna between 23.35 and 23.55, but P/O King failed to become airborne after his port-outer engine failed. The others set course for Orfordness in good weather conditions, to head for the target via a southerly route over France. The conditions remained good, and all cloud had dispersed by the time they reached the target to find only ground haze. The marking at this western aiming-point was both punctual and concentrated, and the Ludford Magna crews bombed on red TIs from 20,000 to 21,000 feet between 02.25 and 02.33. The size of the force ensured that bombing would spill over into the town, and this is precisely what happened, while villages close to the yards were also heavily damaged. Photographic reconnaissance revealed that the railway installations in the east had escaped serious damage, and a second operation would be necessary.

Halifaxes made up the bulk of the force of 331 aircraft assigned to the military camp at Bourg-Leopold in Belgium on the night of the 27/28th. It will be recalled that the 5 Group attack of two weeks earlier had been aborted halfway through because of poor visibility. 101 Squadron was to support this operation with ten Lancasters, led by S/L Morton, while also sending twelve to Aachen as part of a 1, 3 and 8 Group force of 162 Lancasters and eight Mosquitos taking another crack at the Rothe Erde marshalling yards. The two elements departed Ludford Magna between 23.50 and 00.25, and crossed the English coast over Southwold in excellent conditions, which persisted all the way to the targets, which were barely forty miles apart. The crews had been told to adopt a different approach to bomb at Aachen, which involved shedding height at the rate of 1,400 feet per minute and delivering their stores from 10,000 feet. Some 101 Squadron crews complied, but their bombing heights ranged from 7,000 to 13,000 as they ran in between 02.26 and 02.31. The initial red TIs were backed up throughout the raid, and the bombing remained focussed on them. Many fires and explosions were observed, and post-raid reconnaissance confirmed that the yards had sustained severe damage, halting all through-traffic. Collateral damage afflicted a large number of residential and industrial buildings, and the suburb of Forst was flattened. The flak defence was described as moderate, but a number of fighters were seen, and a few combats took place. The Waughman crew was entrusted with another second pilot, P/O Steel, for this, their twenty-ninth sortie, although, for flight engineer, Curly Ormerod, it was the last, and they celebrated by bringing back a bombing photo plotted as a two-hundred-yard overshoot. The attack on the camp at Bourg-Leopold was also highly successful at a cost of a single Lancaster and nine Halifaxes. The Lancaster, LM459, contained the 101 Squadron crew of P/O Allen, who were all killed when it crashed on the island of Overflakee in the Scheldt Estuary while outbound. The other squadron participants bombed from 12,000 to 17,500 feet between 02.05 and 02.14, and returned safely.

The largest of six operations on the last night of the month was against the marshalling yards at Trappes, situated a dozen miles west-south-west of Paris. A heavy force of 211 Lancasters and Halifaxes was made ready, drawn predominantly from 3, 4 and 8 Groups, with ten ABC Lancasters from 101 Squadron in attendance. The squadron was also to support a 1 and 8 Group attack on marshalling yards at Tergnier, near Laon in north-eastern France with nine Lancasters. The raid at Trappes was to be carried out in two phases, each with a specific aiming-point, and the five 101 Squadron crews assigned to the earlier one, at the eastern end, took off shortly before 22.30 led by the newly-promoted S/L Reade. They encountered icing conditions as they made their way south over Lincolnshire, but found only thin cloud over the target with tops at 7,000

Officers of 101 Squadron, Ludford Magna. 'This is a rare photograph because of the very secret nature of the ABC equipment; no photography was allowed. One of the three ABC aerials can be seen under the nose of the aircraft. Shortly after this was taken, eleven were killed on operations.
Back row, l to r: P/O Brown, P/O Friend, P/O Davidson NZ (dec'd), F/O Cooper? (dec'd), F/O Neale? P/O Sharp, F/O Viggers NZ, P/O Cotrell, P/O Cowan, P/O Warburton? P/O Swanson (dec'd).
Middle row, l to r: P/O Whittle, P/O Bardell, P/O Rippon (dec'd), P/O HH King (dec'd), P/O McHattie, P/O Askew? P/O King, F/Lt Wallace, P/O Waughman, F/Lt McKenna NZ, F/O Brown, F/O Davies, F/O Chalmers, F/O Wymark, F/O Rickets, P/O Arnell (dec'd), F/O HF Peacock (dec'd), F/O FJ Scott (dec'd), F/O Holland NZ, P/O Corkhill, P/O Joiner.
Front row, l to r: P/O Crossette, P/O Ball (dec'd), F/O Sutherland, F/Lt Stewart (dec'd), F/Lt Knights?, F/Lt Smith, F/Lt Bryant, F/Lt Hill (Gunnery Ldr), F/Lt Castle (Nav Ldr), F/Lt Gillespie (Station Electrical Officer), S/Ldr Rosevear, W/C Alexander, S/Ldr Tompson, S/Ldr Morton, F/Lt Eagleton (Adj), F/Lt Freeth (MO), F/Lt Bird, F/Lt Tod NZ, S/Ldr Reid, F/Lt Bradley, F/Lt Wilkman, F/O Day, F/O Raine, F/Lt Goeres.' –
Rusty Waughman. NB: note the 'chopper' symbol, top right; gallows humour at its finest... The photograph is not dated but was taken before 8th June 1944, the date on which P/O Algot Arnell and his crew were lost.

feet. The marking was punctual and accurate, and a Master Bomber controlled the attack with clear instructions. The 101 Squadron crews bombed from 8,500 to 9,700 feet between 00.34 and 00.37, and observed large explosion at 00.38, the glow from which was visible for fifteen minutes. Rusty Waughman described the thunderstorms he had to negotiate both out and inbound, and that they almost turned "Wullie" inside-out! Two more members of his crew finished their tours with this one, the thirtieth, and it must have been unsettling to have "strangers" on board for the last few trips. Those from the squadron assigned to the western aiming-point took off between 23.45 and 23.55 led by F/L Goeres and Wallis, and experienced no difficulty in identifying the target visually and assessing for themselves the accuracy of the marking. They bombed from 8,500 to 9,500 feet between 01.59 and 02.02, and watched their bombs fall onto the tracks. They also observed a large explosion at 02.02, before returning home to report a successful operation.

The Tergnier force departed Ludford Magna either side of midnight, and also had to fly through the ice-bearing cloud and electrical storms over Lincolnshire that persuaded some other crews to turn back. P/O Askew was among these, abandoning his sortie at 00.37 when eight miles north of Coningsby. Those reaching the target found clear skies and ground haze, but the latter had no effect on the visibility of the red, green and yellow TIs, which were clearly seen, and their accuracy confirmed visually by the light of the Pathfinder flares. The 101 Squadron crews bombed from 9,000 feet between 02.19 and 02.30, and returned home safely to report a successful night's work. During the course of the month the squadron took part in seventeen operations, and dispatched 196 sorties for the loss of eight Lancasters and seven crews.

'V for Victory', perhaps! Rusty Waughman stands on the access ladder to his Lancaster (Rusty Waughman)

June 1944

June was to be yet another busy month, the opening few nights of which would be dominated by preparations for the impending invasion. Operations began for 1 Group on the night of the 2/3rd, with attacks on railway yards at Trappes, a radar-jamming station at Berneval and gun emplacements in the Pas de Calais area, the last mentioned as part of the continuing deception to draw attention away from the Normandy beaches. Four batteries were identified as justifying attention, and a force from 1 Group was assigned to one near Calais. 101 Squadron was not involved in this operation, but made ready twenty-two Lancasters for other duties, six to provide ABC cover for a predominantly 4 Group raid on the marshalling yards at Trappes, and sixteen for Berneval-le-Grand, situated on the French coast, five miles east of Dieppe. The Trappes element took off first, at 22.40, led by F/L Goeres, and arrived in the target area under clear skies to find the target well-illuminated by Pathfinder flares. Yellow TIs marked out the aiming-point in the centre of the yards, and the squadron crews bombed from 9,000 to 12,000 feet between 00.50 and 00.55. A large red-orange explosion was observed at 00.53, by which time all ground detail had been blotted out by smoke and fires. Rusty Waughman described his thirty-first sortie as a "wizard prang, took a cookie instead of 1,000 pounders…bags of fun and games…. almost full moon. Harry R/G claims JU88-ME109 also seen on fire and seen to explode…" The Berneval element took off between 23.34 and 23.55, led by W/C Alexander with S/L Thompson in support. They found clear conditions at the target and good visibility, and the Pathfinder marking was both punctual and compact. The crews aimed for the red TIs, and plastered the site, mostly from 9,000 feet, between 01.25 and 01.30, facing absolutely no resistance from the ground. They all returned safely to report a job well done.

Coastal batteries dominated the night of the 4/5th, three of them in the Pas-de-Calais as the deception campaign continued with just twenty-four hours to go before the launch of Operation Overlord. 101 Squadron detailed a dozen Lancasters for Sangatte, west of Calais, and they took off between 01.45 and 02.05 led by S/L Reade. They found eight to ten-tenths cloud over the target, with tops at 4,000 to 7,000 feet, and this obscured the ground markers. While some crews caught a glimpse of them through gaps in the cloud, others bombed on their glow, and the 101 Squadron crews released their eighteen 500 pounders each from 4,000 to 11,000 feet between 03.23 and 03.29. They all returned safely, and reported either observing nothing or the occasional flash of a bomb burst reflected in the cloud. Rusty Waughman was diverted to Faldingworth on return, and slept in the mess for a couple of hours before returning to Ludford Magna in a pick-up truck driven by the Ludford Magna station commander, G/C King. He told Rusty that his time was up, and he would not be flying with 101 Squadron again. He was posted to 82 O.T.U as an instructor, and found it to be an all-Australian unit, that didn't take kindly to having a "Pommie Bastard" amongst them.

On D-Day Eve, the Command prepared over a thousand aircraft for operations throughout the night against eleven coastal batteries overlooking the Normandy landing grounds. A number of special operations were also planned to deceive the defenders, including Operations Glimmer and Taxable by 218 and 617 Squadrons respectively, to simulate fleets of ships heading towards Calais, while twenty-four ABC Lancasters of 101 Squadron patrolled known night fighter routes, to jam ground to air communications. No reference was made to the invasion at any briefings across the Command, but crews were given strict heights at which to fly, and were instructed not to jettison bombs over the sea. The 101 Squadron crews took off with empty bomb bays between 22.17 and 23.05, led by W/C Alexander and S/L Thompson. They headed for the Channel to take up positions on their respective beats, where they were to operate between 20,000 and 26,000 feet. P/O Arnell was half way across the Channel and flying in turbulent air, which caused his ABC operator to become

184

severely airsick. Unable to climb above it, he was left with no option other than to turn for home at 00.02. P/O Carson was unable to attain his briefed altitude, and abandoned his sortie when twenty miles off Eastbourne at 00.18. P/O Welsby had been over the same piece of sea when his navigational aids failed, and he, too, had turned back at 00.14. P/O Steel had begun his patrol at 00.06, but, after nineteen minutes, an unexplained vibration required his starboard-outer engine to be feathered, whereupon, both inner engines also cut. A distress call was received at 00.44, and the Lancaster, LL833, was ditched successfully some twenty-five miles off Beachy Head at 00.50. The crew was able to get into the dinghy, and they were picked up safe and well at 02.00 by the destroyer, HMS Orwell. Sgt Finlay had completed two circuits, and was a dozen miles off the French coast at Cayeux-sur-Mer when his instruments failed, forcing him to turn back at 02.31. P/O Brown had completed one circuit, when his ABC and Gee failed and his engines began to overheat, forcing him to give up at 02.34. The other crews completed their patrols shortly after 04.00, and, unknown to them at the time, had made a valuable contribution to the success of the invasion.

Another thousand aircraft were airborne on D-Day night, to attend to nine road and railway targets behind the beachhead. Six 101 Squadron crews were briefed to attack marshalling Yards at Acheres, situated in a loop of the River Seine north-west of Paris. They were part of a 1 Group force of ninety-seven Lancasters, and took off at 00.34, before climbing into eight to ten-tenths cloud, which persisted all the way to the target. Visual identification of the aiming-point was impossible, and only the glow of TIs provided a reference. Some crews went beneath the 7,000-foot cloud base, and found the markers to be fairly well-concentrated near the centre of the yards, and a number of sticks of 500 pounders were seen to fall. However, confusion arose, and the Master Bomber called off the attack, sending the 101 Squadron crews home with their bomb loads intact. Similar operations occupied the following night, when eighteen 101 Squadron crews were briefed for an attack on a six-way road junction in the Foret-de-Cerisy, between Bayeux and St-Lo. They were to be part of a modest force of 112 Lancasters and ten Mosquitos of 1, 5 and 8 Groups, and took off either side of 23.00 led by S/L Reade. The five-tenths cloud en-route had built to ten-tenths by the time the target drew near, but the Pathfinders employed ground markers, which could be seen, although a number of crews bombed on the glow of fires. There was again some confusion, after the Master Bomber issued instructions to bomb the green TIs rather than the reds, which were wide of the aiming-point, but his comments were not authoritative, and some bombs continued to fall around the reds. The 101 Squadron crews delivered their eighteen 500 pounders each from 2,500 to 6,000 feet between 01.31 and 01.50, mostly bombing on the greens, but some on the reds and some on fires after seeing no TIs at all. "Rusty" Waughman's former mount, the recently-repaired ME565, now SR-Q, failed to return home. The crew of P/O Arnell RCAF, who were all killed when ME565 crashed near Saint-Laurent-sur-Mer, close to the American D-Day landing grounds. There were five sightings of enemy fighters in the area of the Cherbourg peninsular, and one of them was almost certainly responsible for the demise of this crew.

101 Squadron crews were rested briefly, while airfields to the south of the beachhead were bombed on the night of the 9/10th, and four railway centres twenty-four hours later. They were called into action next in the early hours of the 12th, to take part in further attacks on railway yards at Evreux, Massey-Palaiseau, Nantes and Tours. The 1 Group target was the first-mentioned, situated midway between Paris and Le Havre, and the eighteen 101 Squadron Lancasters departed Ludford Magna either side of 01.00, led by S/Ls Morton and Reade. P/O Holland lost his port-outer engine on take-off, and turned back, while the others pressed on over heavy cloud, which gave way to lesser amounts over the Channel, but built up again over France to a layer of ten-tenths between 2,000 and 6,000 feet in the target area. Most crews opted to come beneath the clouds, where the markers could be seen to be accurate and well-concentrated. The 101 Squadron crews bombed on red or green TIs from 2,500 to 7,000 feet between 03.19 and 03.25, some hearing the Master Bombers and

others not. S/L Morton saw no markers, and brought most of his load back, and F/Sgt Hopes did likewise. LL751, failed to return after crashing north-east of the target, and P/O Gover RNZAF was killed along with his six-man crew.

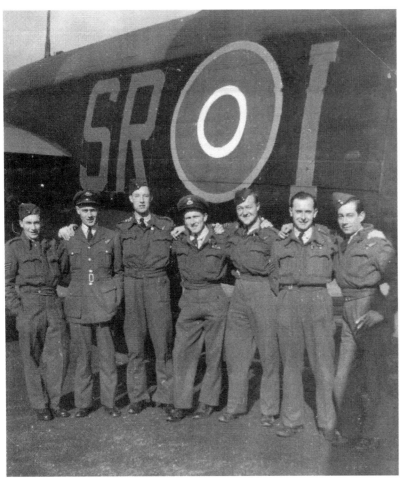

F/Sgt Bob Hopes and crew, with Lancaster SR-I. Left to right: 'Dishy' Dishington (navigator), Merv Wright (bomb aimer), 'Spud' Dullage (flight engineer), Bob Hopes (pilot), 'Mac' MacAteer (air gunner), 'Bigs' Bigsby (air gunner), 'Chuck' Chandler (special equipment operator) (GW).

While 670 aircraft from 4, 5, 6 and 8 Groups continued the attacks on communications targets on the night of the 12/13th, a new oil campaign began at Gelsenkirchen, for which 286 Lancasters of 1, 3 and 8 Groups made up the heavy element. Eighteen of these represented 101 Squadron, led by S/L Reade, and they learned at briefing about a new method of dispensing Window, now at five bundles per minute. The target was the Nordstern synthetic oil plant, which had been attacked before, particularly during the Ruhr campaign, and had proved to be difficult to identify and hit. Departures from Ludford Magna took place in excellent weather conditions between 22.40 and 23.00, but F/O Cook and P/O King turned back early on with engine problems. The outward flight was undertaken over thin cloud, which had cleared by the time the target hove into view, and only ground haze lay between it and the bombers. A new, improved version of Oboe was being employed for the first time, despite which, the initial markers, red TIs, were delivered punctually but inaccurately, and attracted a fair number of bomb loads. Shortly afterwards, red and green TIs were seen to cascade between four and ten miles to the north, and the most northerly were deemed to be on the aiming-point, and were backed up continuously throughout the attack. The 101 Squadron crews were over the aiming-point between 01.00 and 01.11, and delivered their cookie and sixteen 500 pounders each from 18,000 to 20,000 feet in the face of the usual hot reception from the ground defences. Large explosions were observed at 01.05, 01.07 and 01.12, and a column of smoke was rising past 10,000 feet as they turned for home. Night fighters were in evidence for the return leg, and seventeen Lancasters were lost, 6% of those dispatched, but all of the 101 Squadron participants returned safely. The operation was an outstanding success, and the Nordstern plant was put out of action for two weeks, causing a loss of production of a thousand tons of aviation fuel per day.

The first daylight operation since the departure of 2 Group from Bomber Command a year earlier, was directed at Le Havre on the evening of the 14th, to destroy the enemy's fast, light naval craft that posed a threat to Allied shipping supplying the beachheads. 101 Squadron briefed nineteen crews, among which, F/Ls Stewart and S-Wedderburn were the senior pilots on duty. The operation, which involved 221 Lancasters and thirteen

Mosquitos, was to be conducted in two phases, the first one at dusk predominantly by 1 Group, and the second, as darkness fell, by 3 Group. The 101 Squadron contingent took off between 20.40 and 21.05, and, with no early returns, made their way out in excellent conditions that persisted throughout. The target was identified visually, and the 101 Squadron Lancasters deposited eleven 1,000 and four 500 pounders each onto the aiming-point from 17,500 to 18,500 between 22.34 and 22.52. Post-raid reconnaissance confirmed that most of the bombing had fallen where intended, and few, if any enemy vessels had survived intact. A residential district close to the port suffered the destruction of seven hundred houses, and seventy-six civilians were killed, as the inevitable collateral damage took its toll, but the aim of the operation had been achieved.

A similar operation was mounted on the following night at Boulogne, and involved 297 aircraft of 1, 4, 5, 6 and 8 Groups. 101 Squadron contributed nineteen Lancasters, and they would be led by W/C Alexander and S/L Thompson. They took off between 21.05 and 21.30, and flew out in poor weather conditions over England of ten-tenths cloud with a base down at around 2,000 feet. It broke up somewhat over the Channel, but over the target there were thin layers between 8,000 and 12,000 feet, and, although the port could be seen obliquely through the cloud layers by some crews on approach, it was not possible to identify the aiming-point. The first red TIs went down at 22.47, and were clearly visible, and they were backed up continuously throughout the raid. The 101 Squadron crews bombed from 13,300 to 17,000 feet between 22.41 and 22.56, and all returned safely to report concentrated bombing and large explosions. The operation was entirely successful, but the town of Boulogne suffered its worst night of the war, and two hundred civilians lost their lives.

A second new campaign opened on the night of the 16/17th, against flying bomb launching and storage sites in the Pas-de-Calais. 1 Group sent fifty-four Lancasters to the Domleger site, and contributed a hundred, including sixteen from 101 Squadron, to a force of 321 aircraft from 1, 4, 6 and 8 Groups to target the synthetic oil plant at Sterkrade, a district of Oberhausen. Referred to in Bomber Command circles as Sterkrade-Holten, it was known locally as Ruhrchemie A.G. Departure from Ludford Magna took place between 23.00 and 23.41, with S/L Thompson the senior pilot on duty. P/O Carson was forced to turn back with engine problems, but the others pressed on in unfavourable weather conditions of ten-tenths low cloud, which covered the route all the way to the target. The Pathfinder markers quickly disappeared into the cloud, leaving the crews to bomb on the receding glow, and bombing was consequently scattered. The 101 Squadron crews bombed from 18,800 to 21.500 feet between 01.18 and 01.30, and all but one returned to report a scattered attack. Night fighters infiltrated the bomber stream, and, in concert with a spirited flak defence, brought down thirty-one aircraft. LL773 sustained flak damage, and was wrecked in the subsequent forced-landed at the emergency strip at Woodbridge in Suffolk, but S/L Thompson and his crew were able to walk away. P/O Welch RCAF and his crew were less fortunate, and fell victim to a night fighter over southern Holland. LM474 crashed near Volkel, the site of a Luftwaffe fighter airfield, killing the pilot and four of his crew, and delivering the three survivors into enemy hands.

The night of the 21/22nd, Mid-summer's Night, 5 Group entered the oil offensive, and sent two forces out, one of 126 Lancasters and six Mosquitos to attack the Union Rheinische Braunkohle Kraftstoff plant at Wesseling, south of Cologne, and the other, of 120 Lancasters and nine Mosquitos, to hit the Scholven-Buer plant in the north of Gelsenkirchen. 101 Squadron contributed seven ABC Lancasters to the former, and three to the latter, which took off between 23.10 and 23.20 led by S/L Reade and F/L Stewart respectively. Thick, low cloud hid the ground all the way out to the Rhineland, and Wesseling lay under a 2,000-foot blanket of ground haze, with a further 4,000 feet of ten-tenths cloud on top of that. This prevented use of the 5 Group low-level marking method, and bombing went ahead on H2S alone. The glow of red and green TIs could be seen through the cloud, and the 101 Squadron crews carried out their attacks from 18,000 to 20,000 feet between 01.38 and

01.46. The force was badly mauled by night fighters, which hacked down thirty-seven Lancasters, and 44, 49 and 619 Squadrons each lost six aircraft. Two of the missing belonged to 101 Squadron, ME613 crashing at Drunen in Holland, a few miles inland from the Scheldt Estuary. The cause of its demise, and whether it was out or in-bound, is uncertain, as, not only was there feverish night fighter activity, as already mentioned, but there were also reports of considerable flak between the enemy coast and Wesseling. F/O Cook RCAF and three of his crew were killed, and the four survivors fell into enemy hands. LM508 was shot down by a night fighter on the way home, and crashed a little further west in the Biesbosch Estuary, killing two of the crew. P/O Hingley and five others survived and were taken into captivity. A post-war report suggested a 40% loss of production at the plant, but it was probably of short duration. Ground haze up to 2,000 feet attended the outward flight of the Scholven-Buer force, and this was present also over the target, along with a layer of ten-tenths thin cloud extending to 6,000 feet. The conditions were unsuitable here also for the 5 Group marking method, and the attack went ahead on TIs delivered by Pathfinder Oboe Mosquitos. The 101 Squadron trio bombed on red and green TIs from 19,000 to 20,000 feet between 01.42 and 01.49, and all made it home to report explosions, but no genuine impression as to the outcome. P/O King's LL771 was damaged by heavy flak just south of Dortmund on the way home at 01.47, and endured a five-minute engagement with a JU88 over the Dutch coast at Ijmuiden, before escaping to the safety of the North Sea at 02.18. It was only after the war that a secret German report indicated a temporary 20% loss of production.

The remainder of June would be devoted largely to operations against flying bomb sites and railways, and elements of 1 Group were active against a special target during the afternoon of the 22nd, the first genuine daytime operation for a considerable period. The target was an underground V-Weapon site at Mimoyecques in the Pas-de-Calais, which housed a V3 supergun, referred to by Hitler as the "London Cannon". This was because its twenty-five barrels, sunk hundreds of feet into the earth in huge shafts, pointed directly at London, and, when complete, would rain down on the capital three hundred huge high explosive shells per hour, twenty-four hours a day. The workings beneath ground were massive and extensive, and included a railway to keep the guns supplied. The RAF crews would have had no concept of the nature of what they were attacking, and it would have been referred to at briefings as "constructional works". From the air it had the appearance of a slab of concrete, and there was nothing above ground to betray its secrets. 101 Squadron was not involved in this operation, but prepared a dozen Lancasters for that night to attack railway yards at Reims in north-eastern France. They were part of a 1 Group force of 102 aircraft, and took off between 22.30 and 22.39, with F/L Marwood-Tucker the senior pilot on duty. His sortie ended some twenty-five miles out over the Channel when his Gee failed. The others pushed on over patchy cloud, which had increased to nine-tenths at the target, where the initial marking was punctual but scattered, and the Master Bomber had to correct it. Even so, many crews were unable to see the red TIs, and bombed on the glow beneath the clouds. P/O Taylor bombed from 6,500 feet, while the others went in at 8,000 feet between 00.45 and 01.15, with the exception of P/O Homes, who was unable to identify the aiming-point, and decided to retain most of his hardware.

Three flying bomb sights provided employment for 321 aircraft on the 24th, 1 Group detailing one hundred Lancasters for the "constructional works" at Les Hayons, situated between Dieppe and Rouen. 101 Squadron contributed twenty aircraft, which took off either side of 16.00 on a fine afternoon, led by S/L Morton. Scattered patchy cloud lay beneath them as they made their way out over the Channel, and the skies were clear by the time the target was in view. Some fifteen to twenty flak guns opened up at them as they crossed the French coast at Dieppe, and it was probably here, that P/O Harvey's ABC operator was killed. The marking was accurate, but the excellent visibility enabled the crews to identify the aiming-point visually. They bombed from 9,500 to 12,500 feet between 17.40 and 17.47, and the operation appeared to be successful. The crews were up early at Ludford Magna on the 25th, as twenty Lancasters were prepared for an attack on a flying bomb site at Ligescourt, a dozen miles from the coast at Berck-sur-Mer. They took off between 07.25 and 07.45, led by S/L Thompson, and climbed into five-tenths cloud, before setting course for the Channel to pick up the fighter escort. Over the target the skies were clear and the visibility excellent, which allowed the crews a sight of the small wood to the south-west of the aiming-point. 50% of the hundred-strong force bombed visually, and the others on TIs, and the entire site was soon obscured by smoke. There were no losses, and another successful operation was chalked up.

The night of the 27/28th brought a return to railway targets for nineteen 101 Squadron crews, who learned at briefing, that ten would join ninety others from 1 Group to attack the marshalling yards at Vaires, situated ten miles east of the centre of Paris, while the remaining nine were to accompany a 5 Group raid on the yards at Vitry-le-Francois, west of St-Dizier. The latter element was first away from Ludford Magna, shortly before 22.00, and they set course over four-tenths cloud, which would increase to eight-tenths thin layer cloud over the target. P/O Kelly abandoned his sortie at the Channel Islands, when his rear gunner reported sick, leaving the others to continue on to the target. The Mosquito markers delivered red spotfires from low level, which were just visible through gaps in the cloud, and the Master Bomber ordered them to be bombed at 01.44. Shortly afterwards a "stand by" order was issued, and confusion reigned as the Master Bomber told the crews to go home. As no call sign was issued, some crews carried on bombing, and six of the 101 Squadron crews were among these. They released their eighteen 500 pounders from 6,000 to 10,000 feet between 01.45 and 01.56, and a large explosion was observed at 02.08 while they were on their way home. Post-raid reconnaissance revealed damage to the western end of the yards only. The Vaires element took off between 00.43 and 00.53, and made their way southwards in good weather conditions, except, that is, for P/O Taylor, who abandoned his sortie over Lincolnshire with an unserviceable rear turret and "Monica" set. The others pressed on to find the target under clear skies and masked only by ground haze. The Pathfinders were three minutes late in opening the attack, and the Master Bomber had to assess the accuracy of the TIs before backing up those closest to the aiming point. The track and sheds were clearly visible in the light from the TIs, and the squadron participants bombed them from around 14,000 feet between 03.02 and 03.07, and returned safely home to report a successful outing.

Preparations were put in hand during the morning of the 29th for operations later in the day against two constructional works, at Domleger and Siracourt. A force of 286 Lancasters from 1, 5 and 8 Groups included a contribution from 1 Group of ninety-eight aircraft for the former, and ninety-nine for the latter, with nineteen representing 101 Squadron. The Ludford Magna brigade took off between noon and 12.25, led by F/L S-Wedderburn, and climbed into fine weather conditions, which held firm until a few miles from the target, located thirty miles inland from Berck-sur-Mer. There they met five to seven-tenths cloud with tops at 14,000 feet, through which the Pathfinders dropped red TIs at 13.56 and 13.58. These were backed up by six yellows, which fell half a mile to the west of the reds. The Master Bomber had been shot down by flak shortly after crossing the French coast, and his deputy assessed the situation, before instructing the main force to bomb half a mile east of the yellows. Unfortunately, some crews bombed the yellows, and this led to a scattered attack in the early stages, partly caused by gaps in the cloud opening and closing, allowing some crews to see the TIs, others only their glow, and some, nothing at all. The 101 Squadron crews delivered their eleven 1,000 and two 500 pounders each from 11,000 to 13,000 feet either side of 14.00, and a number reported a large explosion at 14.02. P/O McHattie aborted his attack for an undisclosed reason, and P/O King's ME837 was hit by heavy flak over the target, which wounded his mid-upper gunner.

P/O Rippon and crew, lost on 30th June 1944 attacking Vierzon (Aircrew Remembered).

The month ended for 101 Squadron with two operations on the 30th, the first, as part of a 1 Group main force of a hundred Lancasters, against a flying bomb launching site at Oisemont, situated twenty-five miles due east of Dieppe. Sixteen aircraft began taking off from Ludford Magna shortly after 06.00, with F/Ls Marwood-Tucker, Stewart and S-Wedderburn the senior pilots on duty. They climbed into ten-tenths cloud, which persisted all the way to the target, where they were instructed to bomb on navigational aids or DR. All but one of the 101 Squadron crews complied from 12,000 to 14,500 feet between 07.50 and 08.02, and only F/L S-Wedderburn retained his bombs after failing to pick up any instructions. One aircraft from the group managed to get beneath the cloud base, and made a timed run to the aiming point, where no evidence of bombing was observed. That night, ten 101 Squadron Lancasters took off between 22.15 and 22.25 bound for the marshalling yards in the small town of Vierzon, located some fifty miles south of Orleans. F/O Kinman was the senior pilot on duty, the other nine all being of pilot officer rank. They joined up with 108 others from the Group, including six markers from the Special Duties Flight. They encountered ten-tenths cloud outbound, which decreased to three-tenths at the target, but visibility was good enough to employ ground markers, which, in the light of flares, were seen to be a little to the south-east of the aiming point. Further TIs were dropped to the north-west, and instructions were issued to bomb in between. The 101 Squadron crews complied from 7,000 to 9,500 feet between 01.09 and 01.13, and turned for home confident that the site had been squarely hit. Night fighters had been attracted by the flares, and they were highly active over the target and homeward to the Loire. Fourteen Lancasters, 12% of the force, failed to return home, and a bad night for 101 Squadron resulted in three empty dispersal pans at Ludford Magna. DV301 crashed at Langon, a dozen or so miles north-west of the target, killing P/O Brown and his seven-man crew. ME616 came down near Chateaudun, halfway between the target and the coast, and there were no survivors from the crew of P/O Rippon. LL863 was shot down a short distance south-east of the target, and only the pilot, P/O Taylor survived, ultimately to evade capture. His rear gunner, F/L Daniel, had been the squadron's gunnery leader. Post-raid reconnaissance revealed the operation to be highly successful. The squadron operated at twenty-one targets, and dispatched 288 sorties for the loss of ten Lancasters and eight crews.

July 1944

101 Squadron was about to negotiate its busiest month to date, and would average almost one operation every twenty-four hours. To the existing campaigns against oil, railways and flying bomb sites, was about to be added tactical support for the ground forces as they struggled to break out through Caen and into wider France. Flying bomb sites and railways would occupy the first six days and nights, and operations began for the squadron on the 2nd, when five crews took off at 12.40 led by S/L Morton, and set course for the constructional works at Domleger, ten miles west of Doullens, as part of a 1 Group force of 125 Lancasters. They flew over eight to ten-tenths cloud on the outward route, until reaching the target, where a gap opened up that allowed most crews to visually identify the aiming point. TIs confirmed its location, and the 101 Squadron crews bombed from 11,300 to 14,100 feet between 14.14 and 14.19, and the aiming point became completely obscured by bomb bursts.

Railway targets at Orleans and Villeneuve-St-Georges occupied twenty of the squadron's crews on the night of the 4/5th, as part of an overall 1, 6 and 8 Group force of 282 Lancasters. Orleans was assigned to 156 Lancasters of 1 Group, which included six SDF markers and ten ABC aircraft of 101 Squadron, while a further ten joined forces with 6 and 8 Groups for the attack on Villeneuve-St-Georges. The former took off first, either side of 22.30, led by S/L Thompson, and they were followed into the air by the others shortly before 23.00, with F/Ls Stewart and S-Wedderburn the senior pilots on duty. P/O King became indisposed while still over base, and had to return early, and F/O Mackie was an hour and fifteen minutes into his sortie when his Gee packed up. The others continued on over Lyme Regis on the south coast, before setting course for their respective targets, which lay some sixty miles apart. Thick cloud over England gave way to thin layer cloud between 8,000 and 10,000 feet over Orleans, and the crews experienced no difficulty in picking up the assembly point green TIs. A problem with misplaced SDF markers was soon rectified, and the bombing became concentrated right on the aiming point. The 101 Squadron crews delivered their eighteen 500 pounders each from 8,000 feet between 01.30 and 01.37, and returned to report a concentrated attack, during which the Master Bomber's instructions could be heard clearly. There was eight-tenths cloud over Paris with a base at around 8,000 feet, and the Pathfinders opened the attack on time at Villeneuve, dropping TIs in two groups, one to the north and the other to the south of the aiming point. The Master Bomber instructed the main force to bomb the southern group, and the crews were able to identify ground detail in the light of the flares. The 101 Squadron bombing heights ranged from 6,500 to 13,000 feet, and their eleven 1,000 and four 500 pounders each were delivered between 01.14 and 01.19 onto the aiming-point, which erupted in smoke and flames.

The main focus on the night of the 5/6th was on flying bomb sites, but 1 Group briefed 154 crews for an attack on the railway yards at Dijon in east-central France. 101 Squadron made ready eleven Lancasters, which were all airborne by 21.30, led by F/Ls Davies, Marwood-Tucker and S-Wedderburn. They faced ten-tenths cloud until half way across the Channel, when the skies began to clear, and the crews were then able to map-read their way to the target. The Pathfinders opened proceedings in perfect visibility, dropping cascading yellow TIs blind by H2S as a reference for the visual markers, but these were found to be a mile north-west of the aiming point. The Deputy Master Bomber arrived ahead of the Master Bomber, and dropped one red and one yellow TI within sixty yards of the aiming-point. The Master Bomber backed these up with red spotfires, and the main force was called in to carry out its part in the plan. The 101 Squadron crews bombed from 7,000 to 10,000 feet between 01.50 and 02.03, and the aiming-point soon disappeared beneath bomb-bursts and smoke. There was some concern about the bombing creeping back towards the original yellows near the town, and it is possible that some collateral damage occurred.

The advance of British and Canadian ground forces was being held up by a series of enemy-held fortified villages north of Caen. A force of 467 aircraft from 1, 4, 6 and 8 Groups was made ready on the 7th for an attack that evening. The original plan to hit the villages was modified, because of the close proximity of friendly troops and the possibility of a "blue-on-blue" incident. The bombing was brought back to an area of open ground between the northern rim of the town and the villages, and a Master Bomber would be on hand to monitor the attacks on the two aiming-points. Crews greeted with enthusiasm the prospect of becoming involved in the ground war, particularly in daylight, and five 101 Squadron Lancasters took off at 20.00 led by S/L Reade. They headed out across the Channel over seven to eight-tenths cloud between 7,000 and 12,000 feet, which broke up at the French coast to leave a small amount of broken white stuff over the target. The visibility was excellent as the first red TI went down at 21.46, and this was backed-up accurately, before the main force went in to plaster the aiming points. The 101 Squadron crews bombed from 3,500 to 6,500 feet between 21.50 and 22.05, and were well on their way home by the time a further nine 101 Squadron Lancasters began taking off from Ludford Magna at 22.10 to join a 3 Group force in attacking the marshalling yards at Vaires, east of Paris. Eight-tenths cloud at the target had a base at 13,000 feet, allowing the crews to come below and benefit from the excellent visibility. The marking was accurate, and the 101 Squadron crews dropped their ten 1,000 and two 500 pounders each from 11,000 to 12,200 feet between 01.30 and 01.36, and returned to report a successful operation. In hindsight, the bombing at Caen was somewhat counter-productive, and failed to have the desired effect on the enemy ground forces, while making a mess of the northern suburbs of Caen.

A flying bomb storage dump in a wood at Nucourt, twenty miles north-west of Paris, was the target for 213 Lancasters and ten Mosquitos on the morning of the 10th. 101 Squadron provided ten ABC Lancasters led by S/L Reade, which took off shortly after 04.00, and headed for the French coast above ten-tenths cloud, which persisted all the way to the target. No markers could be seen through the cloud, and the Master Bomber instructed crews to bomb on a Gee-fix. The 101 Squadron crews complied from 13,500 to 16,000 feet between 06.01 and 06.12, and returned with no clue as to the outcome. S/L Thompson, F/O Mackie and P/O Smith took off at 18.00 to join a 3 Group force for another attack on the important railway yards at Vaires, east of Paris, but cloud covered the target area, and the Master Bomber sent them home without bombing. They were on their way home when eight Lancasters departed Ludford Magna either side of 21.45 to attack a railway junction at Revigny, a town south-east of Reims in the Marne region of France. They were part of a 1 Group force of 107 Lancasters, including six SDF markers, which flew out in fairly clear skies until some fifty miles from the target, when thin layer cloud slid in and combined with ground haze to create difficult conditions. The Master Bomber's H2S became unserviceable, and he was forced to make a DR run to drop green TIs on the assembly point, before calling in the flare force. Neither he nor his deputy was able to identify the aiming point despite searching for fifteen minutes, and the order was given to abandon the operation. By this time some forty aircraft had bombed on DR, flares, or on what they believed were red spotfires, but as none had been dropped, they were probably Lancasters burning on the ground. The Master Bomber's signal was weak, but all but one from the squadron heard the order and complied. On return, F/O Barrass reported hearing nothing, and bombing on a yellow TI from 3,500 feet at 02.05. Ten aircraft failed to return as a result of collisions, friendly fire and enemy night fighters, and the operation would have to be rescheduled.

It was two nights later, the 14/15th, when a second attempt was made to neutralize the Revigny site, with five 101 Squadron Lancasters joining a 1 Group force of 105 aircraft, while five others supported a 5 Group raid on the yards at Villeneuve-St-Georges. The Revigny-bound aircraft got away from Ludford Magna first, shortly after 21.30, with F/L Marwood-Tucker the senior pilot on duty, and they were followed into the air by the second element at 22.00, led by S/L Thompson. There was ten-tenths cloud at 6,000 feet until the French coast, when it began to break up, and it had decreased to three to seven-tenths by the time the target drew near, with a base at 6,000 to 8,000 feet. Despite a clear patch of sky developing over the target itself, and the extensive use of flares, the Master Bomber and his deputy were unable to identify the aiming-point, and no markers were dropped. The main force crews were orbiting during the deliberations, and were no doubt pleased to be told to take their bombs home. The 101 Squadron representatives complied and returned safely. On return, some crews from other squadrons would claim to have identified the junction and railway lines in the light of the flares. Seven Lancasters were lost for no gain, which meant that another attempt would be necessary. Meanwhile, there was no cloud over Paris, but ground haze hampered the marking, which, even so, was reported to be concentrated. The 101 Squadron crews bombed from 5,700 to 9,000 feet between 01.36 and 01.48, and returned safely to report a successful operation. Post-raid reconnaissance confirmed that the yards had been hit, but much of the bombing had fallen to the east of the intended aiming-point.

The busy month continued for 101 Squadron with two operations to support on the night of the 15/16th. The eight crews were divided equally between a 3 Group raid on marshalling yards at Chalons-sur-Marne, south-east of Reims, and a 4 and 6 Group effort against the previously-visited constructional works at Nucourt. S/L Reade led the Chalons section away first, at around 22.00, but P/O Harvey lost the use of his Gee equipment and had to turn back. The others continued on to encounter seven-tenths thin cloud over the target, where they benefitted from a good marking performance, and bombed from 8,000 to 9,000 feet between 01.32 and 01.38. They returned safely to report a successful operation, which was confirmed by photo-reconnaissance. Meanwhile, the Nucourt section had taken off at 23.40, only for F/Sgt Jenkins to turn back with engine failure. The remaining trio pressed on to encounter seven-tenths thin layer cloud, and conditions that precluded a visual identification of the aiming point. However, the TIs were clearly visible, and the squadron crews bombed from 8,000 to 12,500 feet between 01.45 and 01.52, before returning safely to report a number of large explosions, but no detailed assessment because of the haze. The ORB entry for the 17th is confusing, listing five sorties with take-off times ranging from 03.56 to 12.05, all assigned to the railway yards at Vaires, and all recalled by base.

The 18th would produce a record number of sorties from Ludford Magna, as 101 Squadron was required to take part in four operations. It began with the departure of twenty-four Lancasters either side of 04.00, as part of a 1 Group force of 203 aircraft assigned to attack enemy positions in one of five fortified villages east of Caen in support of the British Second Army's Operation Goodwood. This was just a fraction of the Bomber Command effort, which involved a total of 942 aircraft, in concert with others from the USAAF. England was covered by low cloud, but this began to disperse over the Channel, to leave clear skies and excellent visibility at the target. There was a northern and southern aiming point at Traorne (unable to locate), for the 1 Group crews, and the Pathfinder markers went down on time at the former in the prevailing three-quarter light, and were assessed as accurate. The bombing began a minute early, and the aiming point was soon obscured by dust and smoke, although the TIs remained visible. It was full daylight when the second element arrived to bomb the southern aiming-point, which was also dealt with effectively. The 101 Squadron crews delivered their eleven 1,000 and four 500 pounders each between 06.04 and 06.19, mostly from 6,000 to 6,500 feet, and returned safely to report very concentrated bombing and clear instructions from the Master Bomber. Of the 6,800 tons of bombs dropped during this operation, more than 5,000 tons were delivered by RAF aircraft. The attacks were amongst the most effective carried out by the Command in tactical support of the ground forces.

Many of the crews involved in the morning activity were back in the briefing room during the late afternoon to learn of their respective targets for that night. The Command would be committing almost a thousand aircraft again, principally against synthetic oil and railway objectives, but also on a variety of support and minor operations. When the red tape on the target map was seen to terminate at Wesseling near Cologne, and Scholven-Buer in the Ruhr, it would have brought back memories of the carnage suffered by 5 Group in June, which the 101 Squadron participants had managed to avoid. The last-mentioned was the destination for 153 Lancasters of 1 Group, including eight from 101 Squadron, who would be led by S/L Thompson, while Wesseling was to be a 6 and 8 Group show, supported by six 101 Squadron ABC Lancasters led by S/L Reade. The marshalling yards at Aulnoye, close to the Belgian frontier in north-eastern France, was the target for a 3 and 8 Group force, which would be accompanied by five ABC Lancasters from 101 Squadron led by F/L Stewart, and they were the first to depart Ludford Magna between 22.30 and 22.40. Medium cloud persisted all the way out until the final turning point, when it mostly dissipated to leave good vertical visibility. The Pathfinders dropped green TIs punctually and accurately, and, after the bombing had begun, instructions were received from the Master Bomber at 00.57 to allow a one second overshoot. Four 101 Squadron crews bombed from 9,000 feet between 00.54 and 01.02, but F/O Bursell abandoned his sortie over the target after being delayed by evasive action.

The Wesseling contingent took off between 22.40 and 22.55 to join up with 188 other aircraft, before setting course over low cloud, which dispersed from 02.30°E to leave clear skies and the usual ground haze. The first green TIs went down at 01.14, and the attack was concentrated around them. The 101 Squadron crews bombed from 10,500 to 12,500 feet between 01.14 and 01.18, and returned to report a concentrated raid. This was confirmed by local reports, which told of one thousand high explosive bombs falling within the plant,

P/O Jack Harvey (right) and his crew, with their Lancaster LL779, SR-V. All were lost on the night of 20/21st July attacking the Rhein-Preussen synthetic oil refinery at Homberg. This notorious target, situated on the banks of the Rhine opposite the hotly-defended target of Duisburg, claimed many crews (GW).

destroying 20% of the installations and causing a substantial loss of production. The town was also hit, and 151 houses were destroyed, many of them in the estate occupied by the plant's workforce. Those bound for Scholven-Buer took off between 22.45 and 23.05, but P/O West, P/O Homes and P/O Askew, who had all been involved in the morning operation, turned back with technical failures or sickness. The others headed into seven-tenths thin stratus, which dispersed to leave clear skies over the Ruhr and good vertical visibility. The first red TIs went down a little early at 01.25, and the aiming point marking was maintained throughout the attack. The 101 Squadron crews delivered their cookie and sixteen 500 pounders each from 19,700 to 21,000 feet between 01.29 and 01.33, and returned safely to report numerous fires, and dense columns of oily, black smoke rising to 18,000 feet. A tremendous explosion at 01.29 lasted fifteen seconds, and illuminated the neighbouring factory buildings. According to a local report, almost half of the bombs failed to explode, but, as each Lancaster was carrying four long-delay-fused 500 pounders, perhaps the report was written before they went off! In any event, those that did detonate halted production completely for an extended period.

Another busy night was in store for the Command as crews gathered in briefing rooms on the 20th to learn of their destinations for that night. Twenty-four 101 Squadron crews waited expectantly, and were rewarded with the news that fourteen of them would be supporting a 3 and 8 Group assault on the synthetic oil plant at Homberg, just to the north of Duisburg, while ten others participated in a 1 and 5 Group attack on the marshalling yards and triangular junction at Courtrai (Kortrijk) in north-western Belgium. The former took off first, between 22.45 and 22.59, led by F/Ls Davies, Stewart and S-Wedderburn, but P/O Steel returned some two hours later with an ailing rear gunner. The others climbed into ten-tenths low cloud, which gradually dispersed as they made their way eastwards, and, by the time the target was in sight, the skies were clear, and the visibility impaired only by industrial haze and smoke. The TIs tended to become swallowed up in the murk, but the bombing seemed to find the mark, and smoke was soon rising up to 19,000 feet. The 101 Squadron crews carried out their attacks from 18,000 to 19,200 feet between 01.20 and 01.33, and, those who returned reported a concentrated raid which created many fires. Local reports confirmed that this was another punishing blow to the production of aviation fuel, which had fallen from six thousand tons per day in April to under a thousand tons now, after a succession of attacks by the RAF and USAAF. The success on this night

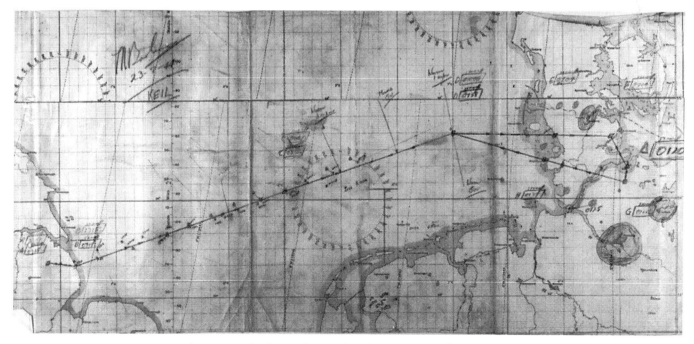

A route map for the attack on Kiel on the night of 23/24th July 1944 (GW).

195

was paid for by the loss of twenty Lancasters, seven of which belonged to 75(NZ) Squadron, four to 514 Squadron and two to 101 Squadron. LL779 crashed in south-eastern Holland at around 01.30, with no survivors from the crew of F/O Harvey RCAF, who, almost certainly, were still outbound at the time. This belief is based on the time and location of the squadron's other loss from this operation, which occurred at 02.29 in north-eastern France. This suggests a direct route out across Holland, and a long, southern withdrawal over Belgium and France to exit the French coast between Boulogne and Dieppe. LL862 was flying at 8,000 feet north of Lille when it was hit by flak, and only the pilot, P/O Meier and his bomb-aimer, both members of the RCAF, survived, the former in enemy hands, while the latter evaded a similar fate.

P/O Smith and his crew failed to return when their Lancaster W4967 crashed in Courtrai (GW).

The Courtrai operation was carried out in two waves, the first by 5 Group on aiming point B. The five 101 Squadron participants took off between 23.10 and 23.20 led by F/L Matthews, and arrived in the target area to find clear skies but thick ground haze extending to 10,000 feet. Despite the poor visibility, the crews were able to identify the river, railway and town, and a red TI was backed up by a green to mark out the aiming-point. F/O Kinman was the first to bomb, at 00.55 from 11,500 feet, without having heard anything from the Master Bomber, and he was unable to assess the accuracy of the raid. The other squadron representatives bombed from 14,000 to 14,800 feet between 00.56 and 01.01, and returned safely to report a concentrated attack, which was confirmed by photo-reconnaissance. The 101 Squadron crews assigned to the attack on aiming-point A departed Ludford Magna either side of midnight as part of a ninety-four strong 1 Group force, and arrived at the target to find improved visibility and prompt, accurate marking. They bombed from 12,000 feet between 01.53 and 01.59, and all but one returned to comment on the accuracy of the bombing and clarity of the Master Bomber's instructions. P/O Smith RCAF and his crew failed to return in veteran Lancaster W4967, which crashed in the target area, killing all but the Canadian navigator, who was taken into captivity.

On the 21st, S/L Morton was awarded an immediate DSO for meritorious service, to add to his DFC and Bar. A major operation against Kiel, the first since April of the previous year, followed on the night of the 23/24th, when the force of more than six hundred aircraft appeared suddenly and with complete surprise from behind a Mandrel (radio counter measures) screen. Nineteen 101 Squadron Lancasters had taken off between 22.40 and 23.05 led by the newly-promoted S/L Matthews, and had flown out over ten-tenths cloud, which persisted all the way to the north German coast. They began to arrive over the target at around 01.20 to find skymarkers in use, and bombed from 17,500 to 22,000 feet between 01.23 and 01.35. On return they described the glow of fires all over the target, and visible for more than a hundred miles into the return journey. The attack had

P/O "Pancho" Hyland, who was of South American origin, and his crew in LM462 crashed near Orleans in France 28/29.7 44 during an operation to Stuttgart (GW).

lasted twenty-five minutes, during which, all parts of the town had been hit, with particular damage inflicted upon the port area and the U-Boot construction yards. The surprise element confused the night fighter controller, and only four aircraft failed to return.

The first of three heavy raids on Stuttgart over a five-night period took place on the 24/25th. Over six hundred aircraft were involved, including fourteen Lancasters provided by 101 Squadron led by S/L Matthews, and they took off between 21.30 and 21.48 into low ten-tenths cloud. P/O James turned back because of a fuel leak, and F/O Kinman would return early from enemy territory with an unserviceable rear turret. The cloud began to disperse over the Channel, and the French coast was crossed under clear skies, until the German frontier was reached, when it built up again to ten-tenths with tops at 10,000 feet in the target area. Skymarkers were in use when the squadron element arrived over the aiming-point at widely ranging altitudes from 16,500 to 21,600 feet between 01.46 and 02.02, and the Master Bomber could be heard controlling the action effectively. There was too much cloud to assess the outcome, but the large glow of fires was reported, and the impression was of a successful operation. Twenty-one aircraft failed to return, but there were no empty dispersal pans at Ludford Magna.

On the following night 560 aircraft, including eight Lancasters of 101 Squadron, were sent back to Stuttgart, while 114 Halifaxes of 4 Group attended to the synthetic oil plant at Wanne-Eickel, situated between Gelsenkirchen and Herne in the Ruhr. The latter were supported by three Pathfinder Lancasters and eight of the ABC variety provided by 101 Squadron. The former took off first, led by S/L Reade at 21.35, and climbed away once more into cloud. For the second night running, P/O James came home early, this time with a rear turret problem, leaving the others to press on to the target, which they found under ten-tenths thin cloud with a base at 16,000 feet. The Pathfinders opened the attack a little early, and established a number of areas of marking, all of which attracted a proportion of the bombing. The 101 Squadron crews delivered their seven 1,000 and four 500 pounders each from 17,000 to 19,000 feet between 01.58 and 02.18, before returning to report somewhat scattered bombing, many fires and smoke. The Wanne-Eickel crews took off between 22.40 and 23.00, with F/L Stewart the senior pilot on duty, and encountered the same cloudy conditions as the

Stuttgart force. Over the target, the thin cloud merged with ground haze to provide poor visibility, but the red and green Pathfinder markers were seen, and most of the bombing fell around them. The 101 Squadron crews bombed from 15,000 to 19,000 feet between 01.12 and 01.19, and observed a number of large explosions, as well as a number of bomb loads falling onto an errant red marker to the north-west. This was not a successful operation, and no serious damage was inflicted upon the oil plant.

The last of the Stuttgart series took place at the hands of an all-Lancaster heavy force of 494 aircraft on the night of the 28/29th, while a simultaneous operation by 307 aircraft of 1, 6 and 8 Groups was directed at Hamburg. In addition to these undertakings, an attack on the flying bomb store in the Foret-de-Nieppe by a 4 Group main force was among a number of minor operations that brought the night's sortie count to 1,126. 101 Squadron prepared twenty-one Lancasters, ten for Stuttgart, six for Hamburg and five for the Foret-de-Nieppe. The Stuttgart contingent departed Ludford Magna first, between 21.40 and 21.50, with F/Ls Marwood-Tucker and S-Wedderburn the senior pilots on duty. Cloud again accompanied the force to the target, as did a large number of enemy night fighters, which picked up the bomber stream south of Paris in the bright moonlight, and remained in contact all the way to the target. 1 Group squadrons alone were involved in eighteen combats during this phase of the operation, six in the area around Orleans, and four near Strasbourg. Stuttgart was covered by a layer of stratus at low level with occasional breaks, but ground markers were visible and plentiful, if scattered, and the bombing appeared to be concentrated around their glow. The 101 Squadron crews bombed on green TIs from 16,000 to 20,000 feet between 01.51 and 02.01, in accordance with the instructions of the Master Bomber, and returned to report fires in three distinct areas, visible for a hundred miles, and a number of large explosions at 01.47, 01.51 and 02.05. A massive thirty-nine Lancasters failed to return in an echo of past campaigns against the Ruhr and Berlin, and LM462 was the 101 Squadron representative among them. P/O Hyland and his seven-man crew all died in the crash six miles north-west of Orleans in France.

The Hamburg-bound element was safely airborne from Ludford Magna by 23.00, led by S/L Matthews. They flew out over nine-tenths low cloud, and found the target under eight to nine-tenths thin cloud with a base now at 12,000 feet. The Pathfinders employed both ground and sky markers, and while the former appeared to be somewhat scattered, the latter were well-grouped. The 101 Squadron crews bombed from 17,000 to 18,200 feet between 01.17 and 01.22, and returned home to report inaccurate ground defences, no night fighters and a large, orange explosion at 01.18. In fact, night fighters were active on the route home, and it was the Halifax brigade that attracted the bulk of their attention, eighteen of them included in the overall loss figure of twenty-two aircraft. There had been a long wait at Ludford Magna after the departure of the Hamburg element, and it was at 02.25 that the first of the Foret-de-Nieppe Lancasters took off, with no pilots above the rank of flying officer. They also encountered thin cloud over the sea, and at the target, where the tops were at around 5,000 feet. Ground haze hampered visibility, but the marking was described as good, and the bombing was concentrated after initially falling short. The 101 Squadron crews delivered their eighteen 500 pounders each from 11,000 feet either side of 04.00, and returned safely to report what appeared to be a successful attack. It had been an expensive night for the Command, with a combined loss of sixty-one aircraft, all from the two major operations.

The final operations of the month were mounted on the 31st, the day on which W/C Alexander's tour as commanding officer came to an end after flying twelve operations with the squadron. He had been a very popular and highly respected commander, who was now succeeded by W/C Everest. That evening, the new commanding officer presided over his first operations, having overseen the preparation of twenty-one Lancasters, ten to support a 5 Group raid on the marshalling yards at Joigny-la-Roche, located fifty miles south-east of Paris, and eleven for a 1 Group attack on the flying bomb store in the Foret-de-Nieppe. The former got away first, between 17.30 and 17.40, and were led by F/L Marwood-Tucker. The thin cloud that had been present over the Channel dispersed to leave clear skies over the target, and the 5 Group markers took advantage of the good visibility to clearly mark the aiming point. The 101 Squadron crews bombed from 12,500 to 14,200 feet between 20.26 and 20.28, and returned safely, highly satisfied with their part in the operation. The Foret-de-Nieppe crews were airborne by 22.00, led by S/Ls Matthews and Reade, and reached the target to find ten-tenths cloud with tops at 4,000 feet. The marking was punctual, accurate and concentrated, and the bombing took place on the glow of TIs, in the case of the 101 Squadron participants, from 12,000 feet between 23.31 and 23.37. On return, the crews were diverted because of adverse weather conditions at Ludford Magna, from where three crews were involved in cross-country exercises. F/O Cornelius and crew were attempting to establish their position, when LL849 clipped trees and crashed at 02.42 near Lichfield airfield in Staffordshire, killing three of the occupants, and injuring the pilot and four others. It had been a hectic month for the squadron, during which twenty-eight operations had resulted in 247 sorties for the loss of four Lancasters and crews, plus the above-mentioned training crash.

Two fuel bowsers and their crews, Ludford Magna, 1944 (GW).

199

August 1944

Sgt Gerhard Heilig (left) was Austrian. His father was a printer and escaped from Vienna after the Anschluss in 1938. ABC operator in the crew of P/O Donaldson RAAF (right), one of only two non-Australian members of the crew (GW).

August would bring an end to the campaign against flying bomb launching and storage sites, but not until the end of the month. In the meantime a concerted assault on them brought operations on each of the first six days. 777 aircraft were detailed to attack numerous sites on the 1st, when the target for fifty Lancasters of 1 Group was the constructional works at Belle Croix les Bruyeres. 101 Squadron sat this one out, its crews enjoying a rare day and night off, but they would find themselves in the thick of the action on all but a single day during the first week. It began on the 2nd with the preparation of ten Lancasters at Ludford Magna, for an attack on one of four constructional works assigned to 1 Group. The plan was that each element would formate on two Pathfinder Mosquitos, and bomb when the first Mosquito released its load. S/Ls Reade and Thompson were the senior pilots on duty as the two 101 Squadron sections took off at 15.22 and 15.35, and made their way towards the south coast over a layer of cloud. This cleared as the Channel slid by beneath, to leave clear skies and excellent visibility over the target at Coquereaux, twenty miles east-south-east of Dieppe. It had proved difficult for the Lancasters to keep up with the Mosquitos, but the bombing went ahead visually from 17,000 to 18,000 feet between 17.41 and 17.45. P/O Steel opened his bomb doors in preparation at 17.37, upon which, his eleven 1,000 and four 500 pounders fell out. A post-raid report suggested that the bombing had been accurate and concentrated on the aiming point, and this was true also for two of the other three 1 Group attacks.

Feverish activity on the morning of the 3rd preceded the take-off from 11.35 of twenty ABC Lancasters, bound for the flying bomb storage site at Trossy-St-Maximin, located north-north-east of Paris on the southern bank of the River L'Oise. This was one of three similar targets on the day's to-do-list, which would occupy the attention of more than eleven hundred aircraft. S/Ls Reade and Thompson were the senior pilots on duty as the squadron climbed away into low cloud, which began to break up as they made their way towards the south. Fortunately, by the time the target hove into sight, the cloud had diminished to three to seven-tenths between

3,000 and 7,000 feet, and the markers were clearly visible on the ground, although most crews were able to pick up the aiming point visually through gaps. The Master Bomber confirmed that the markers were spot-on, and the 101 Squadron element bombed from 11,000 to 14,000 feet between 14.16 and 14.19. It was clear that the attack was concentrated around the aiming point, and the 101 Squadron crews returned home safely, confident that the target had been dealt a severe blow.

Initial orders for the 4th involved a return to Trossy-St-Maximin, but this was cancelled in favour of an attack on an oil production and storage site at Paulliac, located on the western bank of the River Gironde north of Bordeaux. This would require them to fly their longest-yet daylight round-trip, deep into south-western France and back, and the outward leg would take almost five hours to complete. Twenty 101 Squadron Lancasters were made ready, and S/L Thompson was the senior pilot on duty as they departed Ludford Magna between 13.25 and 13.50 to join up with 149 others from the group. In contrast to the previous day, the weather was excellent as they set course for Lands' End, where they would pick up and find comfort in the escort of 100 Group Serrate Mosquitos, Bomber Command's own night fighter arm, which was being employed in an escort role for the first time. The conditions remained ideal all the way to the target, where yellow TIs were seen to cascade over the refinery as the attack opened at 18.00. Most crews bombed visually, the 101 Squadron element doing so from 5,900 to 8,500 feet, untroubled by the defences, and observing the target to disappear under thick, black smoke and flames, which, by the end of the attack, were rising to 17,000 and 4,000 feet respectively.

Three hundred Lancasters of 1, 3 and 8 Groups returned to the region on the following afternoon to hit Pauillac again and two other oil storage depots on the Gironde River at Blaye and Bordeaux. Twenty-one 101 Squadron Lancasters were assigned to the former, and began taking off at 14.10, led by S/Ls Reade and Thompson. P/O Walker lost his port-outer engine over base, and left the others to carry on without him towards the south-west. The weather was once more ideal throughout the operation, and the defences non-existent as the target was reached shortly before 19.00. The bombing was carried out from between 6,500 and 8,500 feet in an eight-minute slot from 18.59 on a visually identified aiming point, guided by the Master Bomber. The attack was clearly concentrated around the aiming-point, and a column of smoke soon reached 2,000 feet. The umbrella of a 100 Group Mosquito escort kept the bombers safe from fighter attack, and not a single aircraft was lost from the three sites, all of which sustained serious damage.

The squadron rested on the 6th, but prepared twenty-three Lancasters on the 7th to take part in operations against five enemy strongpoints facing Allied ground forces south of Caen. Over a thousand aircraft were to be employed in carefully controlled attacks on sites west and east of the Caen to Falaise road, and it was Fontenay-le-Marmion, a couple of miles due south of the town, to which the 101 Squadron contingent was assigned. They took off between 21.05 and 21.30, as part of a 1 Group force of 204 aircraft, and S/L Thompson was the senior pilot on duty. The route out was almost cloud free, and the skies over the target were completely clear, the vertical visibility marred only by ground haze, which was not dense enough to conceal the markers. On approach to the bombing run, the crews could see the green star-shells fired from artillery pieces to identify the aiming point, and the Pathfinders dropped green TIs beneath them for the bombardiers to aim at. Bombing commenced just before H-Hour, and was concentrated around the markers, which soon became obscured by dust and smoke, or were obliterated by bombs. Backers-up kept the aiming point marked until 23.23, when the Master Bomber called a halt, and sent everyone home, including those with bombs still on board. Ten of the 101 Squadron crews bombed from 6,800 to 8,000 feet between 23.23 and 23.26, while thirteen heeded the Master Bomber, and returned their eleven 1,000 and four 500 pounders each to store.

The squadron briefed fifteen crews on the 9th, and divided them equally among three operations by other groups. 5 Group sent 171 Lancasters and fourteen Mosquitos to attack an oil storage dump in the Foret-de-Chatellerault in western France, while 3 Group went for a similar target at Fort-d'Englos, and 6 Group attended to a flying bomb launching site in the Foret-de-Nieppe. The Chatellerault element departed Ludford Magna first, shortly before 21.00, with F/L Marwood-Tucker the senior pilot on duty, and it was an hour later when F/L Porter led away those bound for Fort-d'Englos, and yet another hour before the Foret-de-Nieppe quintet took to the air behind F/L Stewart. Apart from a small mining effort by four crews from Elsham Wolds, this was 1 Group's total contribution to the night's work. The weather outbound for the 5 Group raid was cloudy, but it cleared somewhat towards the target, where haze provided the main challenge. The Mosquito markers found great difficulty in identifying the aiming point, and the main force crews were forced to orbit for about fourteen minutes, during which time two aircraft were seen to collide. The marking was eventually carried out, and the crews instructed to overshoot the green TIs. The 101 Squadron participants complied from 9,500 to 11,000 feet between 00.03 and 00.11, and returned to report a scattered raid. The crews joining 3 Group made their way out in cloudy conditions, which dissipated at the French coast to leave clear skies over the target. F/Sgt Hopes had, by then, abandoned his sortie off the Essex/Kent coast, after DV298 refused to maintain speed and gain height. The others bombed on the Master Bomber's instructions from 13,000 feet between 23.17 and 23.20, and returned to report a concentrated attack, but nothing spectacular, and no explosions were observed. The weather conditions overhead at the Foret-de-Nieppe were similar to those at Fort-d'Englos, but thick ground haze prevented a visual identification of the aiming-point. The initial red TIs were scattered, but the Pathfinder backers-up compensated with well-placed yellows and greens, and most of the bombing fell among these. The 101 Squadron element bombed from 12,000 to 13,200 feet between 00.13 and 00.18, and, again, all seemed satisfied with the quality of their work.

1 Group operated during daylight on the 10th, without calling upon 101 Squadron, but remained largely inactive that night, sending out only a small gardening force and five 101 Squadron Lancasters to support a 4 Group raid on railway yards and a junction at Dijon, in eastern France. They took off at 21.00 with no senior pilots on duty, and climbed into clear skies, which, apart from some low cloud over the Channel, persisted all the way to the target. The initial Pathfinder red TIs overshot slightly, and the Master Bomber ordered the main force to orbit while they were corrected. The 101 Squadron crews bombed on his instructions from 10,800 to 11,600 feet between 00.23 and 00.27, and post-raid reconnaissance revealed the attack to have been effective. On the following evening, four 101 Squadron Lancasters joined 175 others from 5 Group to attack the railway yards at Givors, situated a hundred miles south of Dijon. They took off either side of 20.45 led by S/L Reade, but P/O Donaldson turned back while still over Lincolnshire after an engine failed. The others continued on, and, once at the French coast, the skies cleared, and the target was reached in excellent conditions with good visibility. Ground detail was easily identified by the light of flares, and the 101 Squadron crews bombed on the centre of the green TIs from 9,000 to 10,000 feet at 01.07, as directed by the Master Bomber. Photo-reconnaissance of the site revealed this to be another highly successful raid.

The night of the 12/13th brought multiple operations, and a total of 1,167 sorties, twenty-three of which involved 101 Squadron Lancasters. The two largest operations were mounted simultaneously, one to Brunswick, to test the ability of crews to bomb on H2s without the support of Pathfinders, and the other to the Opel motor works at Rüsselsheim. 1 Group contributed eighty-three Lancasters to the former, of which ten were provided by 101 Squadron, led by S/L Thompson, while nine others from Ludford Magna joined the latter with F/O Balenko the senior pilot on duty. They took off together either side of 21.30, and flew out in clear weather conditions, until the Brunswick force was about fifty miles from the target, where ten-tenths strato-cumulus cloud was encountered. This totally obscured the ground, forcing crews to rely on their H2S to establish position, while others bombed on ETA. The 101 Squadron participants bombed from 18,000 to 21,000 feet between 00.05 and 00.12, aiming at the glow of fires, and those who returned offered a number of opinions on the outcome, ranging from scattered to concentrated and many fires. They reported fires visible for a hundred miles into the return journey, and fierce night fighter activity on the way home from north of Hannover to the Dutch frontier. Three 101 Squadron Lancasters were among twenty-seven aircraft failing to return from this operation, which represented 7.1% of those dispatched. According to Bill Chorley's Bomber Command Losses for this night, DV292 was shot down by a night fighter and crashed at Brockum, about three miles south-east of the Dümmersee. The time of the crash was recorded at 00.10, while the attack on Brunswick was in full swing some eighty miles further east, and this suggests that F/L Tugwell had turned back with some kind of technical issue. All on board lost their lives, and this experienced crew would be missed at Ludford Magna, as would that of F/L Marwood-Tucker, who came down in the Hannover area in LM598, again without survivors. There was at least some good news concerning F/O Atyeo RCAF and five of his crew, who escaped with their lives after the demise of PB258 while outbound over Heverlee in Belgium. They fell into enemy hands, but the wireless operator and ABC operator, sadly, lost their lives. The latter, Sgt Schwarz, whose parents lived in Cricklewood, was of German origin, and disguised the fact by adopting the name Blake for operational purposes. (Bomber Command Losses, 1944. Bill Chorley.) The operation was described by local authorities as heavy, with damage in the central and Stadtpark districts, but no point of concentration.

Meanwhile, P/O Grant had abandoned his sortie to Rüsselsheim at the Suffolk coast because of a failing ASI, and left the others to press on to southern Germany in broken cloud with tops at 8,000 feet. The target lay under just two-tenths cloud, and the marking was described as plentiful and fairly well-grouped, despite which, little damage was inflicted on the factory complex. The 101 Squadron crews bombed on red and green TIs from an average of 17,000 feet between 00.15 and 00.21, and all but one returned to comment more on the night fighter activity over Belgium on the way home, than on the outcome of the raid. Twenty aircraft were missing, 6.7% of the force, and 101 Squadron was represented by ME617, which came down somewhere in southern Germany, killing F/Sgt Jenkins and all but his rear gunner, who was taken into captivity. Also on this night, the squadron dispatched four ABC Lancasters to support an attack by 144 aircraft on enemy troop positions and a road junction north of Falaise, a town inland from the beachhead and south of Caen. S/L Reade led them away at 00.20, and they climbed into clear skies until the French coast, where thin cloud at 2,500 feet covered the ground. The TIs could be seen clearly, as could the bomb bursts, as the squadron crews released their ten 1,000 and four 500 pounders each onto reds and greens from 7,000 feet between 02.16 and 02.20. They returned without incident, and reported observing a few fires and explosions through the cloud.

The squadron enjoyed a day off on the 14th, when another tactical operation was mounted by over eight hundred aircraft in daylight to provide further support for the ground forces in the Falaise area. Seven aiming points were briefed out, all of them close to the advancing Third Canadian Division, and Oboe and visual marking were employed in excellent weather conditions, with a Master Bomber and deputy controlling each aiming-point to try to ensure there were no friendly-fire incidents. Smoke and haze soon made map-reading difficult, and forced the crews down to very low level, but sufficient target indicators were visible to provide a reference point, and, generally, the bombing was accurate. Halfway through the operation, some bombs fell among elements of the 12th Canadian Field Regiment taking shelter in a quarry, and the Master Bomber was unable to prevent around seventy aircraft bombing the area, killing thirteen men, injuring fifty-three others and destroying vehicles and equipment.

In preparation for his new night offensive against industrial Germany, Harris launched a thousand aircraft by daylight on the 15th against nine night fighter airfields in France, Holland and Belgium. 101 Squadron prepared twenty-three Lancasters to divide between the two 1 Group targets of Volkel in south-eastern Holland and Le Culot in north-eastern France. The eleven crews bound for Volkel were all airborne by 10.00, but P/O Nielsen abandoned his sortie over base after losing his starboard-outer engine. F/O Steel was twenty miles out from the Suffolk coast when his starboard-inner began to malfunction, and he, also, turned back. Meanwhile, the dozen squadron Lancasters heading for France had left the ground by 10.14, led by S/L

Lady of the Night... An atmospheric image of a 101 Sqn Lancaster awaiting her next op (GW).

Thompson, with the bulk of the more senior pilots in tow. The weather throughout the operations was perfect, and the crews bound for Volkel could identify the airfield from a considerable distance. The Pathfinders dropped their markers close to the intersection of the runways, and the bombing that followed fell with great concentration around them, to the extent that the aiming-point soon disappeared under dust and smoke. The 101 Squadron crews delivered their eleven 1,000 and four 500 pounders each from 14,000 to 16,000 feet between 12.01 and 12.07, and returned home to report a successful operation. The Le Culot element had been able to map-read to the target from the French coast, and estimated the horizontal visibility as forty to fifty miles. The first red TIs dropped by the Pathfinders fell onto the western edge of the airfield, and the Master Bomber ordered the crews to bomb to the east of these, before putting another TI closer to the aiming-point. The 101 Squadron crews ran in at 14,400 to 17,000 feet between 12.00 and 12.11, and watched their hardware explode close to the intersection of the runways. Returning crews reported a large explosion from the fuel storage area at the southern end of the airfield, and commented on the accuracy of the predicted heavy flak defending the site, which caused some aircraft from the group to come home bearing the scars of battle.

With our very best regards... Armourers pose with a 4,000 lb HC 'Cookie' before loading it onto a Lancaster for delivery to an unwitting recipient (GW).

Harris began his new offensive on the night 16/17th, with operations against the ports of Stettin and Kiel, both of which were supported by elements from 101 Squadron. Eighteen Lancasters were made ready at Ludford Magna, divided equally between the 1, 3, 5 and 8 Group raid on the former, and the 4, 6 and 8 Group assault on the latter. With further to travel, the Stettin-bound element took off first, between 21.05 and 21.15, led by S/L Matthews, and climbed into clear conditions to join up with the 452 other Lancasters over the North Sea. The clear skies persisted all the way across Denmark, but cloud began to build over the Baltic, until a two-thousand-foot-thick band between 15,000 and 17,000 feet greeted the force's arrival at the German coast. Almost miraculously, a patch of clear sky appeared right over Stettin, and the attack was able to take place under predominantly cloudless skies. The marking began two minutes late, but the crews had a plentiful supply of TIs to aim at, and the 101 Squadron crews bombed from 15,500 to 19,000 feet between 01.03 and 01.10, and returned with mixed opinions as to the effectiveness of the attack. Some found the Master Bomber's signal to be weak, and others heard nothing from him. Most commented on the number of fires all over the town, and the consensus was of a successful operation. There was a moderate amount of heavy and light flak to contend with, along with searchlights and night fighters, and F/O Henry and crew fought off two encounters without damage to either party. The operation had, in fact, been outstandingly accurate, and had destroyed fifteen hundred houses and twenty-nine industrial premises. A further thousand houses and twenty-six industrial premises were severely damaged, five ships were sunk in the harbour, and eight others seriously damaged, while eleven hundred people lost their lives.

The 101 Squadron representatives among the Kiel force of 348 aircraft got away between 21.40 and 21.49, with F/L Bursell the senior pilot on duty. They crossed the North Sea under clear skies, but cloud built up towards the Schleswig-Holstein peninsular, until there was six to ten-tenths in layers over the target, with tops at 17,000 feet. Markers were plentiful, but somewhat scattered, and the impression was of overshooting. The 101 Squadron crews bombed on the glow of red TIs from 16,000 to 18,000 feet between 00.11 and 00.18, and returned to report a largely scattered raid. Local authorities admitted to widespread damage in the docks area, and among ship-building concerns, but claimed that a proportion of the bombing had missed the town to the north-west.

1 Group was handed five daytime targets on the 18th, and the briefing of five 101 Squadron crews for one of them took place at Ludford Magna in the morning. They learned that they were to take part in an attack by thirty 1 Group Lancasters on an oil storage depot at Terneuzen, a northern district of the city of Ghent in north-eastern Belgium. This target is sometimes referred to as Ertvelde-Rieme, Riemer being a location a little to the north of Terneuzen. S/L Thompson was the senior pilot on duty as they took off at 12.20, and climbed into cloudless skies, which persisted until approaching the Dutch coast, where there was eight-tenths strato-cumulus between 4,000 and 9,000 feet. The Master Bomber ordered the crews to descend to cloud top height, and to be prepared to descend again to below the cloud base just before H-Hour. It appears that a pass was made by some crews from above cloud to bomb on the glow of the initial TIs, which had overshot, and S/L Thompson was among these, delivering his load from 9,000 feet at 13.49. While the marking was corrected, the crews were forced to make an orbit, and carry out a second bombing run, during which the remaining four 101 Squadron crews delivered their eleven 1,000 and four 500 pounders each from 2,600 to 3,900 feet between 13.57 and 14.00. The target soon disappeared under dust and smoke, before becoming completely enveloped in thick, black smoke, which rose quickly to a considerable height. A large explosion and orange fires confirmed the accuracy of the attack, and the crews returned home satisfied with their day's work.

That night, after briefings during the afternoon, fourteen 101 Squadron crews prepared to take part in three further operations. Proceedings began at Ludford Magna with the departure of five ABC Lancasters at 21.50, which were to join forces with 283 other aircraft from 3, 6 and 8 Groups to attack Bremen, a city left in relative peace for a considerable time. The weather conditions outbound provided clear skies and haze as S/L Matthews led the squadron quintet eastwards, and, although a build-up of cloud threatened shortly before they reached the target area, the city was found to be clear. The markers were closely grouped, and, despite the early bombing undershooting somewhat, it soon became concentrated around the TIs, and a very large area of fire developed. The 101 Squadron crews bombed the centre of red and green TIs from 16,200 to 19,000 feet between 00.15 and 00.20, and contributed to this much-bombed city's greatest ordeal of the war. Over eight and a half thousand apartment blocks were reduced to ruins, and the number of industrial and commercial buildings destroyed or damaged was too great to record. Eighteen ships were sunk in the harbour, sixty-one others were seriously damaged, and the death toll exceeded eleven hundred people.

Thirty-five minutes after the departure of the above 101 Squadron element, F/O Steel and P/Os Farriday and Grant took off for the oil storage depot at Ghent-Terneuzen, which appears as Ertvelde-Rieme in Bomber Command War Diaries. Cloud over the North Sea had dispersed by the time the target hove into sight, and P/O Grant made to open the bomb doors in readiness when some twenty miles away. Nothing happened, and he was forced to turn back and bring his bombs home. The others identified the target in the light of flares, and listened to the clear and concise instructions of the Master Bomber, as he switched the point of attack from one group of TIs to another. The 101 Squadron duo bombed from 10,000 feet at 00.08, and observed the concentrated bombing tending to scatter as the attack developed. Several explosions were noted, along with black smoke rising to a considerable height. The final departures from Ludford Magna on this night involved four ABC Lancasters, which took to the air shortly before 23.00, led by F/Ls Haycraft and Stewart. They were bound for the oil plant at Sterkrade, a district of Oberhausen in the Ruhr. They were to join forces with 230 other aircraft, of which 210 were 4 Group Halifaxes. A small amount of cloud over the target had no effect on the marking, which was well grouped around the aiming point, and concentrated bombing soon resulted in large fires and black smoke rising to 6,000 feet. The 101 Squadron representatives delivered their attacks onto red and green TIs from 17,000 to 18,000 feet between 00.57 and 01.16, and returned safely to report a successful operation.

After a hectic period of operations thus far over the summer, the crews were doubtless appreciative of being able to wake up each morning after a long night's rest, and learn during the course of the day, that they would not be going to war that night. It was something of a paradox that such lengthy spells away from operations soon triggered boredom and a desire to get back on the horse, however lethal that might be. This lull lasted until the night of the 25/26th, when more than thirteen hundred sorties were launched on three major operations and a variety of others of a minor and support nature. Two forces were made ready for southern Germany, the larger, comprising 412 aircraft of 1, 3, 6 and 8 Groups, returning to the Opel motor works at Rüsselsheim, while 5 Group targeted the city of Darmstadt further to the south-east. While these operations were in progress, a Halifax main force from 4 and 6 Groups would target eight coastal batteries around the port of Brest. 101 Squadron was to be involved only at Rüsselsheim, and briefed ten crews, the most senior of which were those of S/Ls Reade and Thompson. They departed Ludford Magna either side of 20.30, and flew out over Selsey Bill in good weather conditions, which would hold for the entire outward leg. There were no early returns, and they arrived in the target area to find it under clear skies and easily identifiable by mostly well-placed and concentrated markers. The defences consisted largely of searchlights co-operating with night fighters, and moderate, although not troublesome, heavy flak in barrage form. A decoy fire site ten miles west-south-west of the target attracted a number of early bomb loads, but the majority were seen to fall around the markers, and a good area of fire developed, sending smoke up to 11,000 feet. The 101 Squadron crews bombed from 16,000 and 18,000 feet either side of 01.00, and eight returned home to report explosions at 00.58, 01.02, 01.09 and 01.10, fires visible for eighty miles into the homeward journey, and intense night fighter activity outbound, over the target and homebound. ME857 crashed at Boult-aux-Bois, a village in eastern France between Reims and the Luxembourg frontier, killing seven of the nine occupants, the bomb-aimer falling into enemy hands, and the rear gunner evading a similar fate. F/L Porter RCAF and his crew were very experienced, and, on this night, were providing operational training for F/O Purkis, who was acting as second pilot. The same was true of F/O Steel RNZAF and his crew, who had F/O Ross RCAF performing the second pilot role. Only the rear gunner escaped from NN705 before it also crashed on French soil, and he managed to retain his freedom. It had been a mature crew, with four members over the age of thirty, and their presence would be missed by all at Ludford Magna. The attack was moderately successful in putting parts of the factory out of action temporarily, but loss of production was not serious.

On the following night, ten 101 Squadron crews joined 362 others in an all-Lancaster main force bound for the port of Kiel, while 5 Group targeted Königsberg at the eastern end of the Baltic, which the enemy was using to supply its eastern front. S/L Thompson led them into the air either side of 20.30, before exiting England over the Lincolnshire coast in good weather conditions that would hold throughout the trip. They arrived in the target area to find the markers well-placed and concentrated within the confines of the town, and, despite the activation of a smoke screen, were able to bomb them from 17,000 to 18,500 feet between 23.11 and 23.18 in the face of a moderate heavy flak barrage, searchlights and intense fighter activity. All returned safely home to report a successful operation, which was confirmed by photo-reconnaissance to have inflicted severe damage in the town centre and surrounding districts, where major fires had been fanned by the strong wind.

The final operations against flying bomb sites were carried out on the 28th, before the Allied ground forces took the Pas-de-Calais a few days later. Twelve sites were targeted by small forces, with Mosquitos providing Oboe marking, but 101 Squadron was not required to take part. Distant targets again occupied a large part of the Command on the night of the 29/30th, when 5 Group returned to Königsberg to deliver an outstandingly accurate attack at the limit of the Lancaster's range, while elements of 1, 3, 6 and 8 Groups raided another Baltic port, Stettin. 101 Squadron made ready twenty Lancasters, all for Stettin, and they took off between 21.04 and 21.30 led by S/Ls Matthews and Reade. They encountered low cloud as far as the Danish coast, where they were met by a large number of enemy night fighters. F/O Balenko abandoned his sortie at 10,000 feet over Denmark at 00.15, after losing his port-inner engine. The others continued on to the Baltic, where they found layers of thin cloud between 12,000 and 17,000 feet, beneath which, visibility was good with a little haze. At the target, flares provided good illumination, and the marking was punctual and concentrated to the north-east of the planned aiming point. The Master Bomber broadcast "Basement 12,000 feet", but not all crews picked up the transmission, and this led to bombing both from below and above cloud through gaps. The 101 squadron crews were carrying a mixture of HE and incendiaries, which they delivered onto the red and green markers from 12,000 to 19,000 feet between 02.01 and 02.15. A large area of fire soon developed, accompanied by a pall of smoke rising to 14,000 feet, and the glow would be visible well into the return journey. Others reported a large explosion at 02.07, and post-raid reconnaissance would confirm the extensive damage in residential and industrial districts, as well as to port installations and shipping. It was another expensive night for 101 Squadron, however, and there were three empty dispersals to contemplate at Ludford Magna next morning. LL757 was carrying the nine-man crew of F/L Stewart, who had P/O Pocock on board as second pilot, and none survived the crash in Sweden. The likelihood is that the Lancaster was fatally damaged during an encounter with a night fighter on the way out over Denmark, and struggled into Swedish airspace to attempt a forced-landing. LM479 came down at Lem, in Denmark's North Jutland region, almost certainly after also encountering a night fighter, and there were no survivors from the crew of F/O Foster RCAF. It seems that ME592 also crashed on Swedish soil, as F/O Piprell RCAF and six of his crew are buried in the same cemetery as the Stewart crew. One man, the bomb-aimer, did survive, however, and evaded capture. Had he landed in Sweden, he would have been interred for a period, but, as there is no mention of internment, he probably parachuted from the stricken aircraft while it was still over Denmark, and was aided in his evasion by local people.

Six hundred aircraft were detailed on the 31st to take part in daylight attacks on nine sites suspected to be storing V-2 rockets. Fourteen 101 Squadron crews were briefed to attack the site at Saint-Riquier, situated five miles east-north-east of Abbeville in northern France. They took off between 13.30 and 13.47 in fair weather conditions, and joined up with thirty-four other Lancasters, before passing over the Sussex coast. It was here that cloud began to form, and was four to seven-tenths at 13,000 feet over the target. Breaks in the cloud allowed the crews to identify an L-shaped wood to the west of the aiming-point, and the red TIs burning nearby. The Master Bomber called for a two-hundred-yard undershoot, and created confusion by changing the direction of attack a number of times. The marking and bombing appeared to be scattered, and when a layer of thick cloud slid across the area, obscuring the TIs, the Master Bomber called a halt to proceedings at 15.38, and sent the force home. Three of the 101 Squadron crews complied with this order, but eleven had already bombed from 11,400 to 13,000 feet between 15.30 and 15.37, and returned home to report accurate heavy flak over the target and at Abbeville. During the course of the month the squadron operated on twenty-five occasions, and despatched 253 sorties for the loss of nine Lancasters and crews.

An illicit photograph of an ABC-equipped Lancaster taking off from Ludford Magna. The crude attempt at censorship highlights the presence of the aerials (GW).

September 1944

The dominant theme in September would be the return to Allied control of the three French ports still in enemy hands. Le Havre would be the main focus of attention during the first two weeks of September, as the Command tried to dislodge pockets of resistance from around it. First, however, 675 aircraft were involved in daylight operations against six airfields in southern Holland on the 3rd, for which 101 Squadron made ready twenty-one Lancasters. The target for this 1 Group element of ninety-nine Lancasters was Gilze-Rijen, while fifty-one others went for Eindhoven to the south-east. They took off between 15.38 and 15.59, led by S/Ls Matthews and Reade, and climbed into rain-bearing low cloud before heading for the coast at Southwold. The cloud decreased during the North Sea crossing, and, although there would be layers over the target at 5,000 and 12,000 feet, it would be insufficient to prevent a visual identification of ground detail. F/O James lost an engine half-way between the English and Dutch coasts, and had to turn back, while the rest of the force found itself ahead of schedule, and having to kill time. They carried out an orbit over the Dutch coast, until being called in at 17.26 by the Master Bomber, who instructed them to bomb on the red TIs, which were confirmed as being accurately placed. The 101 Squadron crews bombed either on these or visually from 9,000 to 13,000 feet between 17.29 and 17.34, before returning safely from what was a successful operation.

Operations against the port of Le Havre would be conducted daily between the 5th and 11th, to dislodge enemy strong-points facing the advancing British forces. Eighteen 101 Squadron crews were briefed for the first of these, as part of a 1 Group force of 159 Lancasters, divided into three waves, each with its own aiming-point. S/Ls Matthews and Thompson were the senior pilots on duty as the first wave departed Ludford Magna between 16.10 and 16.17, the second between 16.28 and 16.40 and the third between 16.47 and 16.53, and climbed into nine-tenths cloud, which gradually broke up as they neared the English Channel. It continued to diminish during the sea crossing, and was no more than three-tenths over the target by the time the first wave arrived. The aiming point could be picked out visually, but there were none of the expected green TIs, and the Master Bomber ordered the force to orbit, while reds were put down at 18.07. There was excellent visibility to aid the crews as they bombed from 10,600 to 12,000 feet between 18.07 and 18.16, and the smoke from this attack could be seen by the approaching second and third waves. The wind ensured that the smoke drifted away from the aiming points, and conditions remained good as the wave two aircraft bombed from a similar height between 18.22 and 18.24. The third wave crews could see the destruction wrought by the first two, and carried out their attacks, still in clear visibility, between 18.42 and 18.47, before returning home to report a successful outcome.

The operation to Le Havre on the evening of the 6th involved 344 aircraft targeting a number of aiming points. The 101 Squadron contingent of sixteen Lancasters was divided between the first and third waves, aiming-points 4 and 6, and the first three Lancasters, containing the crews of S/L Thompson, F/O Grant and S/L Matthews took off respectively at one-minute intervals from 17.15, before climbing into poor weather conditions. They encountered ten-tenths cloud over the Channel with a base at 11,000 feet, and crossed the French coast at 7,000 feet, still with thick cloud above. The Master Bomber was heard at 18.45 giving the basement as 10,000 feet, and as 7,000 feet thirteen minutes later. The marking was punctual, and the red and green TIs stood out clearly in the prevailing murky light. The order was given to disregard the greens and aim for the reds, which were assessed as being well-placed, if a little to the south-west of the aiming-point, and the 101 Squadron trio complied from 6,000 to 7,200 feet between 19.00 and 19.04. The remaining 101 Squadron participants took off between 17.37 and 17.54, and, as they were making their way across the Channel, the second wave was hammering aiming point 5 from 6,000 feet and below, and a large explosion at 17.27, followed by a column of black smoke, suggested that an oil storage dump had been hit. By the time the third wave arrived on the scene, the weather had deteriorated further, and the cloud base had become too low for bombing to take place. The Master bomber began issuing a cancellation order at 17.31, with which the 101 Squadron crews complied. On return at 20.53, F/O Harris overshot the landing, and LL756 ran off the end of the runway and crashed. The crew walked away unhurt, but, after a few days of inspection, the Lancaster was declared a write-off. Two minutes after this incident, F/L Massheder overshot his landing in ND983, and intentionally retracted the undercarriage, presumably to avoid a collision with LL756. The crew was unhurt, but the Lancaster was deemed to be beyond repair.

There was an early start for twenty 101 Squadron crews on the 8th, when Le Havre was the target yet again. They took off between 06.28 and 06.58, with S/Ls Matthews and Thompson the senior pilots on duty, and set course in conditions of heavy cloud, which broke up as they headed south, and then built again over the Channel. F/L Massheder abandoned his sortie thirty miles off the Sussex coast at 07.42 after his bomb sight became unserviceable, and, as the others approached the French coast at 08.16, the Master Bomber was heard to abort the operation because of the adverse weather conditions at the target, and send the crews home. 101 Squadron was not involved at Le Havre on the 9th, when poor visibility in the target area resulted in the Master Bomber calling a halt to proceedings before any of the 250 heavy aircraft had bombed. A massive assault on the port was planned for the following day, when a force of 992 aircraft was assembled, of which 1 Group provided two hundred Lancasters for two aiming points, Bentley 1 and Bentley 2. Twenty-one ABC Lancasters were fuelled and bombed up at Ludford Magna, and they took off between 16.55 and 17.20, with S/L Matthews the senior pilot on duty. They climbed into thin, broken cloud, which dissipated as they flew south, and had cleared altogether by the time the already smoking target loomed on the horizon. The smoke was drifting to the south-west over the town, but the surrounding landmarks stood out clearly in the excellent visibility. The Master Bomber was heard at 18.25 instructing the crews for Bentley 1 to maintain their briefed height, and, at 18.40, called them in to bomb on the red TIs. The 101 Squadron crews were assigned to Bentley 2, and heard the Master Bomber report the first markers overshooting by seven hundred yards. He issued instructions to undershoot these reds, and, meanwhile, more accurate TIs were put down, which the 101 Squadron crews bombed from 8,000 to 10,200 feet between 18.51 and 19.02. All returned home safely to report a successful evening's work.

The squadron was not involved in the final operations against German positions outside Le Havre on the 11th, within hours of which, the garrison surrendered to British forces. That night, 5 Group returned to the southern city of Darmstadt, which it had attacked ineffectively in August. A heavy force of 226 Lancasters included five of the ABC variety, which took off between 21.07 and 21.13 led by S/L Matthews. The outward flight was conducted under clear skies, and it was only on arrival in the target area that eight to ten-tenths very thin cloud appeared with tops at 5,000 feet. This had no adverse effect upon the 5 Group low-level marking system, which worked perfectly, and the illuminating flares and green TIs were clearly visible as the 101 Squadron quintet approached the aiming-point at 23.52. The greens were backed-up by an excellent sequence of red TIs, and the 101 Squadron crews delivered their loads of a cookie, fourteen 500 pounders and incendiaries each from 14,500 feet either side of midnight. They returned safely to report huge fires, which were visible from a hundred miles away, and it was only afterwards, that the full story of the raid was revealed. Districts to the south and east of the city centre were totally destroyed by a firestorm, and the accepted casualty figure now stands at 12,300 fatalities, with a further 70,000 people rendered homeless out of a population of 120,000.

Preparations were made on the 12th for the final major raid of the war on Frankfurt, which was to be carried out that night by 378 Lancasters and nine Mosquitos drawn from 1, 3 and 8 Groups. 1 Group's contribution was two hundred Lancasters, of which thirteen were to be provided by 101 Squadron. A simultaneous raid on

Stuttgart by 5 Group would be supported by nine ABC Lancasters, but it was the former element that departed Ludford Magna first, between 18.17 and 18.31, with S/L Matthews the senior pilot on duty. The weather outbound was clear all the way, and the 101 Squadron participants arrived in the target area as flares went down at 22.52 to illuminate ground detail. Mixed red and green TIs cascaded as the first main force crews bore down on the aiming point, and these were backed up promptly and continuously throughout the attack. The 101 Squadron crews bombed from 16,000 to 18,500 feet between 22.57 and 23.08, and, on return, they were able to report a pall of smoke rising to 5,000 feet as they turned away, and fires visible a hundred miles and more into the homeward journey. They also reported fires still burning in Darmstadt, where, apparently, most of Frankfurt's fire service was still active. Post-raid reconnaissance established that Frankfurt's western districts had sustained severe damage, where industrial and residential property suffered equally.

Meanwhile, the Stuttgart element had taken off between 18.50 and 18.57, with no pilots above flying officer rank, and enjoyed clear skies throughout the operation. P/O Hodgkinson was about ninety miles south-east of Paris when he became ill, and had to turn back, and F/O Hrynkiw's ND924 was hit in the nose by flak at 22.40, when a few miles north of Strasbourg. The bomb-aimer was mortally wounded, and the bomb-sight rendered unserviceable. After tending to his dying colleague, the flight engineer, Sgt Grantham-Hill, assumed bomb-aiming duties, and directed a DR run to an alternative target, believed to be Karlsruhe, where the bomb load of a cookie and incendiaries was delivered from 16,500 feet at 23.00. The other 101 Squadron crews continued on to the target, where visibility was excellent, as was the marking, and they bombed on red TIs from 16,500 feet between 23.11 and 23.17, reporting the glow of fires visible for a hundred miles. A local historian writes that a firestorm occurred, and that the northern and western areas of the city centre were erased on this night, and more than eleven hundred people killed.

The forlorn remains of PB456 following structural failure in flight (GW)

101 Squadron's PB456 took off for a training flight at 19.05 on the 13th, with the crew of F/O Brooks RCAF on board. It suffered structural failure and broke up over Scotland three hours later, and crashed near Dumbarton, killing all seven occupants. After two nights off, nine 101 Squadron crews were briefed on the 15th for an operation that night against Kiel. They were to provide ABC cover for a force of 481 aircraft drawn from 4, 6 and 8 Groups, and took off between 22.28 and 22.45, with F/Ls Bursell and Haycraft the senior pilots on duty. P/O Lyons abandoned his sortie over base for an undisclosed reason, while the others continued on to encounter varying amounts of cloud until reaching the Danish coast, where it began to thin, to leave clear skies and good visibility over the target. Mixed red and green TIs were seen to cascade at 01.08, and they were closely grouped around the aiming point. The 101 Squadron crews bombed from 17,200 to 20,000 feet between 01.14 and 01.28, and reported fires visible for a hundred miles into the return journey. Photo-reconnaissance confirmed severe damage within the town, but also much errant bombing beyond its boundaries.

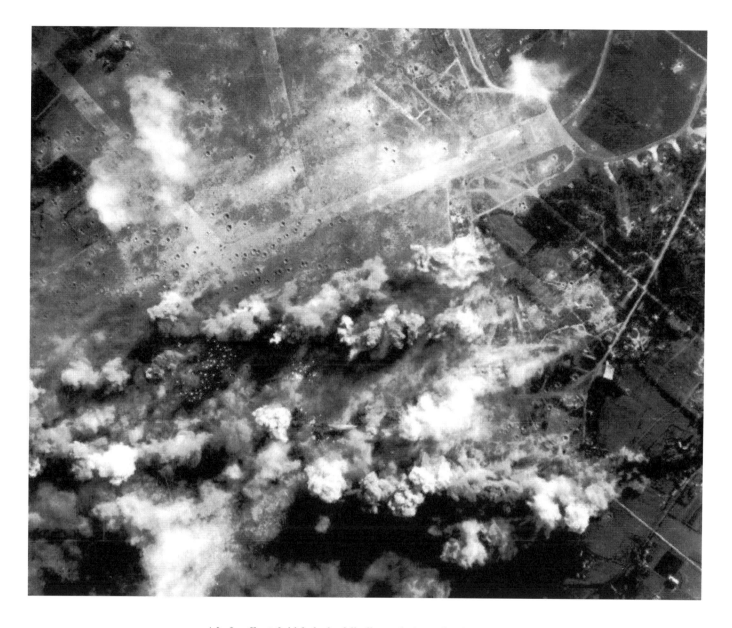

A Luftwaffe airfield feels the full effects of a heavy bomber raid (GW)

On the eve of the launch of the ill-fated Operation Market Garden, which was to begin in the early hours of the 17th, enemy airfields at Leeuwarden and Steenwijk in Holland, and Hopsten and Rheine (Salzbergen), just across the frontier in Germany, were to be targeted by two hundred Lancasters and twenty-three Mosquitos of 1 and 8 Groups. 101 Squadron made ready nineteen Lancasters, seven for Hopsten, and four for each of the others, and it was the Hopsten-bound element that took off first, between 21.29 and 21.47. They were followed into the air by the Steenwijk quartet between 22.12 and 22.20, and, finally, the Rheine and Leeuwarden sections between 00.47 and 01.01. The weather conditions outbound were ideal, and good visibility attended the attacks at each target. The Hopsten crews carried out their bombing runs at 17,000 feet between 23.21 and 23.25, those at Steenwijk from 13,000 feet between 23.45 and 23.47, at Leeuwarden from 11,000 to 11,800 feet between 02.26 and 02.28, and at Rheine from 15,000 feet between 02.49 and 02.54. They all returned home safely to report successful operations, which were confirmed by post-raid reconnaissance.

213

In further support for Operation Market Garden, 112 Lancasters and twenty Mosquitos of 1 and 8 Groups were prepared for an attack on German flak positions on the Island of Walcheren in the Scheldt Estuary. Fourteen 101 Squadron crews were briefed for a site at Westkapelle, in company with seven Lancasters each from 12 and 626 Squadrons at Wickenby. They took off between 16.59 and 17.12, and climbed into fine conditions with just a little cloud, that dispersed to leave clear skies and good visibility over the target. The marking was accurate and concentrated, and the 101 Squadron crews bombed either visually or on red TIs from 11,500 to 13,000 feet between 18.30 and 18.33, before returning home to report a successful outcome. A single heavy attack on Boulogne, involving 762 aircraft on the morning of the 17th, was sufficient to persuade the German garrison to surrender shortly afterwards. 101 Squadron was not invited to take part, and stayed at home also while 5 Group destroyed over 2,600 buildings in Bremerhaven on the night of the 18/19th.

The twin towns of Mönchengladbach and Rheydt were selected for a visit from a 5 Group force on the night of the 19/20th. On this occasion the latter was the principal target in the complex plan, and the Master Bomber for the occasion was the former 106 and 617 Squadron commanding officer and national hero, W/C Guy Gibson VC, of Dambuster fame, who was currently Base Operations Officer at 54 Base at Coningsby. The decision to allow Gibson to act as Master Bomber was somewhat surprising, as he was barely qualified for the role, and there were many far more experienced members of the 5 Group Master Bomber fraternity at Coningsby, like W/C Owen, who had controlled a recent attack at this target, and W/Cs Jeudwine and Woodroffe. Gibson had been agitating to get back into the war before it was over, and didn't want his service to end in a backwater, while others gained the glory by being in at the death. Ten 101 Squadron Lancasters were to provide ABC cover and attack the town centre, and took off between 10.05 and 19.19 with no senior captains on duty. F/O McClenaghan turned back at 20.25 from a position some thirty miles off Dunkerque, and the fact that he was down at 5,000 feet suggests engine failure. The others arrived at the target under clear skies and in good visibility, but found the TIs to be late in going down. It was here that Gibson seemed to experience some difficulty in maintaining control, as the point of attack was shifted from one aiming point to another, and some aircraft bombed markers not assigned to them. Instructions were received to bomb on green TIs, but some crews failed to see any, and aimed instead at fires burning in the centre of the target area, while others did see them and confirmed them as being on the aiming-point. Some crews reported being ordered to bomb greens, only to have that instruction cancelled and changed to reds. The 101 Squadron participants delivered their loads of a cookie and fourteen 500 pounders each from 11,000 feet between 21.49 and 21.57, and returned to report what appeared to be a scattered attack. W/C Gibson failed to return, and the wreckage of his 627 Squadron Mosquito was found on the outskirts of the town of Steenbergen in southern Holland. No conclusive cause of the crash has been established, and it was only after the war, that his identity was finally confirmed.

The first of six operations against enemy strong points around Calais was scheduled for the 20th, and a force of 646 aircraft was made ready, of which 184 Lancasters were provided by 1 Group. They were assigned to aiming points 6C and 6D in the Sangatte area to the west of the town, which were to be attacked in two waves. The thirteen 101 Squadron crews were assigned to the latter, and took off between 15.35 and 15.50, with F/L Massheder the senior pilot on duty. They climbed away into cloudy conditions, which improved as they crossed the Channel, and had broken up considerably since the first wave attack had ended at 16.50. The visibility was more limited now by smoke than by the remaining cloud, but considerable communications interference led to only about 50% of the force picking up the Master Bomber's instruction to descend to 3,000 feet. However, those remaining at 8,000 feet still found the markers to be clearly discernible, and this led to a range of bombing heights for the Ludford Magna gang of anything between 3,000 and 8,000 feet.

They carried out their attacks in an eleven-minute slot from 17.00, and gave encouraging reports to the debriefing team of concentrated bombing.

The squadron spent the following two days kicking its heels, and it was on the afternoon of the 23rd that fourteen crews were called to briefing. They were told of an operation that night to Neuss, a town on the west bank of the Rhine opposite Düsseldorf on the south-western edge of the Ruhr. They were to be part of a force of 549 aircraft drawn from 1, 3, 4 and 8 Groups, of which 1 Group's contribution was 204 Lancasters. F/L Bursell was the senior pilot on duty as they took off from Ludford Magna between 18.54 and 19.11, and climbed towards layer cloud at 10,000 and 18,000 feet, which held until the Essex coast was reached. P/O Hopes didn't get that far, after engine problems forced him to abandon his sortie when right over the 3 and 8 Group stations in Cambridgeshire. The others flew out over Clacton-on-Sea, where the high cloud dispersed to leave ten-tenths at 12,000 feet all the way to the target. It was shortly thereafter that an unfortunate incident accounted for the squadron's NF982 as the various elements of the force reached the rendezvous point. The Lancaster was seen to collide with another aircraft at 20.08, and crash into the sea, taking with it to their deaths the eight-man crew of F/O Mackie. The others reached the target without apparent incident, where a ground-marking plan had been prepared, and, in the absence of skymarkers, crews could only aim at the glow of red TIs through the cloud. Some crews relied on navigation aids to establish their position, and decided to bomb Düsseldorf, which was more easily identified on H2S. The 101 Squadron crews bombed from 16,000 to 19,500 between 21.19 and 21.39, apart from P/O Lyons, who couldn't identify a target, and brought his load home. Bomber Command claimed that the main weight of the attack had fallen into the dock and factory areas, while a local report gave a figure of 617 houses and fourteen public buildings destroyed or seriously damaged.

There was a morning take-off for twenty-one 101 Squadron Lancasters on the 25th, as the campaign against enemy positions around Calais continued. They were part of a mighty force of 872 aircraft, and departed Ludford Magna between 06.45 and 07.12, led by S/L Thompson. By the time they were approaching the French coast, 287 aircraft had bombed through gaps in the low cloud, and the Master Bomber had decided to call a halt to the proceedings. They were sent home with their bomb loads intact, and, no doubt, spent that evening in the local hostelries. It is to be hoped that they didn't overindulge, as twenty-five crews were hauled out of beds very early on the following morning to get ready for a return to Calais. There were to be three aiming points for the 210 Lancasters of 1 Group, all in the Cap-Gris-Nez area, 7A, 7B, and 7C, which, it is believed, were heavy gun emplacements. Take-off from Ludford Magna began at 10.55, with S/L Thompson and the recently-arrived S/L Warner the senior pilots on duty, and the last Lancaster was safely airborne at 11.22. They flew down to the Sussex coast over six to eight-tenths cloud, joining up en-route with the twenty-eight other Lancasters in this wave, and the conditions had not improved by the time the French coast hove into view. They had been assigned to aiming point 7A, which, according to the timings provided in the 1 Group ORB, was the last of the three attacks by the Group. At 12.14 the Master Bomber was heard to give "Basement 7,000", which he reduced to 3,000 feet five minutes later, forcing many crews to orbit to lose the necessary altitude. The visibility below the 3,500-foot cloud base was excellent, and the crews experienced no difficulty in visually identifying the aiming-point, although mostly chose to use the red TIs as their reference. These proved to have undershot the aiming point, and the Master Bomber called for the crews to overshoot by two seconds, then three seconds and finally four seconds. The 101 Squadron crews bombed from 2,600 to 3,200 feet between 12.21 and 12.29, and their loads were observed to fall around the aiming point. A vivid orange explosion occurred on the northern edge of the cliffs at 12.23, and this was followed by a fire of considerable proportions. As the Lancasters withdrew, the wind blew away the smoke to reveal all three aiming-points to be covered by bomb craters.

That night, ten ABC Lancasters took off between 00.49 and 01.05 to join a 5 Group heavy force of 216 Lancasters bound for Karlsruhe in southern Germany. S/L Matthews was the senior pilot on duty as they climbed away into low, broken cloud and set course for the French coast. The cloud built up over the Channel, and formed a thin band of ten-tenths with a base at around 3,000 feet. These were the conditions confronting the crews at the target, despite which, the Mosquito-laid TIs could be clearly seen. The Master Bomber ordered them to be bombed, even though the mixture of reds and green were somewhat scattered and were not firmly established as being on the briefed aiming-point. The 101 Squadron crews delivered their loads of a cookie and cluster bombs from 11,900 to 12,300 feet between 04.00 and 04.06, and reported fires spreading over a wide area. A local report seemed to confirm that the attack was successful, but provided no detail. The work of the ground crews and armourers deserves special mention for preparing thirty-five aircraft for war in a twenty-four-hour period. Little did they know, that they would exceed this figure by a wide margin in the coming month.

The assault on enemy positions around Calais continued on the 27th, but did not involve 101 Squadron. That night, however, 5 Group was scheduled to carry out the first and only major raid of the war on Kaiserslautern, a city in south-western Germany, lying within twenty miles of the frontier with France. 101 Squadron was invited to support this operation with ten ABC Lancasters, and they took off between 22.06 and 22.20, with S/L Warner the senior pilot on duty. The clear skies over England had filled with ten-tenths low cloud over France, and, at the target, had split into two layers, the lower one with tops at 3,000 feet, and the upper one with a base at 6,500 feet. The marking proceeded according to plan, and the Master Bomber could be heard exhorting the crews to overshoot the greens. The 101 Squadron crews bombed from 4,000 to 5,500 feet between 01.03 and 01.14, and the attack appeared to be well concentrated on the aiming-point, and its destructiveness was confirmed in a post-war British survey, which assessed that 36% of the built-up area had been reduced to ruins. This concluded another very busy month for the squadron, during which twenty-one operations had produced 268 sorties for the loss of four Lancasters and two crews.

October 1944

The Command's responsibility to SHAEF was now effectively over, although it would remain on hand to assist the land campaign as required, and Harris could now turn his attention once more to Germany. A second Ruhr campaign would begin towards the end of the first week, but 101 Squadron was first called into action on the 3rd, to provide seven Lancasters among 120 from the group for attacks on the seawall at Westkapelle on the island of Walcheren. Heavy gun emplacements were barring the Allied advance towards the much-needed port of Antwerp, and attacks on them during September had proved to be ineffective, triggering the decision to flood the island, inundate the batteries, and create difficult terrain for the defenders when the Allied ground forces went in. The plan was to send in eight waves of thirty bombers each at fifteen-minute intervals starting at 14.00, and the 1 Group aircraft were to form waves five to eight. The 101 Squadron Lancasters took off between 13.34 and 13.41 led by S/L Matthews, and they met with six to eight-tenths cloud over the Wash, which persisted all the way to the target. The operation had begun on schedule, and the Master Bomber called the crews down to 5,000 feet, below which, the visibility was excellent. The first signs of a breach appeared at 14.02, and by the time the Ludford gang arrived in the target area in the final wave shortly before 15.00, the gap in the seawall had extended to a hundred yards, and the water had already flooded the southern half of the village of Westkapelle. The 101 Squadron crews were each carrying a cookie, eight 1,000

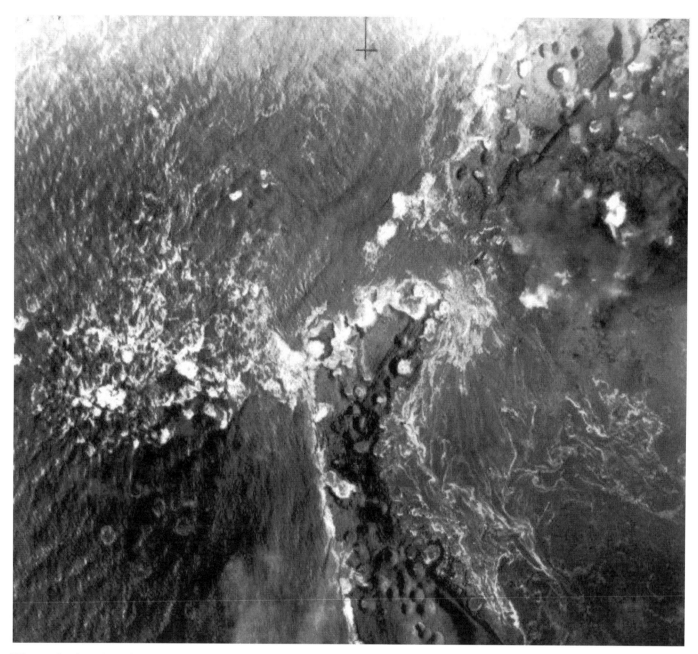

\The sea floods in through the shattered dykes at Westkapelle on Walcheren Island. The island had proved to be a natural fortress for German gun batteries preventing the Allies using the River Schelde to land supplies in the port of Antwerp, until Bomber Command solved the problem

pounders and a single delayed-action 500 pounder, which they delivered from 3,000 to 5,500 feet between 14.54 and 14.57, before returning safely home.

The night of the 5/6th brought a raid on Saarbrücken at the request of advancing American ground forces, which wanted to cut railway communications and block passage through the town. 101 Squadron briefed twenty-six crews, to be divided equally between a 3 and 8 Group assault on the marshalling yards, and a 1 and 8 Group attack on the city itself, taking off two hours apart. Thus, a combined heavy force of 531 Lancasters would be heading for the target, which had not been attacked for two years. The 3 Group effort was scheduled to take place first, and the 101 Squadron participants took off between 17.02 and 17.21, led by S/L Matthews. They encountered ten-tenths low cloud until shortly before the German frontier, when it became thin and broken, and ground haze added to the visibility problems. The marking appeared to be compact, and bomb bursts were observed mostly around them, with, perhaps, a little scattering. The 101 Squadron crews began to bomb from 15,000 feet at 20.33, and, at 20.36, the Master Bomber issued the code-word "Marmalade", the signal to cease bombing, apparently because of the close proximity of US ground forces. The 101 Squadron crews had not been given this particular code at briefing, and continued bombing on red and green TIs until 20.44. F/O Wagner and P/O Hunt abandoned their sorties over the target after hearing the call, but the latter's cookie fell out anyway. LL758 failed to return home after crashing north-east of Liege, and there were no survivors from the crew of P/O Mason.

The second 101 Squadron element took off between 18.50 and 19.02, with F/Ls Bursell and Massheder the senior pilots on duty, and they experienced similar weather conditions on the way to and over the target. Illuminating flares were seen at 22.23, followed by cascading red and green TIs, and the visibility was good enough to confirm their accuracy on the aiming point. The 101 Squadron crews bombed from 14,000 to 15,500 feet between 22.26 and 22.41, but P/O McClenaghan suffered the frustration of his bomb doors refusing to open. A large area of fire soon developed and a number of explosions were observed, including a particularly spectacular one at 22.45, which sent smoke rising to 12,000 feet. As the Lancasters turned away, the city was well ablaze, and its fires could be seen for a hundred miles into the return journey. Post-raid reconnaissance established that road and railway supply routes had been successfully cut, and that 5,882 houses had been destroyed.

The new Ruhr campaign began with the preparation of a force of 523 heavy bombers on the 6th, 293 of them provided by 6 Group in the form of 248 Halifaxes and forty-five Lancasters, and this would be 6 Group's biggest single contribution of the war. They took off in the late afternoon, and delivered another telling blow on this already severely-damaged city. A simultaneous raid by 5 Group on Bremen included nine 101 Squadron Lancasters, which departed Ludford Magna between 17.39 and 17.52 with F/Ls Wood and Massheder the senior pilots on duty. The low stratus cloud over the North Sea dispersed to leave clear skies and excellent visibility at the target, assisted by a bright three-quarter moon, and the marking and bombing proceeded according to plan. The 101 Squadron crews carried out their part from 17,000 to 18,000 feet between 20.26 and 20.30, and returned to report large fires in the target area, visible for 150 miles into the return journey. A local report detailed the destruction of, or serious damage to, 4,859 buildings, and many important war industry factories were included in the list.

1 Group stations were a hive of activity on the morning of the 7th as 254 Lancasters were prepared for a daylight attack on the oil-storage town of Emmerich, situated on the Rhine on the frontier with Holland. The purpose of this operation, and a simultaneous one against Kleve, had nothing to do with oil, but to prevent the towns' use by the enemy to threaten the Allied right flank following the failure of Operation Market Garden. 101 Squadron made ready twenty-six aircraft, which departed Ludford Magna either side of noon, led for the first time by W/C Everest. They climbed away into low cloud and drizzle before turning towards the exit point at Cromer, and the weather began to improve during the crossing of the North Sea. By the time the force reached the enemy coast, it was clear enough for the crews to map-read their way to the target, where the aiming point was easily identified. The defenders responded with accurate predicted flak, and three aircraft were seen to go down during the course of the attack. The green TIs went down on time, slightly overshooting the aiming point, but the following red TIs were accurate and closely grouped. The Master Bomber called the main force in to bomb on them, and the 101 Squadron element complied from 10,000 to 13,000 feet between 14.19 and 14.29. All then returned safely to report a massive concentration of bombing, many fires and explosions, one of which took place at 14.28, and sent black smoke billowing up to 12,000 feet.

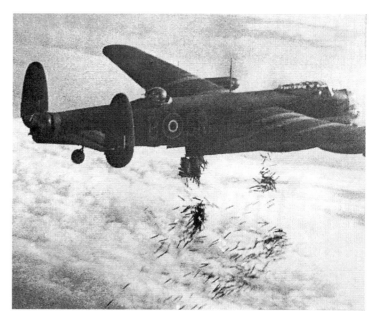

NG128, SR-B drops a typical cocktail of incendiaries, GP bombs and a 4,000lb 'cookie' over Duisburg morning of 14.10.44 with F/O Tibbs RCAF and crew (GW).

Reconnaissance confirmed the outstanding success of the operation, which destroyed more than 2,400 buildings and damaged nearly seven hundred others.

1 Group remained on the ground on the night of the 9/10th, but ten 101 Squadron crews were on duty to support elements of 4 and 6 Groups in a heavy raid on Bochum. They took off between 17.28 and 17.37, with F/Ls Massheder and Woods the senior captains, and climbed into broken, low cloud, which persisted and then built up over enemy territory. By the time they reached the target, there were thin layers of ten-tenths cloud at 12,000 to 16,000 feet, which hampered visibility, and, although some crews caught sight of an occasional TI on the ground through gaps, most were forced to bomb on release-point flares, which compromised accuracy. The 101 Squadron crews' bombing heights ranged from 10,000 to 20,000 feet, and they delivered their eight 1,000 and four 500 pounders each between 20.28 and 20.37. It was difficult to assess the outcome, but some crews reported a concentrated attack with much evidence of fires. In fact, the operation was not successful by recent standards, and caused some modest residential destruction in southern districts.

After a day off on the 10th, twenty crews were briefed during the morning of the 11th for a 1 Group assault on a gun battery at Fort Frederik Hendrik at Breskens, situated on the south bank of the Scheldt. A total of 150 Lancasters was involved at two aiming points, and the 101 Squadron element was assigned to the second one, aiming-point B. They took off either side of 15.00, with S/L Matthews the senior pilot on duty, and climbed through rain-bearing low cloud to clear air at 6,000 feet. F/O Wagner turned back with engine trouble over the sea, while the others continued on, finding conditions improving a little as they made their way towards the enemy coast, and they were met by six-tenths cloud over the target, with a base at around 4,000 feet. This was a considerable improvement on the conditions greeting the aiming-point A crews, who had already been sent home with their bombs because of the impossibly low cloud base. At 16.37 the Master Bomber called "Basement 6,000 feet", and, over the ensuing eight minutes, attempted to bring the second-wave crews down in stages to 4,000 feet, at which altitude they could easily pick out ground detail. The markers slightly overshot the aiming point, but were sufficiently accurate for the purpose in hand, and the bombing was concentrated around them. The 101 Squadron crews carried out their attacks at altitudes ranging from 3,900 to 6,000 feet, aiming at red TIs, and were over the target between 16.50 and 16.57. 101 Squadron's LL771 failed to return, and it was established later that it had crashed at Heille on the Dutch side of the frontier with Belgium, with no survivors from the crew of S/L Matthews.

A mammoth workload lay ahead for the ground crews across the length and breadth of Bomber Command country on the 14th. Their work had actually begun many hours before the first of 1,013 aircraft took off to deliver an important message to the leaders of the Nazi regime and the remaining occupants of Duisburg. Operation Hurricane, which was undertaken in concert with a similar American 8th Air Force effort in the Cologne area, was a demonstration to the enemy of the overwhelming superiority of the Allied air forces ranged against it. Three aiming points were assigned to the 245 participating 1 Group crews, P, Q and the Thyssen Steel Works, and the timings and post-raid reports suggest the last-mentioned to be the specific target for the 101 Squadron element of twenty-four Lancasters. They took off between 06.22 and 06.48, with S/L Warner the senior pilot on duty, and climbed through eight to ten-tenths cloud in layers up to 15,000 feet. A large break in the clouds allowed them to map-read the last few miles up the Rhine, but the target itself was largely covered for most of the giant force. However, it seems that those heading for the steel works were blessed with a sight of the ground until around 08.53, when cloud and smoke drifted across the aiming point. The 101 Squadron crews bombed from 16,000 to 20,000 feet between 08.45 and 09.06, twenty-two of them on the basis of a visual reference, and only two relying upon red TIs. In total, 957 aircraft disgorged over 4,500 tons of bombs from their cavernous bomb bays onto their respective aiming points under a fighter escort, and inflicted huge damage for the loss of fourteen of their number. The Ludford Magna brigade all arrived home safely between 10.54 and 11.41, and, before they had time to cool down, the ground crews were swarming over them to prepare them for a return to Duisburg that night.

The magnificent efforts of the ground crews and armourers enabled 1,005 aircraft to take off either side of midnight, and turn their snouts towards Duisburg, to press home the point about "overwhelming superiority". This meant that 2,018 aircraft had been launched by the Command over a matter of about eighteen hours, and this massive figure had been achieved without a contribution from 5 Group, which would take advantage of the activity over the Ruhr on this night to slip past and finally deliver a devastating attack on Brunswick. The first eleven 101 Squadron Lancasters took off between 22.24 and 22.36, with F/L Woods the senior pilot on duty, and set course for aiming-point Q in company with 107 others from 1 Group. The skies were clear as they crossed the North Sea and enemy coast, and only a little thin, low cloud or industrial haze lay between them and the target. The visibility was good and the markers punctual and closely-grouped around the aiming point. The 101 squadron crews bombed from 20,000 feet onto red and green TIs between 01.28 and 01.34, and a mass of fires quickly took hold, adding to those still burning from the morning attack. A notable red explosion was reported at 01.34, and the glow of fires was visible for 120 miles into the homeward flight. 101 Squadron was not involved in the attack on aiming-point S, which followed, but dispatched thirteen Lancasters to aiming-point R between 00.07 and 00.35, led by S/L Warner. They reached the target to find conditions similar to those prevailing for the earlier elements, and markers were seen from 03.23 onwards. The 101 Squadron crews bombed mostly from 20,000 feet, between 03.25 and 03.35, and, as they left the scene, the entire city seemed to be ablaze. LL774 failed to return to Ludford Magna, and was lost without trace with the eight-man crew of P/O Hunt. Almost nine thousand tons of bombs had been dropped on Duisburg between breakfast time on the 14th and the early hours of the 15th, and a similar ordeal lay ahead for the other Ruhr giants.

The last of fourteen major attacks on the naval port of Wilhelmshaven during the war was mounted on the night of the 15/16th, for which 1 Group contributed seventy Lancasters in an overall force of 506 aircraft from all but 5 Group. 101 Squadron briefed a dozen crews, who took off between 17.27 and 17.44 with F/Ls Parke

220

and Woods the senior pilots on duty. The skies were clear until the midpoint of the North-Sea crossing, when cloud gradually built-up to ten-tenths thin stuff with tops at around 2,000 feet. The ground markers could be seen, however, and their accuracy confirmed by aircraft equipped with H2S, but what may have been spoof green TIs were reported some five miles to the west and north-west of the target, and these attracted some bomb loads. The 101 Squadron crews bombed from 16,000 to 19,500 feet between 19.46 and 19.51, some aiming at red TIs, some at greens, some at fires and one at release point flares, before all returned safely to report a scattered attack. S/L Thompson had now completed his tour with the squadron, and was posted on the 18th to the operations room for non-flying duties.

There were two major operations on the night of the 19/20th, both over southern Germany, one by 5 Group on Nuremberg, and the other, a two-phase effort by 565 aircraft of 1, 3, 6 and 8 Groups, on Stuttgart. 1 Group made ready 251 Lancasters, of which twenty-seven were provided by 101 Squadron, and the fifteen assigned to the first wave, aiming-point D, took off between 16.51 and 17.17, with F/Ls Bursell, Parke and Woods the senior pilots on duty. Flying with F/L Bursell as second pilot was the recently posted-in flight commander, S/L MacLeod-Selkirk. They climbed through low cloud and showers, and headed south to cross the coast at Beachy Head, where conditions improved somewhat, before cloud began to increase over France, and the bombers had to climb through a band ten thousand feet thick to reach clear skies at 16,000 feet. They found the target lying under eight to ten-tenths cloud with tops at 10,000 feet, and most crews, unable to see the TIs, had to rely on skymarking. The raid was planned to last fourteen minutes from 20.30, and it opened on time with groups of parachute flares strung from north to south. The 101 Squadron crews bombed from 15,000 to 17,000 feet between 20.31 and 20.44, and returned to report plenty of fires, but scattered over a wide area. F/L Bursell brought his load home, after flak and incendiaries from above had caused a failure in the bomb-release circuit. The twelve crews assigned to aiming point E departed Ludford Magna between 21.26 and 21.41, led by S/L Warner, and encountered similar weather conditions outbound. Fires from Stuttgart could be seen from approaching aircraft sixty miles away, and some crews would bomb on the glow, while most aimed at the skymarkers. Eighteen minutes had been allotted for this part of the attack, either side of 01.00, and the 101 Squadron crews delivered their ten 1,000 and two 500 pounders each from 14,000 to 17,000 feet between 01.00 and 01.05. They returned safely, and, like their colleagues on the earlier raid, found it impossible to make an assessment of the outcome. It was established later that considerable damage had been inflicted upon central and eastern districts, and that the important Bosch factory had been hit.

A few days of rest preceded a massive assault on Essen on the evening of the 23rd, for which a record force of 1,055 aircraft was made ready, a number which did not include a contribution from the "Independent Air Force". 1 Group contributed 237 Lancasters, of which twenty-seven were provided by 101 Squadron, and they took-off between 16.11 and 16.37 led by S/L Warner. They climbed into scattered cloud, and set course for the French coast for a southerly approach to the target between Cologne and Mönchengladbach. The cloud thickened over the Channel, until the tops were at 23,000 feet, and, it was in mid-Channel that P/O Hrynkiw turned back with instrument failure. F/O McClenaghan was over southern Belgium when engine problems ended his interest in the operation, and he turned back. P/O Harris was about forty minutes from the target when engine problems forced him also to abandon his sortie. The others pressed on, and, by the time the target hove into view, the cloud had become ten-tenths up to 14,000 feet. The Pathfinders had prepared a ground and skymarking plan, and, most crews, being unable to pick out the TIs, aimed at red and green flares. P/O Wagner lost an engine outbound, and had been forced to jettison his cookie just over the Belgian/German frontier in order to maintain height on three. Even so, he was down to 14,500 feet when he let his remaining load of five 1,000 and eight 500 pounders go onto the target at 19.33. This put him and his crew in danger of being hit by falling hardware, not only from his higher-flying 101 Squadron colleagues, who bombed from

18,000 to 21,000 feet between 19.31 and 19.58, but also the rest of the giant force. Fortunately, he and his crew survived, and returned home safely with little to report in terms of an assessment. Some crews observed extensive fires right across the city, but the consensus was of a scattered raid, and a local report detailed 607 buildings destroyed, with a further eight hundred seriously damaged.

Twenty-two 101 Squadron crews were briefed for a return to Essen on the 25th, as part of an overall force of 771 aircraft. The 229 Lancasters of 1 Group were divided between aiming-points J (Krupp works) and G, with the 101 Squadron element assigned to the former, having been given a time-on-target (T.O.T) of 15.27 to 15.44. S/L Warner was the senior pilot on duty as they departed Ludford Magna between 12.51 and 13.13, and proceeded to the target in cloudy, but quite favourable weather conditions. There was ten-tenths cloud with tops at 12,000 feet during the run-up to the target, but isolated breaks appeared, which allowed crews to assess the accuracy of the red and yellow TIs in relation to the Krupp works. The master Bomber ordered the reds to be ignored, and the 101 Squadron brigade bombed visually, or on the yellow TIs or red flares from 16,000 to 20,000 feet between 15.27 and 15.36, and all returned safely home to report a concentrated raid. In the absence of combustible material in Germany's major cities as the result of so many attacks, bomb loads now consisted mainly of high explosives, and the destruction by the smaller force on this day considerably exceeded that of the larger force thirty-six hours earlier. The Krupp works was in a state of paralysis, and other than steelworks and coal mines, the majority of industry had been dispersed to other regions of Germany, robbing Essen of its status as a major centre of war production.

P/O Wagner and crew (GW).

Cologne's turn to face a force of "overwhelming superiority" came on the afternoon of the 28th, when 733 aircraft were made ready to attack two aiming points on the first of what would be a three-raid series. 1 Group detailed 249 Lancasters to be divided 70/179 between aiming-points G and H, and the twenty-five 101 Squadron crews were assigned to the former. S/L Warner and S/L MacLeod-Selkirk were the most senior pilots on duty as the squadron took off between 13.11 and 13.54, and encountered a weather front over the North Sea. At the target there was six-tenths cloud with tops at around 8,000 feet, and the gaps provided most crews with an excellent view of the built-up area, and the opportunity to confirm the accuracy and concentration of the Pathfinder ground marking. They delivered their attacks from 15,500 to 20,000 feet between 15.45 and 16.03, aiming visually on TIs or red flares, and in the face of a moderate barrage of heavy flak. Together with the second phase attack, the operation destroyed 2,239 blocks of flats, fifteen industrial premises and many public buildings, mostly in a line across the city from north-east to south-west.

The 29th brought further attacks on gun emplacements on the island of Walcheren, for which 1 Group contributed seventy-five Lancasters divided equally between three aiming-points at Domburg, situated on the north-western shore. 101 Squadron put up fifteen aircraft, with F/Ls Bursell and Massheder the senior pilots on duty, and they were assigned to the final wave, which saw them taking off between 11.44 and 11.59. They found six to eight-tenths cloud over the target, with a base at 2,000 feet, and, as they approached, the Master Bomber called them down to below the cloud base, where the visibility was excellent. The green TIs had fallen around four hundred yards south of the aiming point, and the Master Bomber ordered the reds to be bombed, the 101 Squadron crews complying from 1,000 to 2,000 feet in a brief slot from 13.31. There was a little undershooting, but the aiming point soon became obscured by smoke, and the Master Bomber instructed the later crews to aim for that. He called a halt at 13.35, and all returned safely home.

A force of 905 aircraft was made ready for another massive assault on Cologne on the 30th, for which 1 Group detailed 251 Lancasters, twenty-three of which were fuelled and bombed-up at Ludford Magna. S/L Warner was the senior pilot on duty as they took-off between 17.29 and 17.52, and flew into ten-tenths cloud, which persisted for most of the outward flight. Over the Channel the cloud tops reached 20,000 feet, but this had lowered to 10,000 to 15,000 feet as the target drew near. F/O Moore must have been fairly close to the target when his rear turret became unserviceable, and he decided to turn back. The others pushed on under a full moon above the cloud, but they found the target to be obscured, and the Pathfinders employed red Oboe skymarkers, which were described as concentrated. These were bombed by the 101 Squadron contingent from 15,000 to 20,000 feet between 20.57 and 21.21, after which, they returned home safely, most to report a concentrated attack. Bomber Command, however, speculated that it had been a scattered and only modestly successful attack, while, in fact, it had been another hammer-blow, which had inflicted further massive damage on the western districts and suburbs of this once proud city.

The final raid of the series was mounted twenty-four hours later by a reduced force of 493 aircraft, including twenty-three Lancasters again from 101 Squadron in a 1 Group contribution of 219 aircraft. F/Ls Massheder and Parke were the senior pilots on duty as they departed Ludford Magna between 17.45 and 18.19, and headed for the south coast over five to seven-tenths cloud. This had increased to ten-tenths over the Channel, and remained so all the way to the target. The Pathfinders delivered red, white and green steady flares by Oboe, and maintained a constant and accurately-grouped supply throughout, which was much appreciated by the crews. The 101 Squadron contingent bombed from 13,000 to 19,000 feet between 20.59 and 21.14, and returned to report the glow of fires beneath the cloud, and, generally, a concentrated attack, with much praise for the Pathfinder effort. According to local reports, most of the bombing had fallen into southern districts,

A Lancaster, identifiable only as SR-V, presumably V – Victory, with her ground and aircrew (GW).

but the level of destruction was less than on the previous two raids. Thus ended another highly intensive month of activity for the squadron, in which it had dispatched 320 sorties on seventeen operations for the loss of three Lancasters and crews.

November 1944

The second Ruhr offensive continued on the 2nd, when a force of 992 aircraft was made ready for an attack on Düsseldorf that night. 1 Group's contribution amounted to 252 Lancasters, of which twenty-five would carry the SR code of 101 Squadron. S/Ls MacLeod-Selkirk and Warner were the senior pilots on duty as the squadron took off between 16.01 and 16.27, and climbed into conditions of low cloud and rain. This began to clear over the Channel, and the target lay under cloudless skies and bright moonlight, with nothing but ground haze and the usual searchlight and flak batteries to protect it. The crews were able to pick out the Rhine and the built-up area in the northern half of the city selected as the aiming point, and the first red TIs went down at 19.11. From that moment, the Pathfinders maintained a constant supply of TIs and skymarkers, although few crews needed to rely on the latter. The 101 Squadron crews bombed from 16,500 to 19,500 feet between 19.13 and 19.36, and returned home to report large explosions, columns of smoke rising to 10,000 feet and beyond, and fires visible ninety miles into the return journey. This places the squadron's attack in the middle of the raid, as the first crews to bomb and return reported seeing fires from sixty miles away, while those at the end could see them from Charleroi in Belgium, some 150 miles distant. It was established later that five thousand houses had been destroyed, along with many important war-industry factories. This proved to be the final major Bomber Command raid of the war on this city.

Bochum's turn to face a "Hurricane" type force came two nights later, when 749 aircraft were assembled, of which 235 represented 1 Group. Twenty-five crews were briefed at Ludford Magna, with S/Ls MacLeod-Selkirk and Warner being joined by the newly-arrived S/L Gundrey-White as the senior pilots. The squadron took off between 17.09 and 17.59, and climbed into nine-tenths cloud, which dispersed gradually over the Channel and the Continent to leave clear skies over the target, with visibility compromised only by the presence of ground haze. The red TIs were seen to fall onto the aiming point, and they and the later accurate greens were maintained throughout the attack, and attracted the main weight of bombs. The 101 Squadron crews bombed from 16,000 to 19,000 feet between 19.31 and 19.46, and, as they turned away, the whole town area could be seen engulfed in a sea of flames. On return, F/O Andrews and crew claimed an enemy aircraft as destroyed, and others confirmed a fierce night fighter response over the target and during the homeward flight, with particular reference to single and twin-engine jet-propelled aircraft. Twenty-eight aircraft failed to return, twenty-three of them Halifaxes, and two of the missing Lancasters were from Ludford Magna. ME865 crashed somewhere between the target and the Dutch frontier, killing F/O Weiss RCAF and his predominantly Canadian crew, and NF936 was lost in the same general area, with no survivors from the crew of F/O Edwards. It had been another outstandingly destructive raid, which had destroyed or seriously damaged more than four thousand buildings, including some housing, steelworks and other war-essential industries. This would be the final heavy raid of the war on Bochum.

Bochum's near neighbour, Gelsenkirchen, was selected to be the next to receive attention as the Bomber Command juggernaut smashed its way across the Ruhr. In the past it had been the synthetic oil plant that had drawn the bombers on, but this time it was to be an area attack to take in the town as well as the oil facility. A force of 738 aircraft was put together on the 6th, of which 221 Lancasters represented 1 Group, twenty-two of them provided by 101 Squadron. They took off between 11.16 and 12.00, with W/C Everest and S/Ls Gundry-White and MacLeod-Selkirk the senior pilots on duty, and climbed into cloud that increased to almost ten-tenths at the Dutch coast. Thereafter, it began to break up, until a gap appeared right over the target, which enabled the early arrivals to pick out the distinctive L-shaped docks to the north-west of the aiming point. Bombing commenced a few minutes early on red and green TIs, the latter assessed as the more accurate, and the Master Bomber, whose transmissions were weak, directed the crews to them. Soon, however, haze began to make it difficult to distinguish the colours, and, at 14.01, the order was issued to bomb any TIs, smoke or on a visual reference, before, at 14.06 the instruction was given to bomb any built-up area. The 101 Squadron crews were over the target at 16,000 to 18,500 feet between 13.50 and 14.03, and all but one returned home to report what appeared to be a scattered attack. The impression was that it had drifted towards the north, but a column of black smoke rising through 10,000 feet suggested that the Nordstern oil plant had been hit. Only five aircraft failed to return, and among them was the squadron's PB692, which crashed in the Eickel area to the east of the target, and there were no survivors from the standard crew of F/O Moore RCAF.

It was, in fact, to the site of F/O Moore's demise that the next operation was directed on the morning of the 9th. The target was the oil plant at Wanne-Eickel, situated no more than three miles east-north-east of Gelsenkirchen, for which a heavy force of 256 Lancasters was made ready, 226 of them provided by 1 Group. 101 Squadron briefed twenty-one crews, with S/Ls MacLeod-Selkirk and Warner the senior pilots on duty, and they took off in a forty-five-minute slot either side of 08.00. They climbed into clear skies, before cloud built up over the North Sea to ten-tenths with tops at 20,000 feet. F/L Parke turned back for an unspecified reason at 09.44, leaving the others to continue on to find the target completely cloud-covered, and tops at 21,500 feet. There was a gap of clear air between 10,000 and 17,000 feet, but this was of no help, and no markers were delivered. Ten minutes before H-Hour the Master Bomber ordered the crews to bomb on H2S, Gee or ETA., and the 101 Squadron crews complied from 14,000 to 22,000 feet between 10.44 and 10.50. It was impossible to assess the outcome, but a local report suggests that the bombing almost entirely missed the town.

Responsibility for the destruction of the Hoesch-Benzin oil plant, located in the Wambel district of Dortmund, was handed to a 1 Group main force of 183 Lancasters, with Pathfinder Lancasters and Mosquitos in support. 101 Squadron made ready nineteen aircraft on the 11th, which took off between 15.42 and 16.04, led by S/L Warner. Having flown to the Ruhr via the northerly approach across Holland on recent occasions, this operation adopted a southerly route, which took it over the English Channel and the French coast. The cloud thickened from 4°E, and had become ten-tenths by the time the Ruhr drew near, and remained so over the target, with tops at 10,000 to 15,000 feet. This provided most unfavourable conditions for bombing, and the crews were forced to seek out the glow of markers through the cloud. Not all had even that to aim at, and resorted to H2S and Gee to establish their position. The 101 Squadron crews bombed from 18,000 to 19,000 feet between 18.59 and 19.07, and returned with little idea of where their bombs had fallen. Remarkably, it seems that the attack was accurate, and local reports confirmed that the oil plant had been severely damaged, along with housing and a nearby airfield.

The 16th was devoted to providing support for the advancing American ground forces between Aachen and the Rhine. 1,188 bombers were assigned to the three small towns of Heinsberg, Jülich and Düren, which lay in an arc from north to east of Aachen behind enemy lines, and Bomber Command's task was to attack them to cut communications to the front. 485 Lancasters and thirteen Mosquitos of 1, 5 and 8 Groups were assigned to Düren, among them twenty-four Lancasters of 101 Squadron, which would be led by S/Ls Gundry-White and Warner. They departed Ludford Magna between 12.36 and 13.07, encountering cloud for most of the way to the target, and, from 15.20, they could hear the Master Bomber calling "Basement" at 10,000 feet. However, fifteen miles from the target the clouds parted, to leave clear skies and just a little ground haze. The crews were able to identify the aiming point visually, and confirm the accuracy of the initial Pathfinder red TIs, which were delivered punctually and accurately where intended. These were soon obliterated, however, and, ultimately, the instruction was to bomb the upwind edge of the smoke. P/O Cooke abandoned his sortie over the target after flak damaged the cable controlling the bomb-release, but the other 101 Squadron crews delivered their typical loads of a cookie, six 1,000 and six 500 pounders from 9,500 to 12,000 feet between 15.29 and 15.35, while the Master Bomber continued to express satisfaction with the quality of the marking and bombing. What the crews left behind them was little more than a heap of rubble, in which 3,127 people lost their lives.

The Group was notified of a return to Wanne-Eickel on the 18th for another crack at the Krupp synthetic oil refinery, and made ready 253 Lancasters as the main force, with 101 Squadron contributing twenty-three of them. They took off between 15.36 and 15.58 led by S/Ls Gundry-White and Warner, and climbed through poor weather conditions of low cloud and mist, which cleared at the French coast. Shortly after crossing the Rhine, a thin layer of stratus slid in at 8,000 feet, and remained in place with occasional breaks over the target. Few crews could pick out ground detail, but the red and green TIs were visible through the clouds, and, apart from one group of greens, were well placed on the aiming point. The bombing was focussed on the main group of reds and greens, and, very soon, a large fire developed, which emitted a column of black smoke seemingly from the refinery. The bombers were met by heavy flak in barrage and predicted form as they carried out their attacks, the 101 Squadron aircraft crossing the aiming point at 15,000 to 19,000 feet between 18.58 and 19.10, before returning home to report a number of large explosions and what looked like a successful operation. Photo-reconnaissance revealed fresh damage to the oil plant, and, according to local reports, the nearby Hannibal coal mine was destroyed.

ME517, SR-M, joined 101 Squadron in late 1944 and saw out the rest of the war with the unit (GW).

It had been some time since the squadron last divided its strength, and the 21st provided the next occasion. It was a day and night of heavy Bomber Command activity, with 1,345 sorties in all, many of them involved in operations against railway installations, oil refineries and canals. The target for 238 Lancasters of 1 Group was the marshalling yards and through-line at Aschaffenburg, situated some twenty miles south-east of Frankfurt in southern Germany. Fourteen 101 Squadron Lancasters were to take part, while seven others provided ABC cover for a 6 Group attack on the Klöckner Werke A.G. oil refinery at Castrop-Rauxel at the eastern end of the Ruhr. All of the most senior pilots, F/Ls Haycraft, Massheder, Parke and Woods, were assigned to the former, as the two elements took off together between 15.15 and 15.45, and climbed into fairly clear skies. Conditions remained excellent for those heading for the Ruhr, while those bound for southern Germany found the cloud building up over France, and it continued to do so until the target was reached. Between 19.00 and 19.12, the Master Bomber and his deputy could be heard in discussions, which culminated in the instruction to bomb on ETA, or on navigation aids, as the target could not be identified in the prevailing conditions. Red TIs were dropped, and their glow could be seen through the clouds by some, and their accuracy confirmed by H2S. There seemed to be plenty of illumination below cloud, and most crews bombed on glimpses of red TIs through gaps or on a large red glow. The 101 Squadron crews carried out their attacks from 11,000 to 14,000 feet between 19.14 and 19.21, and contributed to severe damage within the marshalling yards, although the through lines were not cut. Much of the bombing fell into the central and northern parts

227

of the town, where five hundred houses were destroyed. Conditions over Castrop-Rauxel, meanwhile, were excellent, and the Pathfinders produced an accurate and concentrated marking performance, which the main force crews exploited. Fires soon developed, and there were many explosions and large amounts of black smoke. The 101 Squadron crews bombed from 18,000 to 19,000 feet between 19.00 and 19.05, and contributed to a highly successful raid, which, it is believed, ended all further production on this site.

A few operations were announced and scrubbed over the ensuing few days off, allowing the crews time to draw breath. Worthwhile targets were becoming fewer in a country so expertly destroyed by bombing, and smaller, seemingly insignificant towns, began to find themselves in the bomb sights, particularly if they happened to lie in the path of the retreating enemy forces. The university city of Freiburg found itself a target on the night of the 27/28th for 292 Lancasters of 1 Group, of which nineteen represented 103 Squadron, while eight others provided ABC cover for 282 aircraft of 6 and 8 Groups at Neuss in the Ruhr. With further to travel, the Freiburg element took off first between 16.04 and 16.28, led by S/Ls Gundry-White and Warner, and climbed into clear skies, before setting course to the south-east to exit England at Orford Ness on the Suffolk coast. Cloud began to build over the French coast, and increased to full cover by the German frontier, but dispersed to five to six-tenths, thin and low over the target. Situated in south-western Germany close to the frontier with France, the city was a minor railway centre in the way of advancing American and French forces, but was otherwise of no strategic value. The cloud did not hide the markers, which had been laid by Oboe, using a mobile transmitter in a caravan in France. The Master Bomber instructed the crews to focus on the red and green TIs, until the whole area became obscured by bomb bursts and smoke. At 20.08 he called for skymarkers, and the bombing continued, to leave the built-up area consumed by what appeared to be a single massive fire. The 101 Squadron crews bombed in accordance with the Master Bomber's instructions from 12,000 to 14,500 feet between 19.59 and 20.12, and all returned safely. A particularly large explosion occurred at 20.18, and a pall of black smoke had reached 8,000 feet as the last bombers turned away. It was a devastating attack, during which 1,900 tons of bombs had fallen on this virgin target in twenty-five minutes, and although the railway lines had not been cut, the city sustained massive damage, with two thousand houses destroyed and at least two thousand people losing their lives. The Neuss element took off between 17.05 and 17.12, led by S/L MacLeod-Selkirk, and headed eastwards above seven-tenths cloud, which increased marginally at the target, but could not hide the TIs, which the Pathfinders had planted right on the aiming point. The 101 Squadron crews bombed from 18,000 feet between 20.23 and 20.32, and contributed to another destructive raid, which caused many explosions and created fires visible for a hundred miles into the return journey.

4 Group provided the bulk of the main force for a raid on Essen on the night of the 28/29th, for which 101 Squadron provided eight ABC Lancasters, while a further eight supported a 3 Group G-H attack at Neuss. They took off together between 02.40 and 03.02, with S/L Warner leading the Neuss contingent, and S/L MacLeod-Selkirk those bound for Essen. Both elements adopted the southerly route to the Ruhr via the French coast, where the formerly clear skies began to fill with cloud that had reached ten-tenths by the time the targets lay beneath, with barely twenty miles between them. Skymarkers were required at both locations, and they were rather scattered, and, at Neuss, somewhat erratic, while over Essen there were periods when no markers at all could be seen. The 101 Squadron crews bombed Neuss from 19,000 feet and Essen from 20,000 feet between 05.32 and 05.37, and return home with little to say about the outcome. Later on the 29th, sixteen crews were briefed for an operation to Dortmund by a heavy force of 294 Lancasters, 262 of which were provided by 1 Group. They took off between 11.56 and 12.15, led by S/L Gundry-White, and climbed into five-tenths cloud, which had dispersed completely by the time they exited the English coast at Orford Ness, but built-up again at the enemy coast to become six to eight-tenths in the target area. A combination of sky

and ground marking was employed, but the flares were scattered and the TIs sparse, if well-placed, and could only be seen from directly above. The Master Bomber had little choice but to instruct the crews to bomb visually, upon which the 101 Squadron crews released their loads on a variety of references from 17,500 to 19,500 feet in a five-minute slot from 15.00. All but one returned home with little to report, but the arrival of F/O Lyons and crew was awaited in vain. LM755, a non-ABC Lancaster, was one of six of the type missing, and only the Canadian rear gunner survived to be taken into captivity.

The month ended with another heavy raid on Duisburg by 576 aircraft, drawn predominantly from 4 and 6 Groups, with 8 Group providing the light and heavy markers, and 101 Squadron sixteen ABC Lancasters. There were two aiming points, E for the 4 Group element, and F for 6 Group, each accompanied by eight of the 101 Squadron participants. They took off into cloud between 16.50 and 17.06, with S/L MacLeod-Selkirk the senior pilot on duty. The cloud had built-to ten-tenths by the time the target drew near, and the approaching main force crews could see red TIs cascading into the clouds and disappearing at both aiming points. The Master Bomber immediately changed to skymarking in the form of red and yellow release-point flares, but these seemed to burn out quickly or were shot out, leaving the crews with little to aim at. The 101 Squadron contingent bombed their respective aiming points mostly from 18,000 feet between 20.02 and 20.19, and some reported the glow of fires for some distance into the return journey. Despite the scattered nature of the attack, it was moderately successful, and destroyed a further 528 houses. During the course of the month the squadron took part in fifteen operations, and dispatched 255 sorties for the loss of three Lancasters and crews.

December 1944

The new month began with a heavy attack on the town of Hagen, situated on the south-eastern edge of the Ruhr, ten miles south of Dortmund. It had never been the subject of a major raid before, and now, on the evening of the 2nd, it faced a force of 504 heavies, predominantly from 4 and 6 Groups, with Pathfinder support and seven Lancasters of 101 Squadron to provide ABC cover. They took off between 17.34 and 17.50, with F/L Flint the senior pilot on duty, and climbed into poor weather conditions, which improved as they headed for the south coast and out across the Channel. The cloud built up again from 6°E, and it was at ten-tenths over the target with tops at around 13,000 feet. The markers soon disappeared, and the crews used H2S and Gee to establish their position for bombing, the later ones using the glow of fires as their reference. The 101 Squadron crews bombed on ETA and Gee from 20,000 feet between 20.55 and 21.07, and contributed to a massively destructive attack, which devastated districts in the centre, south and east of the town, destroying or seriously damaging 1,658 houses and ninety-two industrial buildings, along with many more of a public nature. Among the industrial casualties was a factory making accumulator batteries for the new types of U-Boot, which was completely destroyed.

535 aircraft of 1, 6 and 8 Groups were made ready on the 4th for an operation that night to Karlsruhe in southern Germany. 1 Group contributed 259 Lancasters, twenty-four of them belonging to 101 Squadron, which departed Ludford Magna between 16.33 and 16.59 with S/L MacLeod-Selkirk the senior pilot on duty. The weather conditions throughout the operation were generally favourable, with cloud building and decreasing in turns across the Channel and France, and, on arrival over the target, the crews found nine to ten-tenths with tops at around 14,000 feet. As they approached, a few crews were able to see red and green TIs through gaps in the clouds, but the majority had to rely on the glow of greens coming through, and confirm their accuracy by means of H2S or Gee. It was difficult to assess what was happening because of a scarcity of red TIs, and, although the greens were plentiful, they were scattered. The cloud was moving eastwards, and later arrivals were able to identify the built-up area visually. The 101 Squadron crews bombed variously on a

sighting of green TIs, the glow of them, or the glow of fires, and did so from 17,000 to 19,500 feet between 19.28 and 19.43, before return home to report fires visible from up to a hundred miles. The 1 Group ORB mentions one aircraft bombing Stuttgart after failing to identify the primary target, and the 101 Squadron ORB identifies that as P/O Interiano and crew. Severe damage was caused at Karlsruhe, particularly in western and southern districts, at a cost of just two aircraft, but this paled into insignificance when compared with 5 Group's simultaneous assault on the virgin town of Heilbronn, which had the misfortune to sit astride a north-south railway line some fifty miles east-north-east of Karlsruhe and north of Stuttgart. It took but a few minutes to reduce over 80% of the town's built-up area to ruins, and more than seven thousand people died in the firestorm conditions that resulted. This was an example of the kind of target on offer, now that there was precious little left to knock down in the more familiar locations.

The marshalling yards at Soest, a town situated just to the north of the now famous Möhne Dam, was the target for a 4, 6 and 8 Group force of 497 aircraft on the night of the 5/6th. Included in the figure were ten 101 Squadron Lancasters to provide ABC cover, and they took off between 18.11 and 18.21 with no senior officers present. Cloud built up over the Channel, and remained at around seven-tenths, with tops over the target as high as 18,000 feet. Fortunately, breaks in the cloud allowed the crews to observe the close grouping of green TIs around the aiming point, and the bombing was concentrated on them. The 101 Squadron crews bombed from 20,000 feet between 21.18 and 21.32, noting that the town was soon well-alight, and a large, orange explosion was observed at 21.24. They also commented on Hamm burning fiercely after an attack on its marshalling yards by 3 Group. Post-raid reconnaissance revealed severe damage in the northern half of Soest, the location of the railway yards, and that a thousand houses had been destroyed.

Three major operations were mounted on the night of the 6/7th, against the oil refinery at Leuna (Merseburg) a dozen miles or so west of Leipzig in eastern Germany by 1, 3 and 8 Groups, railway yards at Giessen, also in the east, by 5 Group, and Osnabrück in the west by 4, 6 and 8 Groups. 101 Squadron made ready twenty-seven Lancasters, twenty-one of them for Leuna, as part of a massive 1 Group contribution of 294 Lancasters in an overall heavy force of 475 of the type. Six other 101 Squadron Lancasters were to provide ABC cover for the Osnabrück operation, and took off first, between 16.30 and 16.40, led by S/L Gundry-White. They were followed into the air between 16.45 and 17.09 by the others, with S/L MacLeod-Selkirk the senior pilot on duty. The Osnabrück force was routed out over France, and in via the Dutch coast, and encountered poor weather conditions throughout. The target was completely obscured most of the time, with just occasional breaks, through which a few TIs were visible, and two of the 101 Squadron crews bombed on a sighting of these, while the others relied on a Gee-fix. They released their eighteen 500 pounders each from 20,000 feet between 19.41 and 19.48, before returning home to report a scattered attack, which they knew had fallen partly into open country. It was established afterwards, that the railway yards had sustained only slight damage, but a number of important war-industry factories had been hit and 203 houses destroyed.

The Merseburg crews experienced the same unfavourable weather conditions, with complete cloud cover over England, patchy cloud over France, and ten-tenths strato-cumulus over the Leipzig area with tops at 10,000 feet. The early arrivals observed TIs cascading into it, but they were not visible by the time the crews came to bomb, and the Pathfinders quickly changed to skymarking. Release-point flares were in plentiful supply, their accuracy checked by H2S, and, in the absence of instructions from the Master Bomber, they provided the reference for bombing. The 101 Squadron crews carried out their attacks from 17,000 to 20,000 feet between 20.44 and 20.59, with the exception of S/L MacLeod-Selkirk, who was delayed by icing, and was unable to reach the target within the period of the attack. Returning crews reported large explosions and the glow of fires for around sixty miles into the return journey, and post-raid reconnaissance confirmed much damage to the oil plant.

There was a heavy 1 Group presence for the last major night raid of the war on Essen, which was scheduled to take place on the night of the 12/13th. A total of 267 Lancasters was made ready, including a contribution from 101 Squadron of twenty-three, and they were to join with eighty-two Pathfinder Lancasters and 163 Halifaxes of 4 Group to make an overall heavy force of 540 aircraft, with twenty-eight Mosquitos in support. The 101 Squadron element took off between 16.08 and 16.39, with S/Ls Gundry-White and MacLeod-Selkirk the senior pilots on duty, and climbed into poor weather conditions with low cloud, which persisted as they passed out over Beachy Head and set course for the French coast. While they were heading north over Germany the cloud began to clear, but built-up again thirty miles south of the Ruhr to leave the target completely obscured. The Pathfinders were a little late in opening the attack, and a few red TIs were seen to enter the cloud and disappear, whereupon, red release-point flares were dropped, which, initially, were scattered, but soon became plentiful and concentrated. Some crew would complain that they ignited too high, in the region of 18,000 to 20,000 feet, but, generally, the marking and bombing was accurate, and many large explosions lit up the clouds, with a column of black smoke rising up to 20,000 feet. The 101 Squadron crews began bombing the red and green marker flares at 19.31, and continued from 17,000 to 20,000 feet until 19.46, before returning with the general opinion that the attack had been scattered and probably ineffective. In fact, it had been very successful, and had caused much damage to residential and industrial buildings, including the Krupp works, which was now effectively finished as a producer of war materials.

1 and 6 Groups combined to send a main force of 327 Lancasters to Ludwigshafen on the evening of the 15th to bomb the city's northern half and the nearby town of Oppau. Both locations contained an important I.G Farben factory, which were engaged in the production of synthetic oil, and were known to be relying on slave labour. Twenty-five crews were briefed at Ludford Magna as part of a 1 Group effort of 224 Lancasters, and they took off in fair weather conditions between 14.24 and 14.49 led by S/Ls Gundry-White and MacLeod-Selkirk. Cloud came and went over enemy territory during the outward flight, until fifty miles from the target, when a bank of thick stuff appeared with tops at 20,000 feet. Fortunately, it ended abruptly just a short distance from the target, to leave clear skies and visibility marred only by ground haze. It seems that a tail-wind had propelled some aircraft to the target a little ahead of schedule, and they had to orbit to await the arrival of the Pathfinder element. They were on time, and the first red TIs went down at 18.26, and accurate and concentrated bombing began immediately. Release-point flares were also in evidence, but they were ignored in favour of the clearly-observed TIs, and the 101 Squadron crews mostly bombed from 18,000 feet, with a few others at various heights ranging from 15,000 to 19,500 feet. They were over the aiming point between 18.25 and 18.38, and all returned safely to report a concentrated attack with explosions, green and orange smoke, and fires visible for a hundred miles. The Ludwigshafen I.G. Farben factory sustained severe damage and fires, and the Oppau plant was put out of action completely, all for the loss of a single Lancaster.

Another virgin target was the city of Ulm, situated to the south-east of Stuttgart and west of Augsburg in southern Germany. It was similar in nature to the recently-bombed Heilbronn, and as a result of the catastrophic raid there, the local Gauleiter had urged the women and children to evacuate the inner city urgently. Plans were put in place to begin evacuation on Monday the 18th, so that Advent could be observed on the Sunday, but something caused a change of plan, and loudspeaker vans toured the city on Sunday urging the population to leave at once. It proved to be a fortuitous move! Unlike Heilbronn, Ulm contained industry, including two important lorry factories, and there were also military barracks and depots. Twenty-six 101 Squadron Lancasters lined up for take-off at 15.00, with S/Ls MacLeod-Selkirk and Warner the senior pilots on duty, and they all became safely airborne between 15.04 and 15.38. They made their way in cloudy, but fairly good conditions to rendezvous with 250 others from 1 Group to act as the main force, but found the weather deteriorating as they crossed France. Much of the outward flight was spent in cloud, but this cleared at the Rhine to leave excellent visibility, which allowed the crews to map-read their way to the target. Unfortunately, when some twenty miles short, a layer of thin stratus slid in with tops at 2,000 feet to completely obscure the ground. The Pathfinders opened the attack with red TIs at 19.24, but they quickly became swallowed up in the cloud, or were extinguished by the heavy snow on the ground. Release-point flares were dropped at the same time, and, at 19.31, the Master Bomber ordered these to be bombed. The 101 Squadron crews carried out their attacks from 9,500 to 13,500 feet between 19.30 and 19.39, and played their part in an accurate and concentrated raid, which resulted in fierce fires consuming a square kilometre of the built-up area. It would be established later that almost 82% of the city's buildings had sustained damage to some extent, including both lorry factories. There is no question that the evacuation saved many thousands of lives, and restricted the civilian death toll to six hundred. Only two Lancasters were lost, and one of them was 101 Squadron's NG131, which went down over southern Germany, and took with it the experienced, predominantly Canadian crew of F/O Ireland RCAF.

Bonn, a city just south of Cologne, which would become famous after the war as the capital city of Western Germany, had received a number of small-scale visits from the Command during 1944, and was the objective for seventy-seven Lancasters of 1 Group on the 21st, with Pathfinder Lancasters and Mosquitos to carry out the marking of the railway yards. Just six 101 Squadron Lancasters were involved, and they took off between 15.17 and 15.25, led by F/L Wagner. The skies were clear between base and Reading, but cloud had built up to ten-tenths by the time Beachy Head slid unseen beneath, and these were the conditions greeting the Pathfinders as they opened the attack precisely on time. They dropped red TIs, which quickly disappeared into the cloud, leaving a glow, which the early arrivals among the main force bombed. Thereafter, red and green skymarkers were employed, and they were initially confirmed by H2S to be accurate, before they began to become scattered. Five of the 101 Squadron crews bombed on the centre of the red and green flares from 15,000 to 18,000 feet between 18.22 and 18.23, while one arrived six minutes later, and bombed on the glow of red TIs. The expectation of success was not high, and post raid-reconnaissance confirmed that the marshalling yards had not been touched.

Twenty-four hours later the marshalling yards at Koblenz-Mosel came in for attention at the hands of a 1 Group main force of 156 Lancasters, of which fifteen represented 101 Squadron. They took off between 15.15 and 15.30 with F/Ls Parke and Wilder the senior pilots on duty, and joined up with heavy and light Pathfinder elements on the way south. There was ten-tenths cloud until 180 miles from the target, which lay at the midpoint of a line running between Bonn and Mainz. The cloud began gradually to disperse, and there was only a thin layer of stratus of two to four-tenths over the target, with tops at 6,000 feet. The Pathfinders were a few minutes late in opening the attack with TIs, which could clearly be seen in the built-up area of the city between the Mosel and Rhine rivers. Some of the 101 Squadron crews bombed visually on the marshalling yards, while others aimed for the centre of the red and green release-point flares or on smoke, and did so from 15,000 to 19,500 feet between 18.51 and 19.02. A number of large explosions were noted, but it was established later that only the fringes of the marshalling yards had been hit, along with several main lines and two important road bridges. Much of the bombing had fallen onto farm land, and two villages were badly damaged.

Christmas Eve brought attention upon the Cologne-Nippes marshalling yards, which had escaped damage at the hands of a 4, 6 and 8 Group force a few days earlier. This time the job was given to a 1 Group main force, with Pathfinder support, and an overall force of ninety-seven Lancasters and five Mosquitos was made ready. 101 Squadron put up just five aircraft, with F/Ls Herring and Wagner the senior pilots on duty. They took off between 15.03 and 15.15, and headed into low cloud and fog, which dispersed from Reading southwards, and the skies cleared altogether over France.

This artwork suggests that F/L Herring had his own personalised Lancaster! (GW).

The target area was also cloud-free, and, despite the presence of ground haze, the crews were able to identify the target with ease. The Pathfinder marker crews were right on the money, and sent red and green TIs cascading into the railway yards, where they attracted the bombs. The 101 Squadron crews delivered their cookies, 1,000 and 500 pounders from 17,000 to 18,000 feet between 18.29 and 18.32, and contributed to the severe damage inflicted on the tracks and the violent detonation of an ammunition train.

The final Christmas Day was celebrated in traditional style on bomber stations, and relative peace reigned for twenty-four hours. The German break-out in the Ardennes, which had begun on the 16th, and would become known as the Battle of the Bulge, was running out of steam, and 294 aircraft from all groups were sent to attack enemy troop positions around St Vith in Belgium. Eleven 101 Squadron crews were detailed to take part, and departed Ludford Magna either side of 13.00 led by S/Ls MacLeod-Selkirk and Warner. Patches of low fog over the North Sea gave way to clear skies over Belgium, and the crews were able to map-read their way to the target area. Red and green TIs went down accurately on the town, and were soon obscured as the bombs struck home, causing the Master Bomber to issue instructions to aim for the upwind edge of the smoke. The 101 Squadron crews bombed from 10,000 to 12,500 feet between 15.31 and 15.38, and set off home confident in the quality of their work. PB237 was on its way home with the crew of S/L Warner, when it force-landed near Reims at 16.27. The rear gunner, F/Sgt Jackson, did not survive, and whether he died as a result of the landing or through enemy action is not clear.

The group divided its forces on the 28th, when sending 103 Lancasters to Mönchengladbach and a further 133 to attack the marshalling yards again at Bonn. 101 Squadron made ready twenty-two aircraft for the latter, with W/C Everest and S/L Macleod-Selkirk the senior pilots on duty. They took off between 15.17 and 15.45, and flew under clear skies to the south coast and the English Channel, where cloud began to build, and it was at ten-tenths over the target with tops at 8,000 feet and bright moonlight above. The Pathfinders were a little late in opening the attack with ground and skymarkers, but the TIs fell in a fair concentration around the aiming-point, and attracted the bulk of the bomb loads. The 101 Squadron crews bombed from 15,000 to 16,000 feet between 18.44 and 18.50, and all but one returned home to report little in the way of an assessment. The defences claimed just one Lancaster, and that was PB634 of 101 Squadron, in which F/L Parke RCAF and his predominantly Canadian crew all lost their lives. The circumstances of the loss are not known, and, curiously, the pilot and both gunners are buried in Belgium, and the rest of the crew in Germany. The Command's claim that the railway yards sustained serious damage is not borne out by a local report, which suggests that the town bore the brunt of the attack.

1, 6 and 8 Groups combined on the afternoon of the 29th to dispatch 324 Lancasters to attack the synthetic oil plant at Scholven-Buer, in the north-western quarter of Gelsenkirchen. 101 Squadron was on duty with eighteen Lancasters, which took off in a thirty-minute slot from 15.00 led by S/L Gundry-White. The weather was good throughout, but the target was found to be cloud-covered, necessitating the use of skymarkers, which went down precisely at Zero-hour. Their red glow could be seen clearly through the clouds, and the 101 Squadron participants bombed them from 17,000 to 20,000 feet either side of 19.00, before returning safely to report numerous large explosions, smoke rising to 15,000 feet and fires visible for a hundred miles. F/O Gooding reported a collision between his LL772 and another Lancaster, which resulted in damage, and the identity of the other aircraft remains a mystery. A local report detailed three hundred high-explosive bombs hitting the area of the plant, causing fires and inflicting severe damage upon the installations. A further 3,100 bombs fell in other parts of Scholven, causing much residential and industrial destruction, and surface buildings at two coal mines were also hit and severely damaged.

The squadron operated for the final time in the year on New Year's Eve as part of a 1 Group main force of 133 Lancasters, whose crews had been briefed to attack the railway yards at Osterfeld. This was a town located some thirty miles south-west of Leipzig, in an area dotted with synthetic oil production sites, all of which would find themselves in the bomb sights in the coming months. Seventeen 101 Squadron aircraft took off between 14.56 and 15.14 led by S/Ls Gundry-White and MacLeod-Selkirk, and set course for the south coast in cloudy skies, which cleared to an extent over France and Belgium. Unanticipated headwinds of 120 mph were encountered over Belgium, and this delayed the arrival of both the Pathfinders and main force at the target, where the cloud had built again to seven to ten-tenths with tops at 10,000 feet. The first markers were observed at 18.45, but their accuracy could not be determined by the crews in the prevailing conditions. The red TIs seemed to be concentrated around the aiming point, while the greens were scattered, and, although a few crews were able to see the reds through patches of thin cloud, the majority were forced to bomb on the glow of reds. The 101 Squadron crews bombed on a variety of references, including flak, from 18,000 to 20,000 feet between 18.47 and 19.07, and returned to report large explosions at 18.49, 18.53, 18.55 and 19.00. Bomber Command estimated 35% damage to the sidings and 20% to facilities, at a cost of two Lancasters.

The squadron took part in fifteen operations during the course of the month, dispatching 236 sorties for the loss of three Lancasters and two crews. It had been a long and hard-fought year, which had begun with the Command's morale at its lowest point during the dark nights of the Berlin campaign, but was ending with the Allied forces sweeping across Europe into the ever-shrinking Reich. The scent of victory was in the air, but much remained to be done before the proud, resolute and tenacious German forces finally laid down their arms.

Collision damage to the port wingtip of F/O Syd Gooding's LL772. The aircraft collided with another, unidentified, Lancaster on 29th December 1944 during the raid on Scholven. For his skill in bringing his aircraft and crew home, Gooding received the DFC(GW).

101 Squadron photograph, 1945

January 1945

101 Squadron would enjoy a loss-free start to the final year of the war, despite the frequency of operations. However, any thoughts that the defences were spent, were misplaced. Stretched beyond their capacity to defend every corner of the Reich, and hampered by shortages in aviation fuel and experienced crews, the Luftwaffe Tag and Nachtjagd would retain the ability to inflict grievous losses on Bomber Command, and many more crews would be lost before the end came. The Tagjagd did itself no favours when launching its ill-conceived and, ultimately, ill-fated Operation Bodenplatte (Baseplate) at first light on New Year's Morning. The intention to destroy elements of the Allied air forces on the ground at the recently liberated airfields in France, Holland and Belgium was only modestly rewarding, and, in return, the Luftwaffe sacrificed 250 front-line fighters, and a good proportion of the pilots, who were killed, wounded or captured.

The old enemy of Nuremberg became the first major target of the New Year, and would face a heavy force of 514 Lancasters drawn from 1, 3, 6 and 8 Groups on the night of the 2/3rd. 1 Group's contribution amounted to a record 296 Lancasters, of which twenty-one represented 101 Squadron. They took off between 15.04 and 15.35 with S/L MacLeod-Selkirk the senior pilot on duty, and climbed through six-tenths cloud, which thickened over the Channel and remained at ten-tenths until breaking up from 7°E. The target lay under clear skies with excellent visibility, enhanced by the contrast between the built-up area and the snow-covered countryside. A tail wind drove

A crash-landing at Ludford Magna on 4th January 1945 was not the end of the road for NF924, as the aircraft was not struck off charge until May 1947 (GW).

some crews to the target ahead of schedule, and they were forced to orbit until the Pathfinders opened the attack, also a minute or two early. The first salvoes of mixed red and green TIs fell squarely onto the marshalling yards in the centre of the city, and the Master Bomber directed the main force crews to these. The bombing was accurate and concentrated, and the aiming point soon disappeared under smoke, the upwind edge of which became the new aiming-point. The 101 Squadron crews bombed from 16,000 to 19,000 feet between 19.25 and 19.38, and returned safely to report numerous explosions and the glow of fires visible from 150 miles away. Post-raid reconnaissance confirmed this as Nuremberg's worst night of the war, which left more than 4,600 dwellings destroyed, most of them contained in apartment blocks, and two thousand medieval houses were also lost.

In the early hours of the 5th, Lancasters and Mosquitos of 1, 5 and 8 Groups carried out a controversial attack on the small French town of Royan on the east bank of the Gironde Estuary. Acting in response to requests from Free French forces, who were laying siege to the town on their way to Bordeaux, a heavy force of 340 aircraft almost wiped it off the map in a two-wave operation, to which 101 Squadron did not contribute. The tragedy was that the residents had been offered the opportunity by the German garrison commander to evacuate, but two thousand people had opted to remain, and up to eight hundred of these are believed to have

DV302, here coded SR-H, survived an incredible 121 ops with 101 Sqn. The squadron clearly felt that this achievement was worth recording for posterity (GW)

lost their lives. In an ironic twist of war, the town was not taken, and the garrison remained in place until mid-April.

This was to be a momentous month for two of the squadron's veteran Lancasters, DV245 and DV302, both of which were about to achieve a century of operations. DV245 won the unofficial contest, when it was detailed among twenty from the squadron to take part in an operation to Hanover on the night of the 5/6th. F/O Patterson and crew were the occupants as the "old lady" was allowed the honour of leading the twenty squadron participants away at 18.48, to be followed by the others over the ensuing twenty-eight minutes. Having climbed out, they headed for the Lincolnshire coast to join up with 162 others from the group and 501 Lancasters and Halifaxes from 4, 6 and 8 Groups in a very long bomber stream. S/L Gundry-White was the senior pilot on duty, and F/O Meadows the only early return, after his engine controls failed. The route took the bombers across Holland and south of Bremen, at which point the seven-tenths cloud rapidly diminished to leave clear skies over the target. The plan called for the 4 Group Halifaxes to bomb first, about forty minutes ahead of the Lancaster brigade, and the fires from their attack could be seen from a hundred miles away by those approaching. On arrival, most crews found the glare and smoke from the fires obscured ground detail, and it became difficult to assess the accuracy of the marking, although it appeared to be around the aiming-point in the northern half of the city. The 101 Squadron crews bombed from 18,000 to 21,200 feet between 21.49 and 21.55, and returned confident that the operation had been successful. Local reports stated that 493 residential building had been destroyed, and they contained 3,605 separate dwelling units.

Marshalling yards at Hanau and Neuss provided the targets for 482 and 147 aircraft respectively on the night of the 6/7th, both of which operations were supported by 101 Squadron. Ten crews were briefed for the former, an important railway centre located fifteen miles east of Frankfurt, and they took off between 15.37 and 15.59, led by S/L Gundry-White. Also taking off amongst them were seven crews bound for the Ruhr to provide ABC cover for the 3 Group raid at Neuss. Cloud over England diminished over the Channel, but built up again over France, and by the time the Hanau force was within sight of the target, it was at ten-tenths. However, a large, white glow was visible, resulting from the first phase of the operation, to the south-east of which could be seen red TIs at 19.13, and, despite them falling and cascading into the cloud, a strong refection remained for the crews to aim at. The 101 Squadron crews bombed from 19,000 to 21,000 feet between 19.14 and 19.20, and returned to the debriefing room unable to determine what had gone on beneath the white stuff. In fact, the town and its surrounds had endured a torrid time, with a proportion of the bombing hitting the railway yards in the north of the town and rural areas beyond, but much of it also falling to the south into the central districts. A local report estimated that 40% of the town had been destroyed. It was a similar story at Neuss, where the 101 Squadron crews had arrived to find identical weather conditions. They had carried out their bombing runs from 19,000 feet between 18.46 and 18.51, aiming at the glow of red TIs, backed up by release-point flares. They returned safely, unaware that, although the railway yards had been hit, most of the bombing had been scattered over surrounding districts, where 1,749 houses, nineteen industrial premises and twenty public buildings had been destroyed or seriously damaged.

The night of the 7/8th brought Munich into the bomb sights of more than six hundred heavy bombers drawn from 1, 3, 5, 6 and 8 Groups, with 1 Group providing 239 Lancasters. A dozen from 101 Squadron took off between 18.34 and 18.56, with F/Ls Flint, Herring and Wagner the senior pilots on duty. P/Os Boyd and Town returned early for undisclosed reasons, the former early on and the latter after having penetrated deep into enemy territory. The weather was good initially, but varying amounts of cloud and occasional icing conditions made the outward leg challenging, and the target area was hidden by ten-tenths cloud. Stronger-than-forecast winds pushed some aircraft to the target ahead of schedule, and there was a degree of dog-legging and orbiting before the first markers went down at the appointed second. It took some time to establish a concentration of red and green skymarkers, and most of the 101 Squadron crews bombed these from 17,500 to 20,000 feet between 22.29 and 22.39. Bomber Command claimed a successful raid, which would be the last of the war against this city. P/O Kurtzer brought DV302 safely home to complete its one-hundredth operation, and both centurions would increase their tally substantially, although, only one would survive the war.

For most of the Command's heavy units there was an almost unprecedented six nights on the ground after Munich. Only 3 Group was busy, carrying out G-H raids on railway yards on a number of nights, followed up by elements of 4 and 6 Groups on the night of the 13/14th. 1 Group crews were back in the briefing rooms on the 14th, however, to be told they would be joining forces with elements of 5, 6 and 8 Groups that night to attack the synthetic oil refinery at Leuna (Merseburg), west of Leipzig. The plan called for 5 Group to attack first, and for the second phase to go in three hours later, thus committing a total of over 570 aircraft to the operation. 1 Group made available 245 Lancasters, and eight of them lined up for take-off at Ludford Magna shortly after 16.00, to join forces with 5 Group for the first phase attack. The senior pilots as they took off between 16.12 and 16.22 were F/Ls Flint, Gooding and Woods, and they headed out in cloudy conditions, which cleared for a time east of the Rhine, before building again in the target area. The 5 Group marking method worked well, and the 101 Squadron crews were able to aim at red and green TIs, doing so from an average of 16,000 feet, in accordance with the Master Bomber's instructions, between 20.53 and 21.07. The fourteen 101 Squadron crews in the second phase took off between 19.16 and 19.37, led by S/Ls Gundry-White and Warner, they headed for the Sussex coast in good weather conditions over thin cloud, which would prevail throughout the almost nine-hour round trip. The target was reached early by some crews, and found to be covered by ten-tenths thin cloud, with the glow from the 5 Group raid clearly visible, and illuminating flares went down at 23.54, followed by red and green TIs. Although the TIs could be seen, the ground itself was completely obscured, and the Master Bomber experienced difficulty in identifying the aiming point, eventually instructing the main force to bomb on the red and yellow release-point flares. The 101 Squadron crews bombed from 18,000 to 22,000 feet between 23.57 and 00.11, seven of them complying with the instructions, while seven others went for the TIs. Many returning crews thought the operation to be scattered and probably ineffective, when it was, in fact, later found to be among the most devastating attacks on the synthetic oil industry of the war.

A busy night of operations on the 16/17th saw more than 1,200 sorties launched. The largest operation was by predominantly Halifaxes at Magdeburg, while all-Lancaster heavy forces of 328 and 231 attacked synthetic oil refineries at Zeitz-Tröglitz, south-west of Leipzig and Brüx in Czechoslovakia respectively. 101 Squadron was to support both operations, sending eight Lancasters to provide ABC cover for 5 Group at the latter, and twelve as part of a 1 Group contribution of 232 aircraft to the former. They departed Ludford Magna together between 17.27 and 17.48, with F/Ls Flint and Woods the most senior pilots on duty. Cloud over England and the Channel began to disperse over France to leave clear skies in the Leipzig area, with ground haze, while those bound for Brüx would find it totally obscured by ten-tenths cloud. The Zeitz force arrived six minutes ahead of schedule, and the Master Bomber was first heard instructing the crews to bomb at 22.09. The target, the Braunkohle-Benzin plant, was well-illuminated, as the first salvoes of mixed red and green TIs fell on the northern edge of the site, and they would be backed-up continuously. The Master Bomber maintained control throughout, and the attack was both accurate and concentrated, setting off explosions at regular intervals, including one particularly impressive one among storage tanks in the south-eastern corner at

Armourers pose with a Lancaster called 'Zoomer', presumably SR-Z, and a laden bomb trolley. The two visible bombs appear to be christened in honour of Lily and Violets, presumably sweethearts of members of the air or groundcrew. Whoever said romance was dead? (GW)

22.19. The single missing aircraft was the squadron's LM472, in which F/O McGonigle and all but one of his crew were killed. There were two Australian navigators on board, and one survived to be taken into captivity. The fact that burials initially took place in northern Germany, confirms that they were homebound via the planned route, south of Hannover and north of the Ruhr, when the end came.

On the 21st, W/C Gundry-White was promoted from within to become the last wartime commander of the squadron, and he presided over his first operation on the evening of the 22nd, when a benzol plant in the Hamborn district, north of Duisburg's city centre, was selected for attention by a joint 1 and 3 Group main force. 1 Group provided 130 Lancasters, of which eight belonged to 101 Squadron, and they took off between 17.00 and 17.13 with F/Ls Hanney and Watts the senior pilots on duty. There was low cloud between Ludford Magna and the French coast, after which it gradually diminished to leave the target area clear with moonlight and excellent visibility. Crews were able to confirm visually the accuracy of the Pathfinder markers, and, apart from one stray red TI in the docks area, they all fell around the aiming point, and attracted the bomb loads. The 101 Squadron crews delivered their cookie and fifteen 500 pounders each onto red and green TIs from 19,000 feet between 20.01 and 20.12, and returned home full of praise for the work of the Pathfinders. They missed a particularly large explosion at 20.37, which was seen by the last crews to leave the target area, and bombing photos supported the claims of a highly destructive raid. The nearby Thyssen steelworks was also severely damaged after receiving five hundred bombs, and there was collateral damage in adjacent residential districts.

The Group's final activity of the month came on the night of the 28/29th, when contributing 150 Lancasters to a two-phase attack on targets in the Stuttgart area. The first phase was to be directed at the railway yards at Kornwestheim, five miles north of Stuttgart city centre, and the second phase, three hours later, at the Hirth aero-engine factory in the north-western suburb of Zuffenhausen. 101 Squadron briefed eighteen crews for the latter aiming-point, of which seven of flight lieutenant rank were the senior pilots on duty. They took off between 19.36 and 20.03, and flew out in five-tenths cloud as far as the French coast. There were large breaks in the cloud over France, but it built again from the German frontier to leave the target hidden beneath ten-tenths cumulus. The Pathfinders were about three minutes late in opening the attack, by which time some main force crews had decided to bomb. Release-point flares were dropped at 23.30, but these proved to be sparse and scattered. The quantity of flares increased as the attack progressed, and red and green TIs could be picked out through the cloud. Although lacking concentration, there was a good coverage of bombs in the target area, and the 101 Squadron crews added to this from 18,000 to 20,000 feet between 23.30 and 23.45, before returning home to report explosions and the glow of fires. The squadron operated ten time during the month, and dispatched 138 sorties for the loss of a single Lancaster and crew.

LM472, SR-V2, came to grief on the Brüx raid of 16/17th January 1945. The forward ABC transmitter aerial is visible in this photo (GW)

February 1945

February was to be a busy month, as the Command targeted enemy communications in a Germany rapidly collapsing-in upon itself under the weight of advancing ground forces in the eastern and western theatres. The main problem was the weather, which produced challenging conditions during the first week to hamper attempts to deal decisively with targets. Three major operations were to be mounted on the night of the 1/2nd, the largest by 382 aircraft of 1, 6 and 8 Groups against Ludwigshafen, for which 1 Group detailed a massive 277 Lancasters, twenty-five of them representing 101 Squadron. At the same time 342 aircraft of 4, 6 and 8 Groups were assigned to attack Mainz, also in southern Germany, while 282 aircraft of 5 Group plied their trade over Siegen, a town fifty miles due east of Cologne. The 101 Squadron element took off between 15.40 and 16.06, with a host of pilots of flight lieutenant rank leading the way, and climbed into scattered cloud, which dispersed over the Channel, and remained clear over France until 6°E, when it began to build again to nine-tenths in the target area. The Pathfinders opened the attack with cascading red TIs at 19.11, backed up with green TIs, which the main force crews could see on approach, but which became obscured by cloud when directly above. The TIs were backed-up by release-point flares, and the crews mostly aimed for these, the 101 Squadron element doing so from 15,000 to 17,000 feet between 19.16 and 19.26 in the face of little defence from the ground, but a clear presence of night fighters. Twenty-two Lancasters returned to Ludford Magna, where some crews reported a large explosion at 19.40

F/L Harrison and crew. Six were lost and only Harrison and his SDO, Sgt R Whiteford, survived when they were shot down attacking Siegen. The crewmen lost were Sgt JB Breare, flight engineer; F/S RJF Swain, navigator; F/S GH Hillman, bomb aimer; Sgt F Smith, wireless operator; F/S DJ Mackay, MU gunner and Sgt J Squire, rear gunner (GW).

and fires visible from eighty miles away. The attack scattered bombs in many parts of the city, where important railway yards and a road bridge were severely damaged, along with nine hundred houses. After the squadron's single casualty in January, February, in contrast, got off to a bad start, with the failure to return of three Lancasters. JA715 and ME863 collided over France at 19.06 while outbound, and crashed near Sorneville, some seventy-five miles short of the target. F/L Harrison and one of his crew were the only survivors from the former, while none survived from the crew of F/L Boyd RAAF in the latter. PB256 went down in the target area, and the eight-man crew of F/O Clark RNZAF were all killed. This was a Commonwealth crew, which also contained members of the RAF, RAAF and RCAF.

The only large raid of the war on Wiesbaden, a city separated from Mainz to the south by the River Rhine, was scheduled to be delivered by elements of 1, 3, 6 and 8 Groups on the night of the 2/3rd. A heavy force of 495 Lancasters included a 1 Group contribution of 233, of which seventeen represented 101 Squadron, led by W/C Gundry-White. They took off between 20.33 and 21.11, and climbed through layer cloud before setting course for the Channel. F/L McClenaghan turned back at 21.27 after his Gee failed, and left the others to press on to the target, which they found hidden beneath ten-tenths cloud in layers up to 20,000 feet and beyond. Lighter than forecast winds led to the attack opening late, and the markers were completely obscured by the cloud, forcing most crews to bomb on H2S and Gee. The 101 Squadron element delivered their cookies and incendiaries from 18,000 to 20,000 feet between 23.36 and 00.04, and all but one returned home with little to report, other than a very large explosion at 23.46, followed by a column of black smoke rising through the cloud. PD263 did not arrive home with the others, and is believed to have landed in France, before eventually returning to Ludford Magna with the crew of F/O Roberts and continuing its career. A local report confirmed the success of the raid, despite the conditions, stating that 520 houses had been destroyed, along with thirty other buildings, and around a thousand people had lost their lives.

On the afternoon of the 3rd, PB457 was consumed by fire at Ludford Magna while undergoing its seventy-five-hour inspection. Two Ruhr oil-related production sites were the focus of attention on the evening of the 3rd. The Prosper coking plant at Welheim, an eastern district of Bottrop, and situated about five miles to the north-east of Duisburg and Oberhausen, was assigned to a 1 and 8 Group heavy force of 192 Lancasters, including nine from 101 Squadron, while the Hansa benzol plant at Dortmund was given to 3 Group. The Ludford Magna brigade took off between 16.22 and 16.35, led by F/Ls Flint, Hanney and McClenaghan, and climbed away before setting course under clear skies. F/L Hanney aborted his sortie over base for an undisclosed reason, leaving the others to continue on in good weather conditions, which persisted until shortly before the target, where three-tenths low stratus cloud developed with tops at 3,000 feet. The first red TIs went down punctually at 19.26, and were confirmed as accurate, and they were backed up by equally accurate and concentrated greens, which attracted the bombs from above. The 101 Squadron crews attacked from 17,000 feet between 19.30 and 19.39, and contributed to a highly successful operation, which caused extensive damage to the plant.

With the British XXX Corps bearing down on the German frontier near the Reichswald, the towns of Kleve and Goch found themselves in the front line and part of the enemy's defensive system. Bomber Command was invited to destroy them, and that event was scheduled for the night of the 7/8th. A heavy force of 295 Lancasters of 1 and 8 Groups was assigned to Kleve, and this number included twenty-two put up by 101 Squadron, led by S/L Warner. The weather was good as they departed Ludford Magna either side of 19.00, and, having climbed out, they set course for the exit point at Hastings on the Sussex coast. The route out was virtually cloud-free, but a dozen miles from the target it began to build and was at seventh-tenths in a band from 5,000 to 7,000 feet when the raid began at 21.50. The Master Bomber was heard to call "Basement five thousand",

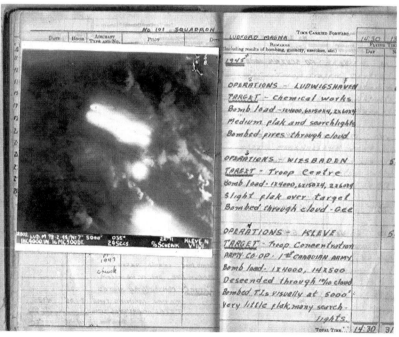

A page from the logbook of F/O Willard Sawyer, RCAF, bomb aimer in the crew of F/L Wilfred Schenk RCAF. The aiming point photo is of Kleve on the night of 7/8th February. It would have been a source of pride to the largely-Canadian crew that their effort was in support of the 1st Canadian Army (GW).

and, as the crews broke cloud, they were greeted by a target brilliantly illuminated and well-marked with red and green TIs. The Master Bomber maintained excellent control throughout, and the 101 Squadron crews bombed in accordance with his instruction from 4,000 to 6,000 feet between 21.59 and 22.15, contributing to the 1,384 tons of high explosives that tore the already evacuated town apart. Sadly, and, unfortunately, it also left difficult conditions for the 15th Scottish Division, which moved in a few hours later.

The final one of three attacks on the oil refinery at Politz since December was planned for the night of the 8/9th, and was to be carried out by elements 1, 5 and 8 Groups in two phases. Situated north of Stettin, it was a long round-trip for the 475 Lancaster crews involved, which had originally included a contribution from 101 Squadron, but its participation, and that of the Wickenby squadrons, was cancelled because of adverse weather conditions over the stations. 1 Group ultimately sent a reduced element of 184 Lancasters, following on two hours after 5 Group, and they contributed to a highly successful operation, that ended all production at the site for the remainder of the war.

The Churchill inspired series of raids on Germany's eastern cities under Operation Thunderclap began at Dresden on the night of the 13/14th, in another two-phase attack begun by 5 Group, employing its low-level marking method. 244 "Independent Air Force" Lancasters dropped eight hundred tons of bombs in a partially successful opening phase, and the fires acted as a beacon to the 529 Lancasters of 1, 3, 6 and 8 Groups following three hours behind. Among these were twenty-one 101 Squadron aircraft, which had taken off between 21.31 and 22.07, led by S/L Warner, and made their way to the target, initially in clear skies until 3°E, when large amounts of broken cloud reached 18,000 feet. This dispersed from 12°E to leave clear skies over the target, although a large bank of cloud threatened a short distance away to the east. The fires from the 5 Group attack were visible twenty minutes from the target, and they were concentrated south of the River Elbe between the marshalling yards and the 1 Group aiming-point. The attack commenced on time with hardly-necessary illuminating flares and red TIs, which were backed up with greens. The 101 Squadron crews delivered their mix of HE and incendiaries from 15,000 to 20,000 feet between 01.29 and 01.45, in the face of scant opposition, and contributed to a further eighteen hundred tons of bombs, which set off the same chain reaction that had devastated parts of Hamburg in July 1943. A firestorm developed of terrifying proportions, which swept through large parts of the city, the population of which had been swelled by an influx of refugees from the eastern front. Initial estimates of the death toll were put at 250,000 people, but a realistic figure of 25,000 has been settled upon in recent years.

This operation has generated a great deal of hysteria ever since Churchill distanced himself from it in an act of betrayal, after being the architect and sponsor of it. Harris unjustly had to bear the condemnation of the German people and others of a pacifist leaning, after Churchill almost accused him in a letter of bombing for the sake of creating terror. Harris did not want to go to Dresden, preferring Berlin for its strategic significance, but he was nagged into it by Chief-of-the-Air Staff Portal on persistent urgings from the Prime Minister. Also, and contrary to the nonsensical claims of some survivors of Dresden, Bomber Command aircraft did not strafe people in the streets. 5 Group Mosquitos may well have come down to rooftop height to carry out their marking duties, but they were not offensively armed. It should be remembered also, that the Americans arrived on the following morning to add to the destruction, and they used escort fighters which had the capability to strafe, although there is no suggestion, or any evidence, that they did so. Even so, one hears no condemnation of the USAAF.

Thunderclap moved on to Chemnitz on the following night for a similar two-phase operation, separated by three hours, this time in the absence of "The Lincolnshire Poachers", otherwise known as 5 Group. A total force of 717 Lancasters and Halifaxes was made ready, of which 202 of the former were put up by 1 Group. 4 Group was to take the early shift, departing their stations after 17.00, and it was between 19.55 and 20.43 that the twenty-one 101 Squadron participants took off from Ludford Magna, led by the newly-promoted S/L Flint. The clear skies over England and the Channel began to fill with cloud from the German frontier, and it was at this point, having just crossed into Germany near Saarbrücken, that F/L Andrew turned back for an unspecified reason. The others continued on to find the target area hidden beneath ten-tenths cloud, with tops in places as high as 18,000 feet. The Master Bomber called for markers at 00.25, but nothing happened, and, four minutes later, he instructed the crews to bomb on H2S and Gee. Release-point flares eventually went down, but disappeared quickly into the cloud, and the 101 Squadron crews bombed on the centre of the glow of red and green "Wanganui" flares from 13,800 to 20,000 feet between 00.28 and 00.39. They returned home safely to report a scattered attack, which was impossible to assess, and there had not even been evidence of the earlier 4 Group raid. Post-raid reconnaissance revealed evidence of bombing in many parts of the city, but most of it fell into open country.

A flurry of losses over a four-day period reminded everyone that bombing Germany was still a very dangerous business. Preparations for the next operation were put in hand on the 20th, when a major assault was planned on the southern half of Dortmund. A force of 514 heavy bombers included twenty-four Lancasters of 101 Squadron, which took off in two phases of twelve aircraft each, the first one between 20.34 and 20.50, and the second between 21.25 and 21.57, the latter led by S/L Warner. They were part of a 1 Group contribution of 271 Lancasters, and climbed away from Ludford Magna into clear skies, which filled rapidly with cloud from 5°E, and was at eight to ten-tenths over the target. The Pathfinders opened the attack punctually with red TIs, which were backed up by greens, and their accuracy confirmed by H2S. Skymarkers were also in use, but these tended to fall short and created a marking creep-back for fourteen miles along the line of approach. The bombing in the early stages was accurate, but, as the cloud thickened, and the glow through the clouds diminished, it became scattered and much of it fell short. The 101 Squadron crews bombed from 17,000 to 21,000 feet between 01.01 and 01.16, and returned home with little to report by way of an assessment. PB671 failed to arrive back with the others, after crashing somewhere between the target and the Dutch frontier, and it was learned later that S/L Warner and four of his crew had escaped by parachute and were in enemy hands, while the remaining three had gone down with the aircraft. The Command claimed a successful operation, but no local report was made in a city descending into chaos.

The final heavy raid of the war on the much-bombed city of Duisburg was handed to 362 Lancasters of 1, 6 and 8 Groups on the night 21/22nd, for which 1 Group made ready 245 aircraft, twenty of them representing 101 Squadron. S/L MacLeod-Selkirk was the senior pilot on duty as they departed Ludford Magna between 19.36 and 20.00, and climbed into conditions of little or no cloud, which persisted until shortly before the target, when a band of stratus a thousand feet thick slid over the city at 15,000 feet to cover it completely. The winds outbound were different from those forecast, and this delayed the arrival of the main force by a few minutes. As they approached, the crews could see the first red TIs cascading at 22.56, but, by the time they arrived to bomb, these had disappeared below the cloud, and no more were evident until 23.08. Some considerable difficulty was experienced in identifying the target, and incendiaries were seen to be dropped all the way from Krefeld to Duisburg. By 23.10 the cloud was beginning to break up, and a better concentration was achieved, and had a Master Bomber been present, he might have been able to compensate for the scarcity of the marking. The 101 Squadron crews delivered their cookies and incendiaries from 16,000 to 20,000 feet between 23.03 and 23.23, mostly aiming at TIs burning on the ground, and all returned safely, some to report large explosions. Post-raid reconnaissance confirmed this as a successful operation.

It had been the intention for Pforzheim to receive its first visit of the war from the Command on the night of the 21/22nd, before the target was changed to Duisburg, but its reprieve was to be short-lived, just forty-eight hours, in fact. The job of destroying it was given to the same combination of groups, and a Film Unit Lancaster was among 367 of the type made ready during the 23rd. At Ludford Magna twenty-five aircraft were bombed up and fuelled for the journey to southern Germany, and they took off between 15.45 and 16.13 led by S/L Flint, before joining up with 233 others from 1 Group. They climbed through ten-tenths low cloud, which persisted until the bombers were over France, where it began to break up, leaving the skies clear and the moon bright as the target drew near. The thin veil of ground haze proved to be no impediment, and the first red TIs went down at 19.54, to be followed quickly by illuminator flares and salvoes of mixed and concentrated reds and greens. Fires took hold rapidly, and the whole town north of the river looked like a sea of flames. By 20.06, the fires were too dazzling for the TIs to be visible, after which the Master Bomber ordered the smoke to be bombed. The 101 Squadron crews carried out their attacks from 6,800 to 9,000 feet between 19.59 and 20.07, and twenty-three returned home to report explosions and fires visible for 150 miles into the return trip. Among the ten missing Lancasters were two from 101 Squadron, PA237, which crashed in southern Germany with no survivors from the standard crew of F/L Watt, and RA523, which was shot down in the target area with the predominantly Canadian crew of F/L McLenaghan RCAF, who all eight of whom survived to be taken prisoner. It took just twenty-two minutes to unload eighteen hundred tons of bombs onto Pforzheim, and seventeen thousand people lost their lives in the ensuing firestorm. This was the third largest casualty figure resulting from a single Bomber Command raid, and was exceeded only by Hamburg and Dresden. 1 Group dispatched 248 Lancasters to Neuss on the 28th, of which twenty-two were provided by 101 Squadron, but they were all recalled shortly after take-off. The squadron completed nine operations during the month, which generated 184 sorties for the loss of six Lancasters and crews.

F/L McLenaghan, RCAF, with his air- and ground crew (Sam Brookes via GW).

March 1945

FIDO BURNING — LUDFORD MAGNA   TAKEN 101/0   S/LDR SLEIGHT.

The handwritten caption says it all: FIDO was a petrol-burner system at selected airfields. The heat raised the air temperature above dewpoint, dispersing the fog, albeit on a very localised basis. However, it allowed a view of the ground in the last few seconds before touchdown and saved countless lives. This photo was taken by S/Ldr Peter Sleight, who joined 101 Sqn from 576 Sqn in March 1945, replacing S/Ldr Macleod-Selkirk as flight commander (GW).

The penultimate month of main force operations would prove to be hugely busy, and began in daylight on the 1st, with the last raid of the war on Mannheim. It was a 1, 6 and 8 Group force of 372 Lancasters and ninety Halifaxes that prepared for take-off that morning, 248 of the former representing 1 Group, of which twenty-two were provided by 101 Squadron. W/C Gundry-White was leading from the front, ably supported by S/L MacLeod-Selkirk, as the last Lancaster at Ludford Magna lifted off the ground at 11.59, and began its climb-out through five-tenths cloud before heading for the south coast. The cloud built from the French coast to ten-tenths, above which the main force maintained good formation, but were three or four minutes late arriving at the target. At 14.47 the Master Bomber was heard asking his deputy if he could see the main force, and, following a negative response, ordered the marker force to orbit until 15.03, when he called for release-point flares. Blue smoke-puff skymarkers went down accurately and in concentration, and the crews were instructed to aim for the centre of these. The 101 Squadron element bombed from 17,000 to 19,000 feet between 15.04 and 15.13, but, on return, the crews were unable to provide an assessment of the results. There was no post-raid reconnaissance or local report, but it is known that many bombs fell on neighbouring Ludwigshafen and its surrounds, where much damage occurred.

Sqn Ldr Peter Sleight DFC, Flight Commander (GW)

The final pounding of the tortured city of Cologne was to follow on the morning of the 2nd, when it would face a total of 858 aircraft attacking in two waves, the first of 703 aircraft, and the second of 155 Lancasters of 3 Group employing G-H. 1 Group put up 244 Lancasters, including twenty representing 101 Squadron, and they would be led by S/Ls Flint and MacLeod-Selkirk. They took off between 06.40 and 07.09, and headed for the south coast under clear skies, which began to fill with cloud as the Channel approached. There was five-tenths cloud over France, but this cleared twenty miles short of Cologne to leave perfect visibility, with only the threat of a large bank hovering to the east of the Rhine. The first crews to arrive found no difficulty in visually identifying the cathedral and Hohenzollern Bridge, but the Master Bomber, whose instructions were not clearly received by many crews, delayed the marking for two minutes, until 09.59, when salvoes of mixed red and green TIs went down. They were reported to have straddled the cathedral to the north and south, and the initial bombing was focussed around them. By 10.01 the markers were obscured by smoke, and later arrivals aimed for the centre of the upwind edge of this. The 101 Squadron crews bombed from 15,700 to 18,000 feet between 09.59 and 10.05, and contributed to further massive damage, which stretched across the main city on the western bank of the Rhine. Miraculously as always, the cathedral escaped more or less intact, but hundreds of people lost their lives. They were spared all but fifteen of the 3 Group bomb loads, after the G-H station failed, but Cologne was now a broken city on the front line, and would be in the hands of American forces within four days.

Operation Thunderclap returned to Chemnitz on the night of the 5/6th, when 101 Squadron detailed twenty-two Lancasters as part of a 1 Group effort of 239. They made up a total force of 754 Lancasters and Halifaxes, which departed their stations in the late afternoon and climbed into ten-tenths cloud, which caused icing problems for 6 Group aircraft, and caused nine of them to crash. Aside from a slight reduction over the Channel and northern France, the complete cloud cover would remain in place all the way to the target. The Ludford Magna brigade took off between 16.29 and 16.53, led by S/L Flint and the newly-arrived S/L Montgomery "Monty" Gibbon, whose thirty-third birthday would begin at midnight, while he was on his way home, but whose time on the squadron would, sadly, be brief in the extreme. The Master Bomber called for "Wanganui" marking (release-point flares), and when these went down at 21.42, they were plentiful and well-grouped, and were confirmed by H2S to be accurate. They quickly disappeared in the cloud, and for a period between 21.55 and 21.58, no markers were visible, and crews were instructed to bomb on any glow they could see. The 101 Squadron crews bombed from 14,500 to 17,300 feet between 21.43 and 22.00, and contributed to severe fire damage in central and southern districts.

The first attack of the war on Dessau, a town some hundred miles to the south-west of Berlin, was mounted on the night of the 7/8th, for which 526 Lancaster were made ready, drawn from 1, 3, 6 and 8 Groups. 101 Squadron donated twenty-three Lancasters to the 1 Group total of 243, and they took off between 16.52 and 17.19, led by the three flight commanders, S/Ls Flint, Gibbon and MacLeod-Selkirk. They climbed through complete cloud-cover, which persisted as far as the Ruhr, where it broke up to five-tenths, but was back up to eight-tenths over the target. F/O Henn had reached the south-eastern edge of the Ruhr when he turned back for an undisclosed reason, and he dropped his bombs on Solingen as a last-resort target. The others continued on, and observed illuminating flares going down at 21.56, followed by red and green TIs, which proved not to be visible through the cloud. Release point flares soon joined the mix, and they were concentrated at first, but became scattered later, as the Master Bomber's instructions suffered from interference after someone in a main force aircraft left a transmitter on. Fortunately, a large break in the clouds at 22.04 provided a clear view of the ground and the many TIs still burning, and some of the 101 Squadron crews were able to take advantage. The squadron participants bombed from 14,000 to 16,000 feet between 22.00 and 22.12, and played their part in the massive destruction that ensued, although, no details are available. This operation brought the squadron's first loss of the month, when PD268 failed to return with the eight-man crew of S/L Gibbon, and no clue to their fate has ever been found.

Two major operations were mounted on the following night, Hamburg by elements of 4, 6 and 8 Groups, and Kassel by a 1 Group main force of 235 Lancasters with twenty-seven 8 Group Lancasters providing the heavy marking function. 101 Squadron made ready nineteen aircraft, but one would fail to take off with the others between 16.59 and 17.44. They climbed out through a layer of ten-tenths thin cloud, which persisted more or less all the way to the target. F/L Hunting lost his port-outer engine over base, but the others pressed on, led by S/L MacLeod-Selkirk, and passed north of the Ruhr, before turning south-east to the target. The attack opened promptly with both TIs and release-point flares, and the former could be picked out clearly through the thin cloud. A break in the cloud provided the crews with a view of the built-up area, and enabled them to assess the marking as accurate. The 101 Squadron crews bombed from 16,000 to 21,000 feet between 21.31 and 21.39, and returned home to report a large area of fire, a particularly noteworthy explosion at 21.37 that produced a mushroom cloud of black smoke ascending to 8,000 feet, and the afterglow visible for a hundred miles and more into the return journey.

A milestone was set on the 11th, when a new all-time record force of 1,079 aircraft took off in the late morning to attack Essen for the last time. 1 Group detailed 240 Lancasters, of which twenty-one were provided by 101 Squadron, led by S/L MacLeod-Selkirk. They took off between 11.32 and 11.54, and climbed through ten-tenths cloud, that persisted throughout the entire operation. F/L Ashes abandoned his sortie at the French coast for an undisclosed reason, leaving the others to press on in excellent visibility above the cloud layer. The Master Bomber called for skymarking, but nothing happened until a few blue-puff markers were dropped at 14.58. Eventually these became evident in greater numbers, and the bombing proceeded according to plan. The 101 Squadron crews bombed from 16,000 to 19,000 feet between 15.00 and 15.06, delivering their share of the 4,661 tons of bombs onto what was a now a city in paralysis. That evening, F/O Collins and F/L Senger took off from Wickenby at 17.27 and 17.32 respectively to lay mines in the Silverthorne area of the Kattegat, and they successfully delivered their loads from around 11,000 feet shortly before 21.00.

Twenty-four hours after Essen, a new record was set, when 1,108 aircraft departed their stations to bomb Dortmund for the final time, and this was a record that would stand to the end of hostilities. 101 Squadron made ready twenty-one Lancasters as part of a 1 Group effort of 244. The Ludford Magna gang took off between 12.52 and 13.26, with W/C Gundry-White the senior pilot on duty, supported by S/L MacLeod-Selkirk. They climbed into clear skies before setting course for the south, but F/Ls Cooke and Harrison abandoned their sorties over base because of engine problems. The others found the cloud beginning to build at Reading, after which it remained present for the remainder of the outwards flight, to become ten-tenths over the target. The marking began punctually at 16.27 with TIs and blue and green smoke-puffs, and, as the TIs could not be seen, it was the latter at which the bombs were aimed under the instructions of the Master Bomber, who maintained excellent control throughout. At 16.35 a mushroom of black smoke, two miles in diameter, burst though the cloud, spiralling up to 8,000 feet, and it would be visible for a hundred miles into the return journey. The 101 Squadron crews bombed from 16,000 to 19,000 feet between 16.30 and 16.38, contributing to the massive 4,851 tons of HE that rained down onto central and southern districts, and put an end to any further industrial production.

Elements of 1 and 8 Groups joined forces on the evening of the 13th, to attack two benzol producers in the Ruhr, the Erin plant at Herne, located between Bochum and Gelsenkirchen, and the Dahlbusch plant, south of the Gelsenkirchen city centre. 101 Squadron added its eleven Lancasters to a 1 Group main force totalling eighty-one, and S/L MacLeod-Selkirk was the senior pilot on duty. They took off between 17.40 and 17.51, and climbed through four-tenths cumulus, which gave way to clear skies over enemy territory and good visibility over the target. Ground detail was obscured by haze, but when the first red TIs were seen at 20.41, and backed up by greens, their accuracy was confirmed by H2S. The 101 Squadron crews were over the aiming-point at 15,000 feet between 20.43 and 20.47, but, sadly, DV298 did not survive its bombing run. It was seen to explode over the target, presumably after a direct hit by flak, and there were no survivors from the eight-man crew of S/L Macleod-Selkirk, whose presence would be missed at Ludford Magna. The others returned home to report many fires and explosions, one at 20.43, accompanied by a large amount of flame, which sent a large amount of smoke up to 5,000 feet.

S/L Peter Sleight was posted in from 576 Squadron to replace S/L MacLeod-Selkirk. He had only recently joined 576 Squadron in the rank of flight lieutenant, and completed just three operations, the recent ones on Mannheim, Cologne and Kassel, before his posting. His flight engineer, P/O Vivian Hazell DFM, was a native of Kingston, Jamaica, and, like the other members of the, reputedly, hand-picked crew, was on his second tour. They were in action immediately as one of seventeen 101 Squadron crews briefed for an attack on the oil refinery at Misburg, on the north-eastern rim of Hannover, on the night of the 15/16th. S/Ls Flint and Sleight were the senior pilots on duty as they took off between 17.10 and 17.43, and were part of a 1 Group main force of 212 Lancasters, with 8 Group providing the marking. Except for the Channel crossing both ways, the operation took place under cloudless skies, and this enabled crews to identify the target visually by the light of illuminator flares. The raid began punctually with red TIs, backed up by mixed reds and greens in great concentration right on the aiming-point, and the Master Bomber called in the main force at 21.12. Almost immediately the target was engulfed in flames, and smoke was observed to rise through 10,000 feet, following an explosion at 21.13. The 101 Squadron crews dropped their mixed load of a cookie, ten 500 and three 250 pounders from 14,000 to 19,000 feet between 21.15 and 21.34, and returned home to report a highly successful operation, characterised by many explosions and fires visible from a hundred miles into the return journey. There was particular praise for the Master Bomber and the Pathfinder element.

The next regular target to host its final raid of the war by Harris's hordes was Nuremberg. 1 Group made ready 231 Lancasters, of which sixteen were provided by 101 Squadron, with S/L Flint the senior pilot on duty. They were to join forces with forty-six other Lancasters and sixteen Mosquitos from 8 Group, while 5 Group went to Würzburg, some fifty miles to the north-west. This would mean a concentration of almost five hundred aircraft converging on southern Germany, and this was likely to attract a night fighter response. The now almost customary early evening take-off had the Ludford Magna crews airborne between 17.10 and 17.43, and, after climbing out, they set course in five-tenths cloud, which increased at the French coast, but dispersed again from 05.30°E to leave four-to six-tenths in the target area with large gaps. They reached the target shortly before 21.30, and found the markers already going down, bang on time and in concentrated fashion. Bombing took place in accordance with the Master Bomber's instructions, mostly on mixed red and green TIs from 15,000 to 18,000 feet between 21.28 and 21.35, and many fires were observed, particularly in southern and south-western districts, and the already devastated Altstadt. The flak defence was light, but a large number of night fighters had made their presence felt between Stuttgart and the target, and on the return route, and many bombers were seen to be shot down. Thirty 1 Group crews reported being engaged, and five made claims of shooting down enemy fighters, three JU88s, one JU188 and a twin-engine jet. Twenty-four Lancasters failed to return, all from 1 Group, and this represented 10.4% of those dispatched. 101 Squadron avoided the carnage, and welcomed all of its sons back to report fires visible from 150 miles into the homeward journey. A local report

S/L Jimmy Havers and wife (GW).

confirmed the effectiveness of the raid, which produced a serious fire area in the south-western district of Steinbuhl, destroyed the gasworks and left 529 people dead.

Operations continued to come thick and fast, and the next target was also in southern Germany. Hanau's railway system had been attacked in January, and now it was time for an area attack, which was to be carried out by a 1 Group main force of 230 Lancasters, supported as always by a strong Pathfinder element. 101 Squadron made ready twenty aircraft, which, unusually for the period, were required to take off between 00.33 and 00.59 on the 19th, led by S/L Sleight They climbed through layer cloud and set course for the south coast and the Channel, cloud building and dispersing all the way out until 8°E, when the skies cleared, but the ground became obscured by thick haze. The first illuminating flares were seen at H-15, and these were

SR-O en route to Bremen on 23rd March 1945 (GW).

followed immediately by both sky and ground markers. The red and green TIs fell in excellent concentration, standing out clearly through the haze, and, when they had been obliterated by the ensuing bombing at 04.37, the Master Bomber issued instructions to bomb the upwind edge of the smoke. The 101 Squadron crews bombed from 10,000 to 12,500 feet between 04.30 and 04.39, and contributed to a highly effective raid, which destroyed 2,240 houses, devastated the Altstadt, and damaged most of the public buildings. All twenty 101 Squadron aircraft returned safely to land at diversion airfields.

1 Group effectively stood down on the night of the 20/21st, dispatching a few Lancasters to lay mines in northern waters, and eleven others from 101 Squadron to provide ABC cover for a 6 and 8 Group attack on the oil refinery at Hemmingstedt, located near Heide on the Schleswig-Holstein peninsular. They took off between 02.05 and 02.20 led by W/C Gundry-White and S/L Flint, and, apart from a little patchy cloud, flew in clear skies to the target. They arrived to find red and green TIs already on the way down, but no instructions from the Master Bomber until after H-hour. The initial markers were found to be misplaced, but once this was rectified, an accurate and concentrated attack followed, which was punctuated by large explosions between 04.31 and 04.35, accompanied by dense columns of black smoke rising to 8,000 feet. The 101 Squadron participants bombed from 8,500 to 11,000 feet, but mostly from 9,000 feet, between 04.30 and 04.33, and returned safely to report another successful outing.

Above: Two photos from the Bremen attack, showing the perils of bombing in tight formation. Another 101 Sqn Lancaster, SR-T, inadvertently demonstrates how numerous aircraft were lost throughout the war due to being accidentally bombed from above (GW).

1 and 8 Groups joined forces again on the night of the 20/21st to attack the benzol plant in the Bruchstrasse district of Bochum. A force of 131 Lancasters and twelve Mosquitos was made ready, of which twenty of the former represented 101 Squadron. They took off between 00.31 and 01.06, with S/Ls Flint and Sleight the senior pilots on duty. They adopted the southern approach to the Ruhr, via the French coast, and encountered little cloud before reaching the target, where the skies were clear and the ground partially obscured by haze. It was insufficient to conceal the TIs that had been delivered punctually by the Pathfinders, and fell in a concentration close to the marshalling yards, just to the south of the planned aiming-point. Thereafter, an accurate attack developed, which created fires and columns of smoke rising to 6,000 feet as the bombers

turned away. The 101 Squadron crews bombed on the centre of mixed red and green TIs from an average of 17,500 feet between 04.14 and 04.19, and returned home to report fires visible for fifty miles into the return journey.

Elements of 1, 6 and 8 Groups were selected to deliver the only heavy raid of the war on the city of Hildesheim, situated south-east of Hannover and south-west of Brunswick. The aiming-point was to be the marshalling yards, but any major operation at this stage of the war was essentially an area attack. A force of 227 Lancasters and eight Mosquitos was made ready   for the daylight operation on the 22nd, and 70% of the town was laid waste, including 3,300 apartment blocks. 101 Squadron did not take part, but girded its loins in preparation for a daylight attack on a bridge at Bremen in concert with 5 Group on the 23rd. Twenty-four Lancasters were made ready at Ludford Magna as part of a 1 Group total of ninety-three, four of which were to drop Window, and they took off between 06.34 and 07.22 led by S/L Sleight and the recently posted-in S/L Jimmy Havers, a veteran of the 1940 Battle of France, when he flew Fairey Battles with 103 Squadron of the Advanced Air Striking Force. He had continued with 103 Squadron until April 1941, when he was posted to 20 O.T.U at Lossiemouth for instructional duties, and his career thereafter has not been established. The weather outbound and at the target was perfect, with excellent visibility, although a smoke screen was in operation. Fortunately, the wind kept the smoke away from the aiming-point, and the crews were able to identify it without difficulty. The plan had called for the 5 Group element to open proceedings, but they were late arriving, and the 1 Group formation leaders started the ball rolling between 09.59 and 10.02. The main body of the 1 Group contingent attacked between 10.04 and 10.07, the 101 Squadron aircraft doing so from 15,000 to 18,000 feet between 09.59 and 10.06, before returning home confident in the quality of their work. Two of the squadron's Lancasters failed to arrive, and one of them was the veteran, DV245, which had been undertaking either its 119th or 122nd operation. It was hit by flak and exploded, before crashing at 10.00 near Moordeich, some five miles south-west of the centre of Bremen. F/L Paterson, his flight engineer and bomb-aimer, were thrown clear, and parachuted into the arms of their captors, but the remaining four members of the standard crew lost their lives. LL755, which had been on squadron charge for almost a year, was heading home, when it crashed at 10.30 some twenty miles south-south-west of Bremen, killing all seven occupants. The pilot, F/O Little RCAF, was an American from New York State, and he and his crew would the last to have their names inscribed in the squadron Roll of Honour. The two missing Lancasters were the last of 171 aircraft of 101 Squadron to be lost on operations.

Operations on the 25th were directed at urban areas through which enemy reinforcements might pass on their way to the Rhine battle area. Elements of 1, 6 and 8 Groups were handed Hannover, for which a force of 267 Lancasters and eight Mosquitos was made ready. 101 Squadron lined up eighteen Lancasters, which took off between 06.34 and 06.53, with S/L Havers the senior pilot on duty. They climbed out through ten-tenths cloud, before heading to the rendezvous point at Wainfleet, which was found to be cloud-free. F/L Meadows had already abandoned his sortie by then, after his starboard-outer engine failed. The others continued on to find the white stuff building up again half way into the North Sea crossing, but it began to disperse from 06.30°E to leave clear skies in the target area. The crews were able to visually identify the built-up areas, the marshalling yards and the river, and the attack opened with accurate bombing, although the bright sunlight made it impossible to distinguish the colours of the TIs. Eventually smoke obscured the aiming-point, and the Master Bomber instructed bombing to be aimed at the upwind edge. The 101 Squadron crews bombed from 17,000 to 18,000 feet between 09.46 and 09.50, and, as they turned away, smoke could be seen rising to 14,000 feet. They all returned safely to report that all bombs appeared to have fallen with the built-up area of the city.

Norman Westby, Rusty Waughman's bomb aimer, demonstrates the tricks of his trade. The complexity of the bomb sight and computer is quite clear in this photo. The lack of flying clothing suggests that this photograph was posed on the ground (Rusty Waughman).

The encirclement of the Ruhr by American forces required just the capture of the town of Paderborn, situated some thirty-five miles due east of Hamm. A force of 268 Lancasters and eight Mosquitos of 1 and 8 Groups was made ready on the 27th, 101 Squadron contributing twenty-two to the 1 Group main force of 225. They departed Ludford Magna between 14.31 and 15.02 led by S/Ls Havers and Sleight, and, after climbing out, headed for the Dutch coast under fairly clear skies. The cloud built once over enemy territory, and there was complete cover over the target. The Master Bomber was heard calling for skymarkers at 17.25, but the first green smoke-puffs did not appear until five minutes later. The early arrivals were forced to orbit, but the crews following behind, who had been preparing to bomb by H2S and Gee, were able now to use the skymarkers as a more reliable reference, while confirming their accuracy by means of navigational aids. The 101 Squadron crews bombed from 16,000 to 17,000 feet between 17.30 and 17.36, and returned to report a cloud of brown smoke ascending to 2,000 feet above the clouds. The operation was an outstanding success, confirmed by a local report, which stated that three thousand separate fires had occurred, and that the town had been virtually destroyed.

The final operation of the hugely busy penultimate month of offensive activity by the Command, was to end with a 1, 6 and 8 Group raid on the Blohm & Voss U-Boot yards at Hamburg, where the new Type XXI vessels were being assembled. A force of 361 Lancasters and a hundred Halifaxes was made ready on the 31st, 201 of the former provided by 1 Group, of which twenty-two stood ready for departure at Ludford Magna.

254

Two unidentified 101 Sqn Lancasters formate on a daylight sortie (GW).

S/L Sleight was the senior pilot on duty as they took off between 06.16 and 06.40, and climbed out through layer cloud, which persisted until 3°E, when it broke up. F/L Andrews lost his port-outer engine over the North Sea, and jettisoned four 1,000 pounders in an effort to climb above 10,000 feet. This he was unable to do, and bombed a heavy flak battery on the southern tip of Texel at 07.52 before turning back. The others pressed on to find the cloud building again from 6°E, and it remained at ten-tenths the remainder of the way to the target. When the leading aircraft of the main force were fifteen minutes out, the Master Bomber warned them to look for smoke-puff markers, and the first of these appeared at 08.43, but only in small numbers. It was a further three minutes before they became plentiful, by which time the bombing was well underway in accordance with the regular instructions coming through from the Master Bomber. Eighteen of the 101 Squadron crews bombed the main aiming-point from 17,000 to 18,500 feet between 08.43 and 08.49, while F/L Wilder and F/Os Henn and Venning were ordered by the Master Bomber to aim for red smoke-puffs over to starboard. All returned safely, most with the impression that the raid had lacked a degree of concentration, but local reports speak of widespread damage in residential and industrial areas in the south of the city and across the Elbe in Harburg, with energy supplies and communications also being hard-hit. The squadron operated eighteen times during the month, and dispatched 330 sorties for the loss of four Lancasters and crews.

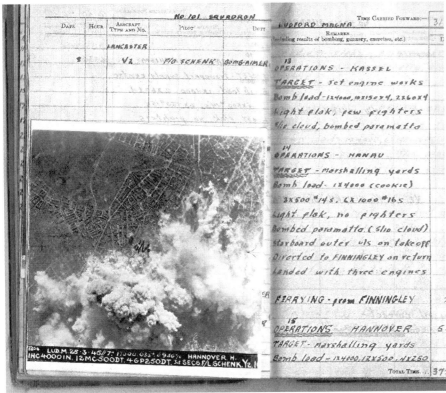

DATE	HOUR	AIRCRAFT TYPE AND No.	PILOT	DUTY
		LANCASTER		
8		V2	F/O SCHENK	BOMB-AIMER

TIME CARRIED FORWARD:— 37:

LUDFORD MAGNA

REMARKS
(Including results of bombing, gunnery, exercise, etc.)

13
OPERATIONS - KASSEL
TARGET - Jet engine works
Bomb load - 1x4000, 10x15ex4, 226ox4
light flak, few fighters
10 cloud, bombed paramatta

14
OPERATIONS - HANAU
TARGET - marshalling yards
Bomb load - 1x4000 (cookie)
3x500 14s, 6x1000 16s
light flak, no fighters
Bombed paramatta (5/10 cloud)
starboard outer u/s on take off
Diverted to FINNINGLEY on return
landed with three engines

FERRYING - from FINNINGLEY

15
OPERATIONS - HANNOVER
TARGET - marshalling yards
Bomb load - 1x4000, 12x500, 4x250

TOTAL TIME 37:

Above: F/O Willard Sawyer and his crew, who had completed 29 ops by the end of hostilities. L to R: F/O Bill Dane, RCAF (navigator), F/S Bernie O'Hallaran, RCAF (mid upper gunner), Sgt Wally Gill (wireless operator), F/L Wilfred Schenk, RCAF (pilot), F/S George Skuce, RCAF (rear gunner), Sgt Fred Davies (flight engineer), F/O Willard Sawyer, RCAF (bomb aimer). Left: Another page from the logbook of F/O Willard Sawyer, with a clear picture of Hannover receiving attention from 101 Sqn. (GW)

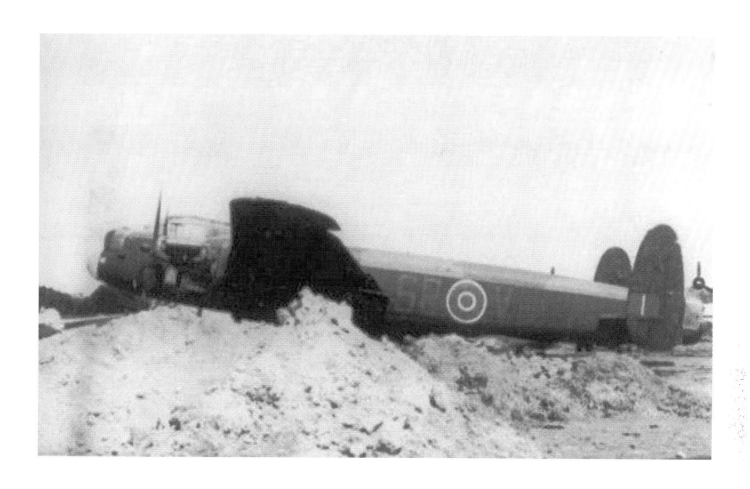

Above: RA597, SR-V, was a latecomer to the squadron, being brought on charge in March 1945. Later operated by 617 and 300 Squadrons, she was struck off charge in 1948.

Left: From late 1944, some squadrons in 1 and 5 Groups were supplied with Lancasters equipped with the Rose Turret. Two 0.5 in Browning M2 machine guns replaced the hitherto ubiquitous 0.303 Brownings. The larger calibre of bullet was considered to be more effective, despite the reduction by two of the number of guns in the rear turret. The turret itself was more spacious and notably open to the freezing air. It was found that the temperature inside the turret, already extremely low, was reduced by only four degrees centigrade. Despite a higher rate of stoppages, the Rose turret was considered to be an improvement on the previous equipment. 400 had entered service with the RAF by the end of the war. (GW)

April 1945

April was a time of mopping up defences, cutting off communications, and finishing off the oil industry, and it began for 1 Group with an operation against what was believed to be a military barracks at Nordhausen, situated 150 miles east of the Ruhr. It was, in fact, a camp for forced workers at the underground secret weapons factory that had been hastily established in caves after Peenemünde. The group provided 210 Lancasters, of which twenty-three belonged to 101 Squadron, and the Pathfinders put up a further thirty-seven and eight Mosquitos. The Ludford Magna gang took off between 13.10 and 13.43, with S/L Jimmy Havers the senior pilot on duty, and flew out over moderate cloud, which thickened as the bomber stream progressed eastwards. By the time the target drew near, there was ten-tenths cloud, and the Master Bomber called the main force down to 8,500 feet at 16.02. Four minutes later, as the bombers approached the cloud tops at around 11,000 feet, the Master Bomber rescinded his original order, and instructed the crews to climb again. This caused confusion, and all semblance of the previously coherent formation was lost. Some futile attempts were made to reform the stream as the Master Bomber called for smoke-puff markers, but these seem to have burst inside the cloud and were not visible. As a last resort, he ordered the crews to "bomb on best navigational aids", and the 101 Squadron crews complied from 12,000 to 14,000 feet between 16.13 and 16.23, without being able to assess the outcome. A single 1 Group crew dropped beneath the cloud base to 5,500 feet, and reported two small fires in the town, but no bombing around the aiming point. F/L West landed LL772 in France after losing an engine on the way home, but the others all arrived back to tell their stories. The target and the town would be attacked again twenty-four hours later by 5 Group, and sustain severe damage. Many friendly foreign nationals would lose their lives in the barracks, while those in the tunnels remained safe from bombs, but endured a hellish existence as they were systematically worked to death.

The night of the 4/5th brought a return to the oil offensive at three sites, Leuna, Harburg and Lutzendorf, and it was for the last-mentioned that 101 Squadron briefed twenty-five crews as part of a 1 and 8 Group force of 258 Lancasters and fourteen Mosquitos. This was one of a cluster of oil refineries, like Leuna, located west of Leipzig, for which the squadron departed Ludford Magna between 21.06 and 21.33, led by S/Ls Flint and Havers. Cloud over England cleared at the south coast, before building up again between 5° and 11°E. It then dispersed again to leave clear skies and good visibility at the target, which was reached after an outward flight of almost four-and-a-half hours. The first Pathfinder ground markers went down at 01.25, and were easily identified by the 101 Squadron crews making their bombing runs at 11,000 to 14,000 feet. They delivered their cookie, ten 500 and two 250 pounders each between 01.28 and 01.38, the later ones on instructions from the Master Bomber to aim at the smoke, which had concealed the T. Is at 01.33. Returning crews reported observing less fire that expected, but a number of large explosions at 01.29, 01.31 and 01.40, accompanied by volumes of thick smoke, suggesting that the attack had been at least moderately effective. In fact the plant had not been decisively damaged, but an attack by 5 Group on the night of the 8/9th would bring an end to all production at the site.

There had not been many extended breaks for the squadron since the start of March, but four days elapsed before the crews were next called to arms on the 9th, this time to carry out an attack on the harbour area at Kiel. Thirty Lancasters were made ready at Ludford Magna, and they were to join a 1, 3 and 8 Group heavy force of 591 of the type. W/C Gundry-White put himself at the top of the Order of Battle, with S/L Flint next, and they took off with the rest of the squadron between 19.28 and 20.11, and headed eastwards across the North Sea. A little cloud was encountered before the enemy coast hove into sight, but the target itself lay under clear skies, with good visibility, and illuminating flares allowed the crews to identify the outline of the fjord and inner harbour. There were two aiming points, and both were well-marked with red TIs, which were backed up by greens. The reds were bombed first, followed by mixed reds and greens, and, finally, greens, before they all became obscured by smoke. The 101 Squadron crews bombed from 12,200 (W/C Gundry-White) to 20,000 feet between 22.32 and 22.41, and, by the end of the attack, the entire area between the aiming-points was on fire, with flames spreading down to the water's edge. A particularly large explosion at 22.35 gave the impression that an ammunition dump had been hit, and thick, black smoke billowing up to a considerable height as the crews turned away, resulted from hits on an oil storage depot. Photo-reconnaissance confirmed the effectiveness of the operation, revealing the Deutsche Werke U-Boot yards to have sustained severe damage, and the other two shipyards had also been hit. The pocket battleship Admiral Scheer had capsized, the Admiral Hipper and the Emden were badly damaged, and adjacent residential districts suffered also.

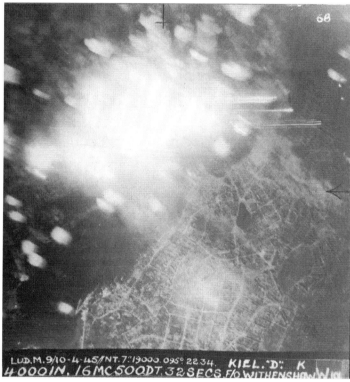

A very clear view of Kiel docks, taken by the bomb aimer in the crew of F/O Withenshaw in SR-W on 9/10th April 1945. Their aircraft was at 19,000 feet; just visible top right is another Lancaster at a much lower altitude (GW).

Twenty-four hours later the target was the railway yards at Plauen, a town in eastern Germany within twenty miles of the Czech frontier. The squadron made ready twenty-five Lancasters as part of a 1 Group main force of 253, and the balance of the heavy brigade of 307 Lancasters was provided by the Pathfinders. S/Ls Flint and Havers were the senior pilots on duty as the 101 Squadron element took off between 18.10 and 18.40, and climbed into clear skies that persisted all the way to the target. The crews were able to visually identify the Weisse Elster River running through the town, and the built-up area to the north where the marshalling yards were located. Illuminating flares and red TIs went down at 23.04, followed by greens three minutes later, and the concentrated bombing that followed soon resulted in the TIs becoming completely obscured by smoke and dust. At 23.10 the Master Bomber instructed the remaining crews to bomb on the centre of the smoke, which was billowing up to 10,000 feet. The 101 Squadron crews bombed from 15,000 to 18,000 feet between 23.08 and 23.15, and returned to report explosions and fires visible for a hundred miles into the return journey. Post-raid reconnaissance confirmed the accuracy of the attack, which resulted in the destruction of 365 acres, or 51% of the town's built-up area.

The final major attack on a German city was directed at Potsdam on the night of the 14/15th, and this would be the first incursion into the Berlin defence zone by RAF heavy bombers since March 1944. A force of five hundred Lancasters from 1, 3 and 8 Groups was made ready, of which twenty-seven proudly carried the SR code. W/C Gundry-White and S/L Sleight were the senior pilots on duty as they departed Ludford Magna between 18.03 and 18.31, and climbed through cloud, which dispersed over the Channel, built-up again over France, but finally disappeared from the Rhine eastwards to leave the target area under clear skies with excellent visibility. The marking commenced six minutes before H-Hour, and, although a little scattered at first, the Master Bomber maintained good control throughout, changing the point of focus as required, and keeping the attack firmly on the aiming-point. The 101 Squadron crews bombed from 17,500 to 20,000 feet between 22.49 and 23.00, and all returned to report many fires and explosions, and an afterglow visible for a hundred miles into the return journey. The raid was confirmed as a success, but some bomb loads spilled into northern and western districts of Berlin.

There were no operations for the squadron over the next three days, and it was early on the 18th when they next assembled in the briefing room to learn that twenty-six of them were to be part of a massive force of 969 aircraft attacking a number of aiming points on the island of Heligoland. The weather for the take-off between 10.20 and 10.45 was excellent, and S/L Sleight led them out over the Lincolnshire coast to join up with the rest of the bomber stream. 1 Group contributed a record 311 Lancasters assigned to two aiming points, the first of which involved the docks and U-Boot pens on the southern end of the Island. The Master Bomber gave a time check at 12.20, before his deputy was heard to report being unable to mark the aiming point. Despite the absence of markers, which would have been obliterated anyway, the whole area erupted under the bombardment, and a few minutes later the northern half received similar treatment. The 101 Squadron crews bombed from 17,000 to 19,000 feet between 12.48 and 12.55, many crews noting a huge explosion, believed to be from an ammunition dump. 617 Squadron was also involved in this operation to deliver Grand Slam and Tallboy "earthquake" bombs, and, as the huge bomber fleet retreated, it left behind a heavily cratered and scarred surface that resembled a moonscape.

As the British XXX Corps moved in on the city of Bremen, Bomber Command was asked to attack enemy strong points in the south-eastern suburbs, where the attack was due to take place in two days' time. 101 Squadron contributed twenty-five Lancasters to a force of 767 aircraft, and they took off in good weather between 15.25 and 15.52 with S/Ls Havers and Sleight the senior pilots on duty. They flew eastwards over cloud, which persisted more or less for the entire outward flight, and, as the first wave approached the target at 17.56, the crews could only catch a glimpse of the ground through gaps. On arrival in the target area, the 1 Group crews found the operation in progress, but heard the Master Bomber's conversation with his deputy confirm that further accurate bombing was not possible under the conditions. Fewer than two hundred aircraft bombed before the Master Bomber called a halt to proceedings, and the entire 1 and 4 Group elements were sent home with their bombs at 18.11.

The final bombing operation of the war to involve 101 Squadron took place on the 25th, when a force of 359 Lancasters of 1, 5 and 8 Groups was dispatched to attack Hitler's 'Eagles Nest' retreat and the nearby SS barracks at Berchtesgaden in the Bavarian mountains. It required an early start, and the twenty-four 101 Squadron participants began taking off at 05.12, with F/O Collett last off the ground at 05.54, on what would be the squadron's final offensive operation of the war. The squadron and flight commanders stayed on the ground, and, no doubt, waved their charges off with a suitable message for them to carry to Adolf, not that he was likely to be at home! P/O Hills had to turn back after three hours because of a failed port-outer engine, while the others pressed on towards southern Germany in good weather conditions. The leading edge of the bomber stream arrived in the target area on time to find that all was not proceeding according to plan. The deputy Master Bomber had been unable to mark the target, and, realising this, the leader of the first wave overshot the final turning point by two-and-a-half minutes, before bringing them back in a wide orbit, which had the

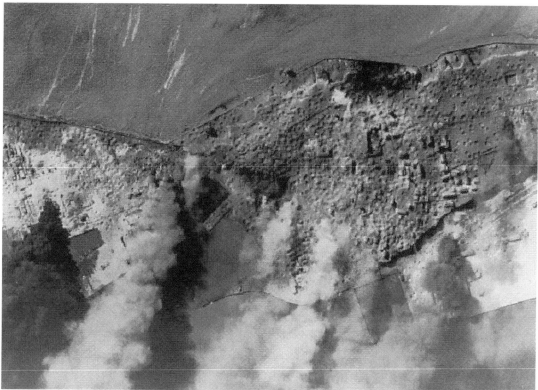

Photos taken before and after the raid on Heligoland of 18th April show the devastation of which Bomber Command was ultimately capable. The port now resembles a moonscape (GW).

Hitler's intended refuge at Berchtesgarten was the target for the squadron's final raid of the war. GW

effect of splitting up the formation, and aircraft began approaching the aiming point from a variety of headings. At 09.45 the Master Bomber ordered the crews to bomb visually if they could, but a minute later a red target indicator went down, which appeared to be accurate, and crews selected whatever was best for them. A concentration of bombs was seen to fall across the SS barracks, and it seems that most fell within the confines of the general target area, causing a column of smoke to rise to 10,000 feet. The 101 Squadron crews bombed from 16,000 to 18,000 feet between 09.48 and 09.57, and returned safely to Ludford Magna after this fitting finale to the bombing war. At 13.52, P/O Phillips RNZAF and crew and Lancaster RE154 had the honour to be the last from 101 Squadron to touch down from an offensive operation.

Operations by other elements of the Command continued during the day and night, beginning with gun batteries on Wangerooge by 4, 6 and 8 Groups in the afternoon, while elements of the "Independent Air Force" went to Tonsberg in Norway that night, to bomb an oil refinery. Then it was all over, and the heavy squadrons' work was done. The humanitarian Operation Exodus began for 101 Squadron on the 27th, when S/Ls Flint and Sleight, F/Os Cairns and Collett and F/Sgt Upcott flew to Brussels and brought back 119 former PoWs to Dunsfold. Sixteen Exodus sorties were carried out by the squadron on the following day, and the first two sorties under Operation Manna, to drop food to the starving Dutch civilians in the enclave still under occupation, were carried out by F/O Collett and F/Sgt Upcott on the 29th. The 30th brought twenty-two Manna sorties, and they would continue until the end of hostilities on the 8th of May, while Exodus would extend for some time into the peace.

Apart from the already mentioned DV245 and DV302, which went on to notch up 121 operations, LL772 also achieved the century milestone, and, likewise, finished on 121. 101 Squadron was a major force in Bomber Command, and completed the war with a record of service which bears comparison with any. Even when 100 Group was established towards the end of 1943, to co-ordinate and carry out the RCM function, 101 Squadron retained its unique role, and even though so tasked, placing its crews more often than most in the firing line, it maintained a fine spirit throughout. This, in itself, is testimony to the quality of its air and ground crews, and the leadership it enjoyed at both squadron and station level. 101 Squadron finished the war with the fourth highest number of sorties in Bomber Command, the second highest number of Lancaster sorties in Bomber Command, the third highest number of Lancaster overall operations in 1 Group, the second highest number of Lancaster sorties in 1 Group, and the fourth highest number of Lancaster operational losses in 1 Group. It was also the only squadron to operate Wellingtons in 2 Group.

Above: Operation Manna was the dropping of desperately-needed food supplies to the Dutch population in remaining pockets of German-occupied territory. It was carried out with the agreement of local German military commanders, whose troops could be seen by low-flying crews, still manning their anti-aircraft guns in case this was a fiendish trick by the Allies. It wasn't, and the Dutch people showed their gratitude for an endeavour which prevented thousands of them from starving. For the crews this was seen as a rewarding way to end their war. Below: For you, Tommy, the war is over... Commencing on 27th April 1945, Operation Exodus saw the repatriation by the RAF of thousands of POWs from France and Belgium after they had been liberated from captivity. In a twist of fate, many returning airmen found themselves being transported by crews from their own squadrons. Lancaster SR-O of 101 Sqn was one of many Lancasters which became de facto troop transports as POWs were released from captivity (GW).

263

And Finally...

A real cause for celebration: the Officers'' Mess at Ludford Magna hosted a celebratory event, probably on VE Day. The photo was contributed by LACW Mary Barber (formerly Bennett), who is in the back row, second from left. The photo has survived the intervening years and was sent to the 101 Squadron Association in September 1991. It is presumed that a good time was had by all! (GW).

On the Ground at Ludford Magna

Left: The library at Ludford Magna. It appears that the staff at the airfield were a studious lot.

Below: A rudimentary NAAFI offered air and ground crews the opportunity for a brew and a cigarette. Note the signs reminding aircrew to empty their pockets before ops of anything that might potentially be of use to the enemy (GW).

Above left: The Ops Room was invariably tense when ops were on. After the departure of the squadron, there was little to do but await any early returns and then the remainder of the squadron. The worst time, inevitably, was after the main body of the squadron had landed and there were aircraft and crews not accounted for.

Above right: 'The Gen Boys?' Not the station's Intelligence Section, but those who were generally deemed to be really in the know: the ground crew.

Left: They also served... A trio of WAAFs relax in a brief moment of peace and quiet.

Below: The Watch Office at Ludford Magna, date unknown (GW).

266

Bomb Loads

The Lancaster was famed for its flexibility as a vehicle for delivering high explosives and incendiaries to the enemy. The composition of each load was dependent on the nature of the target. Area targets, whether residential or industrial, would generally receive an initial dose of high explosive to break open buildings, followed by incendiaries to set the interior of the buildings on fire. As the war went on, some bombs were in short supply as manufacturers could not keep up with Bomber Command's enthusiastic delivery service, and loads became very mixed, increasingly featuring American-produced ordnance. To those on the receiving end, the difference was academic.

Left: This load comprises a 4,000lb 'Cookie' and four 2,000lb bombs.

Below: Along with another cookie, the load comprises a mixture of 1,000lb and 2,000lb bombs.

(GW)

The business end of the Lancaster. A full load of fourteen 1,000lb bombs awaits delivery to an unnamed German customer (GW).

A mixed load; a collection of small bombs, probably 250 lb, along with a 4,000lb 'Cookie' (GW).

Nose Artwork

Crews often regarded aircraft as individuals, especially the ground crews, who considered that they 'owned' their assigned aeroplane and had to pander to their particular mechanical foibles. Personalising the bombers usually took the form of tallies, in the form of a bomb symbol for each successful sortie (typically, trips to Italian targets were celebrated with the painting of an ice cream cone). Many aircraft were named by their crews, or otherwise adorned with images. Often these were of the female form but many were more in tune with the gallows humour of the service, or conveyed a message of vengeance on the Nazi regime. Those depicted here are a few of 101 Sqn's personalised Lancasters. Many other such images are shown throughout this book, so are not replicated here (GW).

271

Members of 101 Squadron Not Featured in this Profile

Above: Air gunners 'Swift' and 'Brown'. The airman on the right is a Flight Lieutenant.
Below: Sgt Williams, Navigator, sitting on an 8,000lb 'blockbuster' (GW)

Above: Two photos of the Lloyd crew. Below left: F/Sgt L Airey.
Below right: F/Sgt Arthur Hamer (GW).

Rogues' Gallery

Photos of unidentified members of 101 Squadron. If you can identify anyone in these photographs and provide information about their time with 101 Sqn, please contact the publisher (bombercommandbooks@gmail.com)

276

101 Squadron

Motto: **Mens Agitat Molem** (Mind over matter)   Code **SR**

Stations

West Raynham	06.05.39. to 06.07.41.
Manston (Detachment)	24.04.41. to 09.05.41.
Oakington	06.07.41. to 11.02.42.
Bourn	11.02.42. to 11.08.42.
Stradishall	11.08.42. to 29.09.42.
Holme-on-Spalding-Moor	29.09.42. to 15.06.43.
Ludford Magna	15.06.43. to 01.10.45.

Commanding Officers

Wing Commander J H HARGROVES	01.04.39. to 05.07.40.
Wing Commander N C SINGER	05.07.40. to 31.03.41.
Wing Commander D ADDENBROOKE	31.03.41. to 04.04.41.
Wing Commander J McDOUGALL	04.04.41. to 05.05.41.
Wing Commander D R BIGGS	16.05.41. to 14.01.42.
Wing Commander T H L NICHOLLS	14.01.42. to 01.06.42.
Wing Commander E C EATON DFC	01.06.42. to 26.01.43.
Wing Commander D A REDDICK DFC AFC	26.01.43. to 27.07.43.
Wing Commander G A CAREY-FOSTER DFC	27.07.43. to 18.01.44.
Wing Commander R I ALEXANDER DFC	18.01.44. to 31.07.44.
Wing Commander M H De L EVEREST	31.07.44. to 21.01.45.
Wing Commander I M GUNDRY-WHITE DFC	21.01.45. to 12.04.46.

Aircraft

Blenheim IV	04.39. to 05.41.
Wellington 1C	04.41. to 10.42.
Wellington III	02.42. to 10.42.
Lancaster I/III	10.42. to 08.46.

CREW MEMBERS KILLED IN ACTION   1094

CREW MEMBERS CAPTURED   178

Operational Record

OPERATIONS	SORTIES	AIRCRAFT LOSSES	% LOSSES
539	6766	171	2.5

	BOMBING	MINING	
	512	27	

BLENHEIM

OPERATIONS	SORTIES	AIRCRAFT LOSSES	% LOSSES
81	618	15	2.4

WELLINGTON

OPERATIONS	SORTIES	AIRCRAFT LOSSES	% LOSSES
150	1253	43	3.4

	BOMBING	MINING	
	133	8	

LANCASTER

OPERATIONS	SORTIES	AIRCRAFT LOSSES	% LOSSES
308	4895	113	2.3

	BOMBING	MINING	
	298	10	

2 GROUP (ALL AIRCRAFT TYPES)

OPERATIONS	SORTIES	AIRCRAFT LOSSES	% LOSSES
88	673	15	2.2

BLENHEIM

OPERATIONS	SORTIES	AIRCRAFT LOSSES	% LOSSES
81	618	15	2.4

2 GROUP WELLINGTON

OPERATIONS	SORTIES	AIRCRAFT LOSSES	% LOSSES
8	66	0	0.0

3 GROUP WELLINGTON

OPERATIONS	SORTIES	AIRCRAFT LOSSES	% LOSSES
135	1161	42	3.6

BOMBING	MINING
122	13

1 GROUP (ALL AIRCRAFT TYPES)

OPERATIONS	SORTIES	AIRCRAFT LOSSES	% LOSSES
316	4932	114	2.3

BOMBING	MINING
302	14

WELLINGTON

OPERATIONS	SORTIES	AIRCRAFT LOSSES	% LOSSES
9	37	0	0.0

BOMBING	MINING
4	5

LANCASTER

OPERATIONS	SORTIES	AIRCRAFT LOSSES	% LOSSES
308	4895	113	2.3

BOMBING	MINING
298	10

Aircraft Histories

BLENHEIM.   **To May 1941.**

L4809	Crashed on landing during air-firing exercise 2.11.39.
L4887	Crash-landed near Lichfield while training 20.11.39.
L4888	To 35Sqn.
L4889	To 35Sqn.
L4891	To 35Sqn.
L4892	To 35Sqn.
L4893	To 107Sqn.
L4894	To 35Sqn.
L4895	To 35Sqn.
L4896	To 17 OTU.
L4897	To Far East.
L4898	To 35Sqn.
L4899	To 86Sqn.
L4900	To 35Sqn.
L4901	To 8Sqn.
L4902	To 51 OTU.
L8870	To 110Sqn and back. Crashed in Hampshire on return from St Malo 26.8.40.
L9250	Crashed on landing at Wittering while training 8.8.40.
L9257	To 2 Group Training Flight.
L9258	Crashed in Norfolk during transit flight 12.6.40.
L9268	From 57Sqn. To 82Sqn.
L9419	FTR from attacks on airfields in occupied territory 19/20.8.40.
L9420	To 8Sqn.
L9421	To 90Sqn.
N3545	To 2 Gp TF.
N3552	From 18Sqn. FTR Brest 3/4.4.41.
N3553	From 18Sqn. To 82Sqn.
N3570	From 40Sqn. Crashed on the beach near Boston while training 2.2.41.
N3574	From 21Sqn. Ditched off Suffolk coast on return from Hamstede 9/10.9.40.
N3616	To 13Sqn.
N6140	FTR Kiel Canal 5.7.40.
N6141	To 13 Gp CF.
N6142	To 5BGS.
N6143	To 5BGS.
N6165 SR-S	Crashed in Norfolk while training 7.3.40.
N6166	From 107Sqn via 35Sqn. To 110Sqn and back via 21Sqn. To 18Sqn.
N6174	From 107Sqn via 35Sqn. FTR Cherbourg 25.7.40.
N6175	From 107Sqn via 35Sqn. Lost 9.7.40. Details uncertain.
N6176	From 107Sqn. Force-landed in Huntingdonshire while training 9.7.40.
N6177	From 107Sqn. To 15Sqn.
N6178	From 107Sqn. Crashed on landing at West Raynham while training 12.1.40.

N6181	From 107Sqn via 35Sqn. To 13 OTU.
N6182 SR-Z	From 107Sqn via 35Sqn. To 139Sqn and back. To 17 OTU.
N6236	From 139Sqn via Wyton. Crashed on approach to West Raynham on return from Wanne-Eickel 23.11.40.
N6238	FTR Hamburg 24/25.11.40.
P4912	From 35Sqn. Crashed near Oxford while training 6.6.40.
P6905	From 35Sqn. FTR from shipping strike 25.9.40.
P6906 SR-K	From 35Sqn. To 13 OTU.
P6908 SR-D	From 35Sqn. To 235Sqn.
P6924	FTR from attacks on invasion ports 18/19.7.40.
P6925	To 110Sqn.
P6953	Crashed in Sussex during operation to Mannheim 16/17.12.40.
P6955	FTR Boulogne 8/9.9.40.
R2788	FTR Boulogne 8/9.9.40.
R3617	To 2 Gp TF.
R3618	To 82Sqn.
R3619	To 82Sqn.
R3689	From 40Sqn. To 60Sqn.
R3752	From 18Sqn. To 54 OTU.
R3801	From 18Sqn. To 107Sqn.
R3803	To 82Sqn.
R3830 SR-V	From 57Sqn. To 82Sqn.
R3845	To Lorraine.
R3846	FTR Wilhelmshaven 18/19.3.41.
T1825 SR-Y	FTR from shipping strike off Boulogne 3.5.41.
T1866	Collided with Blenheim L9250 (101Sqn) after landing at Wittering during training 8.8.43.
T2034	From 18Sqn. Destroyed in air raid at Great Massingham 27.10.40.
T2039	FTR Mannheim 16/17.12.40.
T2047	To 107Sqn.
T2060	Crashed in the Channel 27.8.40.
T2161	To 139Sqn.
T2187	From 18Sqn. To Middle East (missing on flight).
T2234 SR-H	FTR from shipping strike off Boulogne 3.5.41.
T2246	From 18Sqn. Crashed in Lincolnshire during an operation to NW Germany 30.10.40.
T2281	From 139Sqn. Crashed on landing at St Eval on return from Brest 30/31.3.41.
T2437	To 21Sqn.
T2439	Crashed in Dorset on return from Brest 3/4.4.41.
V5460	To 139Sqn.
V5461	To Malta.
V5493 SR-G	FTR from shipping strike off Calais 28.4.41.
V5595	To 21Sqn.
V5651	To 21Sqn.
V5876	From 3SGR. To 82Sqn.
V6034	To 21Sqn.

V6195 SR-B	To 107Sqn.
V6226 SR-C	To 82Sqn.
Z5744	To 18Sqn.
Z5800	To 110Sqn.
Z5801	Abandoned over Devon on return from Mannheim 17.12.40.

WELLINGTON.   **From April 1941 to October 1942**.

L7869 SR-P	From 214Sqn. To 29 OTU.
N2768	From 99Sqn. To 23 OTU.
R1088 SR-O	Crashed in Kent on return from Hamburg 3.8.41.
R1219 SR-R	From 115Sqn. FTR Cologne 10/11.10.41.
R1338	From 40Sqn. To 25 OTU.
R1505	From 115Sqn. To 214Sqn.
R1699 SR-D	From 105Sqn. FTR Turin 10/11.9.41.
R1700 SR-X	To 18 OTU.
R1701 SR-K	FTR Berlin 7/8.11.41.
R1702 SR-F	FTR Brest 24.7.41.
R1703 SR-J	FTR Cologne 31.8/1.9.41.
R1778 SR-G	FTR Hamburg 30.11/1.12.41.
R1780 SR-B/U	Took part in the squadron's first Wellington sortie, against Rotterdam docks, 11/12.6.41. To 11 OTU.
R1781 SR-C	To 12 OTU.
R1800 SR-T	FTR Hamburg 2/3.8.41.
R1801 SR-U	To 419Sqn.
R3295 SR-P	From 99Sqn. FTR Hamburg 30.11/1.12.41.
T2846 SR-S	From 149Sqn. FTR Düsseldorf 13/14.10.41.
T2963 SR-R	
W5715 SR-N	To 301Sqn and back. FTR Kiel 19/20.8.41.
W5716	Took part in squadron's first Wellington operation, against Rotterdam docks 11/12.6.41. To 99Sqn.
X3206 SR-H	To 214Sqn.
X3226	From 9Sqn. Returned to 9Sqn.
X3277	From 419Sqn. To ECU.
X3285 SR-R	From 9Sqn. To 57Sqn.
X3312 SR-U	FTR Duisburg 21/22.7.42.
X3356 SR-P	FTR Hamburg 17/18.4.42.
X3366 SR-H	To 23 OTU.
X3368	To 29 OTU.
X3391 SR-A	From 115Sqn. FTR Nuremberg 28/29.8.42.
X3407	From 9Sqn. To 150Sqn.
X3424	From 9Sqn. To 23 OTU.
X3447	From 115Sqn. Returned to 115Sqn.
X3455 SR-V	From 156Sqn. To 142Sqn.
X3457 SR-R	From 9Sqn. FTR from mining sortie 21/22.9.42.
X3464	From 75Sqn. To 115Sqn.

X3472 SR-D	From 115Sqn. FTR Mannheim 19/20.5.42.
X3473 SR-S	FTR Bremen 3/4.6.42.
X3475	From 156Sqn. To 9Sqn.
X3541 SR-E	From 419Sqn. To 18 OTU.
X3547 SR-P	
X3559	FTR Nuremberg 28/29.8.42.
X3634 SR-T	FTR Wilhelmshaven 8/9.7.42.
X3642 SR-G	From 115Sqn. Crashed on landing at Oakington on return from Essen 10.3.42.
X3647 SR-N	To 115Sqn.
X3648 SR-M	To 425Sqn.
X3649	From 9Sqn. Ditched off Hull following early return from Kassel 27.8.42.
X3650 SR-B	To 27 OTU.
X3651 SR-Z	Crashed on landing at Bourn while training 15.3.42.
X3654 SR-K	FTR Osnabrück 17/18.8.42.
X3655 SR-V	FTR Hamburg 17/18.4.42.
X3656 SR-L	FTR Essen 8/9.3.42.
X3657 SR-Q	Crash-landed at Martlesham Heath on return from Kassel 28.8.42.
X3663	Crashed in Berkshire while training 26.2.42.
X3668 SR-G	Crashed in Cambridgeshire after a collision with 101Sqn CF Stirling N6121 en-route to Hamburg 28.7.42.
X3669 SR-H	FTR Emden 19/20.6.42.
X3670 SR-F	FTR Cologne 30/31.5.42.
X3694 SR-U	FTR Dortmund 15/16.4.42.
X3695	From 156Sqn. To 9Sqn.
X3701 SR-X	FTR Rostock 23/24.4.42.
X3709 SR-J	FTR from mining sortie 2.4.42.
X3753 SR-C	To 29 OTU.
X3754 SR-R	FTR Nuremberg 28/29.8.42.
X3812	To 142Sqn and back via 12Sqn. To 199Sqn.
X3815	FTR from mining sortie 21/22.9.42.
X3960	To 142Sqn.
X3965	To 150Sqn.
X9601 SR-V	Crashed soon after take-off from Bourn while training 18.11.41.
X9806 SR-A	To 75Sqn.
X9818	To 16 OTU.
X9819 SR-V	To 419Sqn.
X9828 SR-K	FTR Frankfurt 24/25.10.41.
X9920 SR-F	To 419Sqn.
X9922	Crashed in Northamptonshire on return from Ostend 20.9.41.
Z1080	To 156Sqn.
Z1081	From 40Sqn. To 214Sqn.
Z1090	To 99Sqn.
Z1095	To 419Sqn.
Z1110	From 311Sqn. FTR Emden 20/21.1.42.
Z1115	FTR Düsseldorf 27/28.12.41.
Z1146	To 419Sqn.

Z1148	To 214Sqn.
Z1569 SR-Z	From 57Sqn. Destroyed by fire after landing at Waterbeach following an operation to Essen 13.4.42.
Z1594	FTR Frankfurt 24/25.8.42.
Z1612 SR-Z	From 156Sqn. FTR Cologne 30/31.5.42.
Z1625 SR-H	To 150Sqn.
Z1658	From 9Sqn. Damaged beyond repair in accident at Bourn 6.8.42.
Z1661 SR-F	To 150Sqn.
Z1662 SR-D	To 16 OTU.
Z1726	To 142Sqn.
Z1748	To 12Sqn.
Z1751	FTR from mining sortie 11/12.7.42.
Z8373	To 214Sqn.
Z8716 SR-D	
Z8840	To 150Sqn.
Z8842 SR-T	To 214Sqn.
Z8854	From 9Sqn. To 75Sqn.
Z8860	Crashed in Cambridgeshire during an operation to Hamburg 30/31.8.41.
Z8891	To 214Sqn.
BJ581	From 57Sqn. To 142Sqn.
BJ583 SR-P	FTR from mining sortie 11/12.7.42.
BJ590 SR-H	FTR Hamburg 26/27.7.42.
BJ606	From 9Sqn. To 12Sqn.
BJ659 SR-T	To 23 OTU.
BJ689 SR-O	FTR Saarbrücken 19/20.9.42.
BJ698 SR-U	FTR Kassel 27/28.8.42.
BJ705	From 57Sqn. To 142Sqn.
BJ711	From 57Sqn. To 142Sqn.
BJ715	To 196Sqn.
BJ768 SR-U	To 142Sqn.
BJ769	FTR Duisburg 6/7.9.42.
BJ796	To 115Sqn.
BJ797	To 115Sqn.
BJ841 SR-B	FTR Düsseldorf 31.7/1.8.42.
BJ844 SR-C	Ditched in the North Sea on return from Osnabrück 17/18.8.42.
BJ847	To 16 OTU.
BJ891	FTR Bremen 4/5.9.42.
BJ897	FTR Essen 16/17.9.42.
BJ961	To 150Sqn.
BJ972	To 150Sqn.
BJ991	To 199Sqn.
BK298	To 142Sqn.
BK299	To 142Sqn.
BK309	To 150Sqn.
BK310	To 150Sqn.
BK311	To 150Sqn.

DV507	To 156Sqn.
DV509	To 419Sqn.

STIRLING **Conversion Flight only. Oakington. From 1.6.42. to 1.10.42.**

N3670	From 7Sqn. To 1657CU.
N6006	From 7Sqn. To 4STT.
N6032	From 7Sqn CF. To 1651CU.
N6039	From 7Sqn. To 1657CU
N6075	From 7Sqn. Crashed in Derbyshire while training 13.7.42.
N6086	From XVSqn. To 1651CU.
N6121 SR-W	From 7Sqn. Collided with Wellington X3668 (101Sqn) over Cambridgeshire while training 28.7.42.
R9303	From 214Sqn CF. To 218Sqn CF.
W7440	From 7Sqn. To 1657CU.
W7447	From 1651CU. To 1657CU.

LANCASTER. **From October 1942.**

R5482 SR-Q	From 97Sqn. Took part in squadron's first Lancaster operation. Crashed while landing at Holme-on-Spalding Moor on return from an air-test 20.12.42.
R5507	From 1660CU. To 1656CU.
W4231	From 83Sqn via 1662CU and 1667CU. To 1LFS.
W4275 SR-A/C	Took part in squadron's first Lancaster operation. FTR Cologne 8/9.7.43.
W4276 SR-D	Took part in squadron's first Lancaster operation. To 207Sqn.
W4309 SR-B	Took part in squadron's first Lancaster operation. To 1667CU.
W4311 SR-F/O	FTR Wuppertal 24/25.6.43.
W4312 SR-H	Crashed on landing at Holme-on-Spalding-moor on return from air-test 23.12.43.
W4313 SR-G	FTR Wilhelmshaven 11/12.2.43.
W4319 SR-N	Took part in squadron's first Lancaster operation. Crashed in North Yorkshire after being engaged by friendly AA fire while on return from a mining sortie 17.12.42.
W4321 SR-P	From 1656CU. First off on the squadron's first Lancaster operation. FTR Berlin 17/18.1.43.
W4322 SR-O	Took part in squadron's first Lancaster operation. To 460Sqn and back. FTR Berlin 27/28.3.43.
W4324 SR-M	FTR Hanover 22/23.9.43.
W4326 SR-C	No operations. Crashed in Wales while training 16.11.42.
W4779	To 1656CU.
W4782 SR-J	Took part in squadron's first Lancaster operation. FTR from mining sortie 8/9.12.42.
W4784 SR-E	FTR Dortmund 4/5.5.43.
W4796 SR-R	FTR Essen 4/5.1.43.
W4833 SR-C	From 100Sqn. To 625Sqn.
W4851	From 156Sqn. To 1656CU.
W4862 SR-E	FTR Essen 12/13.3.43.
W4863 SR-G	Crashed on approach to Holme-on-Spalding-Moor on return from Dortmund 23/24.5.43.

W4882		From 156Sqn. To 1662CU.
W4888 SR-Z/P		FTR Dortmund 4/5.5.43.
W4889 SR-Z		To 1656CU.
W4919 SR-A		FTR Dortmund 23/24.5.43.
W4923 SR-N/N2/N-		Damaged beyond repair during operation to Mannheim 23/24.9.43.
W4951 SR-O/P		FTR Stuttgart 14/15.4.43.
W4966 SR-F/G²		To 166Sqn.
W4967 SR-P		From 626Sqn. FTR Courtrai 20/21.7.44.
W4993 SR-X		To 625Sqn.
W4995 SR-N		To 625Sqn.
W4996 SR-G/G²		To 166Sqn.
W4997 SR-E		To 5MU May 44.
W5009 SR-Z		To 625Sqn.
DV194 SR-V		To 625Sqn.
DV230 SR-T		From SIU. FTR Hanover 18/19.10.43.
DV231 SR-A		From SIU. FTR Berlin 27/28.1.44.
DV236 SR-G		FTR Berlin 15/16.2.44.
DV245 SR-S		FTR Bremen (119th op) 23.3.45.
DV264 SR-L		FTR Nuremberg, shot down by Halifax 30/31.3.44.
DV265 SR-F		FTR Düsseldorf 3/4.11.43.
DV266 SR-U		FTR Hanover 18/19.10.43.
DV267 SR-K		FTR Leipzig 19/20.2.44.
DV268 SR-O/O²		FTR Berlin 26/27.11.43.
DV269 SR-M		FTR Berlin 2/3.1.44.
DV270 SR-E		Crashed in Lincolnshire while training 5.12.43.
DV275 SR-X²		To 463Sqn and back. FTR Mailly-le-Camp 3/4.5.44
DV276 SR-R		FTR Nuremberg 30/31.3.44.
DV283 SR-P		From 44Sqn. Abandoned over Lincolnshire on return from Berlin 17.12.43.
DV285 SR-Q		FTR Berlin 26/27.11.43.
DV287 SR-N		FTR Brunswick 14/15.1.44.
DV288 SR-D/Q		FTR Aulnoye 10/11.4.44.
DV289 SR-T		FTR Berlin 26/27.11.43.
DV290 SR-X		From SIU. Crashed at USAAF Welford on return from Nuremberg 30/31.3.44.
DV291 SR-V		From SIU via 32MU. Crashed on take-off from Ludford Magna when bound for Berlin 22.11.43.
DV292 SR-Y/E/O		From SIU. FTR Brunswick 12/13.8.44.
DV298 SR-E/I/J		FTR Gelsenkirchen/Dahlbusch 14.3.45.
DV299 SR-K²		FTR Berlin 16/17.12.43.
DV300 SR-W		FTR Berlin 16/17.12.43.
DV301 SR-F/Y		FTR Vierzon 30.6/1.7.44.
DV302 SR-J/H		Completed 121 operations. To 46MU.
DV303 SR-U		FTR Berlin 30/31.1.44.
DV304 SR-X		To 61Sqn.
DV307 SR-Z		FTR Berlin 1/2.1.44.
DV308 SR-V		FTR Berlin 1/2.1.44.
DV389 SR-P/X		FTR Aachen 24/25.5.44.

DV407 SR-R/R²/V²   To 46MU.
ED317 SR-Q   From 1656CU. To 100Sqn.
ED320 SR-R/U   From 57Sqn. Destroyed in landing accident at Ford on return from Milan 13.8.43.
ED321 SR-D/E/K   To 625Sqn.
ED322 SR-T   Crashed off Welsh coast on return from Mannheim 6/7.12.42.
ED327 SR-C/D/O/O²   To 166Sqn.
ED328 SR-S   FTR Berlin 23/24.8.43.
ED370 SR-B/D/J   To 103Sqn.
ED372 SR-E/H/K   From 83Sqn. To 166Sqn.
ED373 SR-T/K   FTR Gelsenkirchen 25/26.6.43.
ED374 SR-Z   Crash-landed at Holme-on-Spalding-Moor on return from Lorient 17.2.43.
ED375 SR-V   FTR St Nazaire 22/23.3.43.
ED377 SR-X/O/Q   FTR from mining sortie 27/28.6.43.
ED379 SR-F/L   FTR Pilsen 16/17.4.43.
ED380   To 103Sqn.
ED382 SR-J/J²   To 625Sqn.
ED410 SR-X-/X²   FTR Berlin 3/4.9.43.
ED422 SR-E/E2/H   To 166Sqn.
ED433 SR-F   To 44Sqn.
ED443 SR-B   FTR Essen 21/22.1.43.
ED446 SR-N   Crashed on beach near Hornsea during air-test 20.3.43.
ED447 SR-Q   FTR Hamburg 30/31.1.43.
ED552 SR-Q   Crashed in Yorkshire while training 29.3.43.
ED608 SR-T   FTR Duisburg 9/10.4.43.
ED618 SR-X/X-   FTR Duisburg 9/10.4.43.
ED623   From 626Sqn. To 1LFS.
ED650 SR-L   FTR Krefeld 21/22.6.43.
ED659 SR-T   FTR Berlin 3/4.9.43.
ED660 SR-U-/V   FTR Düsseldorf 25/26.5.43.
ED697 SR-V   FTR Cologne 8/9.7.43.
ED728 SR-Y   FTR from mining sortie 27/28.4.43.
ED736 SR-W   FTR Essen 3/4.4.43.
ED775 SR-Z   Crash on approach to Coltishall on return from Dortmund 24.5.43.
ED776 SR-U-   Crashed while landing at Holme-on-Spalding-Moor on return from Dortmund 5.5.43.
ED807 SR-X   Crashed while landing at Holme-on-Spalding-Moor following early return from Spezia 13/14.4.43.
ED809 SR-W   To 625Sqn.
ED830 SR-X   Crashed on approach to Holme-on-Spalding-Moor on return from Dortmund 5.5.43.
ED835 SR-T   Crashed on approach to Holme-on-Spalding-Moor on return from Dortmund 5.5.43.
ED841 SR-R   From 156Sqn. To 166Sqn.
ED951 SR-P   To 625Sqn.
ED987 SR-A-   FTR Bochum 12/13.6.43.
EE137 SR-U/A   To 166Sqn.
EE182   To 103Sqn.
EE192 SR-Y   FTR Berlin 23/24.8.43.

JA715 SR-M²/C	From 156Sqn. Collided with ME863 and crashed in France during operation to Ludwigshafen 1/2.2.45.	
JA863 SR-U²	FTR Hamburg 27/28.7.43.	
JA926 SR-A	FTR Mannheim 5/6.9.43.	
JA928	To 83Sqn.	
JA965 SR-K²	From SIU. Shot down by intruder near Wickenby on return from Hanover 28.9.43.	
JA977 SR-J	From SIU. FTR Mannheim 23/24.9.43.	
JB128 SR-U²	FTR Berlin 2/3.12.43.	
JB142 SR-Y	To 166Sqn.	
JB149 SR-R²	FTR Berlin 3/4.9.43.	
JB150 SR-S/P²	FTR Berlin 31.8/1.9.43.	
JB151 SR-H	To 166Sqn.	
JB718 SR-Q	From 12Sqn.	
LL750 SR-P	FTR Friedrichshafen 27/28.4.44.	
LL751 SR-F	FTR Evreux 11/12.6.44.	
LL755 SR-R/R²/U	FTR Bremen 23.3.45.	
LL756 SR-Z/Q	Crashed on landing at Ludford Magna on return from Le Havre 6.9.44.	
LL757 SR-W	FTR Stettin 29/30.8.44.	
LL758 SR-A	FTR Saarbrücken 5/6.10.44.	
LL771 SR-L/S/Y	FTR Breskens 11.10.44.	
LL772 SR-R/R²	From 626Sqn.	
LL773 SR-U/D	Crashed at Woodbridge on return from Sterkrade 17.6.44.	
LL774 SR-U	FTR Duisburg 14/15.10.44.	
LL779 SR-V	FTR Homberg 20/21.7.44.	
LL829 SR-J/A	From 626Sqn.	
LL832 SR-K²	FTR Nuremberg 30/31.3.44.	
LL833 SR-O	Ditched in the Channel during D-Day support operation 6.6.44.	
LL849 SR-O	From 626Sqn. Crashed near Lichfield while training 12.8.44.	
LL860 SR-R/I	FTR Schweinfurt 26/27.4.44.	
LL861 SR-H	FTR Nuremberg 30/31.3.44.	
LL862 SR-L/K	FTR Homberg 20/21.7.44.	
LL863 SR-H/M	FTR Vierzon 30.6/1.7.44.	
LM161 SR-E/F		
LM312 SR-U	To 166sqn.	
LM318 SR-Y	FTR Gelsenkirchen 25/26.6.43.	
LM325 SR-J/U-	FTR Mülheim 22/23.6.43.	
LM341 SR-L	To 166sqn.	
LM363 SR-P	FTR Berlin 2/3.12.43.	
LM364 SR-N²	FTR Berlin 2/3.12.43.	
LM365 SR-H	From SIU. FTR Düsseldorf 3/4.11.43.	
LM367 SR-C	From SIU. FTR Brunswick 14/15.1.44.	
LM368 SR-B	To 467Sqn.	
LM369 SR-I/W	To 1656CU.	
LM370 SR-K²	FTR Berlin 18/19.11.43.	
LM371 SR-T	FTR Berlin 29/30.12.43.	

An unidentified crew pose alongside LM457 in her time as SR-G (GW).

LM387 SR-O   FTR Berlin 20/21.1.44.
LM389 SR-Y   Crashed in Yorkshire on return from Berlin 17.12.43.
LM395 SR-Q   FTR Dortmund 22/23.5.44.
LM417 SR-S/A   FTR Mailly-le-Camp 3/4.5.44.
LM457 SR-A/G/V²   SOC 2.1.45.
LM459 SR-K   FTR Bourg Leopold 27/28.5.44.
LM462 SR-V²   FTR Stuttgart 28/29.7.44.
LM463 SR-N²/K   FTR Nuremberg 30/31.3.44.
LM464 SR-U²/E   Crashed in Suffolk on return from Frankfurt 18/19.3.44.
LM467 SR-Z/J   FTR Mailly-le-Camp 3/4.5.44.
LM472 SR-T/V²   From 626Sqn. FTR Brüx 16/17.1.45.
LM474 SR-N²/X²   FTR Sterkrade 16/17.6.44.
LM479 SR-C/F   FTR Stettin 29/30.8.44.
LM493 SR-X   FTR Friedrichshafen 27/28.4.44.
LM508 SR-P   FTR Wesseling 21/22.6.44.
LM596   To 626Sqn.

One of a number of Lancasters that bore the squadron code SR-D. The serial number cannot be discerned, but this aircraft was on charge in late 1943 / early 1944 (Rusty Waughman).

LM598 SR-M²   FTR Brunswick 12/13.8.44.
LM755 SR-N   FTR Dortmund 29.11.44.
ME305 SR-N/N²
ME310 SR-Z/X
ME419 SR-V²
ME494 SR-I
ME517 SR-M
ME518 SR-P
ME558 SR-Q   FTR Stuttgart 15/16.3.44.
ME564 SR-J/Z   FTR Mailly-le-Camp 3/4.5.44.
ME565 SR-W/Q   FTR Foret de Cerisy 7/8.6.44.
ME566 SR-S/X   FTR Brunswick 14/15.1.44.
ME590 SR-C   To 1651CU.
ME592 SR-T/D   FTR Stettin 29/30.8.44.
ME613 SR-L²/M²   FTR Wesseling 21/22.6.44.
ME616 SR-B   FTR Vierzon 30.6/1.7.44.
ME617 SR-N   FTR Rüsselsheim 12/13.8.44.
ME618 SR-J   FTR Nuremberg 30/31.3.44.
ME619 SR-U   FTR Düsseldorf 22/23.4.44.
ME837 SR-L

ME847 SR-D	To 300Sqn.
ME857 SR-C	FTR Rüsselsheim 25/26.8.44.
ME863 SR-I/K	Collided with JA715 (101Sqn) and crashed in France during operation to Ludwigshafen 1/2.2.45.
ME865 SR-X/K	FTR Bochum 4/5.11.44.
ND983 SR-D/B	Crashed while landing at Ludford Magna on return from Le Havre 6.9.44.
NF924 SR-C	Crash-landed at Ludford Magna 4.1.45.
NF933 SR-L²	
NF936 SR-F	FTR Bochum 4/5.11.44.
NF954 SR-W	Crashed at Ludford Magna 21.3.45.
NF982	FTR Neuss 23/24.9.44.
NF983 SR-D/B	Collided with another aircraft over the sea while bound for Neuss 23/24.9.44.
NG128 SR-B	
NG129 SR-Z	
NG131 SR-M²/W	FTR Ulm 17/18.12.44.
NG139 SR-W²	
NG402 SR-C	
NG405 SR-L	
NN705 SR-O	FTR Rüsselsheim 25/26.8.44.
NX569 SR-W	
NX572 SR-S	
NX575 SR-U	
NX579	
NX609 SR-S/A/A²	
NX610 SR-F2	
PA237 SR-R/V	FTR Pforzheim 23/24.2.45.
PA238 SR-Z/Z²	
PA281 SR-J	
PB237 SR-M	FTR St Vith 26.12.44.
PB256 SR-P	FTR Ludwigshafen 1/2.2.45.
PB258 SR-V	FTR Brunswick 12/13.8.44.
PB350 SR-G	
PB399 SR-T/J	
PB456	Crashed in Scotland on exercise 13.9.44.
PB457 SR-V	Destroyed by fire during maintenance at Ludford Magna 3.2.45.
PB573	From 170Sqn. Returned to 170Sqn.
PB634 SR-U	FTR Bonn 28/29.12.44.
PB671 SR-M	FTR Dortmund 20/21.2.45.
PB673 SR-V/Y	From 626Sqn. To BCIS.
PB692 SR-K²	From 626Sqn. FTR Gelsenkirchen 6.11.44.
PB748 SR-Y	From 150Sqn.
PB788 SR-E/E²	
PB800 SR-N	
PD268 SR-O	FTR Dessau 7/8.3.45.
PD396 SR-O/A	
RA523 SR-I	FTR Pforzheim 23/24.2.45.

RA595 SR-Q
RA597 SR-V
RE138 SR-W/D²
RE154 SR-X²   The last Lancaster to touch down from a 101 Squadron offensive operation.
RE157 SR-R
RE161 SR-L²
RE162
RE163 SR-T²
RF125 SR-K
RF187 SR-S   From 12Sqn.
RF261 SR-B
RF262 SR-H²
RF263
RF264 SR-H
RF268

HEAVIEST SINGLE LOSS: 30/31.03.44. Nuremberg. 7 Lancasters. 6 FTR. 1 crashed on return.

PA238, SR-Z was another Lancaster that survived her time with 101 Squadron (GW)

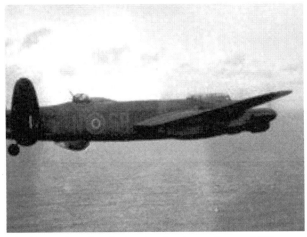

SR-N, serial unidentified, at low level over the sea (GW).

Printed in Poland
by Amazon Fulfillment
Poland Sp. z o.o., Wrocław